Navigating Boundaries

THE ASIAN DIASPORA IN TORRES STRAIT

Navigating Boundaries

THE ASIAN DIASPORA IN TORRES STRAIT

EDITED BY ANNA SHNUKAL, GUY RAMSAY
AND YURIKO NAGATA

Australian
National
University

eVIEW

Published by ANU eView
The Australian National University
Acton ACT 2601, Australia
Email: enquiries.eview@anu.edu.au
This title is also available online at press.anu.edu.au

National Library of Australia Cataloguing-in-Publication entry

Title: Navigating boundaries : the Asian diaspora in Torres Strait
            / Anna Shnukal, editor ; Guy Ramsay,
            editor ; Yuriko Nagata, editor.

Edition: Second Edition.

ISBN: 9781921934377 (paperback) 9781921934384 (ebook)

Notes: Includes bibliographical references and index.

Subjects: Asian diaspora.
            Asians--Migrations--Queensland--Torres Strait Islands.
            Asians--Queensland--Torres Strait Islands.
            Asia--Emigration and immigration.
            Torres Strait Islands (Qld.)--Emigration and immigration.

Other Creators/Contributors:
            Shnukal, Anna, editor.
            Ramsay, Guy Malcolm, editor.
            Nagata, Yuriko, editor.

Cover design and layout by ANU Press

Cover: Donald Friend (1915–89)
[Thursday Island] Manuscript Collection MS5959/33/113
For an account of Friend's visit to the Torres Strait in 1946–47 see *The Diaries of Donald Friend, Volume 2*, Paul Hetherington, ed., Canberra: National Library of Australia, 2003.
Reproduced courtesy of the National Library of Australia.

First published 2004 by Pandanus Books
This edition © 2017 ANU eView

We dedicate this book to
the people of Torres Strait.

Acknowledgements

We wish to acknowledge the support we have been given over many years by the people of Torres Strait and we dedicate this book to them. We are also grateful for financial support from the Australian Research Council, the University of Queensland and the School of Languages and Comparative Cultural Studies at the University of Queensland. We thank all the contributors to this volume and gratefully acknowledge the assistance given to us by the staff of the Queensland State Archives, John Oxley Library, National Archives of Australia, National Library of Australia, Australian War Memorial Library, Noel Butlin Archives Centre (The Australian National University), Royal Historical Society of Queensland Library; and by Judith Ramsay, Colin Sheehan, Michael Stubbins, Rodney Sullivan and Evelyn Suzuki.

Contents

List of Tables and Figures

Introduction

THE COMING TOGETHER of diverse peoples in a defined geographical space implies the prior navigation of geopolitical or physical boundaries and the subsequent navigation of social and cultural boundaries. To move from place to place is necessarily to navigate the boundaries between places, an experience that is invariably stimulating and ultimately enriching for its participants, producing cooperation and conflict in the forging of a new identity. New spatial borders, social values, economic interactions and political positionings are claimed, challenged and negotiated to produce new, if also transient equilibria. What has come to be known as 'multiculturalism' is now the norm of Australian contemporary urban society. Although this is viewed as a recent innovation, even a historical aberration, in fact, Australia's cultural pluralism has many antecedents in the nation's pre-colonial and colonial period, its 'polyethnic past'. One example is Torres Strait in north-eastern Australia, a region uniquely positioned at the confluence of the Australian continent, South-East Asia and the Pacific. Here, as in other 19th-century northern centres, the convergence of Australian Indigenous people, Asian and other 'Coloured' immigrants and European colonists created a polyethnic society, whose members have, through time, forged the social and familial connections that underlie the claim of their descendants to be a single people. Thursday Island, the regional commercial centre, was predominantly an Asian town from its inception until its wartime evacuation in 1942. For three generations, the majority of its population was born in Asia or was of Asian descent. Our book examines facets of the complex history of Asian Torres Strait, which continues to evolve and influence the present.

In the context of Torres Strait, 'boundary' is a salient, multifaceted concept. On one hand, it refers to artificially imposed maritime borders of geopolitical origin; more metaphorically, it refers to actual and perceived social and cultural divisions among ethnic groups. Both concepts are examined in the following chapters. For the Islanders of Torres Strait, South-East Asia and the

Pacific, however, the notion of the shifting sea as a boundary is alien, the inverse of the European terrestrially focused perception. The boundaries of their sea territories are marked by naturally occurring, fixed and prominent land masses, such as reefs and rocks. Their surrounding territorial seas are not boundaries, i.e., constraining features of their environment, which serve to separate them from their island and mainland neighbours, but rather maritime highways, which connect them with others for reasons of trade and ritual. Thus, for the diverse peoples who came to inhabit Torres Strait, the sea emphasised connection through trade, navigation and kinship.[1] We wish to emphasise this 'cross-cultural difference in constructions of the sea',[2] which is crucial to an understanding of subsequent historical events in Torres Strait. We also stress the cultural affinities among the sea-oriented peoples of the small-scale, resource-poor islands of Torres Strait, Asia and the Pacific. These affinities enabled them — indeed, predisposed them — to find common ground, which predated their shared experiences of labour in the fisheries, life in a remote British colonial town under the White Australia Policy and pervasive prejudice expressed through administrative and legislative control. Subsistence farmers and fisherfolk on their islands of origin, they also shared a similar maritime physical environment and marine practices, tropical climate and seasons, flora and fauna, and modes of life, including longstanding, accepted protocols for establishing trading relationships. Their world views, too, coincided, resonating in similar myths based on the significance of the sea for the founding and sustenance of their societies. Social values emphasised the principles of mutuality and reciprocity; kinship and sharing underlay all significant social relationships. Trade was a necessity for all of these peoples and it was the sea that made possible their navigation to a wider world.

These cultural traits, combined with the strategic geographical position of Torres Strait, which today shares a northern border with two separate nation-states, proved immensely conducive to the development of the region as a vital maritime trading centre during the late 19th and early 20th centuries. During this time, Asian migrants flocked to the region to forge new connections and contentions with Islanders and European colonists alike.

Academic Scholarship

Ann Curthoys, among others, has noted the 'parallels in discourse, policy and practice' between Indigenous Australians and Asians during the first half of the 20th century, which 'continued to be rarely spoken together'.[3] Academic historiographical and anthropological paradigms and the relative lack of available documentation have meant that, until recently, most scholarship of

Torres Strait has focused on Indigenous and colonial histories, relegating the numerically significant Asian presence to the margins.

Two 1970s theses by Armstrong, on 19th-century Japanese immigration to Queensland, and Evans, on the polyethnic society of pre-World War I Thursday Island, were exceptions, as was Chase's article on Aboriginal-Asian relations on Cape York.[4] The Japanese contribution to the pearl-shell and pearl-culture industries has now been extensively documented by Bach, Armstrong, Sissons, Ohshima, Ganter and Haig;[5] the impact of internment during World War II by Nagata;[6] and the musical contribution by Hayward and Konishi.[7] Kehoe-Forutan's PhD thesis deals in part with the contemporary experience of Thursday Islanders of Asian heritage;[8] and other scholars, inside and outside the academy, have begun to document aspects of Asian immigrant community experience in Torres Strait: Gatbonton, Ileto and Perdon for the Filipinos; Staples and O'Shea and Manderson for the Indonesians; and Swan, Sparkes and Weerasooria for the Sri Lankans.[9]

More than two decades ago, historian Hank Nelson called for a detailed study of Torres Strait 'from 1850 with its apparent extremes of frontier violence, conflict and alliance between different races and economic interests in pearling and trading, and government shifts between neglect and heavy paternalism', which would reveal much about racial 'behaviour, attitudes and legislation' in Australia.[10] Since then, Nelson's concerns have been addressed by the book-length studies of Ohshima, Beckett, Singe, Sharp, Ganter, Mullins and Osborne and in many theses and journal articles.[11] No one, however, has attempted the nuanced and comprehensive examination of the five major Asian diasporic communities of Torres Strait — Chinese, Japanese, Filipino, Indonesian and Sri Lankan — and their interrelationships, which is the subject of this volume.

Our book addresses this gap in scholarship, illustrating the richness of the Asian experience in Torres Strait and its influence on local social and cultural values, micro-economies and positionings from multiple viewpoints. It highlights the interconnections and contentions among the Asian groups and between them and local Indigenous and European people; more specifically, how ethnic community boundaries were — and continue to be — 'navigated' in Torres Strait. By examining community boundaries, which 'raise questions of power as broadly construed, differentially distributed, and socially constructed',[12] we hope to demonstrate the impact on ethnic relations of government policies of social control, the effects of which continue to the present. Our book is also a celebration of members of past communities who, despite many difficulties, successfully navigated physical and cultural boundaries to make successful lives for themselves and their families in Torres Strait.

Navigating Boundaries

An appreciation of the Asian experience in Torres Strait and the geopolitical and socio-cultural boundaries navigated by each individual and community requires an understanding of the broader historical context. In Chapter One, Paul Battersby discusses the notion of 'boundary' as a legally constituted geopolitical border, examining the location and legitimacy of Australia's present-day maritime border with its closest northern neighbours, East Timor, Indonesia and Papua New Guinea. Battersby portrays the border as historically problematic, not least because of the failure of all attempts to impose cultural uniformity on people within surrounding nation-states. This is clearly illustrated by A. R. Wallace's proposed geographical division between Australasia and the western Indonesian archipelago, known as the Wallace Line. Battersby argues that this demarcation of divergence in the biological composition of human, animal and plant species indigenous to these respective regions is neither congruent with geopolitical reality in the mid-19th century nor with the significant social interaction and cultural exchange between northern Australia and the Malay world at that time. While Federation in 1901 brought stricter demarcation of 'Australian' political and cultural space, global economic forces, entrenched traditions of Malay mariners and the vastness of the Australian coastline worked against the total closure of the Commonwealth's northern borders. Battersby demonstrates how the porousness of this imposed boundary has increased over time: in the second half of the 19th century, an ever-increasing number of Asians came to work in northern Australian maritime and agricultural industries and, at the same time, European Australians increasingly ventured into South-East Asia as tourists, business travellers and mining entrepreneurs. He contends that the social and cultural importance of these exchanges was masked by the ideology of White Australia and is only now coming to light at a time when nation-statehood itself faces an uncertain future.

In Chapter Two, Anna Shnukal and Guy Ramsay present an overview of Torres Strait Islander/Asian/European interaction. The chapter briefly documents the historical periods during which the Asian diaspora flourished and then declined: from first contact to the pearling boom; subsequent Asianisation of Thursday Island, the regional centre; Federation and its legislative impact; World War II and its immediate aftermath; and postwar decline. The chapter provides for those unfamiliar with the region a broader framework within which to situate the succeeding chapters, in which different interpretations of 'boundary' come to the fore.

Chapters Three to Seven of this book draw on extensive archival documentation and a widely dispersed body of existing sources, including local oral narratives, to document the histories and experiences of people from the five major Asian communities that came to define the Asian diaspora in the Torres Strait: Chinese, Filipino, Indonesian, Japanese and Sri Lankan. Each chapter illustrates to varying degrees what Clifford has defined as 'the main features of diaspora: a history of dispersal, myths/memories of the homeland, alienation in the host ... country, desire for eventual return, ongoing support of the homeland, and a collective identity importantly defined by this relationship'.[13] It is here that the notion of 'boundary' as a socio-cultural division emerges. Group members clarify inter-group differences by emphasising 'the characteristics of one's group as a whole',[14] which then 'become[s] a pragmatic basis for the formation of interest groups and networks, social resources for pursuing individual and communal utilities'.[15]

Guy Ramsay examines the Chinese community of Thursday and nearby islands, documenting the reasons for the arrival of the Chinese, their contributions to and connections with the local community and the broader Chinese diaspora, and their observance of culture and traditions. Through Ramsay's chapter, the dynamic of communal boundary-marking by the Chinese, as exemplified by Chinese business practices, can be measured against the government-propagated discourses of exclusion and threat, evidenced by legislation that curtailed rights of naturalisation, restricted family reunion and forbade Chinese contact with Indigenous women. Ramsay's chapter also portrays the continual presence on Thursday Island of a Chinese community, whose members, while greatly diminished in size by the 1942 evacuation, have successfully mediated ethnic and local identities, but who today face the dual challenges of Native Title and regional autonomy.

Whereas the majority of settlers from insular South-East Asia made their homes on Thursday Island, Torres Strait's commercial heart, some individuals and families settled on other islands. Anna Shnukal examines three little-known, independently established Filipino and Malay communities: the Filipino community on Ngarupai (Horn Island), c. 1889–1942; and the Malay communities on Badu (Mulgrave Island), c. 1890–c.1906, and Port Lihou, 1939–42. Shnukal gives an overview of the rise and fall of each community, celebrating the ways in which members of marginalised Asian groups, through their navigation of inter-group and interpersonal connections, subverted the constrictions placed on them by the dominant European minority and created new 'place-based' identities predicated on ethnic origin, kinship, custom and the multiple connections of daily life.

Reynaldo C. Ileto's chapter complements Shnukal's study of the Filipino Horn Island community by focusing on the experience of the Filipino entrepreneur, Heriberto Zarcal, who arrived on Thursday Island in 1892. Although in many ways an atypical immigrant, Zarcal's story exhibits almost all the features of members of the early 'Filipino-Australian' diaspora: successful involvement in the maritime industries, commercial and social integration into the local community, naturalisation, and continued links with events in the homeland. His story underlines the fluidity of boundaries for members of a diasporic community, where local endeavour frequently intertwines with connections with one's homeland. Ileto's chapter reconstructs Zarcal's highly successful career as a merchant, dealer in pearls and owner of a large fleet of pearling vessels. It probes the implications of the racist diatribe against his naturalisation as a British subject in 1897 and documents the material support he offered to the Philippine revolutionary forces, whose representative in Australia he later became.

The Japanese presence in Torres Strait has been the most widely studied. Scholars have generally emphasised a 'sojourner' community, which dominated the pearl-shelling industry until World War II and continued its involvement in the region's pearl-culture industry until the 1970s. In this book, Yuriko Nagata, who has previously documented the experiences of internment, repatriation and return to prewar Australian communities, traces the continuity of their presence, giving the concept of 'Japanese Thursday Islanders' its full historical integrity. The chapter not only synthesises a widely dispersed body of information and evidence published in Australia and Japan, but examines Japanese integration into the diverse local community of Torres Strait through intermarriage with Torres Strait Islanders, Malays, Chinese and Europeans. The contribution of Japanese women who worked and lived on the island is for the first time integrated into the historiography of the Japanese community, which has hitherto been almost exclusively male-based.

In the final chapter of this section, Stanley Sparkes and Anna Shnukal draw on newspaper accounts, archival records and family histories to document the personal and business lives of the Sri Lankan community. The first 'Cingalese' (as Ceylonese — Sri Lankans — were then called) arrived in Torres Strait independently in the 1870s, but a distinctive community was not created until the importation of 25 indentured Sri Lankans in 1882. Those first settlers became watermen (boatmen) and sailors, living in a recognised 'Cingalese quarter' in Thursday Island on Victoria Parade. Some of them became small businessmen: boarding-house keepers, billiard-room proprietors, shopkeepers, boat-owners, gem and curio hawkers and fishermen. They were joined in the

1890s by a 'second wave' of immigrants, part of a move by Sri Lankan professional jewellers to seek outlets for the gem trade in South-East Asian ports. The authors assess the commercial, religious, social and cultural contributions made by the Sri Lankans to the wider community and demonstrate how the foundations were laid for the most prominent business enterprises established by Charles, De Silva, Mendis, Mowlis and Saranealis.

These chapters deal with specific communities, yet they illustrate the emergence of implicit and explicit socio-cultural boundaries and their navigation by individuals and families. This is so among Asian groups and with other resident groups. These boundaries are porous to a degree, yet they also underpin imbalances in power relations. Indeed, the social, economic and political jurisdictions of cultural groups in Torres Strait were substantially 'enframed' by the exercising of colonial power and authority. Thus, Whites governed paternalistically over the Indigenous people of the region — their experience of paternalism continued into the 1980s — and hegemonically over the Asian 'visitor'. These constraints were formalised in legislation such as the various Queensland Aboriginal Protection Acts and the Commonwealth policies of White Australia, as well as marine industry regulations and indenture agreements. Local, state and Commonwealth policies also directly or indirectly affected every aspect of community life in Torres Strait, as the following chapters demonstrate.

Two government officials between them shared extraordinary power over the lives of the inhabitants of the strait. The first was the Government Resident, the supreme government representative in the region; the second was the local Protector of Aboriginals. There could at times be friction between the two, but during the colonial period it was the Government Resident who prevailed. After the Resident's death, the Protector became more powerful, as the Torres Strait Islanders became subject to the restrictions of the Aboriginal Protection Acts.

Jeremy Hodes' Chapter Eight explores the paternalistic 'rule' exercised by the first and most influential Government Resident, Hon. John Douglas, a former premier of Queensland, who served in Torres Strait from 1885–1904. It exposes what we today would perceive as contradictions in the man who, on the one hand, feared the effects of large-scale Chinese and Japanese immigration on the Britishness of Australian society — as premier in 1877, Douglas was instrumental in preventing Chinese from entering Queensland — and yet who numbered Chinese and Japanese individuals among his friends; a man who was benevolent towards and admiring of Torres Strait and Pacific Islanders and yet a strong supporter of the White Australia Policy. We must view Douglas, arguably the most influential figure in Torres Strait colonial history, who would never have considered himself a racist, in the context of his time. His dislike of the Japanese presence evolved into acceptance, powerless as he was to end their dominance of the Torres Strait fisheries. Hodes' chapter portrays the rhetoric of the White Australia Policy in collision with reality, and is a fascinating account of how the Asian communities in general, and the Japanese in particular, were seen through the eyes of the chief government representative in the region during the early years of the White Australia Policy.

Regina Ganter's Chapter Nine focuses on the exercise of authority by the second-most important government powerbroker, the Protector of Aboriginals, whose authority reached its height during the inter-war years. In her chapter, Ganter reveals how government officials sought to prevent contact between Asian and Indigenous people, making evident the discursive sentiment that underpinned their actions. At a time when a growing community of 'Coloured' people blurred the boundaries between Asian, Indigenous and White populations, Ganter documents the story of a 'mixed-race' family in Torres Strait, whose life was strongly imprinted by the efforts of bureaucrats to manage and contain 'pernicious associations' with the Indigenous population. Her chapter demonstrates the profound impact that Asian contact had on Aboriginal policy and the resistance offered by Coloured communities to the paternalistic grip of the Department of Native Affairs.

Despite the administrative and legislative obstructions put in place by colonial authorities, a blurring of cultural boundaries at the social level in Torres Strait becomes more evident through time.

> In the multi-racial society that existed on Thursday Island in the pre-World War I period, the various ethnic groups were faced with an interactional dilemma. On the one hand they were attempting to retain their own transplanted or indigenous cultures in a new environment, while at the same time trying to maintain or improve their status in the developing community. On the other hand, it was necessary to have a certain degree of ethnic group interrelationships in order to sustain the society as a working entity. Competition and exclusiveness amongst the different nationalities was therefore tempered by a forced interdependence.[16]

As more stories emerge about the ways in which Asian and Torres Strait Islander individuals and families subverted the intentions of racially based legislation and racist officials to navigate increasingly meaningless borders, we can trace their success in new hybrid cultural forms. Bhabha has stated that '[i]t is at the level of the interstices that the intersubjective and collective experiences of nationness, community interest, or cultural value are negotiated'.[17] Cultural exchange, which accompanied socio-cultural integration, has profoundly influenced the development of *ailan pasin* ('island custom'), a fusion of Indigenous, Pacific and Asian elements. Anna Shnukal's Chapter 10 adduces a range of Asian influences on Torres Strait contemporary cultural expression: in ethnic identity, cuisine, intoxicating substances, plants, gardening techniques, clothing, architecture, religion, funeral and burial practices, and reflected by vocabulary borrowed from Tagalog, Bahasa Indonesia, Japanese and Chinese into Torres Strait languages.

The significant contribution made by immigrant Asian groups to the music and performance culture of Torres Strait is the subject of Karl Neuenfeldt's Chapter 11. Using excerpts from the *Torres Straits Pilot*, Neuenfeldt documents how, along with other cultural artefacts and practices, migrants from Japan, Indonesia, the Philippines and elsewhere in Asia brought their music and musicianship with them to the region. Neuenfeldt argues that the rich musical culture of Torres Strait Islanders today is the result of these diverse Asian musical influences combining with the equally diverse music of the Melanesian, Polynesian, Aboriginal and European peoples of Torres Strait. His chapter examines some of the musical traces of Asia found in particular songs of the Torres Strait repertoire, songs that are remembered and sung primarily by the older generation, who grew up in Torres Strait before World War II. Neuenfeldt also demonstrates how recent recordings are reintroducing the songs to Torres Strait Islanders living in the Torres Strait and those who have migrated to the Australian mainland.

The final chapter of the book provides a more personal insight into the Asian experience in Torres Strait. Proffering a multiplicity of viewpoints, local voices narrate individual stories of Torres Strait people of Asian ancestry. Their stories complement the academic insights of the preceding chapters, enabling this book to provide a unique, comprehensive interpretation of the cultural dynamics of this significant and enduring site of Asian engagement in Australian history and society.

Footnotes

[1] Torres Strait Islanders, indeed, did not consider the colonially constructed geographical boundary particularly salient until the proposed border change with Papua New Guinea in the 1970s threatened their unity. This political minefield, with its profound implications for the division of a unified people, was settled by a treaty in 1978 and the establishment of a Protected Zone, which allowed continuity of traditional connections with friends and family.

[2] Jackson, S. E. 1995. 'The water is not empty: cross-cultural issues in conceptualising sea space.' *Australian Geographer*, Vol. 26, No. 1. pp. 87–96, at p. 89.

[3] Curthoys, A. 'An uneasy conversation: the multicultural and the indigenous.' In J. Docker and G. Fischer (eds), *Race, Colour and Identity in Australia and New Zealand*. Sydney: University of New South Wales Press. p. 25.

[4] Armstrong, J. B. 1970. 'The question of Japanese immigration to Queensland in the nineteenth century.' MA Qual. thesis, University of Queensland. Evans, G. 1972. 'Thursday Island 1878–1914: a plural society.' BA Honours thesis, University of Queensland. Chase, A. K. 1981. 'All kinds of nation: Aborigines and Asians in Cape York Peninsula.' *Aboriginal History*, Vol. 1, No. 5. pp. 6–15.

[5] Bach, J. P. S. 1955. *The Pearling Industry of Australia: an account of its social and economic development*. Canberra: Department of Commerce and Agriculture. Armstrong, J. 1973. 'Aspects of Japanese immigration to Queensland before 1900.' *Queensland Heritage*, Vol. 2, No. 9. pp. 3–9. Sissons, D. C. S. 1977. 'Karayuki-san: Japanese prostitutes in Australia, 1887–1916.' *Historical Studies*, Vol. 17, No. 68. pp. 323–41; Vol. 17, No. 69, pp. 474–88. Sissons, D. C. S. 1979. 'The Japanese in the Australian pearling industry.' *Queensland Heritage*, Vol. 3, No. 10. pp. 8–27. Ohshima, G. (ed.) 1983. *Toresu Kaikyo no Hitobito: People of the Torres Strait*. Tokyo: Kokon Shoin. Ganter, R. J. 1991. 'Images of Japanese pearl-shellers in Queensland: an oral history chapter in Australia-Japan relations.' *Royal Historical Society of Queensland Journal*, Vol. 14, No. 7. pp. 265–85. Ganter, R. J. 1994. *The Pearl-Shellers of Torres Strait*. Melbourne: Melbourne University Press. Ganter, R. J. 1999. 'The Wakayama triangle: Japanese heritage of north Australia.' *Journal of Australian Studies*, No. 61. pp. 55–63, 221–2. Haig, K. 1999. 'By the bounty of the sea: industry, economy and society in maritime Japanese immigrant communities in Hawaii and Australia, 1890s to World War II.' BA Honours thesis, Harvard University.

[6] Nagata, Y. 1996. *Unwanted Aliens: Japanese internment in Australia*. St Lucia: University of Queensland Press. Nagata, Y. 'Japanese Australians in the postwar Thursday Island community.' *Queensland Review*, Vol. 6, No. 2. pp. 30–43.

[7] Hayward, P. and J. Konishi. 2001. 'Mokuyo-to no ongaku: music and the Japanese community in the Torres Strait (1890–1941).' *Perfect Beat*, Vol. 5, No. 3. pp. 46–65.

[8] Kehoe-Forutan, S. 1990. 'Effectiveness of Thursday Island as an urban centre in meeting the needs of its community.' PhD thesis, University of Queensland.

[9] Gatbonton, M. 1988. 'Filipinos in Queensland.' In M. Brandle and S. Karas (eds), *Multicultural Queensland: the people and communities of Queensland: a bicentennial publication*. Brisbane: Ethnic Communities Council of Australia and the Queensland Migrant Welcome Association. pp. 59–64. Ileto, R. C. 1993. 'Philippine-Australian Interactions: the late nineteenth century.' In R. C. Ileto and R. Sullivan (eds), *Discovering Australasia: essays on Philippine-Australian Interactions*, Townsville: James Cook University of North Queensland, Department of History and Politics. pp. 10–46. Perdon, R. 1998. *Brown Americans of Asia*. Sydney: Manila Prints. Manderson, L. 1988. 'Malays.' In J. Jupp (ed.), *The Australian People: an encyclopedia of the nation, its people and their origins*. North Ryde: Angus and Robertson. pp. 691–3. Staples, J. and K. O'Shea. 1995. 'Thursday Island's Asian heritage: an oral history.' Unpublished typescript in possession of Anna Shnukal.

Sparkes, S. J. 1988. *Sri Lankan Migrants in Queensland in the Nineteenth Century*. Brisbane: S. J. Sparkes. Swan, B. 1981. 'Sinhalese emigration to Queensland in the nineteenth century: a note.' *Journal of the Royal Australian Historical Society*, Vol. 67, No. 1. pp. 55–63. Weerasooriya, W. S. 1988. *Links Between Sri Lanka and Australia: a book about the Sri Lankans (Ceylonese) in Australia*. Colombo: Government Press.

10 Nelson, H. 1982. 'Looking North.' In G. Osborne and W. F. Mandle (eds), *New History: studying Australia today*. Sydney: Allen and Unwin. pp. 142–52, at pp. 142–3.

11 Ohshima, G., *Toresu Kaikyo no Hitobito*. Beckett, J. R. 1987. *Torres Strait Islanders: custom and colonialism*. Cambridge University Press. Singe, J. 1989. *The Torres Strait: people and history*. St Lucia: University of Queensland Press. Sharp, N. 1993. *Stars of Tagai: the Torres Strait Islanders*. Canberra: Aboriginal Studies Press. Ganter, R. J., *The Pearl-Shellers of Torres Strait*. Mullins, S. P. 1994. *Torres Strait: a history of colonial occupation and culture contact, 1864–1897*. Rockhampton: Central Queensland University Press. Osborne, E. 1997. *Torres Strait Islander Women and the Pacific War*. Canberra: Aboriginal Studies Press.

12 Rodman, M. and M. Cooper. 1996. 'Boundaries of home in Toronto housing cooperatives.' In D. Pellow (ed.), *Setting Boundaries: the anthropology of spatial and social organization*. Westport: Bergin and Garvey. pp. 91–110, at p. 95.

13 Clifford, J. 1997. *Routes: travel and translation in the late twentieth century*. Cambridge: Harvard University Press. p. 247.

14 Tajfel, H. 1981. *Human Groups and Social Categories: studies in social psychology*. Cambridge University Press. p. 258.

15 Comaroff, J. and J. Comaroff. 1992. *Ethnography and the Historical Imagination*. Boulder: Westview. p. 60.

16 Evans, G., 'Thursday Island 1878–1914', p. 35.

17 Bhabha, H. K. 1994. 'Frontlines/borderposts.' In A. Bammer (ed.), *Displacements: cultural identities in question*, Bloomington: Indiana University Press. pp. 269–72, at p. 269.

Thursday Island Harbour, 1900.
Courtesy of John Oxley Library, Brisbane (Item No. 14338).

CHAPTER ONE

Mapping Australasia

Reflections on the permeability of Australia's northern maritime borders

Paul Battersby

On 18 December, 1978, Australia and PNG signed a treaty delimiting their respective sovereignties in the Torres Strait. The treaty established three boundaries: a seabed boundary that marks the Australia-PNG maritime border, an Australian fisheries protection line extending north to encompass three islands adjacent to the PNG coast and mutually recognised as sovereign Australian territory, and a protected zone extending from the PNG coast to a line south of the seabed boundary. Recognising historical cultural ties between communities on the PNG south coast and the Torres Strait Islands, the treaty permits freedom of movement within the protected zone for 'traditional inhabitants' of this area and apportions a share of commercial fisheries to PNG.[1] Adding to the complex overlay of maritime jurisdictions to Australia's north, the Australian Government insists that, under the United Nations Convention on the Law of the Sea (1982), the 'natural prolongation' of Australia's continental shelf allows the delineation of seabed boundaries much closer to East Timor and Indonesia than the Australian mainland. Inherited British colonial territories of Christmas Island, a mere 186 nautical miles south of Java, and Ashmore Island in the Timor Sea give further legal weight to Australia's northward maritime 'boundary creep'. In another minor concession to the fact that juro-political borders disrupt established patterns of human interaction, fishermen from the Indonesian island of Roti are given heavily circumscribed access to 'traditional' fishing grounds around Ashmore Reef.[2]

The ensuing patchwork of superimposed seabed boundaries, exclusive economic zones and protected areas aptly illustrates the paradox of territoriality in an allegedly borderless world.

Geopolitical borders, write Thomas Wilson and Hastings Donnan, are 'always domains of contested power'. Inseparable from their frontiers, 'zones of varying width which stretch across and away from borders', they are defined as much by the movement across them of people, money, merchandise and ideas as they are by the actions and decisions taken in the centres of political power.[3] This essay explores the economic and social dynamics at the margins of Australia and Asia in the late 19th century, crudely disrupted and subsequently masked by the ideology of Australian nation-statehood. Until Federation heralded stricter demarcation of national political and cultural space, anchoring northern Australia to a southern axis, the waters separating Australia from the Indo-Malaysian Archipelago were a vast lake across which roamed adventurers, migrants, guest workers and tourists from Europe and Asia. Integral to the story of northern development, these Austral-Asian economic, social and cultural transactions also point to a still under-recognised cosmopolitanism at the southern fringes of this once open Australasian maritime frontier.

Geographical Imaginings

The English naturalist, Alfred Russel Wallace, claimed in *The Malay Archipelago* (1869) that 'no two parts of the world differ so radically in their productions as Asia and Australia'.[4] Yet Wallace believed that the 'biogeographic' boundaries of Asia stopped at Bali, to the east of which lay the 'Austro-Malayan' subregion of the Indo-Malaysian Archipelago. Reflecting on the structure of this subdivision, he wrote subsequently in *Australasia* (1879), that the Australian continent 'forms its central and most important feature'.[5] Wallace based his conclusion on the presence of distinctly Australian fauna east of a continuous dividing line, the Wallace Line, separating Bali from Lombok, Borneo from Sulawesi, and the southern Philippines from the Moluccas. Allowing that 'along the line of junction intermigration and commixture have taken place', he claimed the distribution of human characteristics confirmed the accuracy of his zoological observations.[6]

Wallace's Australasia spanned the entire Indo-Malaysian Archipelago, New Guinea, Australia, New Zealand and the South-West Pacific. He was dismayed at the *Encyclopaedia Britannica*'s contraction of his geographical idea to encompass Australia and New Zealand only, and maintained in his later study of Australia and New Zealand, also titled *Australasia* (1893), that the island continent was 'geographically a southern extension of Asia'.[7] Wallace's

Line remains a point of reference for biogeographers, although the 'faunal split' between Australia and Asia moved gradually eastward as geographers and naturalists applied different criteria, from the distribution of mammals to freshwater fish, to map its precise delineation. Even Wallace revised his line in 1910 to exclude Sulawesi from the Austro-Malayan division to eliminate some of the ambiguities caused by overlapping faunal zones.[8] Modern archaeologists define the vague geographic frontier bisecting Wallace's Australasia as an 'intermediate zone' named Wallacea, between 'Greater Australia' bounded by the edge of the Australian continental shelf, and Wallace's Indo-Malayan division of the archipelago.[9] A consequence of the historical mobility of fauna, flora and humans across open water in island South-East Asia, this 'intermediacy' renders impossible the delineation of precise and inclusive 'natural' boundaries.

At which point then should the narrative of interactions between northern Australia and the Indo-Malaysian Archipelago begin? In human terms, the story of contact predates the arrival of the voyages of Captain Cook by tens of thousands of years. In his seminal study of contact between northern Australia and the Malay world, Charles Campbell MacKnight asserted the centrality of sea voyages in Australian and South-East Asian history.[10] His is a compelling logic. Indigenous Australians were the first 'accidental' navigators to reach the Australian continent through the archipelago some 40,000 years BP.[11] At the end of the last Ice Age, rising sea levels cut northern Australians adrift from their ancestral moorings, but maritime communication remained salient in localised economic and cultural interactions between island and coastal communities along the northern shores of Greater Australia. From localised beginnings, the maritime peoples and entrepots of island South-East Asia built a vast and intricate trading system which, by the first millennium CE encompassed eastern Africa, the Persian Gulf, India and southern China. According to the South-East Asianist, Oliver Wolters, this system comprised a single ocean bound together by the propensity to trade, in which the sea was perceived as a means of communication, not a prohibitive or defensive barrier.[12]

Not until the 16th and 17th centuries did northern Australia reconnect with the Australasian maritime milieu as Portuguese, Dutch and British navigators made 'accidental' landings along the north-west coast. Contemporaneous with the arrival of European explorers and colonisers, the commercial reach of the seafaring Bajau Laut from southern Sulawesi slowly extended towards northern Australia in the 18th century. A pivotal maritime people in the bêche-de-mer (trepang) trading chain reaching northward to China, the Bajau roamed the eastern Indo-Malaysian Archipelago harvesting their catch for Makasarese traders. Depleted trepang stocks forced the Bajau to probe for new fishing grounds south to Ashmore Reef in the early 1700s and the Coburg Peninsula by 1780 at the very latest, according to anthropologist James Fox.[13] From the Kimberley coast, Kayu Jawa in Malay, to the Coburg Peninsula and the western Gulf of Carpentaria, known to the Bajau as *Marege*, Aboriginal and Malayan cultural spheres overlapped for more than a century until Australian fisheries law, part of an alien and inflexible British politico-legal regime, forced the Bajau to retreat from their traditional Indo-Australian fishing grounds.[14]

Looking far beyond the expanding boundaries of European colonisation, British merchants, navigators and early New South Wales governors alike appreciated the potential value of a 'new Singapore' in northern Australia. Matthew Flinders hinted at the commercial and strategic advantages presented by the 'proximity' to British India trade routes of the coast from Cape Arnhem to Melville Island in his account of his circumnavigation of Australia.[15] Fort Dundas (1823), Raffles Bay (1827) and Port Essington (1838–49) in what is now the Northern Territory were established to attract commerce southwards from the Netherlands Indies and link northern Australia through maritime trading networks to Britain's Far Eastern empire. Poorly planned and provisioned, and only intermittently resupplied, these early experiments failed. Major Australian population centres had no need of such an entrepot. Asia-bound ships sailing from Sydney through the Torres Strait more than doubled in number from 15 to 41 a year between 1832 and 1838.[16] Population growth in NSW increased demand for tropical foodstuffs, such as sugar, which, by the 1840s was sourced primarily from Java and the Philippines. Sugar imports from Java reached 16 million pounds weight in 1842, more than three-quarters the total volume imported for that year.[17] Ready markets for sealskin and sandalwood in China gave impetus to the creation of early Australian maritime corporate empires. Sydney entrepreneurs such as Robert Towns, whose merchant fleet ranged as far north as Canton, secured rich cargoes of tea, coffee, sugar and tobacco to satisfy the appetites of Australian consumers.[18] Australia was the largest and second-largest market for Philippine sugar and coffee respectively in 1847. A decade later, it was the largest market for both commodities, with the bulk of imports entering through Sydney.[19]

As Australasia emerged as a field of colonial Australian commerce, the region's richness and strategic significance tempted some to speculate on the future shape of the Dutch Empire. To Australasian colonisers, the Dutch stood between Australia and the dream of a greater British Empire in the East. The Anglo-Dutch Treaty of 1824 recognised the Indies as a Dutch sphere of interest, but at the time, Dutch power reached barely across the island of Java and parts of Sumatra. The Van Delden Proclamation of 1828 enlarged Dutch claims to incorporate western New Guinea, but, as Nicholas Tarling writes, they 'had to accept that their tenure in the Archipelago itself was in a sense conditional'.[20] Britain exerted indirect influence over northern Borneo in the 1840s and watched on disdainfully as the remainder of the eastern archipelago was hastily incorporated into the Netherlands Indies. British policy-makers, however, hesitated to extend Britain's territorial reach beyond what was deemed necessary to advance British economic interests and protect major shipping lanes from foreign threats.[21] Concern for peace and order were common justifications for British colonial interventions, lest potentially hostile powers take advantage of local political instability and establish a strategically sensitive foothold near the vital arteries of British commerce. Colonial Australians were therefore careful to address these concerns when urging the northward expansion of British influence.

Eager to emulate the achievements of Thomas Stamford Raffles, Sir George Ferguson Bowen, first Governor of Queensland, harboured boundary-less aspirations towards the archipelago. Claiming 'destiny' as his guide, Bowen anticipated a 'convergence' of Asian and Pacific trade routes to Australia's north. Advocating the creation of another northern outpost at Cape York overlooking the Torres Strait, he advised the Secretary of State for the Colonies that a settlement properly garrisoned would 'command the whole of the commerce between the South Pacific and the Indian Ocean'. Citing Raffles as his inspiration, he envisioned the Torres Strait would replicate the Strait of Malacca in its commercial and strategic significance. But further:

> A station at Cape York could not fail to extend the influence and *prestige* of Great Britain over the Indian Archipelago; while it would form a link between the possessions in Australia, India, and China, [assure] the possession of the north and north-east coasts of the Australian Continent 'and, as it were close the ring fence with which we have girt the fifth quarter of the globe'.[22]

Consolidation of British rule on the Australian continent could, Bowen conjectured, lead to the enlargement of Britain's eastern possessions to incorporate 'New Guinea, and *other portions of the Indian Archipelago*' (emphasis added). Expressing the hope that 'the Moluccas shall be freed from the trammels in which they have hitherto been bound', Bowen envisioned an arc of islands from New Guinea through the Moluccas to northern Borneo shaded in imperial red on the map of Britain's empire in Asia.[23]

Bowen declared that the 'tide of colonisation in Queensland is sweeping onward at the rate of about two hundred miles each year'.[24] Confident in the '*assimilating* powers of the Anglo-Saxon race', he echoed the sentiments expressed by Edward Gibbon Wakefield some 30 years earlier and embraced the prospect of Asian immigration. Branding as 'Luddites' those responsible for assaults on Chinese miners at Buckland River and Lambing Flat in NSW, he asserted that Asian migrants were essential to the development of tropical industries in Queensland. Bowen's claims lent intellectual justification to demands from Queensland businessmen for 'the successful cultivation of a race habituated to labour in a tropical climate'.[25] Thus would the template for British colonial achievement be transposed to Queensland to build a new Australasian colony replete with a bustling northern emporium, an extensive hinterland yielding tropical products for a global market and a Coloured underclass of 'coolie' labour ruled by a new class of White Rajahs.

The dream of a 'new Singapore' proved illusory. Cut off from the hub of the Torres Strait pearling industry by a maritime boundary that restricted Queensland's maritime jurisdiction to three miles from the Cape York coast, the settlement of Somerset (1864–77) languished. Denied the capacity to levy tax on cargoes of pearls and bêche-de-mer, the settlement also struggled to attract trading vessels passing through the strait.[26] Apart from some sputtering attempts to initiate regular steamer traffic between Queensland and the archipelago, an eagerly anticipated steamer service to Batavia (present-day Jakarta) and Singapore failed to materialise. Ironically, the growth of sugar industries in Queensland and NSW arrested demand for imported sugar from Java and the Philippines. With the archipelago's declining importance in eastern Australia's sugar trade, shipping companies were unwilling to bear the commercial risk of running a regular steamer service through the Torres Strait without additional financial incentives. The belief persisted, however, that the Australian colonies, Queensland especially, had important interests to protect and advance in the archipelago.

Prospects for a northern emporium improved with two unilateral maritime border revisions in 1872 and 1879. The first, instigated by the Palmer Government, enlarged the Queensland Government's maritime jurisdiction from three to 60 miles. The urgent need to regulate labour recruitment was used to justify this revision and the subsequent annexation of the strait during Sir Thomas McIlwraith's first term as premier, which pushed Queensland's northern maritime border to within half a mile of the New Guinea coast.[27] With a ready tax base thus appropriated to fund the apparatus of State control, Thursday Island supplanted Somerset as the commercial and administrative hub in the strait. Riding the expansion of the pearling industry, Thursday Island became a frontier outpost of the Queensland colonial state and a forward base for Australian enterprise in New Guinea and the Indies. As one 'North Queenslander' wrote to the *Straits Times*, the colonisation of Cape York offered

Thursday Island views, 1910.
Courtesy of John Oxley Library, Brisbane (Item No. 180490).

the perfect opportunity to 'command the commerce of a large portion of Australia, of the Indian Archipelago, and of the islands of the Pacific'.[28]

Thursday Island's international significance increased with the inauguration of the Torres Strait Mail Line in 1874. To divert the flow of migrants to Queensland, the Palmer Government offered a £20,000 annual subsidy as an inducement to the British-owned Eastern and Australian Mail Steam Company Limited (E & A) to connect with the P & O service in Singapore and bring Brisbane within 44 days of London via Brindisi.[29] Articles in the Singapore and Brisbane newspapers heralded the Torres Strait route for the 'smoothness' of the voyage and the picturesque beauty of the archipelago, but the monthly service struggled to capture the imagination of Australian tourists or British migrants. A. H. Palmer stood by the mail line his government had created by taking his family on a trip to Batavia in 1874, but the Torres Strait Mail Line carried a mere 101 saloon passengers from eastern Australia to Batavia and Singapore in its first year. British migrants preferred the long-established south-coast shipping routes rather than transhipping at Singapore and enduring the tortures of cramped steerage quarters and the suffocating tropical heat of the archipelago.[30] Although E & A insisted that their service terminate in Sydney rather than Brisbane, the Queensland Government persisted with the venture because it was assumed that migrants from Britain would eventually opt for the Torres Strait route, and because Asian emporia beckoned as potential export markets for Queensland's primary industries.

Commercial necessity dictated that good relations be nurtured with the Netherlands Indies, but, at the level of popular debate at least, the intermediacy of the archipelago continued to invite speculation. The Australian novelist, Marcus Clarke, thought the cultural divide between northern Australia and South-East Asia would one day be transcended. In terms strikingly resonant with modern theories of cultural globalisation, Clarke wrote in *The Future Australian Race* (1877) of 'that abolition of boundaries' brought by 'waves of social progress', which made it 'easier for men to change skies, to change food, to intermarry, to beget children from strange loins'.[31] Like Bowen, Clarke appreciated the powerful forces that were reshaping the geopolitical map of Asia. As railways and steam shipping routes converged to increase the frequency and speed of international interactions, so Clarke envisaged a civilisational split in Australasia, not between the Australian continent and the archipelago, but at a line south of Brisbane.

According to Clarke, a 'luxurious and stupendous civilisation' would one day evolve encompassing northern Australia, New Guinea, the Moluccas and 'parts adjacent', leaving southern Australia and New Zealand to form a residual European cultural sphere.[32] Clarke's 'waves of social progress' were already changing the northern Australian socio-cultural terrain. Chinese miners from the NSW and Victorian goldfields moved north into Queensland as new gold rushes broke out around Gympie, Ravenswood and Charters Towers. Ships brought more guest workers and settlers from southern China through the Torres Strait to Cairns and Cooktown in the 1870s. 'Malay' and Filipino pearl divers and lugger crews added to northern Queensland's multi-ethnic population.[33] Given the fractious nature of Queensland politics, the idea that increased social and commercial exchanges between northern Australia and the archipelago could reconfigure political boundaries was hardly romantic speculation. Separationists in northern and central Queensland have campaigned since the mid-1860s for the creation of a new colony, partly to liberate their taxes but, equally important to regional business interests, so that the north could be populated with cheap 'coolie' labour recruited from as far afield as India and China. Hot climates, after all, wrote Clarke, naturally induced despotism and slavery.[34]

Acts to establish the Federal Council of Australasia in 1885 anticipated the possibility of external territorial realignment. In defining the council's terms of inclusion, 'Australasia colony', the legislation read, comprised the six Australian colonies, New Zealand and 'any British colonies which may be hereafter created within Her Majesty's possessions in Australasia'.[35] Coveted by business interests in Sydney and Brisbane, eastern New Guinea had been the subject of inconclusive negotiations between the Queensland Government and the Colonial Office for possible British annexation in the preceding decade. But for a disagreement over responsibility for funding the creation of a new British colony, we might remember John Douglas and not McIlwraith as Queensland's most aggressively expansionist premier.[36] Acting with the support of southern colonies, McIlwraith annexed New Guinea's south-eastern quarter in 1883, alleging that a German presence in north-eastern New Guinea presented a threat to Australian and wider British interests in the Pacific.[37] Preoccupied in Burma and Malaya, Britain reluctantly agreed to establish and run the new territory as a British protectorate, funded by the Australian colonies, if only to clarify German, Dutch and now British territorial claims on the island.

Nonetheless, the Netherlands Indies Government remained distrustful of British intentions and, with Germany, was hostile towards Australian commercial activity in the eastern islands. Dutch and German sensitivities were undoubtedly heightened by the expanding frontiers of Australian enterprise and the cavalier attitude of many Australian maritime entrepreneurs. From the 1880s, Australian pearling fleets roamed as far afield as Labuk Bay in British North Borneo (Sabah) and the Sulu and Mergui Archipelagos in search of new fishing grounds.[38] Australasian colonial expansion remained a matter of public debate as late as 1892, when the *Straits Times* reported that certain Australian business interests were openly advocating a pre-emptive Australian-led invasion and occupation of Portuguese East Timor.[39] Responding to an international controversy ignited by imprisonment of the captain of the Sydney-registered whaling ship, the *Costa Rica Packet*, at Ternate in the Moluccas, one German newspaper was in no doubt as to Australian ambitions:

> If they could do just what they liked in Sydney, the German flag would not much longer fly in New Guinea, and on the Marshall or Bismark Islands, and in fact that the Australians wish to arrogate to themselves the right of being the 'boss' in the Malayan Archipelago, has been proved by their uncouth conduct in the matter of the pearl fisheries of the Aru Islands.[40]

Across New Frontiers

Suspicion and disdain lurked beneath the surface of bilateral relations, but Australian social and business connections with the Netherlands Indies deepened in the late 19th century. In anticipation of a lucrative trade in dairy produce and frozen beef from Queensland, the British India Steam Navigation Company (BISN) secured the Queensland mail contract in 1881, earning an increased subsidy in return for terminating their fortnightly mail service in Brisbane. As many as 200 British migrants a month passed through the archipelago along the Torres Strait route with the BISN. New Australian, Dutch, German and Japanese-owned steamer services opened the doors to Manila, Kobe and Hong Kong in the 1890s. Australia's primary and secondary ports were integrated into a network of transoceanic steam shipping lines connecting Australia to Asia and the wider world. Thomas Cook and Son offered currency-exchange services, travellers' cheques, telegraphic money transfers and round-the-world tickets to metropolitan and colonial leisure classes. In a single transaction, Australian tourists and business travellers could purchase the right to circumnavigate the globe by land and sea.[41]

Australians travelling to Asia for the first time crossed many boundaries. For the thousands of Britain-bound saloon passengers who endured enforced stopovers at Asian port cities as their steamers refuelled, the changing cultural scenery was little more than an engaging novelty. For a significant minority, however, disembarkation was the beginning of a journey of meaning that, even for the British-born, revealed the depth of attachment to their Australian home. Yorkshire-born Henry Copeland, New England MLA in the NSW Parliament, wrote of 'a genuine regret at leaving Australia behind us' and with it the reassuring continuum of everyday routines symbolised by the 'two-penny post'.[42] Confronted with glaring cultural differences, the likes of Copeland found that attributes of 'Australia' were a frame of reference against which they gauged new environments and experiences — sometimes with surprising results.

Cast adrift in an unknown world, 'new chum' travellers noticed a perceptible transformation of the land and seascape as they crossed the Arafura Sea. Even the coastline of tropical north Queensland could not compare with the sights that greeted Australians as their steamer crossed the Wallace Line and entered the Bali Strait. New landscapes were quickly followed by the appearance of markers of new cultural terrain. Steaming towards the Java Sea, Copeland noted in his travelogue, *A Few Weeks with the Malays*, that 'curious' sailing craft signalled entry into a new cultural space, populated by a 'strange people'.[43] From the comfort of their gilded saloons, travellers were greeted by the 'curious' lateen sails of Chinese junks, forested tropical islands and the exotic 'perfumes' of luxuriant tropical flora.

Mackay parliamentarian Hume Black reported 'disgust and revulsion' at the sight of rickshaw-drawers in Singapore 'being entirely opposed to Australian ideas of freedom'.[44] Yet Black enjoyed the company of one Rajah Impey, a fellow shareholder in the Australian-owned and operated Raub Australia Gold Mine at Pahang on the Malay Peninsula, who greeted him on his arrival at Port Klang and shared his carriage on a train journey into the interior.[45] Preconceived notions of Oriental despotism were frequently contradicted by the experience of interpersonal contact with Asian elites. Copeland lauded Chinese merchants for their entrepreneurial flair and their bourgeois values: property, law, order and trade. He struggled to digest the culinary productions of Dutch Eurasian culture, but reserved his strongest criticism for the British. He was concerned at the effect of climate on the moral character of British colonisers, suggesting their penchant for servants resulted from heat-induced idleness. Entertaining a vague notion that one day Australians might assume

the 'white man's burden' somewhere in Britain's eastern empire, he observed
that the tropics were suitable only for European north Queenslanders, who were
biologically adapted to the stresses of equatorial temperatures. Envisioning
Australia's commercial integration into Britain's eastern empire, Copeland
reminded his readers of the economic logic for a central Australian railway
linking southern capitals to Darwin from whence steamer services would open
markets for Australian produce in Malaya and India.[46] The Netherlands Indies
by contrast was but an exotic detour.

Founded on an uneasy accommodation between the imperial powers over
respective colonial jurisdictions, trade and tourism encouraged the
domestication of Australia's near-Orient. A deliberate policy of tourism
development transformed Java into a popular tourist destination for Australians
travelling the Torres Strait route to Asia and Europe. After the bourgeois
fashion for 'going to the hills', sanatoriums were established at Sindanglaya,
Soekaboemi, Garoet (Garut) and Tosari, enhancing the appeal of sightseeing
excursions to the restored Hindu temples of the Dieng Plateau and the fabled
Buddhist shrine of Borobudur.[47] Such was the demand for tourist travel that the
Australian shipping company, Burns Philp, open a specialised travel department
to market Asian holidays. Featuring Java, 'Garden of the East', their 1913
edition of *Picturesque Travel Under the Auspices of Burns Philp & Company Ltd*,
directed tourists to the island's 'majestic ruins'. In the romanticised cultural
space of the East Indies, potential tourists were enticed by standardised images
of an exotic Oriental paradise in which dwelled passive and contented subjects
ruled by a benign imperial power.[48]

Trusted Australian investors were also welcome in the Indies. 'Willie'
Jack, partner in the north Queensland firm, Jack and Newell, operated a gold
mine at Kuandang on the Minhassan Peninsula on the island of Sulawesi in
partnership with Dutch investors from Amsterdam during the 1890s.[49] Burns
Philp strengthened their trading links with the Netherlands Indies by
establishing their 'Island Line' steamer service and opening an office in
Samarang in 1908.[50] Brisbane pearling magnate James Clark secured a pearling
concession near the Aru Islands with partner E. Munro in 1904. Becoming
consul for the Netherlands in Queensland the next year, Clark extended his
business empire to Ceram, where his family grew cocoa, coffee, sago and rubber
until 1942.[51] Australians could and did marvel at the wonders of Borobudur,
prospect and mine for gold throughout the Netherlands Indies, and secure
markets among the Dutch Eurasian population for Australian meat, dairy
products, flour, coal, jams and pickles.

Cultural distances between European Australians and the indigenous
populations of the Indo-Malaysian Archipelago were substantial. 'A far wider

space than the Arafura Sea separates us and them' wrote an early Australian tourist to Asia.[52] But, acceptance of Asian cultures was as essential for the productive management of a multiracial workforce in northern Australia as it was for commercial success in Asia. 'Malay' workers were, like their Filipino counterparts, highly regarded by employers in the Australian pearling industry, and were much less likely than Europeans to break the law. Writing of the Filipino presence in the Torres Strait, Rey Ileto describes how Asian and Australian businesspeople valued their mutual contributions to the prosperity of local industry.[53]

Further south, the introduction of more stringent limitations on the recruitment of Kanaka labour by the Griffith Government in 1885, forced sugar planters to also look northwards to the archipelago to meet their labour needs. North Queensland's 'Malay' community swelled from less than 300 to nearly 1,100 in 1886 as labourers, mainly from Bantam and Sunda on the island of Java, but also from Pahang on the Malay Peninsula, were brought to work on cane fields from Innisfail south to Mackay and Maryborough.[54] At Mourilyan Plantation, Javanese were considered 'cleaner in their habits than kanakas' and better suited to plantation labour.[55] It was a measure of the flexibility of work practices that indentured Javanese were permitted to work under Javanese supervisors, 'mandoors', and, when in breach of company regulations were 'punished by their own code of laws'.[56] Admitted to the fringes of more populous districts, Javanese sugar workers more readily caught the public eye and were noted for their assertiveness. As one J. O'Halleram, manager at the Innisfail Estate, told the Queensland Royal Commission into the sugar industry, 'They are a class of labour that, if they can best you they will best you and keep you bested.'[57]

Public debate about the 'Malay' character at the time of the 'Black Labour' Queensland election in 1888 highlights the political dynamics of White Australia. Objecting to the repayment of wage advances, a legal requirement under the terms of their labour contract, 50 Javanese plantation employees protested their cause in the main street of Mackay. The *Mackay Mercury* seized on an opportunity to mount a vigorous campaign against the importation of Javanese labour. Depicting Javanese as violent delinquents who 'ran amok' and threatened 'defenceless white people with their long bladed krisses', the *Mercury* invoked images of 'Malay' savagery popularised in the writings of explorers and naturalists such as Wallace.[58] Discontented with wages and working conditions, Javanese plantation employees frequently 'absconded', but incidents of violent assaults involving Javanese workers were rare. Public fears were, however, further heightened by events at Normanton in June 1888, where a Javanese called Sedin 'ran amok' killing three Europeans and igniting an outpouring of race-hate by the town's White population.[59]

Thursday Island Harbour, 1935.
Courtesy of John Oxley Library, Brisbane (Item No. 42746).

Race relations were reportedly strained by the growing South-East Asian presence in Normanton, mostly internal migrants from Thursday Island.[60] Before public order could be restored, rioters themselves ran amok causing £5,000 in damage to non-European property in a wild orgy of destruction. Unsurprisingly, the fact that several 'Malays' disarmed Sedin before police intervened earned scant attention in the Queensland press. The *Townsville Herald* vindicated the White townspeople's malevolence as a 'cleansing of its [Normanton's] Asiatic plague'.[61] Acutely conscious of Queensland's tarnished reputation for race relations, Thomas McIlwraith described the rioters' behaviour as a disgrace to the colony but promptly suspended the transportation of another 2,000 Javanese indents preparing to embark in Singapore and Batavia.[62]

Concerned about the welfare of its colonial subjects, and about Queensland's territorial designs, the Netherlands Indies banned labour recruitment in its eastern islands.[63] The Normanton riot merely confirmed Queensland's international image as a predatory, labour-hungry colony. McIlwraith eased restrictions on the recruitment of Pacific Island labour, thereby reducing the need to obtain labour from Malaya and Java, but Javanese were still recruited into the Queensland sugar industry, in much smaller numbers, until all non-White immigration ceased in 1901. By then, an image of the 'savage Malay' was embedded in the popular imagination alongside the Yellow Peril as a physical and moral threat to the security of White Australia.

Guest workers from Malaya and Java who entered Queensland and remained, as Rey Ileto states in relation to Filipinos, merely transferred their allegiance from one colonial power to another.[64] But the creation of the Australian nation-state severed them from their cultural roots and forced these Indo-Australians to negotiate new political identities while confronting the harsh reality of their place as cultural fringe dwellers who were denied a voice in the politics of Australian nationalism.

Australia or Austral-Asia?

With the exception of New Guinea, the convergences foreshadowed by Bowen did not work towards an expanded British empire in the eastern archipelago. The unrealised idea of Australasia as a federation of British, Asian and Pacific colonies owes more to the exigencies of British foreign policy than to a failure of Australian political imagination. In its place emerged the conviction shared by many among Australia's commercial and political elites that Asia, and maritime South-East Asia in particular, was a natural sphere of Australian business enterprise. Nineteenth-century geographical ideas could still be mobilised to justify these more modest ambitions. Presaging Australian policies of 'engagement' with South-East Asia in the 1990s, J. J. Long's commissioned report on trade prospects with the Netherlands Indies and Malaya stressed mutual interests with neighbouring states born of geographic proximity and economic complementarity. He wrote:

> It is not without interest, in view of the nature of my investigations, to note that the inhabitants, the language, the flora, fauna, and the geological formation all support the theory that these islands, large and small, are really but the highland remains of a vast and extensive continent which formerly united Australia to Asia. The corollary, of course, is that they constitute a natural geological outlet for Australian trade, the volume of which — once … it has attained the possible of normal times — should advance automatically with the increasing prosperity and population of the islands.[65]

Long lamented the slow pace at which Australian business took up the challenge of Asia, but the frontiers of Australian business enterprise crept steadily outwards. In the 1890s, Australian prospectors, gold and tin miners could be found across an arc starting in New Guinea and stretching to the Malay state of Kelantan on the Malay Peninsula. Twenty years later, this mining frontier reached the tin districts of Phuket and Ranong on Siam's west coast, where Australians from Hobart, Melbourne and Sydney formed business alliances with prominent Sino-Thais — much to the chagrin of British competitors.[66] The idea of Australasia as a necessary commercial sphere for Australian business persists in Federal Government hopes for an Austral-Asian free trade area, the AFTA-CER. Asian business migrants, valued for their entrepreneurship and investment capital, are today generally welcome in Australia. Australian companies and company managers operate throughout the South-East Asian region, while Asian counterparts deal profitably from corporate 'branch offices' in Australia's capital cities.

The idea of the Indo-Malaysian Archipelago as a protective barrier persists in contemporary defence thinking. Recognising the impossibility of a fortress Australia, Paul Dibb defined the strategic significance of island South-East Asia and the south-west Pacific, which formed Australia's 'area of direct military interest'.[67] Continental defence entailed the development of military links with northern neighbours, which, before and since the collapse of the old imperial order, have proved difficult to manage. The vastness of Australia's coastline made 19th-century defence planners acutely aware that Australian strategic interests were intertwined with the political affairs of the archipelagic states to the north. Relations with the Netherlands Indies were, as they are with its successor state today, consequently tinged with mutual suspicion. Australian strategic interests in PNG and, more recently, Australia's leading role in the independence of East Timor, add important third-country considerations to the calculation of maritime border security. Even the Howard Government, despite downgrading Indonesia's relative significance to Australian defence interests, understands that maritime borders cannot be 'protected' by force alone.

There is a tendency to lament the demise of 'comprehensive engagement'[68] with South-East Asia, and yet relations with Australia's northern neighbours have historically ebbed as much as flowed as either trade or military security dominated official concerns. The resurgence of a strident anti-Asia rhetoric in the 1990s goaded Australians into accepting a recidivist conservative agenda. Paul Keating's vision that Asia might be a source of national regeneration is not shared by enough Australians to permit the immediate revival of Australasia as a cultural ideal. Perhaps the word Australasia evokes too many awkward memories. From imperialist aspiration to the presumption of Australia's natural right to membership of an Asian political community, Australasia can imply the subordinacy of Asia. The term also attracts criticism from Rey Ileto for creating a misleading 'indeterminacy' in 'crossing two fictions', Australia and Asia.[69] As a historical concept, however, Australasia is a reminder that 19th-century conceptions of Australia's 'region', albeit based on a contentious geographical idea, extended deep into the Indo-Malaysian Archipelago. Further, the word captures the intermediacy of the northern Australian maritime milieu and the reality of peaceful accommodation between diasporic Asian communities and Australians, too often drowned out by the strident rhetoric of race and nation.

Footnotes

[1] An added complication, the treaty also recognises Australian territorial seas surrounding
15 'Australian' islands north of the seabed boundary. 'Treaty between Australia and the
Independent State of Papua New Guinea concerning Sovereignty and Maritime Boundaries in the
area between the two Countries, including the area known as Torres Strait, and Related Matters.'
(Sydney, 18 December, 1978.) In Joint Committee on Foreign Affairs and Defence, 1979, *The
Torres Strait Treaty: Report and Appendixes*, Canberra: AGPS. pp. 5, 7, 8–11.

[2] Applications of the natural prolongation principle seriously affected the tenor of recent
negotiations between Australia and the newly independent state of East Timor over seabed
resources in the Timor Gap. Joint Standing Committee on Treaties. November 1997. *Australia-
Indonesia Maritime Delimitation Treaty*. 12th report. Commonwealth of Australia. pp. 11–13.
Sherlock, S. 2001–02. 'The Timor Sea Treaty: are the issues resolved?' Research Note, No. 45.
Parliament of Australia: Department of the Parliamentary Library.
http://www.aph.gov.au/library/pubs/RN/2001-02/02rn45.htm

[3] Wilson, T. M. and H. Donnan. 1998. 'Nation, state and identity at international borders.'
In T. M. Wilson and H. Donnan (eds), *Border Identities: Nation and State at International Frontiers*,
Cambridge: Cambridge University Press. pp. 9–10.

[4] Wallace, A. R. (1869) 1989. *The Malay Archipelago: The Land of the Orang-Utan and the Bird of
Paradise*. Singapore: Oxford University Press. p. 25.

[5] Wallace, A. R. 1879. *Australasia*. London: Edward Stanford. p. 2. See also Van Oosterzee, P. 1997.
Where Worlds Collide: the Wallace Line. Melbourne: Reed Books. pp. 23–7.

[6] Wallace, A. R., *The Malay Archipelago*, p. 592.

[7] Wallace, A. R. 1893. *Australasia, Vol. 1. Australia and New Zealand*. London: Edward Stanford.
p. 2.

[8] Shermer, M. 2002. *In Darwin's Shadow: The Life and Science of Alfred Russel Wallace*. Oxford:
Oxford University Press. pp. 122–3. Van Oosterzee, op. cit., pp. 34–8.

[9] Jones, R. 1998. 'The fifth continent: problems concerning the human colonisation of Australia.'
In T. Murray (ed.), *Archaeology of Aboriginal Australia: A Reader*, Sydney: Allen and Unwin.
pp. 104–5.

[10] Macknight, C. C. 1976. *The Voyage to Marege: Macassan Trepangers in Northern Australia*.
Melbourne: Melbourne University Press. pp. 9–13.

[11] Allen, J. 1998. 'When did humans first colonise Australia?' In Murray, T. (ed.), op. cit., pp. 50–5.

[12] Wolters, O. W. 1982. *History, Culture, and Region in Southeast Asian Perspectives*. Singapore:
Institute of Southeast Asian Studies. p. 39.

[13] Fox, J. J. 1998. 'Reefs and shoals in Australia-Indonesia relations: Traditional Indonesian fishing.'
In A. Milner and M. Quilty (eds), *Australia in Asia: Episodes*, Melbourne: Oxford University Press.
pp. 118–9.

[14] Macknight, C. C., op. cit., p. 89.

[15] Flinders, M. 1814. *A Voyage to Terra Australis, Vol. 2*. London: G. W. Nichol. pp. 247–8.

[16] Howard, D. 1931–32. 'The English activities on the north coast of Australia in the first half of the
nineteenth century.' *Proceedings of the Royal Geographical Society of Australasia, South Australian
Branch*, Vol. 33, Session 1931–32. p. 103.

[17] Staples, A. C. 1966. 'Maritime Trade in the Indian Ocean.' In G. C. Bolton and B. K. de Garis
(eds), *University Studies in History*, Perth: University of Western Australia Press. pp. 101–14.

[18] Broeze, F. 1900. 'Australia, Asia and the Pacific: The maritime world of Robert Towns,
1843–1873.' *Australian Historical Studies*, Vol. 24, No. 95, October. pp. 222–7.

[19] Legarda y Fernandez, B. F. 1955. 'Foreign Trade, Economic Exchange and Entrepreneurship in the
19th century Philippines.' PhD thesis, Harvard University. pp. 180–9. New South Wales
Parliament. 1858. 'Statistics of New South Wales from 1848 to 1857.' *Legislative Council Journals*,
2nd Parliament, 1st Session, Vol. 3. p. 427.

20 Van der Veur, P. W. 1966. 'The Van Delden Proclamation of 1828.' In Van der Veur, P. W., *Documents and Correspondence on New Guinea's Boundaries*, Canberra: Australian National University Press. p. 2–4. Tarling, N. 1994, 2nd Ed. *The Fall of Imperial Britain in South-East Asia.* Kuala Lumpur: Oxford University Press. p. 27.

21 Tarling, N., op. cit., pp. 27–31.

22 'George Ferguson Bowen to Secretary of State for the Colonies, 9 December, 1861.' *Letterbooks and Despatches to the Secretary of State for the Colonies*, Vol. 2, 18 November, 1859–14 December, 1863. QSA GOV/23.

23 Ibid.

24 'Bowen to Secretary of State for the Colonies, 3 November, 1862.' *Letterbooks and Despatches.* QSA GOV/23.

25 'Bowen to Secretary of State for the Colonies, 5 November, 1862.' *Letterbooks and Despatches.* QSA GOV/23. 'Sir Charles Nicholson to Governor of Queensland, Queensland Legislative Assembly.' *Votes and Proceedings* (hereafter QLA V&P), Vol. 1, 1861. pp. 647–9.

26 Mullins, S. 1994. *Torres Strait: A History of Colonial Occupation and Culture Contact, 1864–1897.* Rockhampton: Central Queensland University Press. p. 88.

27 White, M. W. D. 1981. 'Establishment of the Queensland Border in the Torres Strait.' In P. J. Boyce and M. W. D. White (eds), *The Torres Strait Treaty: A Symposium*, Queensland: Australian Institute of International Affairs, and Canberra: Australian National University Press. pp. 16–24.

28 *Straits Times*, 10 October, 1874.

29 *The Australian Handbook and Almanac and Shippers and Importers Directory for 1875.* 1875. Melbourne: Gordon and Gotch. p. 314.

30 Nicholson, I. H. 1996. *Via Torres Strait: A Maritime History of the Torres Strait Route and the Ships' Post Office at Booby Island.* Nambour: Roebuck Society. pp. 260–1.

31 Clarke, M. 1877. *The Future Australian Race.* Melbourne: A. H. Massina & Co. p. 3.

32 Ibid., p. 20. Clarke emphasised the Moluccas, but his vision of Australasia extended to Singapore and Malacca.

33 Philipps, L. 1980. 'Plenty More Little Brown Man: Pearl-Shelling and White Australia in Queensland, 1901–18.' In E. L. Wheelwright and K. Buckley (eds), *The Political Economy of Australian Capitalism*, Vol. 4, Sydney: ANZ Book Company. p. 60.

34 Clarke, M., op. cit., p. 18.

35 Federal Council of Australasia Acts. 1886. *Votes and Proceedings*, Vol. 2, 1886. Queensland Legislative Assembly. p. 1035.

36 'Earl of Carnarvon, Secretary of State for the Colonies, to Sir A. E. Kennedy, Governor of Queensland, 29 January 1877.' PRV 8231-1-1, QSA.

37 Meaney, N. *A History of Australian Defence and Foreign Policy 1901–1923: Volume 1, The Search for Security in the Pacific 1901–1914.* Sydney: Sydney University Press. pp. 17–8.

38 Tregonning, K. 1958. *Under Chartered Company Rule: North Borneo, 1881–1946.* Singapore: University of Malaya Press. p. 95. *Straits Times*, 27 May, 1892, and 12 September, 1892.

39 *Straits Times*, 14 December, 1892.

40 Extract from the *Cologne Gazette* quoted in the *Straits Times*, 1 August, 1894. Captain John Bolton Carpenter was charged with piracy and transported to Makassar for trial. 'Report from the Select Committee on the Costa Rica Packet Case together with the proceedings of the Committee and minutes of evidence.' 1893. *Votes and Proceedings*, Vol. 51. New South Wales Legislative Council. pp. 171–219.

41 Battersby, P. 1993. 'Influential Circles: The Philippines in Australian trade and tourism, 1840–1926.' In Reynaldo C. Ileto and Rodney Sullivan (eds), *Discovering Australasia: Essays on Philippine-Australian Interactions.* Townsville: James Cook University, Department of History and Politics. pp. 62–3.

42 Copeland, H. 1883. *A Few Weeks with the Malays.* Singapore: Straits Times Press. p. 5.

43 Ibid.

44 *Straits Times*, 24 February, 1891.

45 Ibid.

46 Copeland, H., op. cit., pp. 10, 29.

47 Reed, R. 1976. 'Remarks on the colonial genesis of the hill station in Southeast Asia with particular reference to the cities of Buitenzorg (Bogor) and Baguio.' *Asian Profile*, Vol. 4, No. 6, December. p. 558.

48 *Picturesque Travel Under the Auspices of Burns Philp and Company Ltd*, No. 3, 1913. Sydney: Burns Philp and Company. pp. 108–12. Battersby, P. 1993. 'Tourists of Substance: Australian travellers and tourists in Island Southeast Asia, 1866–1913.' Honours thesis, James Cook University, Townsville.

49 *Straits Times*, 5 November, 1890; 8 October, 1890; 9 March, 1891. *Townsville Herald*, 7 February, 1891. *North Queensland Register*, 13 June, 1894. *Cairns Argus*, 26 August, 1896.

50 Buckley, K. and K. Klugman. 1983. *The History of Burns Philp: The Australian Company in the South Pacific*. Sydney: Allen and Unwin. p. 182.

51 *Townsville Daily Bulletin*, 9 August, 1912. Mercer, P. 1981. 'Clark, James (1857–1933).' In *Australian Dictionary of Biography*, Vol. 8, 1891–1939, Melbourne: Melbourne University Press. pp. 9–10.

52 *Brisbane Courier*, 23 May, 1874.

53 'Malay' was the racial term used to categorise divers and crew recruited from the archipelago, irrespective of socio-cultural differences. For an extended discussion of Filipinos in the Torres Strait, see Ileto, R. C. 1998. *Filipinos and their Revolution: Event, Discourse and Historiography*. Manila: Ateneo de Manila University Press. pp. 117–34.

54 *Queensland Census*, 1886. pp. 360–5.

55 'J. Gullard, Mourilyan Sugar Company, to Chief Secretary, 27 July 1886. Introduction of Javanese into Queensland.' QLA V&P, Vol. 3, 1889.

56 'Report of the Royal Commission appointed to inquire into the general condition of the sugar industry in Queensland Together with minutes of evidence.' QLA V&P, Vol. 4, 1889. p. 84.

57 Ibid., p. 71.

58 *Mackay Mercury*, 10 March, 1888.

59 Queensland Legislative Assembly. 1888. *Parliamentary Debates*, Vol. 55. pp. 296–7.

60 *The Queenslander*, 25 July, 1885.

61 *Townsville Herald*, 23 June, 1888.

62 Queensland Legislative Assembly, op. cit., pp. 296–7.

63 *Townsville Herald*, 22 December, 1888.

64 Ileto, R. C., op. cit., p. 122.

65 'Report of the Commissioner Senator the Honourable J. J. Long on Java and the East Indies, Singapore and the Straits Settlements.' Commonwealth Parliamentary Papers, Session 1917–18–19, Vol. 5. p. 1069.

66 Battersby, P. 1996. 'No Peripheral Concern: The international political implications of Australian tin mining investment in Thailand, 1903 to the 1950s.' PhD dissertation, James Cook University, Townsville.

67 'Report to the Minister for Defence by Mr Paul Dibb.' March 1986. *Review of Australia's Defence Capabilities*. Canberra: AGPS. p. 3.

68 Australia's Regional Security. Ministerial Statement by the Senator the Hon. Gareth Evans QC, Minister for Foreign Affairs and Trade, December 1989. pp. 15, 44–5.

69 Ileto, R. C., op. cit., p. 119.

Labourers in the pearl-shell industry, 1936.
Courtesy of John Oxley Library, Brisbane (Item No. 106579).

CHAPTER TWO

Tidal Flows

An overview of Torres Strait Islander-Asian contact

Anna Shnukal and *Guy Ramsay*

Torres Strait Islanders

The Torres Strait Islanders, Australia's second Indigenous minority, come from the islands of the sea passage between Queensland and New Guinea. Estimated to number at most 4,000 people before contact, but reduced by half by disease and depredation by the late-1870s, they now number more than 40,000. Traditional stories recount their arrival in waves of chain migration from various islands and coastal villages of southern New Guinea, possibly as a consequence of environmental change.[1] The Islanders were not traditionally unified, but recognised five major ethno-linguistic groups or 'nations', each specialising in the activities best suited to its environment: the Miriam Le of the fertile, volcanic islands of the east; the Kulkalgal of the sandy coral cays of the centre; the Saibailgal of the low mud-flat islands close to the New Guinea coast; the Maluilgal of the grassy, hilly islands of the centre west; and the Kaurareg of the low west, who for centuries had intermarried with Cape York Aboriginal people. They spoke dialects of two traditional but unrelated languages: in the east, Papuan Meriam Mir; in the west and centre, Australian Kala Lagaw Ya (formerly called Mabuiag); and they used a sophisticated sign language to communicate with other language speakers. Outliers of a broad Melanesian culture area, they lived in small-scale, acephalous, clan-based communities and traded, waged war and intermarried with their neighbours and the peoples of the adjacent northern and southern mainlands. The sea was their chief source of sustenance, wealth and mythology. Pragmatic, courageous fishermen, hunters, agriculturalists, warriors and long-range traders, whose complex exchange networks extended from the headwaters of the Fly River to the eastern coast of Cape York, they were largely protected from outside incursion by the dangerous currents, submerged reefs and shifting sandbanks of the strait itself, one of the least navigable passages in the world.

First Contacts

Oral accounts narrate the visits of Chinese and possibly Indonesian fishermen, who harvested trepang (bêche-de-mer) for the Chinese market long before European arrival in Torres Strait.[2] These men did not interfere with the Islanders nor seek to settle, but came each fishing season, traded peacefully and returned to their homes. The early 17th-century Japanese pirate, Nagamasu Yamada, is said to have visited Torres Strait and buried treasure on Booby Island.[3] British and French interest in the strait was sparked by its navigation in 1606 by Luis Vaez de Torres, after whom it is named, but it was not until the late 18th and early 19th centuries that relatively safe routes began to be mapped by naval surveyors.

Meanwhile, as Pacific stands of sandalwood and trepang became exhausted, European sandalwooders and trepangers moved westward in a search for fresh supplies, making exploratory trading visits from the 1850s and establishing stations on some north-eastern and central Torres Strait islands by the mid-1860s. Crews of 'coloured men' or 'Kanakas' (Pacific Islanders, Chinese and Malays) — the terms are often used interchangeably — under the nominal control of European boat captains, at times terrorised the Torres Strait Islanders, stealing their garden produce and women, killing those who resisted and burning their houses and canoes. An increasing through-traffic of sailing boats meant an increasing number of wrecks and murdered sailors, whose severed skulls were the preferred regional currency.

Responding to geopolitical and humanitarian concerns, the Queensland Colonial Government established its first (short-lived) official presence in the region in 1863 — a garrison at Port Albany and, a year later, a settlement at Somerset — for reasons of defence, trade and as a seamen's refuge. Having failed in all of its objectives, Somerset, originally hailed as 'the Singapore of Australia', was abandoned in 1877 and the settlement removed to Thursday Island under the supervision of the Police Magistrate, Henry Majoribanks Chester.[4]

The trepangers, while answerable to little but their own commercial interests, had begun to reach accommodation with the Islanders in a bid to further those interests. Some young men joined the station workforces and their sisters formed alliances with the European and Pacific Islander trepangers, giving birth to children who were usually adopted into the mother's family. This new equilibrium was again disturbed when, in 1869, commercial quantities of pearl shell were taken from the Tudu (Warrior Island) reefs to Sydney.[5] Word of the opportunities spread throughout the ports of Asia and the Pacific and triggered the pearl rush of the 1870s and 1880s, when thousands of men from all parts of the world made their way to Torres Strait, eager to pursue dreams of wealth. By then the Torres Strait Islanders had been 'pacified' and offered only a token resistance to the newcomers, whose arrival affected every aspect of their traditional life and custom. Again, young men from surrounding islands and the northern and southern mainland coasts joined the pearlers, being paid not in money but in food, and women were given as wives. Pearling stations were established throughout the strait, but the majority were located on the islands adjacent to Thursday Island, traditionally Kaurareg territory.[6]

Pearling and the Introduction of Asian Marine Workers

Of all the marine industries, the most lucrative was pearl shell, which, from 1870 until the introduction of the diving dress in 1874, depended almost exclusively on Pacific Islander and local Indigenous 'swimming divers', male and female.[7] Adoption of the diving dress rescued the industry from the consequences of its over-exploitation of island reefs and changed its nature.[8] The dress enabled divers to descend to great depths — up to 15 fathoms — in their search for pearl shell; and led to the importation of lower-paid Asian indentured labour and ethnic specialisation within the industry. The first generation of elite 'dress' divers were Europeans, who are said to have taught Polynesians and Filipinos the art of diving, before being displaced by them. The latter, in turn, were replaced by Japanese divers and tenders. Melanesians and 'Malays' (an omnibus term for the inhabitants of insular South-East Asia and beyond) tended to be less well-paid crewmen, as were Chinese and Sri Lankans. The British owners preferred ethnically mixed crews, despite their tensions, lest a group of disaffected 'countrymen' make off with boat and booty. Few records were kept of the very first Asian seamen to join the fisheries and even fewer have survived. Chinese, Filipinos, Indonesians and later, Japanese, travelled independently or semi-independently to Torres Strait from the early 1870s, lured by the same dreams of wealth and opportunity that had attracted so many others, but the Asian population remained low until the mid-1880s.

Wishing to exercise some control over the marine industries and tax the proceeds, the Queensland Colonial Government sought the approval of the

British Imperial Government to extend Queensland's maritime boundary and bring its offshore islands within the jurisdiction of the Colonial Government. In 1872, the maritime boundary was extended to include islands lying within 60 miles of the Queensland coast, including islands in the Torres Strait; in 1879, it was extended further to incorporate islands outside the 60-mile limit. These annexations extended British sovereignty over the islands (though not the waters) of Torres Strait at a time when Great Britain, France, Germany, the Netherlands, Russia and Spain all sought to extend the boundaries of their existing colonial empires through annexation of islands in the Indian and Pacific Oceans (see Paul Battersby's Chapter One, this volume).

The Pacific Island Labourers Act of 1880 and subsequent amendments foreshadowed the eventual cessation of Pacific Islander labour: the pearlers' response was mass importation of identured South-East Asian labour, which marked the beginning of a shift in fisheries labour dominance from Pacific Islanders to Asians.[9] It also created the earliest Torres Strait Asian communities, which were to endure for 60 years. Towards the end of 1881, a vast new pearl bed was discovered, later known as 'the Old Ground', extending many kilometres south-west of Mabuiag. Seeing a lucrative business opportunity, James Burns, of Burns Philp & Company imported 50 'Malays' on three-year contracts from Singapore and, shortly afterwards, imported half that number of Sri Lankans as boatmen.[10] Citing the successful Singaporean venture, Burns almost immediately applied to the Colonial Secretary of Ceylon to engage a further 100 Sri Lankans from Galle.[11] According to Sissons, in November of 1883, 'the first group of Japanese recruited under contract for the industry were brought to Thursday Island by the master pearler, Capt. John Miller. There were 37 in this group.'[12] After free immigration was permitted under the Anglo-Japan Treaty of Commerce and Navigation of 1894, the Japanese became the most numerous community, taking virtual control of the industry by the late 1890s and displacing the other groups (see Table 2.1).

The Hon. John Douglas, chief government official from 1885 to 1904, the heyday of the industry, outlined the historical trajectory as follows:

> [A]t first the shellers, finding that it was impossible to get sufficient white men who would ship in their boats, had recourse to Malays and Manila men, both of whom were found suitable for the purpose. Then came the Japanese, who appeared to be not only suitable as employees, but who very soon showed that they could not only work for others, but that they could work for themselves. They bought and built boats, and fitted them out, obtaining licences, and winning for themselves a position and a standing which could not be questioned. Would they appropriate the industry? It looked very like it. In numbers they were rapidly increasing, and in co-

operative capacity they proved more than a match for the Europeans or the Manila men. Then it was discovered that the Asiatic Japanese is an alien, and it was scarcely to be expected that we could license aliens to take our profitable pearl shell from our territorial waters. And thus it came about that the licensing of boats, which up to that time had been unlimited, was thenceforth restricted [in 1899 after intense political manoeuvring] to British subjects.[13]

In 1877, Thursday Island had become the new site of the government settlement. The Police Magistrate, H. M. Chester, having overseen the removal of the settlement from Somerset, reported to the Colonial Secretary that on the day he took charge the population comprised about a dozen European government officials, the crew of the government cutter, a Chinese gardener and 17 non-Europeans serving prison sentences for striking work.[14] By about 1885, the first Thursday Island census enumerated a population of 307, the majority of them Asian immigrants: 139 Europeans, 77 Malays, 49 Filipinos, three Chinese, seven Japanese, 20 Sri Lankans, four Arabs and 16 local Indigenous people.[15] This mirrored a general increase in the Asian population of Torres Strait, which by then comprised 'nine tenths of the employees in the fisheries'.[16]

Thursday Island, an Asian Port

The appointment of John Douglas as Government Resident, the highest public official in the strait, began a period of expansion for Thursday Island and its Asian communities, which ended soon after his death in 1904. This was not entirely coincidental: Thursday Island, like the rest of the region, depended for its prosperity on the pearl-shelling industry, the fortunes of the Asian communities rising and falling with the profitability of the fisheries. In 1885 and 1886, several shellers left with their crews for newly discovered beds in Western Australia, not returning until 1889–90. There was another downturn during the depression of the 1890s; in 1905, when most of the fleet moved to Dutch waters; and during the depression of the 1920s. But Douglas deserves the credit for encouraging the social harmony and surprisingly good community relations that prevailed during his period of office. His 'benevolent paternalism' ensured an impartial local court and honest police force and he reinstated previous measures of local government for the Torres Strait Islanders, as well as generally encouraging naturalisation and entrepreneurial activity among the Asian immigrants, some of whom had found profitable niches in the trochus and trepang industries. Undoubtedly, his most significant political victory while Government Resident was in quarantining the Torres

Table 2.1: Nationalities of men engaged in the marine industry based on Thursday Island, 1885, 1896–1938

Year	Japanese	Malays	Filipinos	T. S. Islanders	Europeans
1885	132	257	147		30
1896	511	270	212		51
1897	651	268	182	72	54
1898	790	247	251	174	86
1899	707	174	319	206	53
1900	619	217	237	279	65
1901	551	207	253	285	67
1902	624	194	205	289	41
1903	617	197	217	306	67
1904	739	231	188	307	68
1905	539	64	52	201	17
1906	460	51	42	131	7
1907	524	30	59	183	17
1908	498		44	148	9
1909	508		35	253	15
1910	528		18	205	14
1911	533	259	21	215	17
1912	631	115	19	224	22
1913	655	82	22	190	7
1914	427	58	17	161	3
1915	193	40	16	214	3
1916	422	40	18	197	3
1917	358	21	21	312	39
1918	576	32	14	229	8
1919	613	31	13	244	13
1920	600	12	2	147	
1921	377	63		216	
1922	407	67		130	30
1923	492	50		172	21
1924	411	42	2	191	15
1925	488	29	3	136	3
1926	528	36	1	148	6
1927	510	65		137	6
1928	542	59		111	6
1929	580	58		393	7
1930	488	38	1	354	7
1931	293	23	2	419	8
1932	339	20	2	447	6
1933	327	16	2	469	10
1934	352	24	3	742	14
1935	320	27	2	895	15
1936	335	56	3	349	16
1937	412	71	3	362	16
1938	429	55	3	211	5

Sources: Figures for 1885, 1896–97 from Annual Reports of the Government Resident for Thursday Island; for 1898–1938, abbreviated from Schug (1995: 154–7).

Strait Islanders from the restrictions of Queensland's Aboriginals Protection and Restriction of the Sale of Opium Act 1897, which confined mainland Aboriginal people to reserves and appointed local 'protectors' with wide powers.[17]

The last years of the 19th century were the height of Thursday Island's influence as the centre of the pearling and associated industries. The island was also home to five flourishing Asian communities, which together constituted the majority of the population (see Table 2.2). Generally speaking, each group filled an ethnically specialised economic niche: Chinese were market gardeners, cooks and small-shopkeepers; Filipinos were divers and trepangers; Indonesians were crewmen and shell-packers; Japanese were divers and tenders; Sri Lankans were boatmen, jewellers and pearl dealers. Despite the strains of poverty and crowded living conditions, reciprocity was the societal norm and interpersonal relations were generally harmonious. This is the thrust of residents' memories and court records and the conclusion of most official reports. Residents came together in their daily activities and recreational pursuits, for special events such as concerts, dances, boxing matches, and to celebrate the Chinese and Malay new years, the Buddhist *Wesak* and the Japanese Festival of Lanterns.

Admittedly, there existed economic and ideological divisions that promoted inter-group rivalries. The structure of the labour system, which was supported ideologically by the 'racial hierarchy' then in vogue, fed tensions that could erupt in assaults, brawls and sometimes murder. Chinese-Japanese and Filipino-Pacific Islander antipathy is well documented, but there were also occasional fights between Filipinos and Malays,[18] Filipinos and Chinese,[19] Malays and Sri Lankans,[20] Malays and Japanese,[21] Japanese and Sri Lankans,[22] and Japanese and Filipinos.[23] Cooperation and conflict, amity and enmity[24] are two sides of the same coin and historians are free to emphasise what best suits their argument.[25] The widely acknowledged hierarchy among the Asian groups was based partly on their specialised status and earnings within the pearling industry,[26] but was also supported ideologically by the supposedly scientifically proven 'hierarchy of races'. The Europeans were at the apex and the mainland Aboriginal people at the base, with Torres Strait Islanders just above them; in between came, in descending order, the Japanese, Chinese, Sri Lankans, Filipinos and Malays. Even the Anglican Bishop of Carpentaria, denouncing changes in Queensland's protection policy in his address to the third Synod of the Diocese of Carpentaria on Thursday Island in July 1935, subscribed to the almost universally held belief in the importance of race as a crucial determinant of individual achievement: not only could its importance 'not be ignored or underrated', he said, but '[t]he inheritance of different races is something given which cannot alter'.[27] The hierarchy and the now-discredited ideas of 'race' it embodied touched the lives of every inhabitant of Torres Strait. It regulated interpersonal and inter-group relations in almost every domain between the 'Black', 'White' and ethnically mixed 'non-Aboriginal' 'Coloured' inhabitants, the latter a socially and administratively ambiguous category, which might approximate either 'Black' or 'White' according to the dictates of policy. Even children were not exempt. Segregated schooling meant that Chinese and Japanese children generally attended the 'White school', whereas the children of Malays and Filipinos who were not educated at the convent school attended the 'Coloured school' along with children of Indigenous descent. 'Race', along with religious considerations, also came into play when the immigrants (and later their children) came to marry: there could be considerable loss of prestige if Chinese or Japanese chose spouses from Filipino, Malay or Indigenous families.

The racial hierarchy as an idea was so pervasive it was reflected, whether by accident or design, in the spatial location and configuration of the different communities on Thursday Island, where, by the turn of the 20th century, the majority of Torres Strait's Asian-heritage families had made their homes. Most of the Europeans, inheritors of 'Western civilisation', made their homes in spacious bungalows on the hillside above the western corner of the township, then known as Port Kennedy, near the present-day hospital. Most of the immigrants from Asia, 'Eastern peoples', congregated in the small, overcrowded cottages, shops and boarding houses of the Asian quarter, close to shore on the eastern side, up from the Post Office and between Summers and Hargrave Streets, an area commonly known as 'Yokohama'. It was here that a smaller and less distinct 'Malaytown' also emerged, alongside the billard rooms, gambling dens and brothels that served the island's large itinerant population. The Chinese and Sri Lankan communities proved the exception, positioning themselves — geographically and socially — between the European and Asian quarters (see Figure C). Chinese merchants generally resided behind or above their businesses in the centre of the retail precinct of Port Kennedy, near the corners of Douglas and Blackall Streets, while market gardeners lived on their plots, situated mostly north of the township. Sri Lankans lived in a recognised 'Cingalese quarter' at the eastern end of Victoria Parade. Even the cemetery was racially sectionalised:

> The layout of Thursday Island cemetery reads like a social map of Thursday Island, both last century and up to about the 1960s. On the top of the hill are the white 'bush aristocracy', and government officials; next are ordinary European Protestants; coming down the hill over the road are the Roman Catholics, then South Sea Islanders, Japanese, Chinese and Malay, with Torres Strait Islanders again over the road; and right at the bottom the (mostly young) Japanese divers who died in their hundreds working the pearl boats.[28]

View of Thursday Island, 1900.
Courtesy of John Oxley Library, Brisbane (Item No. 14339).

Newcomers found Thursday Island 'to be more like an Asian than an Australian town'.[29] It was the first 'Asian' port encountered by outbound passengers from eastern Australia, the last by inbound passengers. It was our 'gateway to the East', possibly to become 'a second Hong Kong'. British colonial architecture, manners, legal and cultural institutions may have dominated the western end of the island, but visitors who ventured into the small shops and alleyways of 'Malaytown' and 'Yokohama' at the eastern end were both attracted and repelled by the 'Eastern' exoticism they found there. 'There were Japanese divers, barefoot Malays in loose sarongs, Chinese in blue trousers, skull caps and pigtails',[30] selling 'turtle steaks, which they carried draped over bamboo poles',[31] Japanese women in kimonos, a Japanese temple near the Post Office,[32] 'a tiny tin Buddhist temple and an equally small Chinese Joss house'.[33] At a time when many British-Australians feared the social and economic effects of Asian intrusion into Australian society and when racial prejudice was widely institutionalised and internalised, the Asianness of Thursday Island elicited complex responses from visitors. Frank Hurley in 1920 was amused and affronted:

> The populace are a heterogeneous collection from Malay [sic], China, Japan, and natives from neighbouring islands. These intermarry and the offsprings are puzzles of racial complexity and mixture. The shops appear to be mostly controlled by Chinese and Japanese. There is a considerable white population; but these appear to be exclusively traders or lugger owners. The wants of the town being supplied by Asiatics. Thursday Island is a Satire on the White Australia Policy.[34]

Wilkins, in about 1925, was fascinated and condescending:

> Thursday Island is in itself a most charming and beautiful spot, but
> nothing that man has done has tended to improve it. A few straggling
> shops line the main street, and a few residential houses are scattered here
> and there. On a low-lying section backed by dilapidated boat-houses are
> what are known as the Oriental quarters, but the sordid, rusty iron
> buildings in no way resemble the equally filthy parts of the Orient which,
> even in spite of the dirt, maintain a picturesqueness that is entirely missing
> at Thursday Island.[35]

Table 2.2: Asian and European population of Thursday Island, 1877–1914

Year	Chinese	Japanese	Filipinos	Malays	Sri Lankans	Europeans
1877*	included in the 700 'natives'	included in the 700 'natives'	included in the 700 'natives'	included in the 700 'natives'	included in the 700 'natives'	50
1878*	included in the 683 'natives'	included in the 683 'natives'	included in the 683 'natives'	included in the 683 'natives'	included in the 683 'natives'	31
1879*	included in the 720 'natives'	included in the 720 'natives'	included in the 720 'natives'	included in the 720 'natives'	included in the 720 'natives'	17
1880*	9	included in the 213 Asians	included in the 213 Asians	included in the 213 Asians	included in the 213 Asians	28
1883*						c.90
c.1885	3	7	49	77	20	139
1886	included in the 800 'natives'	included in the 800 'natives'	included in the 800 'natives'	included in the 800 'natives'	included in the 800 'natives'	400
1890	38	22	25	36	22	270
1892	52	32	61	90	43	582
1893	61	179	207	189	32	362
1894	101	222	98	149	38	651
1895	84	233	119	131	38	626
1896	84	233	119	117	30	626
1897	73	331	92	87	48	571
1898	77	619	70	63	40	608
1899	71	440	103	64	54	574
1900	74	385	79	53	48	614
1901	114	304	83	62	54	705
1902	89	384	90	80	54	686
1903	98	351	82	60	43	740
1904	126	509	110	77	45	880
1906	101	309	81	74	33	734
1907	97	522	48	41	19	639
1909	80	190	49	32	14	663
1910	81	238	53	53	14	662
1911	106	191	36	37	10	559
1912	96	189	32	50	11	630
1913	85	182	33	78	11	613
1914	88	232	31	44	11	662

*Figure includes total fisheries population.
Sources: for 1877–84, 1886–92, 1894, 1896–1914 from Evans;[36] for c.1885 from Census, Thursday Island;[37] for 1893 from Map of Thursday Island;[38] for 1895 from *Annual Report of the Government Resident, Thursday Island*, 1894–95. Note that official sources are inconsistent and it is not until 1890 that we can compare ethnic groups in Torres Strait with any accuracy.

From Federation to World War II

Federation of the Australian colonies brought great changes to the circumstances of the Asian communities in their dealings with Europeans. The first Commonwealth legislation passed by the new Parliament was the Immigration Restriction Act of 1901, which was overtly discriminatory and deliberately sought to exclude immigrants who were not White and did not speak English. While pearling industry employees were specifically exempted, the import was clear. A number of amendments followed, each more restrictive. In January 1904, the Commonwealth Naturalisation Act of 1903 came into force, giving the Commonwealth responsibility for the naturalisation of 'aliens' (non-British subjects). It replaced the Queensland Aliens Act of 1867, which had excluded Asians (and Africans) only on the grounds of being unmarried and less than three years resident in Queensland. Now Asians (and other non-Europeans) were denied the right to apply for naturalisation and, even if resident in Australia, to bring their wives and children into the country. Typical of the personal difficulties faced by long-term immigrants who had made their homes in the Torres Strait was that of Punchi Hewa Mendis, a Sri Lankan who 'had married a Sinhalese lady, but on account of the White Australia Policy, she had not been permitted to live with her husband in Australia. So each year he had been obliged to visit her in Ceylon.'[39]

These new laws had long been mooted and, allied with the economic effects of the 1890s depression and the heightened emotions of the time, many Asian immigrants feared violence, incarceration or deportation and returned home.[40] Of those who stayed, a significant number accompanied the exodus of the pearling fleets to the Aru Islands in 1905 after shell prices fell sharply and limitations were placed on the hiring of non-White crews. Some returned, but the shelling industry never recovered its former profitability and the region began its economic decline. There were times of apparent recovery: shell brought good prices during the last half of 1919, for example, which encouraged the entry of some small operators; but they fell again in 1920 and prices for all marine produce generally remained low for most of the 1920s.[41] The indenture system continued until the late 1930s; the pearling industry was the only exception to the White Australia Policy, but the success of the Japanese as entrepreneurs led their European rivals to restrict Japanese indenture and access to the ownership of the means of production. Despite this, the Japanese continued to increase their dominance of the industry, which remained substantially in their hands until the outbreak of World War II.

Issues affecting the Torres Strait Islanders also came to impact on the local Asian population. After John Douglas's death in 1904, Brisbane bureaucrats lost no time in pressing for the inclusion of Torres Strait Islanders in the Protection Acts, largely for reasons of administrative convenience and control, but also influenced by ideological imperatives. In March 1906, the Home Secretary officially transferred all administrative responsibility for Islanders from the Government Resident to the local Protector of Aboriginals.[42] In 1912, most of the outer islands were gazetted 'reserves' and the Protector consolidated his control even further over the lives of local Indigenous people, including their interactions with members of the Asian communities. Torres Strait Islanders could not reside on Thursday Island or travel elsewhere without permission. Asian-Indigenous families residing on the outer islands were given a stark choice: if they remained on reserves, they would be classified as 'Aboriginals' and treated legally as wards of the Protector and fully subject to his authority; if they came to live on Thursday Island or adjacent non-reserve islands, they would be free people but, equally, they would be forced to forgo association with their Indigenous relatives. As 'Coloureds', they were again victims of 'the enframing practices of state and institutions', defined by Rodman and Cooper as 'methods of dividing up and containing space and people in ways that are made to seem natural and neutral but are in effect disciplinary mechanisms of order and control'.[43]

With the decline of the pearling industry, the long-term immigrants from Asia who had married and settled on Thursday and surrounding islands found manual and semi-skilled work in allied industries. While members of the first generation retained their distinctive dress, language and customs within defined communities, and preferred intra-ethnic marriage as far as possible, many of the early distinctions and antagonisms were elided over time through deep friendships, inter-group marriages and adoptions that transcended ethnic and religious differences. Their locally born children, educated together in the Coloured and convent schools, began to identify and refer to themselves as 'Thursday Islanders' or 'Thursday Island half-castes' and to intermarry in their turn. Tom Lowah, born in 1914 to a Solomon Island father and Murray Island mother and brought up on Thursday Island, writes:

> We had at least three different races of children with whom I went to school, and the parents were so friendly with mine that it made us feel we were all related ... Two of my Aunts, now deceased, were both married to Javanese [and adopted their husbands' religion of Islam].[44]

Ironically, the official policies of segregation, at their height during the 1920s and 1930s, were (unintentionally) blurring ethnic and religious boundaries among the Asian communities. Unlike most local Europeans, the Asian immigrants were on the whole remarkably tolerant of difference in everyday life: the Japanese diver, Kew Shibasaki, for example, was a Buddhist who married a Muslim Malay; one of his children became a Christian.[45] This tolerance was even more marked among the second generation of locally born children of Asian-Indigenous descent. This is what one would expect of a culturally rich, but economically and politically oppressed minority living side by side in a small, bounded location. In what was, in retrospect, an unofficial socio-cultural experiment on the part of the Queensland Government, the largely undifferentiated perception, categorisation and treatment of Thursday Island's 'half-caste' population promoted the formation and consolidation of a self-conscious third group identity. The outcome proved a challenge to existing legal classifications, forcing the authorities to proliferate increasingly absurd 'racial' categories (see Regina Ganter's Chapter Nine, this volume).

Also during the inter-war years, the 'half-caste' population began to be affected by the general unrest that had been building up for some time in the region as a reaction to the actions of the local Protector. Resentment came to a head with the passage of the Aboriginals Protection and Restriction of the Sale of Opium Acts Amendment Act of 1934, which redefined the term 'half-caste' to include many of the hitherto 'free' people of Thursday Island of Asian-Indigenous descent. This new act extended the Protector's control to yet another sector of the local population — citizens of Thursday Island of Asian-Indigenous descent, who until then had been exempt from the provisions of the act. The Bishop of Carpentaria was moved to speak out publicly against the Government, calling the restrictions 'a threat to their liberties and the free use of their property'.[46] Possibly encouraged by this unexpectedly overt opposition to official policy, the Islanders working 'company boats' organised their first challenge to European authority. In early 1936, they went on strike, eventually forcing the Government to make a number of concessions. The most significant was the passage of The Torres Strait Islanders Act 1939, which, for the first time, legally recognised the Islanders as a separate group of people. While various motivations for the strike are adduced by Beckett,[47] Sharp's definitive accounts demonstrate that at its core was 'a great cultural refusal' to accept the increasingly restrictive conditions imposed on the Islanders by the workings of the Protection Acts.[48] The Asian contribution to the climate of anti-government sentiment on Thursday Island and its role in mobilising that sentiment, which led to the repeal of the Protection Acts and the appointment of a more conciliatory protector, is yet to be documented.

The War Years and Their Aftermath

The intervention of World War II relegated to the background this complex and difficult situation, which had brought State and Church into open conflict after years of covert antagonism. The war years marked a turning point in Indigenous-European and Indigenous-Asian relations across all of northern Australia. In 1939, the National Security (Aliens Control) Act came into operation, requiring the registration of all aliens over the age of 16 and restricting their movements.[49] Anticipating hostilities with Japan, barbed-wire fencing and other supplies had already been delivered to Thursday Island to secure the Japanese quarter. At the outbreak of the Pacific War in 1941, the navy commandeered all vessels and the military authorities on Thursday Island took over the administration of Torres Strait, transforming Yokohama into a temporary internment camp for the Japanese residents. Until they were transferred to the permanent camps on the mainland, daily life continued within the wire fence.[50]

Torres Strait's strategic position and its perceived vulnerability to Japanese attack led to the evacuation in 1942 of the European and 'Coloured' populations from Thursday Island and other non-reserve islands. This effectively destroyed the prewar Asian communities and their distinctive hybrid culture. The majority of evacuees remained on the mainland; only a minority of the prewar Asian families returned to Thursday Island and they were, for the most part, of mixed Asian and Asian-Indigenous heritage. They found their former houses, businesses and community buildings looted, damaged or destroyed by the Australian soldiers stationed there, who also destroyed the houses of the Horn Island Filipino community.[51] In the midst of the destruction, the returnees set about constructing new lives in a radically altered sociopolitical and economic environment. They turned their energies inwards towards rebuilding family businesses, rather than outwards towards reconstructing the prewar Asian communities, even if this had been possible. Yokohama's buildings and Japanese temple had been destroyed by the army and the once-flourishing Japanese Society, Japanese Brethren's Society and Youth Club were never reorganised.[52] The Buddhist temple, located near the present Post Office, had also disappeared, along with the early Sri Lankan community that had sustained it.[53] The old Malay Club premises had been co-opted for other purposes, although there was a token meeting of the club once each month, where members would gather for a while and talk. Malaytown continued to exist after the war as a remnant community in decline, but it too disappeared with the deaths of its original members in the 1950s and 1960s.[54] Without the constant infusion of newcomers from Asia, none of the previous demarcated communities could be reconstituted either physically or ideologically, racial segregation was about to be discarded as government policy and it became clear that the future lay in affirmation of a new identity.

The postwar Queensland Government's policy was 'to emphatically oppose any infiltration of Japanese or other Indents to the Queensland Pearling

View of Thursday Island, 1941.
Courtesy of John Oxley Library, Brisbane (Item No. 177693).

Industry'.[55] In 1949, only 15 Asian indents were so employed, all of them prewar residents, who were 'permitted to continue in the Pearling Industry after the war only after their circumstances had been fully and carefully investigated by the Government'.[56] The prewar Asian numerical superiority on Thursday Island was further eroded in relative terms by the influx of Torres Strait Islanders, who had previously been barred from residence.

Soon after the war, the Islanders, almost 800 of whom had served in the Australian Defence Forces stationed on Thursday Island, began to call for significant improvements in infrastructure and services, promised to them in return for their involvement in the war effort. Controls on their movement began to be relaxed and many came to live on Thursday Island, beginning the process of re-indigenisation of the island and other former Kaurareg lands. In 1947, a group of Islanders was for the first time given permits to work on the mainland, setting in train the diaspora that today sees the great majority of Islanders living away from the strait. Buoyed by the postwar decolonisation of the Pacific, some prescient leaders of Pacific descent called for measures of self-government and even the creation of a separate and autonomous territory.

Nevertheless, the Queensland Government maintained its paternalistic policies toward Indigenous people, within and outside Torres Strait, until the mid-1980s. By contrast, legislative restrictions on Asian groups were being relaxed gradually as the White Australia Policy became untenable. The postwar rise of communism in China had caused some unease among the authorities with regard to the Chinese population of Australia and this extended to the strait. Local Whites, however, saw no real threat to their political and economic dominance by the now very diminished Asian presence, especially since the remaining Asians had had little alternative to assimilation with Whites in postwar society. Such sentiment was evident in the relaxed response by the Thursday Island community to the arrival of large numbers of illegal Asian fishermen in the 1970s and 1980s.[57]

The Islanders' successful struggle against the Commonwealth Government's decision to change their border with PNG and divide them as a people, which was ratified by treaty in 1978, increased their sense of unity and confidence in political action. In 1981, the Townsville-based Torres United Party argued in the Australian High Court that the 1879 annexation of the outer islands was invalid. Although this move for sovereignty was unsuccessful, it led indirectly to the 1992 'Mabo' decision of the High Court, which recognised traditional Indigenous rights to land. That decision, together with the proposed transition to regional autonomy in Torres Strait, given substance by a 1997 report by the Commonwealth House of Representatives Standing Committee on Aboriginal and Torres Strait Islander Affairs, have seen an inversion of previous ethnic power dynamics. Torres Strait Islanders are today far more confident in their Indigenous identity and the older generations have neither forgotten nor forgiven their differential treatment and their personal humiliations 'under the act'. The most recent challenges to locals of Asian descent have arisen from within the strait itself as postwar paternalism has yielded to Indigenous self-determination. Having reclaimed their lands and now preparing to reclaim their seas, some Islanders wish to impose new descent-based boundaries and deny the Asian history of Torres Strait. Once-influential members of the Asian communities now struggle to find a voice, while 'blended' families find empowerment chiefly in their Indigenous ancestry.

Acknowledgements

We gratefully acknowledge the assistance of Ali Drummond, Yuriko Nagata and Colin Sheehan.

Footnotes

1   About 700 years ago, the period from which oral tradition dates the settlement of the Torres Strait islands by their present-day inhabitants, there was a transition between a warm dry period, the Little Climatic Optimum, and a cool dry period, the Little Ice Age. This led not only to a cooling of the temperature but, more importantly, a sea-level fall of possibly one metre. This, says Nunn, was 'one of the most profound environmental changes within the last 1,200 years' of Pacific history.

Its importance lay in the fact that most of the population depended largely on resources, particularly protein, which they gathered from offshore reefs and on their lowland crops. The drop in sea level meant that the most productive parts of the offshore coral reefs were killed off and the crops withered, possibly within 10 to 20 years. Nunn estimates a decline of about 80 per cent in the food resource base of those communities, leading to competition for scarce resources, warfare and abandonment of coastal settlements for areas with greater food resources. Nunn, P. Interview with Robyn Williams, *The Science Show*, ABC Radio National, 12 April, 2003. http://www.abc.net.au/rn/science/ss/stories/s821596.htm. Retrieved 15 April, 2003.

2   Haddon, A. C. 1935. 'Reports of the Cambridge Anthropological Expedition to Torres Strait.' *Ethnography*, Vol. 1. Cambridge University Press. p. 88. Based on information from Rev. W. H. MacFarlane, Church of England priest of the Torres Strait Mission, 1917–33.

3   Alan Rix, pers. comm. to Anna Shnukal, June 1998.

4   In 1865, a government committee reported that it had been led to believe that Somerset 'may not improbably become the centre of a considerable traffic with the Chinese, Malay, and Polynesian traders, provided that it be constituted a "free port", and earnestly invite consideration to the desirability of removing all restrictions which may have the effect of deterring Asiatics from free commercial intercourse with that settlement'. 'Report of the Joint Committee of Legislative Council and Legislative Assembly appointed 11 May 1865 to inquire into and report upon … steam communication.' 17 August, 1865, *Queensland Votes and Proceedings*. p. 7.

5   'Police Magistrate, Somerset, to Colonial Secretary, 6 September, 1870.' Extracts from *Letterbook No. 1 of Police Magistrate, Somerset Settlement, 28 July 1869–1 October 1871*. Typescript B1414, Mitchell Library.

6   The various islands of the Prince of Wales Group, which became home to the Asian immigrants and their descendants — Muralag (Prince of Wales Island), Ngarupai (Horn Island), Keriri (Hammond Island) and Waiben (Thursday Island) — form part of traditional Kaurareg territory. The Kaurareg are linked through blood and legend to the Islanders immediately to their north and to the Aboriginal people of Cape York. As owners of the islands which became the hub of European occupation and which were coveted by Europeans for exploitation as sites of pearling stations and as agricultural and grazing land, the Kaurareg suffered most from the effects of colonisation. They were removed from their heartland of Muralag (Prince of Wales Island), first to Keriri (Hammond Island) in about 1892 and from there to Mua (Banks Island) in 1922. In 1947, they began to reclaim their ancestral lands through a process of resettlement (Harris, A. 1996. 'A short recent history of the Kaurareg.' *Land Rights Queensland*, April 1996. p. 12.) and, five years after initiating their claim, were granted Native Title to some of their former territories in 2001. The background negotiations, however, brought into the open still-unresolved tensions between the traditional owners and later settlers.

7   'Report on the Fisheries in Torres Strait by Police Magistrate, Thursday Island, to Colonial Secretary, 29 April 1882.' COL/A339, Queensland State Archives (hereafter QSA).

8   'Report of The Royal Pearl-shell and Bêche-de-mer Commission.' 1908. *Queensland Parliamentary Papers*. p. xlvii.

9   While the importation of Malays was a boon to the chronically labour-starved shellers, it was viewed with disfavour by the Police Magistrate. 'Malays [being Muslims] as a rule do not drink and are apt to use the knife when molested by drunken South Sea islanders. I have heard of several affrays of this nature within the last few weeks, but as Europeans are not employed in the boats it is impossible to get evidence.' 'Police Magistrate, Thursday Island, to Colonial Secretary, 29 September 1882, COL/A347/5304, QSA.

10   'Twenty five (25) coolies from Ceylon imported by Burns for shelling boats are they placed on ships articles or kept under original agreement.' 'Police Magistrate, Thursday Island, to Colonial Secretary, 4 September 1882.' In letter 4742 of 31 August, 1882. COL A/346, QSA.

11   Weerasooriya, W. S. 1988. *Links Between Sri Lanka and Australia: a book about the Sri Lankans (Ceylonese) in Australia*. Colombo: Government Press. p. 139.

12   Sissons, D. C. S. 1977. 'Japanese in the Northern Territory 1884–1902.' *South Australiana*, Vol. 16, No. 1. pp. 3–50, p. 5.

13   Douglas, J. 1902. 'Asia and Australasia.' *The Nineteenth Century and After*, No. 52, July–December. pp. 43–54, p. 50.

14   'Police Magistrate, Thursday Island, to Colonial Secretary, 25 September 1877.' COL/A246/4892, QSA.

15   Thursday Island census of c.1885, A/18963, QSA. Thomas McNulty wrote to the Attorney-General on 13 October, 1883: 'This is a small quite [sic] little place the Government Buildings being the larger portion of which there is six dwellings there is two Hotels one store and four private houses.' COL/A370/5183, QSA.

16   'Police Magistrate, Thursday Island, to Under Colonial Secretary, 28 July 1884.' COL/A397/5557, QSA.

17   This legislation provided the model for later similar laws in South Australia and the Northern Territory.

18   'Charlie vs Joe Reis and Francis for assault, 17 February 1885.' CPS13D/P1. 'Hassan Ah Mat vs Santiago for assault and battery, 29 June 1893.' CPS 13D/S1. 'Santiago vs Hassan Ah Mat for assault grievous bodily harm, 29 June 1893.' CPS 13D/S1. 'Police vs Lucio Del Rosario for wilful murder of one Hassan, 10 February 1904.' CPS13D/P11, QSA.

19   'Ah Foo vs Louis Castro for assault, 29 January 1890.' CPS 13D/P3. 'Yee On Wah vs Carlos Gar, Gregorio Geraldino, Pantalcon Asur, Mariano for unlawful assault, 30 July 1902.' CPS 13D/S2. 'Yee On Wah vs Carlos Gar, Gregorio, Pantalcon, Mariano for assault, 30 July 1902.' CPS13D/P10. 'Yee On Wah vs Feliciano for wilfully and unlawfully destroyed panes of glass the property of Yee On Wah, 1 August 1902.' CPS 13D/S2, QSA.

20   'Police vs Miskin for disorderly conduct in Victoria Parade, 7 January 1890.' CPS 13D/P3, QSA. Miskin was arrested for fighting with a Malay before a crowd of about 70 men, threatening 'a general engagement between the Cingalese and the Malays'.

21   'Awong vs Assa for sureties, 15 August 1902.' CPS13D/P10. See also 'Sergeant Pro Inspector of Aboriginals, Cairns, to Commissioner of Police, Brisbane, 28 May 1912, re Japanese and Malay disturbances'. POL/J36, QSA.

22   'Police vs Kicumato for assaulting one Saris Appu, 21 July 1902.' CPS13D/P10, QSA.

23   'John Nakashiba vs Fernando Gusman for assault, 25 July 1902.' CPS13D/P10, QSA.

24   McNiven, I. J. 1998. 'Enmity and amity: reconsidering stone-headed club (*gabagaba*) procurement and trade in Torres Strait.' *Oceania*, No. 69. pp. 94–115.

25   See, for example, the different interpretations of Evans, G. 1972. 'Thursday Island 1878–1914: a plural society.' BA Honours thesis, University of Queensland. p. 114, and Ganter, R. 1994. *The Pearl-Shellers of Torres Strait*. Melbourne University Press, p. 30.

26   Sissons, D. C. S., 'Japanese in the Northern Territory 1884–1902', p. 13, quotes a report by K. Watanabe to the Japanese Government on conditions of Japanese abroad in 1893 to the effect that the ordinary Japanese in Darwin and Thursday Island received £3–5 per month and the better divers £7–8; this compared with the £20 per year received by most of the Filipinos. Writing of Broome, Edwards claims that a good diver 'could make a fortune in a few seasons by the standards of the poor fishing villages of Japan or the waterways of Singapore, Koepang, and Manila, which produced the tough, spare little men who had the courage to wear the copper helmet'. Edwards, H. 1983. *Port of Pearls: a history of Broome*. Adelaide: Rigby. p. 72.

27   Extract from the published version in *Yearbook of the Diocese of Carpentaria* for 1935. A/58853, QSA.

28   Staples, J. and K. O'Shea. 1995. *Thursday Island's Asian Heritage: an oral history*. Unpublished typescript in possession of Anna Shnukal. pp. 10–11.

29   Thomas H. Crowe, who drove cattle from Rokeby Station in about 1903. Quoted in Pike, G. 1983. *The Last Frontier*. Mareeba: Pinevale. pp. 97–8.

30   Holthouse, H. 1999. *The Australian Geographic Book of Cape York*. Terrey Hills: Australian Geographic Pty Ltd. p. 52, of Thursday Island c.1893.

31   Holthouse, H. 1976. *Ships in the Coral*. South Melbourne: Macmillan. p. 119.

32 Amira Mendis, pers. comm., April 1999.

33 Jones, E. 1921. *Florence Buchanan: the little Deaconess of the South Seas*. Sydney: Australian Board of Missions. p. 18.

34 Hurley, J. F. 'Diary entry for 13 December, 1920.' MS 883, Diary A, Item 7, National Library of Australia.

35 Wilkins, G. H. 1928. *Undiscovered Australia: being an account of an expedition to tropical Australia to collect specimens of the rarer native fauna for the British Museum, 1923–1925*. London: Benn. p. 126.

36 Evans, G, 'Thursday Island 1878–1914', pp. 26a–g.

37 A/18963, QSA.

38 TR1794/1 Box 25, QSA.

39 Lock, A. C. C. 1955. *Destination Barrier Reef*. Melbourne: Georgian House. pp. 131–2.

40 'When the White Australia Policy was introduced, the Asians on T. I. were frightened about being sent away. They feared being rounded up and most returned home.' Amira Mendis, pers. comm., April 1999. Weerasooriya, W. S., op. cit., p. 160, states that they left Torres Strait because of fear that they would not be allowed to return home under the new regulations.

41 Annual Reports of Department of Harbours and Marine for 1919–29. The marine industries were also severely disrupted by the influenza pandemic, which reached Torres Strait in Feburary 1920.

42 'Under Secretary, Home Secretary's Office, Brisbane, to Government Resident, Thursday Island, 21 March 1906.' A/69463, QSA.

43 Rodman, M. and M. Cooper. 1996. 'Boundaries of home in Toronto housing cooperatives.' In D. Pellow (ed.), *Setting Boundaries: the anthropology of spatial and social organization*, Westport: Bergin & Garvey. pp. 91–110, p. 95.

44 Lowah, T. 1988. *Eded Mer: my life*. Kuranda: Rams Skull Press. p. 65.

45 Staples, J. and K. O'Shea, *Thursday Island's Asian Heritage*, p. 10.

46 *Yearbook of the Diocese of Carpentaria* for 1935.

47 Beckett, J. R. 1987. *Torres Strait Islanders: custom and colonialism*. Cambridge University Press. pp. 52–4.

48 Sharp, N. 1980. *Torres Strait Islands: a great cultural refusal: the meaning of the maritime strike of 1936*. Bundoora: Department of Sociology, School of Social Sciences, La Trobe University. See also Sharp, N. 1993. *Stars of Tagai: the Torres Strait Islanders*. Canberra: Aboriginal Studies Press.

49 Nagata, Y. 1996. *Unwanted Aliens*. St Lucia: University of Queensland Press. p. 41.

50 Ibid., p. 68.

51 Ina Mills Titasey to Monica Walton Gould, pers. comm., 1991.

52 Kikkawa, J. 1988. 'Japanese in Queensland.' In Brändle, M. and S. Karas (eds), *Multicultural Queensland: the people and communities of Queensland: a bicentennial publication*. Brisbane: Ethnic Communities Council of Australia and the Queensland Migrant Welcome Association. p. 136–45, p. 137.

53 Weerasooriya, W. S., op. cit., p. 155.

54 Ali Drummond to Guy Ramsay, pers. comm., November 1999.

55 'Under Secretary, Premier and Chief Secretary's Department, Brisbane, to State President, Demobilised Sailors, Soldiers and Airmen's Association of Australia, Brisbane, 15 July 1949.' TRE/A13838/51/11559, QSA.

56 Ibid.

57 The local attitude was in stark contrast with the recent government response to illegal Asian arrivals, which almost led to the exclusion of Torres Strait from the Australian Migration Zone in 2002.

Chinese boat in Thursday Island Harbour, 1930.
Courtesy of John Oxley Library, Brisbane (Item No. 78910).

CHAPTER THREE

The Chinese Diaspora in Torres Strait

Cross-cultural connections and contentions on Thursday Island

Guy Ramsay

The Chinese have maintained a long historical presence in Australia. Their mainland experience, driven by opportunity and fortune yet encumbered by racial prejudice and exclusion, has received a great deal of scholarly attention in the past three decades.[1] This narration of the Chinese diaspora in Australia has until recently focused on a racial binary of White settler versus minority group. In colonial Australia and beyond, the Chinese were seen as intruders, the 'other'. A State-constructed discourse of 'threat' nourished and legitimated dominant society's fears of the Chinese presence. This resonated clearly in dominant perceptions of competition for economic resources, such as gold and retail commerce; drug trafficking in opium and alcohol; sexual competition and anti-miscegenetic sentiment in regard to Chinese 'bachelor societies'; post-World War II fears of communist expansion; and, more recently, illegal immigrants and boat arrivals.

A new generation of Australian historical studies, however, has extended discussion of the Chinese diaspora beyond this White-minority binary.[2] Recent studies of mainland communities have decentred the racial narrative to incorporate a third space of Chinese-Indigenous connections. Normative racial boundaries have been successfully inverted by placing the oppressed at centre stage and the oppressor at the sidelines, revealing a more complex and nuanced experience of triangulated group relations (Chinese–Aboriginal–White).[3] This study extends such work beyond the context of mainland Australia to examine the Chinese diasporic experience within an even more complex site of cultural pluralism — Thursday Island, in Australia's north-east. This story of a diasporic Chinese community sustaining and crossing boundaries within a prevailing multicultural milieu elaborates the connections, contentions and intersections that were experienced among politically subjugated but numerically dominant 'minorities': Chinese, Torres Strait Islander, Aboriginal, Japanese, Indonesian, Filipino and Sri Lankan. A hitherto undocumented but distinctive racial narrative emerges in this chapter, that of the presence on Thursday Island of a longstanding Chinese community, which, while ostensibly subject to the hegemony of White colonial society, subtly undermined the latter's cultural dominance through connections and contentions with an array of other Asian and Indigenous cultures.

Navigating a Presence

The Chinese presence in Torres Strait predates the establishment of a government settlement on Thursday Island in 1877. Oral tradition tells of Chinese junks visiting islands in search of bêche-de-mer.[4] Chinese men were often employed as engineers, sailors, stewards and cooks on steamers and fishing vessels that plied the strait before and after settlement of Thursday Island.[5] Within the strait, however, Thursday Island became the principal site of Chinese migration during the late 19th century. Here, the Chinese were to establish over time a significant presence numerically, economically and, to a limited extent, politically. Yet scholarship on the multicultural island community to date has failed to examine this experience in any detail.[6] This chapter aims to address this oversight.

In fact, the Chinese, as Chester, Thursday Island's first Resident Police Magistrate, reported in 1877, were the first of the Asian nationalities to arrive on the island:

> I have this day taken charge of the settlement at Thursday Island [on 25 September, 1877]. The population comprised only the Police Magistrate and Mrs Chester and their son Neville, Pilot Allan Wilkie (a married man) and the crew of the government cutter *Lizzie Jardine*, Coxswain William Richard Scott and four water police constables [one of whom was James Simpson], Edmonds Lechmere Brown (who was dividing his time between Thursday Island, Somerset and the fishery), a Chinese gardener and sixteen or seventeen South Sea Islander prisoners serving sentences for striking work.[7]

While the Chinese market gardens on Thursday Island — like those on the Australian mainland — produced a welcomed supply of fresh vegetables, before long, the aforementioned Chinese gardener had become a target of contention. Chester complained in 1879 that:

> A number of valuable pearls are obtained during each season's fishing; these are invariably secreted by the men employed, and sold either in Sydney, or on board the mail steamers, the loss to the owners representing a considerable sum yearly. As the pearls never come into possession of the owners it is impossible to identify them or to convict any one of stealing them. A Chinaman living here, whose ostensible means of support is a garden, is the principal buyer, or agent in effecting a sale on board the mail boats, and has carried on this traffic with impunity for the last twelve months. I would suggest:
>
> 1st That it should be made unlawful for any Polynesian, Asiatic, or other person employed in the fisheries, not being the manager or owner of a fishing station, to have pearls in his possession, or to traffic in them under a penalty of six months with hard labour, and forfeiture of the pearls to his employer.
>
> 2nd That if pearls are found on any person not employed in the fisheries, the onus of proof that he is lawfully possessed of the same should be thrown on such person, with a like penalty in default, and forfeiture of the pearls.
>
> 3rd That any person buying or receiving pearls from any person employed in the fishery should be punished in like manner; with power to search suspected persons. All proceedings to be summary as it would be ruinous for owners to leave their stations to prosecute offenders.[8]

Within a decade, the number of Chinese on Thursday Island was climbing. On a visit to Torres Strait in September 1885, Mackellar, a travel author, recorded that:

> A very large number of Chinese arrives, and learnt at Thursday Island that a new law had been passed in Australia, and that they could not land there without paying a certain sum and having a sort of passport with their photograph attached. Here was a dilemma. They would all have had the great expense of returning to Normanton [in Queensland's Gulf country], or perhaps China; but a man in the store who had a camera saw his chance and offered to do their portraits at £5 a head! They jumped at it, and he reaped a harvest. As his photographic work is of the poorest description, and as every Chinaman to our eyes — especially in a portrait — looks much like every other one, the results cannot be of much use, but it is complying with this ridiculous law.[9]

As the pearling industry expanded, so did the Chinese presence on Thursday Island. Early census data show a rapid growth in Chinese numbers on Thursday Island from 1890 (see Table 3.1). This was driven by economic migration, particularly from the far north coastal and Gulf regions after Queensland's gold rush and the completion in 1889 of the Pine Creek railway, which had employed more than 3,000 Chinese.[10] In addition, the introduction of restrictive anti-Chinese immigration legislation in the Northern Territory during 1888 saw an exodus of 1,690 Chinese — numbers dropped from 6,122 in 1888 to 4,432 in 1889 — with many heading eastward to far north Queensland.[11]

Thursday Island was an important stop-off for boats travelling between Australia and Asia. As boats journeyed to and from China and the coastal ports of Queensland, Chinese seamen and labourers would therefore come and go.[12] It was as convenient to travel to the state capital, Brisbane, as to return to Singapore or southern China. This is demonstrated in incidents such as that in January 1895 when a man named Ah Bow was deemed by the Thursday Island court to be 'of unsound mind' and, within a month, was sent off 'home' on board a vessel bound for Hong Kong.[13]

The continued importance of Thursday Island to maritime navigation between Asia and Australia early last century, and the significance of this to the Chinese residing on the island, are illustrated by two visits by important people almost exactly 30 years apart. The first was the arrival there of Mei Quong Tart, a prominent member of Sydney's Chinese community, an outspoken opponent of opium smoking and 'an old friend' of the Government Resident, Hon. John Douglas, while on a journey to China with his family.[14] The second was the brief stopover by Chan On Yan in June 1923.[15] Chan was the representative of Dr Sun Yat Sen, patriarch of the ruling Nationalist Party (Kuomintang) in China. Recalled to China 'on business' — at the time of the rise of the Chinese Communist Party after its founding in Shanghai by Chen Duxiu and Li Dazhao in 1921 — he had been placed under police protection during his voyage home on the S.S. *Victoria*.[16] Police intelligence had uncovered a planned assassination attempt by members of the Chinese Masonic Society.[17] Despite the threat to his life by known 'enemies of his government in China', Chan On Yan disembarked from the steamer and was reported to have 'visited the town on two occasions during his stay here, interviewing several leading Chinese of the island at their respective residence'.[18]

Table 3.1: Chinese population, Thursday Island 1877–1913[19]

Year	Males	Females	Children	Total Chinese	Total Thursday Is
1877	1			1	c.32
c.1885	3			3	307
1886	4			4	c.500
1890	37	1	0	38	526
1892	50	2	0	52	1067
1893	61	0	0	61	1441
1894	94	3	4	101	1409
1896	71	3	10	84	1354
1897	56	4	13	73	1344
1898	51	3	4	58	1702
1899	62	3	6	71	1515
1900	67	2	5	74	1431
1901	61	3	8	72	1437
1902	78	3	8	89	1645
1903	77	4	10	91	1515
1904	102	6	18	126	1619
1906	73	5	21	99	1432
1907	75	5	17	97	1353
1909	58	4	18	80	1281
1910	58	4	19	81	1371
1911	81	4	21	106	1318
1912	71	3	22	96	1321
1913	64	5	16	85	1365

Thursday Island's strategic maritime importance and the 'Chinese connection' are also demonstrated by the Federal Government's expressed concern over illegal Chinese arrivals through the port post-Federation. Reports in 1905, 1909, 1918 and 1920 reveal prime ministerial fears of an 'influx' of Chinese 'New Chums' via Thursday Island and other northern ports.[20] Although related police investigations in 1905 asserted that there was 'hardly an opportunity ... for Chinamen to arrive by overseas boats', a 1918 report subsequently claimed:

> Henry Suzuki, Petrie Terrace [Brisbane], a Japanese, informed the Police that he had been told by some of his countrymen that both Japanese and Chinese had been in the habit of gaining illicit admittance into the Commonwealth by the following means. When ships anchor outside Port Darwin, Thursday Island ... and other Northern ports, they disembark into small portable boats and then land upon some unfrequented part of the coast.[21]

While opportunities for arrival by sea on to Thursday Island abounded, travelling through Cape York to White mainland settlements would have proved quite hazardous!

Dominant Discourses of Exclusion

Given the itinerancy inherent in maritime settlements and the growth of strong anti-Chinese sentiment across the colony, it is remarkable that a community of Chinese market gardeners, merchants and tradesmen prospered for so long on Thursday Island. Part of the community's success derived from the fact that the Chinese created businesses and provided skills that were essential to the long-term viability of the island settlement. A small number even successfully applied for naturalisation. These included probably the earliest arrival, Jimmy Ah Sue, born in Canton, and naturalised in August 1887 at the age of 30; another early arrival, Ah Sang, was naturalised in April 1893 at the age of 31; Tai Yit Hing, a 28-year-old storekeeper, was naturalised in July 1902; and 42-year-old George Sing, born in Canton, who, in September 1900, married Ah Bow, was naturalised in October 1902.[22] At the time, Sing had already resided on the island for 10 years and had five children, 'all brought up in the English Church': Lilly (born 1897), Poy Lun (1898), Ah Chun (1899), Celia (1900) and Chilli (1902).[23]

The number of naturalisations is, however, rather low when compared with that of other non-White 'aliens' during the same period, especially given the large number of Chinese on the island and their significant input into the local economy. The reason may be that few Chinese were married and the Alien's Act of 1867 clearly stipulated that:

> No Asiatic … shall be entitled to be naturalised as a British subject [in Australia] unless such alien shall be married and shall have resided in the colony for a period of three years. Provided that the wife of the said alien shall, at the time of his being so naturalised, reside with him in the colony.[24]

Moreover, prevailing racial discourses of the time placed Chinese — along with Indigenous people — at the lowest rungs of the Darwinist order. The *Queensland Figaro* in October 1883 'predicted that some day the menial work of the universe will be all done by Chinamen and negroes, whilst the Caucasian race is to fill the high places of the earth, and the other races are to be squeezed out of existence altogether'.[25] A *Bulletin* article from August 1886, entitled 'The Chinese in Australia', was similarly outspoken:

> Disease, defilement, depravity, misery and crime — these are the indispensable adjuncts which make the Chinese camps and quarters

loathsome to the senses and faculties of civilised nations. Whatever neighbourhood the Chinese choose for the curse of their presence forthwith begins to reek with the abominations which are forever associated with their vile habitations. Wherever the pig-tailed pagan herds on Australian soil, they introduce and practice vices the most detestable and damnable — vices that attack everything sacred in the system of European civilisation.[26]

Indeed, the Sydney newspaper, *The Telegraph*, on Wednesday 8 May, 1899, reported the tracing of a local leprosy outbreak to the Thursday Island Chinese community:

> Statements are current to the effect that a family, certain members of which had developed symptoms of leprosy, had reached one of the Sydney suburbs from Queensland. It is now ascertained that the family formerly resided at Thursday Island, and had a boy afflicted with the disease in the Dunwich lazaret. The family recently took up their residence at Ashfield, and a neighbour a few days ago informed the local police that the condition of the face of a little girl who accompanied the new residents warranted the presumption that the unfortunate child was leprous … So far as can be ascertained, the leprosy is traceable to a Chinese boy who acted as nurse to the children and who, it is stated, frequently sucked their feeding bottles to see if they worked properly. This man afterwards developed the dread disease.[27]

On 1 January, 1901, the Queensland colony became a state in the Commonwealth of Australia. The Commonwealth soon enacted the Immigration Restriction Act, which served to legitimate the discourses of fear and bigotry marginalising the Australian Chinese community. There were no naturalisations for Chinese residing on Thursday Island between 1902 and World War II. Naturalisation of Chinese and the immigration of their families were prohibited by the Commonwealth Nationality Act of 1903.[28]

Chinese contributions to the Thursday Island community and the remoteness of the place from the seats of government, however, allowed a more inclusive sentiment to prevail. After the end of conscription during World War I, a recruiting drive for volunteers led the Bishop of Carpentaria to request that locally born men of Chinese descent be included:

> I should be very glad to know if there is any possibility of half castes being accepted as recruits for the Army. There are several of them in these parts who were very anxious to enlist a year ago, and who might be got now if it were quite certain they would be accepted. They are a fine stamp of men — Some half caste Chinese with white women as mothers. They have

really been very badly treated as they answered the call of the Prime
Minister some 16 months or more ago. Papers were sent to them and they
answered yes, and then were turned down. The confidential committee
tried hard to have the embargo taken off them and failed.

As the conditions have changed so much during the last few months, and
as the Referendum means that volunteers have to be got to make up the
Reinforcements it seems possible you might be willing to accept these as
volunteers now, who were rejected before Universal Service was definitely
rejected. If anything can be done will you write to the Secretary of the
War Committee in Thursday Island.[29]

Chinese — but not Indigenous, 'Malay' or Filipino — children were
welcome at the local school.[30] A memorandum from Albert Edward Kelly,
acting head teacher of the Thursday Island State School, to the Director of
Education in March 1942, however, reveals that approval did not extend to
children of Chinese-Islander heritage. His reasons reveal some of the workings
of the caste system then in operation on the island:

Chinese and caste [sic] Chinese-White … live as white people and are
accepted in white society … Chinese-Islanders are not accepted probably
because they attended the 'Coloured School' … The admission of
Chinese, Japanese and Chinese-White has been accepted because they
reach a high standard mentally and morally and are always clean and tidy
and provide healthy competition for the white children and live as white
people. Other coloured children fail to reach a very high standard
probably because of their wretched living conditions and are classed as
undesirable pupils in the State School … At present, I suggest that those
to be admitted be: those accepted as white or predominantly white,
Chinese, Japanese and half-caste Chinese-Whites … but public opinion
desires as white a school as possible.[31]

Despite the general policy, one schoolmaster did remove all the Chinese
children from the school and sent them to the 'Coloured school'. When he left,
they returned to the state school.[32]

Connections and Contributions

We have seen already how the Thursday Island Chinese managed in part to
subvert the State-sponsored racist discourses that sought to disempower them.
This was due mainly to their small numbers and their contribution to the local
economy, which provided access to White domains generally denied their
mainland countrymen.[33]

Thursday Island picture theatre and Chee Quee's store on Douglas Street, 1923.
Courtesy of John Oxley Library, Brisbane (Item No. 698444).

Until World War II, the Chinese on Thursday Island worked in a number
of occupations, predominantly service-oriented (see Table 3.2). The occupations
broadly mirror those traditionally undertaken by Chinese residing on the
Australian mainland.[34] Of course, many Chinese had moved to Thursday Island
after economic opportunities on the mainland had disappeared after the gold
rush and, despite the economic fluctuations of the region's maritime economy,
many eventually established prosperous, long-term business enterprises, catering
to countrymen and other resident communities alike. Ah Sang, for example,
was the local baker for more than a decade before and well after Federation.
Tommy Ah Sue, too, ran a bakery for more than 16 years after Federation.
Joseph Chin Soon was a tailor for nearly 20 years. King Woh ran a store and a
lodging house and was a signwriter for a similar period of time. George Sing,
Wing Sing Wah, Sam Hop, See Kee and Lai Foo all conducted longstanding
retail businesses, of which the latter two still remain today. Their enterprises
were often extensions of their experiences in other thriving Chinese centres of
coastal far north Queensland: King Woh had a merchant firm in Port Douglas,
near Cairns, during the 1880s and 1890s; George Sing was a general merchant
for 10 years in Cooktown and four years in Cairns before coming to Thursday
Island in 1892; and Ah Hing, Ah Foo, Ah San, Lai Foo and See Kee were all
from Cooktown, the port of entry for the 1870s gold rush.[35]

As key contributors to the local economy, Chinese businessmen played a significant role in supporting the broader Thursday Island community.[36] Until the evacuation of the island in 1942, they supplied the inhabitants with commodities from Asia, as exemplified in the following 1936 advertisement:

> 'Just arrived by SS. Taiping. Fresh and Best Chinese Rice, 11s. per mat, or 3 1/4 lb for 1s.' Salt eggs, sweet prawn, Chinese sausage, Chinese peanut toffee, bean sauce, bean curd, salt olives, ginger, etc. 'All the above goods are for cash only. Ring up your order early, and I will deliver it right to your door. Buying from me, not only are you saving pounds, but you are also getting the Best Goods. A. See Kee, Cash Store.'[37]

Chinese businessmen were also key benefactors to local community organisations. The list of subscribers to the Jubilee Benevolent Fund in 1897 included Sun Loy Goon, George Sing, Quong Seng, On Cheong, Hop Woh, Tommy Ah Sue and Ah King.[38]

Only Chinese leased and worked the market gardens that served the local community. As early as August 1887, Lady Annie Brassey, the wife of the First Lord of the British Admiralty, who visited the island on the *Sunbeam* in 1887, had commented on the vegetables grown on the islands opposite Thursday Island by the 'invaluable Chinese'[39] — most probably the market gardens on Prince of Wales Island later tended by Ah Loong (1891–1907) and Wong King (1907–13).[40] Market gardens became the sole domain of the Chinese, who readily transferred leases from community member to community member. A garden located at the north-east of Thursday Island (present-day Rose Hill) changed hands from James Ah Sue (who had obtained the lease in 1890) to Tong Sing (1891), to George Bow (1891) and to Gee Woh (1901, written off in 1922).[41] Tong Sing's lease was invalidated 'on account of his being an Asiatic Alien, not naturalised in Queensland',[42] yet many of similar status were 'allowed to remain in informal occupation on a yearly tenure' since the authorities deemed it 'essential for the health of the Thursday Island residents that these gardens be carried on'.[43] A garden located in the north-west (present-day Tamwoy) changed hands from George Ah Gow (leased in 1900) to Ah Luk (1902), to Pang Bow (aka Ah Man, 1904), to Tseng See Kee (1918), to Francis Asange (1940);[44] another from Ah For (1900) to Ah Yet (1900), to Tseng See Kee (1915, written off in 1922).[45] To the west (near Green Hill) there were gardens leased by George Nicholson (1889), Ah Man (1900), Ah Sing (1902), Sue Shing (1910) and Hoo Ping (1930).[46] In many instances, leases changed hands when owners returned to China. There remained up to four market gardens on Thursday Island until the evacuation during World War II.[47]

Table 3.2: Occupations of Chinese resident on Thursday Island (and nearby islands) pre-World War II

Occupation	Name	Year cited[48]
Baker	Ah Sang (aka Sun Tai Lee, Sun Ty Lee; later Asange)	1888–91, 1899, 1901, 1902, 1905
	Ah Mee	1890
	Tommy Ah Sue	1899, 1900, 1905, 1916
	George Lai Foo	1939
Carpenter	Kam Tai (aka Goon Dai)	1900
Cook	Sam Ah Chin	1884
	Ah Bow	1885
	Ah Loong	1895
	Chang How	1899
	Tommy Low Shung	1899
	Yuen Chow	1902
	Ah Gee	1904
Doctor (Chinese medicine)	Ching Kin Ting	1899
Fisherman	Ah Bow	1891
Fruit-seller	Ching Chong	1900
	Ah Gee	1903
	Chin Yuen	1904
Gardener (some may have just been market garden lessees)	Sam Ah Chin	1884
	On Lee	1888 (Prince of Wales Is.)
	Ah Kwong	1891
	Jimmy Sue	1891 (Hammond Is.)
	Lee Sat	1891
	Ah Loong	1891–1907 (Prince of Wales Is.)
	Ah Sing	1892
	Ah See	1894
	Law Luk Kee (aka Lu Lu Kee, Loo Look Kee)	1894
	Ah Man	1905 (Hammond Is.)
	Wong King	1907–13 (Prince of Wales Is.)
	Chin Jung	1937–39
	Chin Wong	1937–38
	Chong Sang	1937–40
	Pa Wa Co.	1937–42
	Ah Fat	1939–40
	Francis Augustine Asange	1940
	Chong Yong Lem	1940

continued over

Table 3.2: continued

Occupation	Name	Year cited
Importer-exporter	Chow Bow	1897, 1899
Jeweller	George Bow	1891
Lodging House Keeper	Jimmy Ah Sue	1885, 1887
	King Woh (aka Wang Woh, Kwong Woh Leong, Ah Man)	1901
Nightman (collector of human excreta)	Ah Gee	1891
	Ah Loong	1892
Pearl-sheller	Jimmy Ching	1894
	James Foy	1906
	Law Luk Kee (aka Lu Lu Kee, Loo Look Kee)	1907
	Lai Fook	1908, 1910–12
Seaman	Ah Sing	1877
	Ah Sam	1883
Shop Assistant	Ah Chu	1895
	Hong Chop Son	1901
Sign-writer	King Woh (aka Wang Woh, Kwong Woh Leong, Ah Man)	1900
Storekeeper	Sin On Lee	1888
	Ah Sang (aka Sun Tai Lee, Sun Ty Lee; later Asange)	1888, 1890
	Wong Fat	1888, 1890
	Lai Foo	1888, 1903–28
	Ah Foo	1890
	Jimmy Ah Sue	1890
	See Foo	1890
	Tommy Lee	1890
	Ah Hing	1891
	King Woh (aka Wang Woh, Kwong Woh Leong, Ah Man)	1891, 1895, 1900, 1902, 1903
	George Nicholson	1891, 1899
	Yuck Wah	1892
	Sun Loy Goon	1894
	Low Shung	1894
	Loo Look Kee (aka Law Luk Kee)	1895
	Hong Wong Ling	1895
	Ah Ling	1895, 1900
	Pon Kew	1896–1900
	Tung Sung Woh	1897, 1905
	Tommy Ah Sue	1897, 1899, 1900

continued over

Table 3.2: continued

Occupation	Name	Year cited
Storekeeper continued	George Sing	1897, 1901, 1902, 1904, 1905, 1916
	Ah Chang	1899
	Long Kee Jang	1899
	Chow Bow	1899, 1901, 1905
	Ah King (aka Ah Kim, Ah Kin)	1899, 1903
	On Cheong	1900
	See Kee	1900, 1903, 1905, 1909, 1913, 1916
	Kwong Seng (aka Quong Seng)	1901
	William Sam Hee	1901
	Ah Sing	1902
	Tai Yit Hing (aka Lai Yet Hing)	1902
	Lay King	1903
	Ah Kum	1903–13
	Lai Fook	1903–13
	Kum Hun Chong & Co.	1903–42
	Ming Lee	1904
	Ah Ken (aka Pong Keng)	1904 (Mabuiag Is.)
	Wing Sing Wah	1905, 1916
	Chong Quin Lem	1911
	Sam Hop	1911–42
	Chong Yong Lem	1912–19
	Lai Too Fook	1913–28
	Way Hop Chong & Co.	1913
	Wih Sung Tiy & Co.	1913
	Sun Chong	1916
	Hom Yuen	1916, 1931
	Sam Hop	1922, 1931, 1932, 1939
	James Chee Quee	pre-1927
	Chin On Laifoo	1928–37
	Moo Kim Kow Chee Quee (M. J. Chee Quee & Co.)	1928–39
	George Laifoo	1937
	George Ah Sang (Asange)	1939
Store Manager	Chop Sun Heong (spelling unsure)	1903
Tailor	Ah You	1891
	Ah Chong	1904
	Ah King (aka Ah Kim, Ah Kin)	1904
	Hop Woh Shing	1905
	Joseph Chin Soon	1910, 1911, 1928
	Chin Daw	1916
	Kwong Tai Cheong	1916, 1931
Washerman	Ah Man	1904

Contentions and Criminality

Chinese businesses and services provided venues for communal interaction and contention. While the retail businesses were clearly essential to all community groups on Thursday Island, racial discord often surfaced, as we see from these excerpts from Courthouse records of the time:

> Sam Mitchell, an African American, states as plaintiff in a trial: 'I went to Mrs Jimmy Ah Sue's. I was outside the shop on the sidewalk and asked for Mrs Ah Sue's husband. She said, "He is in bed asleep. You got a very bad dog. He bit my husband["] … She called me a black nigger, ["]You rotten teeth, you black son of a bitch. How dare you come speak to me["].' [49]

> Mowen, a [Muslim] diver residing on Thursday Island gave evidence in a trial: 'I no got water at my house. I take two buckets. Yuck Wah say, ["]come inside and I get key.["] I go inside. Yuck Wah take piece of wood, hit my hand, he try hit my head. He no give key, he fight me. I go outside and ask, ["]What for you make fool of me. The ground belong me where well is.["] I no tell Yuck Wah I will put poison in well and kill Chinamen. I no tell him I cut tail off.' [50]

> William Burchell, another American-born 'coloured' labourer living on Thursday Island, explained to the court: 'About 6 o'clock I was standing in the door of my shop in Douglas St, T. I. Mrs Ah Sange came along the footpath and said, "Oh you dirty blackfellow you stink" and told her own children who were with her to call me a blackfellow — "smell him" — and a "binghie he stinks".' [51]

> King Woh, a storekeeper, claimed in a trial: 'Another Japanese owes me 15/- and I asked him for the money. I saw the other Jap had money and asked him … [The Japanese who owed me money] thought I wanted to fight the other Jap and so he assaulted me.' [52]

Galassi also notes many attested attacks by Japanese on Chinese. [53]

Chinese-run communal recreational spaces — highly stigmatised symbols of the Chinese diaspora across Australia — played a significant role in the Thursday Island cultural experience at the turn of the 20th century. Gambling houses and opium dens, in particular, as the more visible and documented of these spaces, served as social domains for the local Chinese community to meet and fraternise, and as sites of interaction with members of other cultural groups. Though popular, they were nevertheless illegal and subject to frequent raids by local police. The following extract from a police report on gambling at Fing Luck's house in Hargrave Street on 19 September, 1894, is typical:

> I saw a number of men around a table with a lot of coins — Chinese …
> Chinese cards and markers for fan tan … The house in Hargrave Street
> has been used as a gaming house for [the] last month or six weeks … There
> were at times 30 people there … people of all colours. All foreigners. I saw
> them playing Fan Tan. I am acquainted with the nature of Fan Tan. It is a
> game played for money.[54]

When the police raided William Sam Hee's house in October 1901, they
found a predominantly Japanese and Chinese clientele,[55] but many other
ethnicities, including Europeans, participated and the raids continued well into
the 1930s.[56] The most common games were fan-tan, che fa and pak-a-poo.[57]
Che fa and pak-a-poo are essentially lotteries. A Thursday Island police officer's
evidence against Ah Bow on 6 May, 1901, states:

> The ticket I produce is a [che fa] lottery ticket with animals on it … The
> tickets bear the names of the animals to be backed. The numbers on this
> ticket produced correspond with a list of the animals. This ticket is written
> in Chinese and each character means an animal or an insect. When a
> person backs one of these animals the ticket is then passed in. Supposing a
> person backs an animal, it is marked on the list which one is backed and
> the amount put on, if you wish you tell the Chinaman which you want to
> back and he backs it for you. The ticket is then passed in to the banker
> who gives a receipt for the ticket. The stakes are passed in with it. After all
> the tickets are in, the envelope containing the winning number is taken
> down from over the door by the banker or conductor and opened … The
> ticket is taken out from the envelope and what is the winning number is
> called out and those who have backed that ticket draw the money.[58]

Fan-tan is more sophisticated. Rolls provides a vivid description of the
game:

> The croupier sits at the end of a long table. In front of him is a big pile of
> porcelain buttons, or any round counters … In Australia they often used
> the worthless brass cash. A narrow ledge prevents any sliding off the end of
> the table. The croupier, always with his arms bare, spreads the counters
> with his fingers so that none overlap, bunches them together again in a
> flat-topped mound with the edges of his palms, then takes his zhong … a
> small tin rice bowl in Australia … inverts it over the counters, jiggles it till
> its rim touches the table all round, and pushes it away to a clear space. He
> lifts the cup, reaches out with a short polished ebony wand, divides the
> pile in two and rakes the counters quickly towards him four at a time from
> one pile, then the other. The betting is on how many will be left — one,
> two, three or four … As well as on single numbers, bets can be laid on odds
> or evens, or on corners to bracket two numbers.[59]

Although the Gaming Act of 1850 and the Suppression of Gambling Act of 1895 had rendered fan-tan, pak-a-poo and che fa illegal, 'these Acts were more of a nuisance to the Chinese [in north Queensland] than a severe restraint upon their activities'.[60]

The Chinese gaming houses on Thursday Island were highly organised. The gamblers would group together in one room of the venue, with another room serving as the office for the manager. Two clerks stood outside this room and passed tickets on to the conductor in the gaming room.[61] A 'cockatoo' would stand outside and watch for police.[62] Some prominent businessmen were also gaming leaders. In January 1902, the police expressed concern about the existence of an organised gambling ring led by Ah Sang, Ah Sam, Sang Chong and Ah Sue, all respected within the wider community.[63]

As sites of multicultural intersection, Chinese gaming sites, too, were at times the venues for disputes, usually fomented by aggrieved clients who suspected the Chinese of cheating. A disturbance during September 1900 between Chinese and Japanese men originated 'in the Chinese gambling house … near Yokohama [the Asian quarter on Thursday Island]'.[64] In June 1902, police noted that Ah Sing — a gaming-house keeper and opium seller — 'has made several complaints … about Japanese throwing stones at his house'.[65]

When improper activities brought members of the Thursday Island Chinese community into contact with the local court, treatment was normally even-handed and equitable.[66] While trials were conducted in English — with a Chinese defendant 'sworn in accordance with the custom of his country' — interpreters were provided for those with a poor command of English.[67] Ah Que, Charlie Sam Yuen, George Sing, Lai Foo and Chee Quee all served as court interpreters between 1894 and 1921.[68]

Cross-Cultural Contacts and 'the Act'

For centuries, opium smoking was also a common form of recreation for many Chinese. Some of them continued the practice after migration to Australia. As on the mainland, the opium problem on Thursday Island was attributed to the Asian presence, particularly the Chinese.[69] In January 1895, the local police reported that Ah Ling's shop in Victoria Parade was 'fitted with bunks all round, pipes, opium, and lamps and mats. It is an "opium den"'.[70] In July 1899, two years after passage of the Queensland Aboriginals Protection and Restriction of the Sale of Opium Act — which prohibited the selling of opium to Aboriginal people — Ah King, 'a Chinaman … of unsound mind' who was known for 'lurking around opium dens', was put on trial for precisely that offence. At his trial, a police officer informed the magistrate that opium abuse was 'common among the Malays and Chinese. Significant complaints have been made to me about the existence of opium dens. It is openly practised by the Malays and Chinese.'[71] The Northern Protector of Aboriginals, Walter E. Roth, was also present and condemned the prevalence of opium abuse among 'Blacks' and its connection with the Chinese community.[72]

The selling and smoking of opium were eventually criminalised by Commonwealth legislation in January 1906, but opium abuse by Chinese and non-Chinese alike continued well beyond this date.[73] Before then, permits to sell opium were held by a number of Chinese on Thursday Island. At the aforementioned trial of Ah King, M. T. McCreery, Senior Sergeant of Police on Thursday Island, states:

> I am informed by the Inspector of Police that there are a certain number of persons who have permission from the Collector of Customs, some being wholesale dealers and others retail dealers. The Customs Department furnishes me with a monthly return of the opium sold. The returns show the number and names of the purchasers of opium. The sale of opium is now almost uncontrolled in Thursday Island and there are several shops or dens where it is sold habitually. From the information I have there are about a dozen people who are authorised to sell opium on Thursday Island. The Defendant [Ah King] is not to my knowledge one of those who is authorised.[74]

In 1902, there were 10 permit holders on Thursday Island; in 1904, there were 15. The Chief Protector of Aboriginals had lamented: 'It seems extraordinary to me that places like Cooktown [with 16 licences] and Thursday Island [with 10 licences] should have a greater number of "permits" in force than Brisbane which has only nine'[75] — the clear implication being that this was because of a large Chinese presence in the two far northern townships. The Aboriginals Protection and Restriction of the Sale of Opium Act of 1897 in theory had 'prohibited the sale of opium by any person not a legally qualified medical practitioner or pharmaceutical chemist … [h]owever this provision was counteracted by the issue of special licences enabling reputable merchants to sell opium'.[76] Roth considered such permits not only illegal, but morally reprehensible, given the tragic outcomes arising from opiate addiction among Queensland's Indigenous population:

> These so-called permits to sell opium (both wholesale and retail) are not issued for any stated periods, and not a few of the Protectors, the officers administering the very Act for the suppression of the illicit supply of the drug, are aware of the Europeans or Asiatics to whom they have been granted. Cases have even occurred where an individual has been charged

with illegally supplying opium, and has tried to defend his action by showing a permit.[77]

Roth criticised the issuing of permits free of charge and pointedly recommended enforcement of the letter of the act against 'Chinamen'.[78]

It is true that opium peddling had long been a problem on Thursday Island. The first recorded conviction after Douglas's arrival as Resident Magistrate occurred on 5 January, 1885, when Ah Bow, a ship's cook, was charged for smuggling opium allegedly brought from Cooktown.[79] Convictions continued at fairly regular intervals until 1928, when Ah Wah was fined for possession.[80]

During the colonial period, Chinese cultural tolerance of opium consumption invariably came into conflict with mainstream repugnance towards its abuse. When Sun Loy Goon was tried in October 1894 for selling opium at his Victoria Parade store, he pleaded to no avail that 'it is customary for my countrymen to smoke opium'.[81] According to Manderson, such attitudes prevailed across Australia.

> The Chinese smoked opium … It was for them a recreational drug like alcohol or tobacco. Like any such drug, therefore, there were occasional users, regular users, abusers and addicts; there were houses in which the smoking of an opium pipe was regarded as a social courtesy, and others where it was a serious business.[82]

While Sun's case was dismissed because the 'sale had not been completed', another storekeeper, Low Shung, was convicted of the same offence the next month.[83] Low had originally begun selling to his Muslim client, Omar, when they resided in Croydon some 1,000 kilometres away on the mainland.[84]

Opium dens were generally to be found in, or adjoining, private residences. The home of storekeeper Ah See in Hastings Street came under the notice of the police in April 1890:

> [T]he premises were in a very dirty condition, there was no closet [toilet]. There is a water-course running through the allotment occupied. The occupier has a large number of fowls, probably a couple of hundred. The fowl house was in a very filthy condition with a very nasty smell coming from it. I entered the tenement occupied by the defendant. It appeared to be used as a place for smoking opium. There was a lamp and opium pipes … There was all sorts of rubbish lying about the place. The water [course] was defiled by the presence of human excreta …[85]

Although the Chinese dominated the selling of opium on Thursday Island, others, such as the Malay Ahmat family, also operated small smoking dens:

> Papa had this little den at the back of our house and a few Chinese used to
> come there and … at different times they used to go to their places to
> smoke opium and it wasn't illegal in those days or no one made any drama
> about it … I ended up in there one day — Mama told me never to go near
> there … There's these Chinese chaps lying on the bench with these long
> pipe things with a thin candle burning in the centre … He just pointed to
> another pipe on the counter … [Mama] came in … and she just grabbed
> me and gave me the biggest hiding I ever got for being in there … When
> Papa died that was the end of our den.[86]

The Aboriginals Protection and Restriction of the Sale of Opium Act
not only proscribed opium selling to Aborigines — by inference by Chinese —
but impacted heavily on other activities that brought Chinese and Indigenous
residents of Thursday Island into contact. The recruiting of Indigenous pearl-
shelling labour by Chinese, for example, was forbidden, in effect excluding
Chinese from the fisheries industry.[87] Chinese-Indigenous liaisons were
prohibited: Ah Young was fined in May 1910 for 'permitting [an] Aboriginal
female to be upon premises in his occupation' and again two years later for
supplying liquor;[88] Hom Yuen was fined in January 1918 and again in August
1929 for keeping the company of an Aboriginal woman and was refused
permission to marry a 'half-caste' woman in 1916.[89]

Rare exceptions were made. In December 1905, the local Protector,
O'Brien,

> went to Hammond Island [near Thursday Island] to investigate a rumour
> re supplying of opium. I found that a Chinaman, Ah Man, was living at a
> garden with a (lawfully married) aboriginal wife, and although I found a
> small quantity of opium, I could find nothing to justify the belief that his
> wife had taken to the habit. In fact, she expressed her disgust at the idea of
> her husband smoking. I have not prosecuted the husband for being in
> possession of opium, mainly on account of the difficulty of maintaining his
> wife during any term of imprisonment to which he might be subjected.
> She is a Burketown woman, and has no tribal friends here.[90]

Generally, though, Chinese-Indigenous marriages were rarely sanctioned
by the Protector, even when — as in Hom Yuen's case — supported by
'character references from the Mayor, the Town Clerk, a Justice of the Peace
and six other Europeans'.[91] Local Protector Lee-Bryce made it clear in a 1916
correspondence that he did 'not approve of our women marrying aliens, and the
making of a precedent would result in numerous applications by Chinamen and
others who merely desire the girls for their own purposes'.[92] The act was
ultimately successful in its anti-miscegenetic intent, since between its passage
and 1914 no marriages between Chinese and local Indigenous people took place
on Thursday Island.[93]

Postwar: starting anew, under suspicion

A significant, yet, due to the White Australia Policy, ever-diminishing Chinese presence endured on Thursday Island until World War II. With the outbreak of the Pacific War, however, Chinese residents were evacuated south. On 28 January, 1942, 20 Chinese left on the *Zealandia* and *Ormiston*.[94] They remained on the mainland during the war, although the See Kees were trapped in occupied Hong Kong while on holiday and were unable to return until 1947. One local of Chinese ancestry, Joseph Chin Soon (Taylor), served alongside the Torres Strait Islander servicemen during the war. In 1944, he was redeployed south, however, when Islander servicemen objected to the fact that he, along with other Thursday Island 'Malays', were being paid full Australian Military Forces wages.[95]

Only four families returned after peace was declared in 1945. Those who returned were the established merchant families, Lai Foo and See Kee, and those of Chinese-Indigenous heritage, Chin Soon and Asange.[96] The Lai Foos were the first to return soon after the war, with the See Kees coming later, in 1947. Arriving on Thursday Island, the families had to 'start all over again'.[97] Their shops and houses, along with the Joss house, had been looted or destroyed by members of the Australian forces during the occupation. The Lai Foos rebuilt, with the See Kees renting from them on their return. A market gardener also returned to the island early on and set up a plot near the current site of the high school.[98] He remained until 1950, when he moved to Cairns. The See Kees took over the plot but closed it down in 1952 — pearling brought in more money. Thereafter, fresh vegetables had to be shipped in. Individual Chinese also came: William Ah Loy, a storekeeper who married a local Japanese woman; Frederick James Yen Foo, Robert Lee Way, Wing Kong Lee and Charles Thomas Sue San, all storekeepers who later retired or left.[99]

With time, businesses were re-established and the Chinese families, although numerically fewer compared with the prewar period, again came to dominate the local retail sector, 'owning one-half of the shops on the main business street, Douglas Street'.[100] Indeed, this drew the attention of Federal Government officers after the communist victory in China in 1949. A security report dated December 1949, two months after the communist victory, saw George Laifoo as

> the most astute and the wealthiest ... business man on the Island ... own[ing] five (5) stores, two (2) Billiard saloons and three (3) taxis and is a power to be reckoned with ... Next in importance would probably be George Asange, also with a Chinese background. He is a member of the Town Council and conducts a store.[101]

View of former Chinese market garden site, 1997.
Courtesy of Guy Ramsay.

In fact, at the time, officers bluntly asked Thursday Island Chinese, 'Are you a communist?'[102]

As before the war, the contributions of the Chinese community provided them with privileges despite their continuing 'minority' status. In the local cinema during the 1950s, for example, they sat upstairs with the Whites; 'Malays' and Islanders were downstairs in the front, with 'half-castes' at the back.[103] This saw Robert Lee Way create a disturbance one night when he and his Malay girlfriend were refused admission to the upstairs section.[104]

Seafaring Chinese once again navigated a presence on Thursday Island during the late 1960s and 1970s with captured illegal Taiwanese fishing boats being detained there:

> In late 1976 there were five Taiwanese vessels anchored under guard in Port Kennedy and because it frequently takes months to repatriate the seamen detained, there were anything up to one hundred Taiwanese roaming the streets of Thursday Island. Naturally they were patronised by the local Chinese community. Some obtained jobs with businessmen moving goods, labouring and painting, and by working for forty dollars a week they undercut local unskilled labour (mainly Islanders) … The fishermen from the steel-hulled vessels tend to be more sophisticated than the clam gatherers. They drink at the hotels, frequently acquire Island

girlfriends and are accepted by the community with its usual hospitality. Some even moved into houses on the Tamwoy Reserve as the guests of sympathetic Islanders. Surprisingly there seems little resentment about the lost jobs, for as one Islander put it: 'They come from a very poor land and we are sorry for them.'[105]

With 'the act' now a historical relic, the Chinese visitors were free to mix with Islanders. Thursday Island Chinese, too, married into the two cultural groups that had come to dominate the island postwar: Islander and White. Nevertheless, some still 'went back' to find Chinese marriage partners.

By the late 20th century, however, power dynamics in the region had shifted dramatically from the White to the Islander communities. The catalyst, the 1992 High Court Mabo decision, recognised Native Title for the strait's Mer Islanders and, by precedent, all Indigenous communities where connection with traditional lands had been maintained. Successful claims over Thursday Island by the Kaurareg people and a push for Torres Strait regional autonomy have thus altered the positions of 'minorities' on Thursday Island — the Chinese are no longer the 'significant power group in the town' that they became in the 1980s.[106] Some continue to see their future in the region — Liberty See Kee, for example, is a Torres Shire councillor — while others have or plan to leave. In conclusion, the Chinese diasporic presence on Thursday Island, though little known outside the island, has a long and rich history, evidence of the community's success in maintaining a cultural boundary within a prevailing multicultural milieu. The significant contribution of Chinese to Thursday Island set their 'birthright' there, in connection and contention with other cultural groups on the island. As power dynamics continue to shift in the region, the future position of the Thursday Island Chinese community or those residents with Chinese ancestry remains to be seen.

Acknowledgements

I gratefully acknowledge the assistance of Joseph Ahmat, Judith Ramsay, Richard See Kee and Anna Shnukal.

Footnotes

[1] See: Choi, C. 1975. *Chinese Migration and Settlement in Australia.* Sydney: Sydney University Press. Evans, R., K. Saunders and K. Cronin. 1993. *Race Relations in Colonial Queensland: a history of exclusion, exploitation and extermination.* St Lucia: University of Queensland Press. Giese, D. 1997. *Astronauts, Lost Souls and Dragons: conversations with Chinese Australians.* St Lucia: University of Queensland Press. Jones, T. 1997. *The Chinese in the Northern Territory.* Darwin: Northern Territory University Press. Ling, C. 1988. 'Chinese in Queensland.' In M. Brandle and S. Karas (eds), *Multicultural Queensland: the people and communities of Queensland: a bicentennial publication.* Brisbane: Ethnic Communities Council of Australia and the Queensland Migrant Welcome Association. pp. 19-25. Loh, M. 1989. *Dinky-di: the contributions of Chinese immigrants and Australians of Chinese descent to Australia's defence forces and war efforts 1899–1988.* Canberra: AGPS. May, C. 1984. *Topsawyers: the Chinese in Cairns 1870–1920.* Townsville: James Cook University, History Department. Rolls, E. 1992. *Sojourners: flowers and the wide sea.* St Lucia: University of Queensland Press. Rolls, E. 1996. *Citizens: flowers and the wide sea.* St Lucia: University of Queensland Press.

[2] Anderson, K. 2000. 'Thinking "postnationally": dialogue across multicultural, Indigenous, and settler spaces.' *Annals of the Association of the American Geographers,* Vol. 90. pp. 381–91. Ganter, R. 1998. 'Living an immoral life – "coloured" women and the paternalistic state.' *Hecate,* Vol. 24. pp. 13–40. Ramsay, G. 2003. 'Cherbourg's Chinatown: creating an identity of place on an Australian Aboriginal settlement.' *Journal of Historical Geography,* Vol. 29, No. 1. pp. 109–22.

[3] Sibley, D. 1995. *Geographies of Exclusion: society and difference in the West.* London: Routledge. p. 44.

[4] Coral, C. [Rev. W. H. MacFarlane] 1925. 'When shadows lengthen, yarns of old identities of Torres Strait: Maino and the warriors of Tutu.' *The Queenslander,* 20 June, 1925. p. 11. Langbridge, J. W. 1977. 'From enculturation to evangelisation: an account of missionary education in the islands of Torres Strait to 1915.' BA Honours thesis, James Cook University. p. 23. Haddon, A. C. 1901. *Head Hunters: Black, White and Brown.* London: Methuen. p. 88.

[5] D'Albertis, L. M. 1880. *New Guinea: what I did and what I saw,* 2 vols. London: Sampson Low. 'S. McFarlane, Somerset, fifth voyage of "Ellengowan", 20 March–1 April 1875.' *London Missionary Society Papuan Letters.* Microfilm M91, John Oxley Library, State Library of Queensland (hereafter JOL). 'Police Magistrate, Somerset, to Colonial Secretary, 6 May 1876.' *Extracts from Records of Somerset, Cape York 1872–77.* MS.Q 589, Mitchell Library. 'Police Magistrate to Colonial Secretary, 12 February 1873.' Ibid. 'Torres Strait and a trip to Deliverance Island.' *Brisbane Courier,* 29 September, 1877. p. 3.

[6] Evans, G. 1972. 'Thursday Island 1878–1914: a plural society.' BA Honours thesis, University of Queensland. Ganter, R. 1994. *The Pearl-Shellers of Torres Strait: resource use, development and decline, 1860s–1960s.* Melbourne University Press. Kehoe-Forutan, S. 1991. 'The effectiveness of Thursday Island as an urban centre in meeting the needs of its community.' PhD thesis, University of Queensland. Nagata, Y. 1999. 'Japanese-Australians in the post-war Thursday Island community.' *Queensland Review,* Vol. 6, No. 2. pp. 30–44. Sissons, D. C. S. 1979. 'The Japanese in the Australian pearling industry.' *Queensland Heritage,* Vol. 3, No. 10. pp. 8–27.

[7] 'Police Magistrate, Thursday Island, to Colonial Secretary, 15 January 1878.' COL A/252, Queensland State Archives (hereafter QSA).

[8] 'Police Magistrate, Thursday Island, to Colonial Secretary, 24 April 1879.' COL A/277/1787, QSA.

[9] Mackellar, C. D. 1912. *Scented Isles and Coral Gardens: Torres Straits, German New Guinea and the Dutch East Indies.* London: Murray. pp. 48–9.

[10] Ling, C., 'Chinese in Queensland', pp. 22. Richard See Kee, pers. comm., November 1999.

[11] Choi, C., *Chinese Migration and Settlement in Australia,* p. 35. Jones, T., *The Chinese in the Northern Territory,* pp. 59, 69.

12   Boats bound for Asian ports would dock at least once a month, according to Richard See Kee, pers. comm., November 1999. See also Rolls, E., *Citizens: flowers and the wide sea*, p. 313.

13   *Court Book, Thursday Island, Clerk of Petty Sessions Deposition and Minute Book* (hereafter *CPSDMB*). pp. 250, 297. CPS13D/P6, QSA.

14   'John Douglas to Robert Douglas, 19 May 1894.' Letter in possession of Andrew and Lorraine Douglas, Brisbane. Many thanks to Jeremy Hodes for the transcription.

15   'Report by Constable M. Mulcahy, 22 June 1923.' POL/J1: Chinese (general), QSA.

16   'Report by Queensland Police Commissioner, 15 June 1923.' POL/J1, QSA.

17   Ibid.

18   Ibid. 'Report by Constable M. Mulcahy, 22 June 1923.' POL/J1, QSA.

19   Ramsay, G. and A. Shnukal. 2003. ' "Aspirational" Chinese: achieving community prominence on Thursday Island, northeast Australia.' *Asian and Pacific Migration Journal*, Vol. 12, No. 3. p. 343.

20   POL/J1: Chinese (general), QSA.

21   'Report by Inspector of Police, Cairns, 22 September 1905.' POL/J1, QSA. 'Report by Queensland Commissioner of Police, 4 September 1918.' POL/J1, QSA. Fears of illegal immigration extended to other Torres Strait islands as well. A memorandum dated 7 January, 1931, from the Torres Land Agent regarding the application by T. E. Thompson, Secretary of the Torres Strait Canning Co., for the lease of Deliverance Island, notes, 'Mr R. Hockings, Parbury House, rang up this morning in regard to Special Leases 1732 and 1541. In the course of conversation he stated that he understood there was a proposal before the Department to lease Deliverance Island. He desired to notify the Dept that it was rumoured — and he thought there was a good deal of truth in the rumour — that Chinese and Japanese were being surreptitiously introduced into Australia and that they were being landed on Deliverance Island.' 'Correspondence re Islands on the Queensland Coast, November 1920–December 1932.' Queensland Department of Public Lands (hereafter QDPL). LAN/AK140, QSA.

22   'Naturalisation.' *Queensland Public Records Historical Resource Kit, Part 3*. 1989. Brisbane: QSA.

23   Home Office file on naturalisation of George Sing. HOM/A41, QSA.

24   May, C., *Topsawyers*, p. 288.

25   Evans, R. et al., *Race Relations in Colonial Queensland*, p. 20.

26   Manderson, D. R. A. 1998. 'The first loss of freedom: early opium laws in Australia.' *Australian Drug and Alcohol Review*, Vol. 7. pp. 439–53, at p. 445.

27   'Isolated leper suspects 1896–1906.' *The Telegraph*, Wednesday 8 May, 1899, Sydney. In POL/J22, QSA.

28   Choi, C., *Chinese Migration and Settlement in Australia*, p. 39. Walsh, K. 2001. *The Changing Face of Australia: a century of immigration 1901–2000*. St Leonards: Allen and Unwin. p. 43.

29   'Bishop's Correspondence, 24 February 1917.' OM.AV 61/2, JOL.

30   *The Parish Gazette*, Vol. 37, No. 3, 1 March 1939. p. 5.

31   'Albert Edward Kelly, Acting Head Teacher, State School, Thursday Island, to Director of Education, Department of Public Instruction, 9 March 1942, re Admission of Coloured Children.' EDU/Z2676, QSA.

32   Sadako and Evelyn Yamashita to Anna Shnukal, pers. comm., 28 July, 1998.

33   For more information on how Thursday Island Chinese obtained social status and regard within the broader community, see Ramsay, G. and A. Shnukal, '"Aspirational" Chinese.'

34   Choi, C., *Chinese Migration and Settlement in Australia*, pp. 30–1.

35   CPSDMB, CPS13D/P6, QSA. p. 8. Home Office file on naturalisation of George Sing, HOM/A41, QSA. May, C., *Topsawyers*, p. 303. 'Naturalisation', *Queensland Public Records Historical Resource Kit, Part 3*. Richard See Kee, pers. comm., November 1999.

36   Hurley, J. F. 'Diary entry for 13 December, 1920.' MS 883, Diary A, Item 7, National Library of Australia.

37   *Torres Straits Daily Pilot and New Guinea Gazette* (hereafter *Torres Straits Pilot*), 2 April, 1936.

38   *Torres Straits Pilot*, 5 June, 1897, and 3 July, 1897.

39 Evans, G., 'Thursday Island 1878–1914', p. 23.
40 Informal Lease Files (IL168), QDPL, TR1817/1, QSA.
41 Special Lease Files (SL440), QDPL, TR1794/1, QSA.
42 Ibid.
43 Special Lease Files (SL676), QDPL, TR1794/1, QSA. Informal Lease Files (IL24), QDPL, TRI817/1, QSA.
44 Special Lease Files (SL622), QDPL, TR1794/1, QSA.
45 Special Lease Files (SL676), QDPL, TR1794/1, QSA.
46 Special Lease Files (SL426 and SL729), QDPL, TR1794/1, QSA. Informal Lease Files (IL69), QDPL, TR1817/1, QSA. George Nicholson was Chinese.
47 Richard See Kee, pers. comm., November 1999.
48 *Annual Report, Queensland Office of the Chief Protector of Aborigines.* 1905. p. 10. A/18963, QSA. *Cash Book 1929–1932, Thursday Island Court House*, in possession of Anna Shnukal. *Census — Coloured Aliens.* 1908. POL/J2, QSA. Communist Party of Australia. 11 December 1949. *Activity and Interest in Thursday Island.* pp. 12–13. A6122/40, Item 273, National Archives of Australia (hereafter NAA). CPSDMB, CPS13D/P1–13, QSA. Diocese of Carpentaria. *Register of Thursday Island Baptisms 1920–1928.* Evans, R. et al., *Race Relations in Colonial Queensland*, p. 312. Magistrates Court, Thursday Island, *Bench Record and Summons Book* (hereafter *TIBRSB*). QS787/1, Items 1–4, QSA. 'Naturalisation', *Queensland Public Records Historical Resource Kit, Part 3. Parish Gazette*, 1 February, 1913. p. 7; 1 February, 1927. p. 4; and 1 February, 1939. p. 8. *Queensland Post Office Directory including Papua (New Guinea) 1917–1918.* 1918. Brisbane: H. Wise and Co. pp. 380–1. *Queensland Post Office and Official Directory.* 1906. pp. 409–10. Ramsay, G. and A. Shnukal, ' "Aspirational" Chinese.' *Register of Firms*, Thursday Island, 1903 61, QS744/1, QSA. 'Report of A. S. Cairns, Schoolteacher at Mabuiag.' In *Annual Report of the Government Resident, Thursday Island*, 1904. 'Northern Protector of Aboriginals to Under Secretary, Home Department, Initiation of Aborginals etc. Act at Thursday Island, 20 November 1899.' p. 7. A/69491, QSA. *Thursday Island Census.* 1885. A/18963, QSA. *Torres News*, 12 January, 1965. *Torres Straits Pilot*, 8 September, 1888; 21 June, 1890; 6 March, 1897; 4 November, 1899; 16 December, 1899; 6 January, 1900; 3 March, 1900; and 8 December, 1922.
49 *CPSDMB*, p. 331, CPS13D/P3, QSA.
50 *CPSDMB*, 28 September, 1892, CPS13D/P5, QSA.
51 *CPSDMB*, 24 December, 1901, CPS13D/P10, QSA.
52 *CPSDMB*, p. 383, CPS13D/P10, QSA.
53 Galassi, F. 2001. 'From Nippon to North Queensland: Japanese pearl-divers in the 1890s.' *Journal of the Royal Historical Society of Queensland*, Vol. 17, No. 12. pp. 545–58, at p. 553.
54 *CPSDMB*, pp. 1–6, CPS13D/P6, QSA.
55 *CPSDMB*, p. 395, CPS13D/P9, QSA.
56 'Thursday Island Notes.' *North Queensland Register* (Townsville), 7 May, 1932. p. 74.
57 *CPSDMB*, p. 394, CPS13D/P9, QSA.
58 *CPSDMB*, p. 160–1, CPS13D/P9, QSA.
59 Rolls, E., *Citizens: flowers and the wide sea*, p. 350–1.
60 May, C., *Topsawyers*, p. 292.
61 *CPSDMB*, p. 165, CPS13D/P9, QSA.
62 *CPSDMB*, p. 152, CPS13D/P9, QSA.
63 *CPSDMB*, p. 202, CPS13D/P10, QSA.
64 *CPSDMB*, pp. 294–5, CPS13D/P8, QSA.
65 *CPSDMB*, pp. 212, 214, 224, CPS13D/P10, QSA.
66 Jeremy Hodes' Chapter Eight (this volume) elaborates on the local criminal justice dealings on Thursday Island.
67 *CPSDMB*, p. 312, CPS13D/P4, QSA.
68 *CPSDMB*, CPS13D/P1–13, QSA; TIBRSB, QS787/1 Items 1–4, QSA.

69 Evans, R. et al., *Race Relations in Colonial Queensland*, p. 94–5.
70 *CPSDMB*, p. 243, CPS13D/P6, QSA.
71 *CPSDMB*, pp. 329, 331, CPS13D/P7, QSA.
72 *CPSDMB*, p. 333, CPS13D/P7, QSA.
73 Brown, R. 1986. *Collins Milestones in Australian History: 1788 to the present*. Sydney: William Collins. p. 428. Rolls, E., *Citizens: flowers and the wide sea*, p. 408.
74 *CPSDMB*, 12 July, 1899, CPS13D/P7, QSA.
75 Queensland Office of the Northern Protector of Aborigines. 1902. *Annual Report*. p. 10.
76 May, C., *Topsawyers*, p. 292.
77 Queensland Office of the Chief Protector of Aborigines. 1904. *Annual Report*. p. 8.
78 Ibid., p. 9.
79 *CPSDMB*, p. 345, CPS13D/P1, QSA.
80 *TIBRSB*, 1 February, 1928, QS787/1 Item 3, QSA.
81 *CPSDMB*, p. 48, CPS13D/P6, QSA.
82 Manderson, D. R. A., 'The first loss of freedom', p. 443.
83 *CPSDMB*, p. 118, CPS13D/P6, QSA.
84 Low claimed during the trial, 'I no sell [Omar] opium that night. I sell him opium at Croydon.' *CPSDMB*, p. 122, CPS13D/P6, QSA.
85 *CPSDMB*, p. 255, CPS13D/P3, QSA.
86 Joseph Ahmat, pers. comm., November 1999.
87 Ganter, R., *The Pearl-Shellers of Torres Strait*, p. 105.
88 *TIBRSB*, 19 May, 1910, QS787/1 Item 1, QSA. *TIBRSB*, 28 December, 1912, QS787/1 Item 2, QSA.
89 'Chief Protector of Aboriginals to Under Secretary, Home Department, 24 June 1918.' A/58769, QSA. Evans, R. et al., *Race Relations in Colonial Queensland*, p. 312. *TIBRSB*, 4 January 1918, QS787/1 Item 2, QSA. *TIBRSB*, 6 August 1929, QS787/1 Item 3, QSA.
90 Queensland Office of the Chief Protector of Aborigines. 1905. *Annual Report*. p. 10. The Burketown region was a common site of Chinese-Indigenous contacts, due to its close proximity to the Northern Territory. It was from the Territory that a large population of Chinese migrated eastward into far north Queensland after legislative restrictions took effect in 1889.
91 Evans, R. et al., *Race Relations in Colonial Queensland*, p. 312.
92 'Lee Bryce, Residency, Thursday Island, to R. A. C. Hockings Esq., Thursday Island, 26 September 1916.' A/69433, QSA.
93 Evans, G., 'Thursday Island 1878–1914', pp. 53, 81.
94 Nagata, Y. 1996. *Unwanted Aliens: Japanese internment in Australia during WWII*. St Lucia: University of Queensland Press. p. 89.
95 Conditions of service, native units Torres Strait Islanders enlisted in the forces, 1943–53, A1308/762/1/135, NAA. Draft 271/1/882, Conditions of service, natives of Papua New Guinea [and Torres Strait Islanders], Extract from 'Nine Thursday Island "Malayans" serving along side Torres Strait Islands to be withdrawn and reallocated', MP742/1/247/1/1290, NAA. See also See Kee, Vanessa. 2002. *Horn Island: in their steps on Horn Island 1939–45*. Horn Island: Vanessa and Arthur See Kee.
96 Richard See Kee, pers. comm., November 1999.
97 Ibid.
98 Ibid.

99 *Register of Firms*. Thursday Island, 1903–61, QS744/1, QSA.

100 Kehoe-Forutan, S., 'The effectiveness of Thursday Island as an urban centre in meeting the needs of its community', p. 98.

101 Communist Party of Australia. 11 December, 1949. *Activity and interest in Thursday Island*. pp. 12–13, A6122/40, Item 273, NAA.

102 Richard See Kee, pers. comm., July 2002.

103 Richard See Kee, pers. comm., November 1999.

104 Ibid. Japanese were excluded from the local tennis club at some stage.

105 Singe, J. *1989. The Torres Strait: people and history*. St Lucia: University of Queensland Press. pp. 138–9.

106 Kehoe-Forutan, S., 'The effectiveness of Thursday Island as an urban centre in meeting the needs of its community', p. 231.

Opening of the Horn Island Catholic Church, Ascension Thursday 1933.

F. J. Doyle, 'Thursday Island', *Annals of Our Lady of the Sacred Heart*,
1 September, 1933, p. 569.

CHAPTER FOUR

'They don't know what went on underneath'

Three little-known Filipino/Malay communities of Torres Strait[1]

Anna Shnukal

This chapter introduces three little-known Filipino/Malay 'outstation' communities, which arose on islands in Torres Strait between about 1890 and 1942. Smaller and more transient than their home communities on Thursday Island, they existed at a time when Europeans exercised stringent control over the movements, marriages and marine employment of the Asian population of Torres Strait. They have their own intrinsic historical interest, as well as shedding light on the activities of two numerically large and culturally rich, though economically and politically subordinated, Asian groups and the contributions made by their locally born wives and children. They are the only Asian communities that were established independently by their members away from Thursday Island, although they had the tacit official sanction that was essential for their survival. Once that sanction was withdrawn, they could not endure. Self-initiated, self-reliant, self-governing Asian (and Pacific Islander) communities such as these illustrate some of the ways in which immigrants pursued their economic and family interests in prewar Torres Strait. Such communities subverted the control of the dominant European minority and call into question previous assumptions about the apparently passive response to it. Two of them demonstrate intriguing continuities and discontinuities between first- and second-generation residents and thus illustrate the emergence of a new social identity, predicated less on ethnic origin than on local connections and a common sensibility bred from physical proximity and shared life experiences. This place-based identity eroded ethnic boundaries and promoted inter-group marriages. The result was a new generation, locally born and of mixed descent, which forced policy-makers to multiply 'racial' categories in an increasingly desperate attempt to maintain their control (see also Regina Ganter's Chapter Nine, this volume).[2]

Despite the light they shed on Asian-Indigenous-European social relations, there is little discussion of these outstation communities in the literature, with the exception of Osborne and Perdon,[3] and a few accounts appearing in popular magazines, newspapers and unpublished correspondence and reports.[4] Because so little has been written about the Filipino/Malay diaspora in Torres Strait, I have sought to clarify some general issues before introducing the communities that are the subject of the chapter.

Community

I define 'community' here as a spatially bounded aggregation of individuals and families, bound by bonds of ethnic origin, social values, kinship and intermarriage, with each member fulfilling a multiplicity of social roles and with some (unspecified) temporal continuity. To qualify for inclusion here, they must also have been self-initiated and acknowledged as predominantly Filipino or 'Malay' in values, outlook, customs and way of life.

Fitting these criteria are three communities: one on Horn Island, one on Badu and one at Port Lihou (see Figure D).[5] I do not discuss the early polyethnic settlements of the Prince of Wales Group (including Thursday Island), in which no single group predominated, nor, despite the Filipino descent of most of its pioneers, the Roman Catholic mission on Keriri (Hammond Island), which was established with government approval and oversight and where the prevailing ethos was religious rather than overtly socio-cultural. Also excluded from this overview are the families of mixed Filipino/Malay-Indigenous descent, who settled on the outer islands.[6] These families constituted a spatially scattered 'outsider' minority, dominated numerically and culturally by Torres Strait Islanders. Unlike their 'free' cousins on non-reserve islands, the descendants were designated as 'Aboriginals' and have always identified primarily as Torres Strait Islanders.

'Malay' and 'Filipino' as Problematic Terms

The word 'Malay' in 19th-century northern Australia was an omnibus geographical and racial term, which obscures rather than clarifies geographical origins.[7] It does not readily translate into contemporary geopolitical realities.

At times it refers to Macassarese and Buginese, and at other times to divers from the Sulu Islands, north of Sarawak; it also refers to Malays from the Straits Settlements and the Federated Malay States, to people from Koepang, Timor, including both those of Portuguese-Malay descent and natives of the islands of Roti, Sawu and Alor, and occasionally also to Javanese and Filipinos, or Manilamen.[8]

For Martinez, 'Malay' was an 'ambiguous colonial construction which was loosely based on notions of 'racial' grouping'.[9] She notes that in prewar Darwin — like Thursday Island a polyethnic pearling port — the term 'encompassed a number of different ethnic groups including peoples from Singapore, Java, Maluku, Timor and Sulawesi'. In Torres Strait, the term appears to have included not only 'natives of Java and the Straits Settlements', but all the peoples of insular South-East Asia, i.e., of modern-day Borneo, East Timor, Indonesia (Dutch East Indies), Malaysia, the Philippines, Singapore and Thailand (Siam), who were physically characterised as having lighter skin and straighter hair than 'Papuans'. Sometimes different groups are enumerated independently, such as the Javanese and Koepangers. This was not a reflection of Indigenous categories but rather of the nature of the legal treaties signed by Great Britain with other powers, to which the Australian colonies were subject.[10] That is, the men were classified and treated differently under law depending on whether their original islands were colonial possessions of Germany, Great Britain, the Netherlands, Portugal or Spain. This classification had ramifications for those who wished to settle permanently, marry, seek naturalisation and engage in business in the Australian colonies.

The majority of the 'Malays' came from the Dutch East Indies; the 'Manila men' from the Philippines, a Spanish colony before 1898. When the prominent Filipino businessman, Heriberto Zarcal, was naturalised on 17 May, 1897, it was on the grounds of being 'a native born of a European State', i.e., a Spanish subject (see also Reynaldo Ileto's Chapter Five, this volume).[11] He had simply to attend before a Magistrate's Bench and take the oath,[12] his lawyer arguing

> that the Philippine Islands, the birthplace of Mr Heriverto Zarcal is a Spanish possession and as such might be said to be a portion of a European State, and entitles Mr Zarcal to receive a Certificate of Naturalisation under Section 5 of the Aliens Act of 1867.[13]

Confusing the issue even further is the fact that the term 'Malay' was even more broadly generalised in the popular imagination:

> Though we called them Malays they were an assortment of Eastern people, and included men from all over the Malay Archipelago, from Ceylon and

parts of India, and from lands even farther afield [including North Africa]. Most of them had been attracted to North Queensland by the pearl-shell industry at Thursday Island, considerable numbers being employed as crews on the luggers; others found work ashore in that town of varied nationalities.[14]

Sometimes, 'Malay' and 'Kanaka' were used interchangeably:

> These men [pearl-shell station labourers], who are spoken of under the comprehensive term of 'Kanakas', are for the most part Malays: the remainder being a motley collection of Manila men, Fijians, natives of New Hebrides, and brown-skinned Polynesians from various Pacific Islands.[15]

Although 'Malay' and 'Manila men' could be synonyms in the official documents of 19th-century north Queensland, 'Manila men' is less problematic. It generally referred to people from the Philippine islands, the term 'Filipino' being far less common in Torres Strait. The majority of the 'Manila men' came from coastal villages of Cebu, Leyte, Luzon, Masbate, Panay and Samar, but a minority came from the Philippines dependency of the Marianas, including Guam.[16] Once settled in Torres Strait, some married local Indigenous women from the strait and Cape York, some married British immigrants, while others sought wives from the convents of Portuguese Macao and Hong Kong.[17] Few of the wives were Philippines-born. The Europeans of Thursday Island branded them all as 'Manila', but the conflation rankled:

> The frequency with which the term 'Manila' is applied erroneous [sic] to many men and women is resented by proper Manila residents of the island. A distinction should be made between Manilas and other Philippinos. There is but one real Manila woman on Thursday Island, Mrs Denas Lampane [Demas Lampano]; the other are either natives of Hong Kong, Macao, or other eastern place, born of Portuguese parents. A term 'Manila' should only be given to those Philippino people who are, properly speaking, natives of Manila city or the provinces of which it is the capital.[18]

Beyond the geopolitical and racial distinctions lay a religious dimension. 'Malays' were predominantly Muslim, the 'Manila men' Roman Catholics. On Thursday Island, for the most part, the two groups lived in separate boarding houses, practised different customs and tended to marry within their faiths. There were occasional fights between them, but the grievances may have been more personal than racial.[19] Catholic Filipinos celebrated their (legally recorded) marriages in church;[20] Muslims tended to celebrate their 'Malay fashion', contracted between families but not officially recorded. As such, they were not recognised by the colonial authorities who viewed them as 'often only legitimised prostitution'.[21]

Yet another complication arises from the local inter-war usage of 'Malay', 'Coloured' and 'Thursday Island half-caste' as synonyms. The terms were used interchangeably to refer to the residents of Thursday Island of mixed heritage (mostly Filipino/Malay/Indigenous), who were technically exempted from control by the Protection Acts and compulsorily evacuated to the mainland, along with Europeans, in 1942.

First Arrivals

It is not known exactly when men from insular South-East Asia began to arrive in Torres Strait. The standard historical works are vague, generally adducing the early 1880s. There is, however, evidence that from 1870, the year that commercial quantities of pearl shell were first discovered, Filipinos and Indonesians were being brought to the strait by European captains to dive for shell and to gather bêche-de-mer.[22] In 1873, Frank Jardine, Police Magistrate at Somerset, wrote of the possibility of engaging 'three Kanakas or Manilla men' as boat crews for one-third the wages of Whites.[23] The movement of men to the region was facilitated by the commencement of the Singapore mail service to Somerset in 1873,[24] and the introduction of diving apparatus in 1874 provided opportunities for 'Malays' to earn high wages as divers and tenders. Payment for divers was rarely less than £200 a year, a vast sum by the standards of the day. Although non-Europeans earned considerably less, they were still better paid than most of their countrymen.

> Many get between £6 and £10 per month and a levy of so much per ton on their own catch; one diver at one of the stations gets a fixed sum of £250 a year and no levy; at another station the divers employed get £5 a month and £20 per ton on the amount of shell they get; last year these divers must have taken close on £340 apiece.[25]

Tumultuous political events at home, such as the Cavite uprising in the Philippines in 1872, the Dutch invasion of Aceh in 1873 and the beginning of British colonisation of the Malay Peninsula in 1874, the new mail service and the rapidly expanding marine industries, brought many men to Torres Strait and there are numerous references to 'Malays' working in various capacities during the mid- to late 1870s.[26]

Those first individuals made their way independently to Torres Strait during the pearl rush, like the many hundreds of seamen from all over the world. Few immigration controls existed before Federation of the Australian colonies and little documentary evidence remains of their movements. Labour was in short supply across all of northern Australia and, as early as 1846, enterprising sea captains had begun to look to South-East Asia to recruit crews and general labourers.[27] The first documentary evidence of similar enterprises in Torres Strait is when Captain Francis Cadell brought 20 'Malays', probably from either Guam or the Marianas, to work in the fisheries in March 1877.[28] He told the local Police Magistrate that he had shipped them 'with the consent of the Spanish Authorities and in the presence of the British Consul'.[29] By 1879, 'Malay' indents were being imported from Singapore and islands of the Dutch East Indies, with bonds being entered into to return the men to their port of engagement,[30] and, in the next year, 213 'Malays and Asiatics' made up a little more than one-quarter of the workforce of 801 people employed on the 11 pearl stations (the Chinese were enumerated separately).[31]

In 1877, the Somerset settlement was removed to Thursday Island. No 'Malays' were among the official party that accompanied the removal, but at least five 'Malays' were among the 23 striking prisoners transferred across to the new lockup: Juan Francis, Kitchell, Alli Java, Aurelio Rido and Sulliman.[32] Individuals also continued to sign on privately in Australian ports for service on the pearling boats and stations. One of them,

> Domingo, a Manilla man, signed articles for the lugger *Mamoose* as boat hand in Sydney on 17th August 1881 … This man was sent to Thursday Island in the N. I. steamer *William McKinnon* to serve in any of the boats or on the station belonging to O'Hagan and Macalister. The *William McKinnon* arrived at Thursday Island on the 27th August 1881.[33]

Domingo was accompanied by two countrymen, one of whom had been staying in the same Sydney boarding house. Domingo, like many others, was probably alerted to employment opportunities by a 'Malay' maritime network in Asian and Pacific ports similar to the Pacific Islander network. On Thursday Island, they lived in the boarding houses of Malaytown, owned or run by their countrymen, who lent them money, supplied them with liquor (beer, not spirits for many Muslims) and provided gaming rooms.

By the time of the first Thursday Island census in about 1885, and henceforth in most government reports, 'Malays' and 'Manila men' were formally distinguished.[34] Less than a decade after the establishment of the settlement, they were numerically dominant and together outnumbered Europeans: 77 'Malays' (one of whom was a woman) and 49 'Manila men' out of a total of 307, of whom 139 were Europeans. The newly arrived Catholic priest wrote to his superior in 1884 that there were 'about forty Filipinos' living on Thursday Island and 'about four hundred Catholics from Manila scattered amongst the various islands. They were there fishing for pearls.'[35]

Mass Indenture

The rapid increase in the 'Malay' population was the direct result of systematic mass indenture. For some time it had become apparent that Pacific Islander labour, hitherto the mainstay of the maritime industries, was to be curtailed and the pearlers were desperate to find new and reliable sources of supply. Unlike the previous hit-and-miss system, in which individual firms employed stowaways, crews of passing vessels or men recruited from southern Australian ports, the pearlers began to rely on middlemen to supply their labour requirements from Asian ports, usually Singapore (then also a British colonial possession). Large groups of seamen were collected by an agent and signed a shipping agreement under the supervision of the Shipping Master at Singapore for a fixed term (from 18 months to three years) at a fixed rate of pay. The agreements were subsequently ratified and confirmed by his counterpart on Thursday Island and the men were then allotted to firms as required. At the end of their period of indenture, they were expected to return to their port of origin,[36] but some re-signed at the end of their term while still on Thursday Island.[37]

The scheme's antecedents can be traced to the actions of the local Police Magistrate, H. M. Chester. Shortly before the annexation of the outer Torres Strait islands in 1879, he had written to the Colonial Secretary requesting a boat to enable him to supervise and control the fisheries and soon-to-be-annexed islands. To save money, he suggested that he 'should be authorised to get the Malay crew from Singapore by mail steamer, cost about £30'.[38] The request was granted and, in June 1879, he 'wrote to Capt Ellis, Master Attendant at Singapore, requesting him to select a suitable crew of Malays who will probably arrive by the down Mail in July'.[39]

In early 1882, the first consignment destined to be sent to work at various pearling stations was imported by the trading firm, Burns Philp & Co. Ltd. Among them was the Filipino, Lothario, who arrived 'with a batch of other Malays and Manilla men from Singapore' in 1882 and was alloted to a station on Mabuiag.[40] A second group of 49 men was shipped by the S.S. *Hungarian* in November 1882 and the agreements were ratified on Thursday Island on 22 December, 1882.[41] With one exception, all were either Malay or Filipino.[42] They signed articles for three years at 7 dollars a month and received three months advance on their wages in Singapore.

Once alloted to the shelling stations, the men's agreements could be transferred or terminated by the managers. Some were guaranteed a passage back to their home port on expiry of their contracts but some were not, a source of discontent that often found its way into the local court. The majority were employed as seamen. Abdul Rahman, however, was employed as a general servant to cook and wash for the clerks at Burns Philp & Co., although he complained to the court that he 'didn't sign to cook and wash'.[43] The original consignment details have been lost but we can gauge the success of the enterprise by court details and other primary sources: agreements were signed on 31 November, 1883, 14 July, 1884,[44] and 15 November, 1884;[45] 60 'fresh men' arrived in early April 1885, with a further 90 expected later that month;[46] and 60 arrived on 26 September, 1885.[47] By the outbreak of World War II, when the practice effectively ceased, many hundreds of 'Malays' had worked as indentured labour in the fisheries of Torres Strait (see Table 2.1). Only a small number, however, settled there permanently.

The fortunes of the Filipino/Malay communities of Torres Strait were ultimately decided not so much by individual decision as by external circumstances: the prosperity of the marine industries on which their livelihoods depended, official tolerance, legal and administrative restrictions and the outbreak of war. The relative numerical strength of the two communities declined abruptly in 1905 as a result of the departure of mainly Malay and Filipino crews to Dutch waters in September of that year, regional economic decline, the restrictions of the White Australia Policy and Aboriginal Protection Acts and the deaths of some older members. Indentured Malay and Filipino labour continued to be imported until the outbreak of World War II,[48] but it was far outnumbered by Japanese.

Some Characteristics of the Malay/Filipino Immigrants

Unlike the Chinese, Japanese and Sri Lankans, the Malay and Filipino immigrants tended to marry local Indigenous women, although the Filipinos also sought wives from the convents of Portuguese Macao and Goa.[49] They were encouraged to become naturalised by the Government Resident, Hon. John Douglas, and 16 did so between 1886 and 1900 (see Table 4.1).[50] For Douglas, naturalisation was reserved for immigrants of any ethnic origin who 'had proved themselves worthy of such a privilege', who were married, of good reputation, 'possessed of means' and able to speak and write English.[51] The importance of naturalisation lay in the fact that, while it was not a precondition for residence or marriage, it was so for property ownership, boat-licensing and leaseholding. Under the terms of the Immigration Restriction Acts, indents could apply each year for their Certificate of Exemption. For long-term residents in work and of good character, this was a mere formality. This situation changed after Federation, however, and particularly stringent restrictions on long-term residence and marriage were in place during the inter-war years. Nevertheless, even during this period, a number of indents managed to circumvent official disapproval and marry the locally born daughters of the original immigrants. Generally speaking, it was the families of Asian-Indigenous descent who returned to Thursday Island after the war. By then, inter-group marriage had rendered the former ethnic barriers almost meaningless and, with few exceptions — the Malay Club, for example — there was no real push to reconstitute the institutional foundations of the prewar communities.

Table 4.1: Naturalised Malays/Filipinos, 1886–1900

Name and occupation	Place of birth	Date of naturalisation
Batchoo, diver	c.1849 at Macassar	26 June, 1886
Pedro Galora, diver	c.1840 at Cebu, Philippine Islands	10 April, 1889
Anthony Spain (Antonio Puerte), tailor	c.1863 at Cebu, Philippine Islands	16 April, 1889
Raphael Louis Castro, diver	c.1854 at Vigan, Philippine Islands	29 April, 1889
Tayib, diver	c.1862 at Singapore	30 November, 1891
Henrique Elarde, pearl-sheller	c.1863 at Philippine Islands	16 May, 1892
Ambrosio Lucio Artigoza (Alcala), pearl-sheller	c.1867 at Philippine Islands	16 May, 1892
Benito Lanzarote, billiard-room proprietor	c.1865 at Philippine Islands	23 June, 1892
Tolentino Conanan, pearl-sheller	c.1856 at Philippine Islands	23 June, 1892
Matthew Roderick (Matteo Rodriguez), pearl-sheller	c.1862 at Philippine Islands	23 June, 1892
Marcos Peres, diver and boatowner	c.1852 at Philippine Islands	29 June, 1892
Marcelino Rapol, diver	c.1863 at Philippine Islands	7 April, 1894
Nicholas de la Cruz, diver	c.1864 at Philippine Islands	7 April, 1894
Pablo Remedio, pearl-sheller	c.1864 at Philippine Islands	24 January, 1895
Pedro Guivarra, pearl-sheller and diver	c.1869 at Philippine Islands	11 December, 1896
Heriberto Zarcal, jeweller and pearl-sheller	c.1864 at Philippine Islands	17 May, 1897

Source: Register of aliens naturalised 1876–92. SCT/CF35-37, QSA.

The occupational range of Filipinos and Malays was more diverse than is generally recognised: bêche-de-mer fisher, billiard marker, billiard-room proprietor, boarding-house keeper, carpenter, commission agent, cook, deck hand, crew, diver, foreman, goldsmith, hairdresser, jeweller, labourer, laundryman, lugger-owner, pearl-sheller, pump hand, sail-maker, servant, shell sorter, shell packer, skipper, store clerk, storekeeper, storeman, tender, waterman, woodcutter. Depending on status and marital circumstances, they were housed in dormitories or cottages on the pearling stations of the Prince of Wales Group adjacent to Thursday Island — Goods, Muralag, Ngarupai, Wai Weer Islands[52] — or rented small dwellings on Thursday Island, or spent the off-season in boarding houses run by Filipinos and Malays on the eastern end of Thursday Island itself, among the small gambling shops, opium dens, bathhouses and brothels of Malaytown. Here, the police rarely penetrated without provocation. A minority of married Malays and Filipinos, however, established themselves in more secluded communities, close to countrymen and kinfolk, away from the segregation and prejudice of the European-dominated spaces and surveillance by Europeans. It is those communities that are the subject of this chapter.

The Filipino Community of Horn Island (c.1889–1942)

The best-documented and longest-lasting of the three independently established and self-reliant communities was located at Ngarupai (Horn Island), directly south of the township of Thursday Island and easily accessed by boat. It was settled by a small number of naturalised Filipino divers, who had married local Indigenous women and had become marine entrepreneurs. Their main motivation was apparently their desire to raise their families among countrymen of like mind, away from the crowded conditions of Port Kennedy, and to pursue their economic interests without constant oversight.

Horn Island is a large, low island, bounded on three sides by mangroves and mud flats,[53] but there is a good beach on the north-west side.[54] Like others of the Prince of Wales Group, it forms part of Kaurareg traditional territory and Kaurareg births on Horn Island are attested (in later marriage records) from the 1870s. Many of those who survived the early depopulation were removed to other islands by government decree but began to return after World War II. The returning Kaurareg first settled on Galora family land but, in deference to the prior claim, established present-day Wasaga village not far away to the south-west.[55]

In 1894, commercial quantities of alluvial gold were discovered on Horn Island, causing a flurry of excitement and attracting mainly European miners to the field. The island was officially proclaimed a gold field on 31 August, 1894, Mining Homestead Leases were granted on the east side and operations began immediately.[56] Several mines were established and a small township surveyed in

1896. By 1897, however, the mines were declared unprofitable, the companies were in debt, prospecting was 'pretty well dead' and most of the miners had left.[57] Some prospecting continued until the turn of the century but, with the exception of a single mine reopened in about 1990,[58] 'the hills of Horn Island were claimed by Malayans and Filipinos who built houses, grew vegetables, paw paw fruit, bananas and pineapples'.[59]

In fact, at least five years before the discovery of gold in the eastern part of Horn Island, the 'Malayans and Filipinos' had established a small outstation for themselves on the north-west foreshore 'from the location of today's Wongai Hotel along the beach to the site of the present wharf complex'.[60] In October 1889, a few months after his naturalisation, the Filipino diver, Pedro Galora, known locally as Peter Manila, and his wife, Clara Gonelai from Mabuiag (Jervis Island), were living in their own house on Horn Island.[61] They may even have moved there soon after their marriage in June 1888, on the understanding that Galora's application for a lease would be approved. Thursday Island Courthouse records and the *Somerset Register of Births* attest that also squatting there between 1889 and 1890, when the situation was regularised by the granting of Galora's lease, were four of his countrymen, who formed the nucleus of the community: Raphael Louis Castro (Louis Manila) and Caroline, his Aboriginal wife from Somerset;[62] Gregorio Leon Fabian (or Pavian) and his wife, Kuruwara Philomena from Gebar (Two Brothers Island), whose third child, Clara, was the first child born to the community in 1889;[63] Pablo Remedio and his wife, Caroline from Mer (Murray Island); and Ramon Roas and his wife, Mary Ann Kass (or Kias) from Mua (Banks Island).

On 1 June, 1890, Galora, who became the community's unofficial spokesman and mediator with outsiders, took out Special Lease 415 on three acres of ground on the western side of the island for a fishing station. The lease was granted for 21 years at an annual rental of £4.10 for the first seven years.[64] In November 1890, the rest of the island was opened for Occupation Licence.[65] Ellen McNulty, widow of the publican on Thursday Island and an astute businesswoman, took out a lease of 10 acres in December 1892 to run cattle, but it was cancelled in August 1901.[66] It specifically excluded Galora's lease, which was paid to 31 May, 1896, and written off on 1 February, 1897.[67] No further leases were granted and, by 1902, there were 'no reservations, occupations, licences or pastoral leases issued for Horn Island, nor are there any been issued for the last twelve months by the Crown'.[68] Squatters were sighted on the southern shore of Horn Island, perhaps Kaurareg, woodcutters or discharged seamen such as the 'Malay', Charlie Omar, who lived simply on fish he caught illegally in traps.[69] The island's mangrove stands were a source of timber and firewood for Thursday Islanders and groups of woodcutters would set up temporary shore camps. Since the island was now Crown land, they needed fuel licences to cut them down: in July 1902, the 'Malays', Dayman, Osen, Bendara, Solomon and Nariga, were charged with cutting timber on Crown lands at Horn Island without licences and Dayman was fined a total of £3.7.4.[70] He had constructed a 'humpy' on the south-west part of the island and had piled up the wood in front of it. Dayman gave evidence that he had been punting over to Horn Island and cutting firewood for about eight years for his countryman, Thomas Bolan Toulasik. Toulasik, a Timorese storekeeper on Thursday Island, employed him on contract, paying him 14/- a cord for long wood and 7/- a cart-load for short wood.

The island's reversion to Crown land did not affect the Filipino community of Horn Island, which was generally left alone by local authorities. Presumably this was in recognition of the families' long residence and good behaviour and the difficulties of resettling them on Thursday Island, much of which was reserved for military use and where children of Asian-Indigenous descent were becoming an embarrassment to officialdom. The community grew steadily to about 150 in 1895, after which there was a decline to 113 in 1900, 92 in 1902 and 42 in 1903, followed by an increase to 49 the next year and to 73 in 1906.[71] Among its early attested members were Gregorio Aguere and his wife, Emilia Wanto from Cape Grenville; Pedro Assacruz and his wife, Kodo from Batavia River; Nazario Orbulio (Bullio) and his wife, Maria Inez from Hong Kong; Matteo (Matthew) Canendo and his wife, Katie Wanto from Cape Grenville; Jaspar Cornelius; Thomas Dorales; Florentio Manantan and his wife, Kondia from Batavia River; Mariano; Dorotheo San Miguel and his wife, Lizzie from Batavia River; Sylvestre Laurentino Petro Lima (Leon Sylvestre) and his wife, Maria Migel from Cape Verde. Lucio Jerusalem (Hermida) and his wife, Marsela from Seven Rivers, are recorded as living for a time in Mariano's house. Charles Hodges and his wife, Dinah Walton, who were related by marriage to the Assacruz family of Horn Island, also had a house there for a time. There were almost 70 recorded births on Horn Island between 1889 and 1932 (see Table 4.2), but this is an underestimate, since not all births were recorded and some children, e.g., Henry Victor Hodges and Mary Galora Bowie, were born on Thursday Island to families resident on Horn Island. The list also includes children who did not survive to adulthood and at least one, Jena Ah Boo, who was born at the gold-mining camp, when her father was mining at Horn Island.[72]

Table 4.2: Horn Island births 1889–1932

DOB	Name	Father	Father's POB	Mother	Mother's POB
10/8/1889	Clara	Leon Gregorio Fabian	Philippines	Philomena	Gebar, TS, Q
5/1/1890	Joseph	Pablo Remedio	Philippines	Caroline Maria Lifu	Mer, TS, Q
20/2/1891	Sebelo	Ramon Roas (Raymond)	Philippines	Mary Ann Kass	Mua, TS, Q
19/11/1891	Ambrosio	Pedro Galora	Philippines	Clara Gonelai	Mabuiag, TS, Q
13/6/1892	Antonia Inez	Nazario Orbulio (Bullio)	Philippines	Maria Inez Francisco	Hong Kong
29/12/1892	John	Ramon Roas (Raymond)	Philippines	Mary Ann Kass	Mua, TS, Q
27/4/1893	Pedro	Dorotheo San Miguel	Philippines	Lizzie	Batavia River, Q
c.1894	Mercedes	Nazario Orbulio (Bullio)	Philippines	Maria Inez Francisco	Hong Kong
14/2/1894	Mathias Victor	Pablo Remedio	Philippines	Caroline Maria Lifu	Mer, TS, Q
23/2/1894	Kitty	Etam	Java	Topsy	Seven Rivers, Q
10/4/1894	Scholastica	Matthew Canendo	Philippines	Kathleen (Katie) Wanto	Cape Grenville, Q
27/1/1895	Bridget	Dorotheo San Miguel	Philippines	Lizzie	Batavia River, Q
10/6/1895	Maria Theresa	Ramon Roas (Raymond)	Philippines	Mary Ann Kass (Kias)	Mua, TS, Q
5/7/1895	Mary Cecelia	Usop	Singapore	Mona	Batavia River, Q
15/12/1895	Maria Theresa	Pedro Assacruz	Philippines	Kodo	Batavia River, Q
4/2/1896	Andreas (Andrew)	Matthew Canendo	Philippines	Kathleen (Katie) Wanto	Cape Grenville, Q
29/6/1896	Mary	Moyden	India	Maggie	Torres Strait, Q
2/6/1898	Marcellino	Matthew Canendo	Philippines	Kathleen (Katie) Wanto	Cape Grenville, Q
c.1899	Catherine Jaira	Solomon Amboyn	Borneo	Saradha	Nagi, TS, Q
13/4/1901	Pattiemo	Solomon Amboyn	Borneo	Saradha	Nagi, TS, Q
4/3/1902	Casimero	Florentio Manantan	Philippines	Kondia	Batavia River, Q
4/3/1902	Sam (Zitha)	Florentio Manantan	Philippines	Kondia	Batavia River, Q

continued

Table 4.2: continued

DOB	Name	Father	Father's POB	Mother	Mother's POB
c.1903	Jessie	Jimmy Malay (Goentjoel)	Java	Para	Cape Grenville, Q
4/8/1903	Dominica	Gregorio Aguere	Philippines Q	Emilia Wanto	Cape Grenville, Q
12/10/1903	Jelany	Solomon Amboyn	Borneo	Saradha	Nagi, TS, Q
14/11/1903	Adolfo	Pedro Assacruz	Philippines	Kodo	Batavia River, Q
26/2/1905	Napsia	Usop	Singapore	Mona	Batavia River, Q
11/8/1905	Milon Henry	Mile Bin Lehou (Botaweer)	Java	Cassamina Seden	Prince of Wales Island, TS, Q
13/11/1905	Magno Stanislaus	Magno Lloren	Philippines	Felicia Pitt	Halfway Island, TS, Q
28/3/1906	Sisto	Pedro Assacruz	Philippines	Kodo	Batavia River, Q
18/5/1906	Catharina	Emilio Pelayo	Hong Kong	Johanna Fabian	Thursday Island, TS, Q
19/6/1906	Ismail	Solomon Amboyn	Borneo	Saradha	Nagi, TS, Q
16/10/1906	Incarnacion	Telesforo Aguilar	Philippines	Minnie Savage	Croydon, Q
7/2/1907	Isabella	Magno Lloren	Philippines	Felicia Pitt	Halfway Island, TS, Q
24/2/1907	Maria Trinidad	Juan Blanco	Philippines	Annie	Cape York, Q
20/6/1907	Esa	Usop	Singapore	Mona	Batavia River, Q
5/4/1908	Lorenzio	Magno Lloren	Philippines	Felicia Pitt	Halfway Island, TS, Q
9/9/1908	Agnes	Felix Mayor	Philippines	Johanna Fabian	Thursday Island, TS, Q
16/11/1908	Jena	Hassan Ah Boo	Singapore	Lass Seden	Thursday Island, TS, Q
17/1/1909	Cyriaca	Lucas MacBire	Philippines	Diana	Seven Rivers, Q
18/5/1909	Celestina	Juan Blanco	Philippines	Annie	Cape York, Q
23/11/1909	Cecilia	Eustachio Sim	Philippines	Maria Eusebia Galora	Thursday Island, TS, Q
12/12/1909	Rosalina	Cornelio Francis Villanova (Garcia)	Puruma, TS, Q	Antonio Bullio	Horn Island, TS, Q
24/12/1909	Gelanie	Massat Solomon	Somerset, Q	Charlotte Hodges	Thursday Island, TS, Q
24/12/1910	Philomena	Juan Blanco	Philippines	Annie	Cape York, Q

continued

Table 4.2: continued

DOB	Name	Father	Father's POB	Mother	Mother's POB
28/1/1911	Juliana	Lucas MacBire	Philippines	Kondia	Batavia River, Q
14/8/1911	Joseph	Cornelio Francis Villanova (Garcia)	Puruma, TS, Q	Antonio Bullio	Horn Island, TS, Q
8/10/1911	Henry Frederick Solomon (Massat)	Massat Solomon	Somerset, Q	Charlotte Hodges	Thursday Island, TS, Q
3/7/1912	James	Harry Hodges	Burke Island, TS, Q	Ellen Cecelia Edgar	Gregory Downs, Q
8/11/1912	Alphonso			Mercedes Bullio	Horn Island, TS, Q
16/4/1913	Maria	Lucas MacBire	Philippines	Kondia	Batavia River, Q
16/4/1913	Michael	Lucas MacBire	Philippines	Kondia	Batavia River, Q
9/10/1913	Martha	Massat Solomon	Somerset, Q	Charlotte Hodges	Thursday Island, TS, Q
11/7/1914	Jessie Ellen			Marian Moyden	Morecambe Bay, Q
22/7/1914	Mariano Manuel (Celestino)	Cornelio Francis Villanova (Garcia)	Puruma, TS, Q	Antonio Bullio	Horn Island, TS, Q
8/9/1914	Ambrosia			Mercedes Bullio	Horn Island, TS, Q
16/10/1914	Osman	Massat Solomon	Somerset, Q	Charlotte Hodges	Thursday Island, TS, Q
12/11/1914	Gilbert Henry	Harry Hodges	Burke Island, TS, Q	Ellen Cecelia Edgar	Gregory Downs, Q
24/1/1915	Jack	Willie Smoke	Timor	Pattiemo Amboyn	Horn Island, TS, Q
29/7/1915	Horace	John Raymond	Horn Island, TS, Q	Jenon Abrahams	Thursday Island, TS, Q
23/10/1915	James William Hodges	Massat Solomon	Somerset, Q	Charlotte Hodges	Thursday Island, TS, Q
12/11/1915	Unnamed male	Harry Hodges	Burke Island, TS, Q	Ellen Cecelia Edgar	Gregory Downs, Q
20/10/1916	Freddy (James William Massat)	Massat Solomon	Somerset, Q	Charlotte Hodges	Thursday Island, TS, Q
28/4/1918	Emma Emily Massat	Massat Solomon	Somerset, Q	Charlotte Hodges	Thursday Island, TS, Q

continued

Table 4.2: continued

DOB	Name	Father	Father's POB	Mother	Mother's POB
10/1/1920	Charles William Hodges	Joseph Lee	Mabuiag, TS, Q	Charlotte Hodges	Thursday Island, TS, Q
6/1/1922	Dora	Joseph Lee	Mabuiag, TS, Q	Charlotte Hodges	Thursday Island, TS, Q
27/5/1929	Dinah Gertie	Joseph Lee	Mabuiag, TS, Q	Charlotte Hodges	Thursday Island, TS, Q
18/9/1930	Peggy Norina Charlotte Hondo	Joseph Lee	Mabuiag, TS, Q	Charlotte Hodges	Thursday Island, TS, Q
8/1/1932	Pauline (Polly) Alice	Joseph Lee	Mabuiag, TS, Q	Charlotte Hodges	Thursday Island, TS, Q

Sources: *Somerset Register of Births and Marriages*; *Missionaries of the Sacred Heart Register of Baptisms* 1884–94; tombstone inscriptions.

The original nucleus of Filipino settlers shared a number of attributes beyond their geographical origin, deep Catholic beliefs and attachment to the Church. All had left the Spanish colony of the Philippines for the British colony of Queensland before the period of mass indenture, attracted to Torres Strait by employment opportunities, and they received good wages as pearl-shell divers. All continued to work in some capacity in the marine industries, some in small family businesses. All married local Indigenous women, decided to make Torres Strait their permanent home and were naturalised. Their wives were baptised in the church and their locally born children were brought up as Catholics. Prudent men, they had each saved enough money to invest in a small cutter (Galora the *Maria Eusebia*, Fabian the *Rosy* and Remedio the *Joseph*), registering with the Thursday Island Shipping Master as men-in-charge. Some began as pearl-shellers, socially among the most prestigious occupations in the strait, but oscillated as circumstances demanded between the more capital-intensive pearling industry and other niches, working bêche-de-mer and trochus along the eastern coast of Cape York with the assistance of their Aboriginal kinship networks. These were family businesses and relied for success on the labour of wives, affinal kin and even children. The women worked on the boats during the bêche-de-mer season, cooking, looking after children, gathering wood for the beach smokehouses and preparing the trepang for packing and export to the Chinese market; Aboriginal relatives provided labour in return for food and tobacco; and children dived for trepang and collected wood from shore. The businesses prospered and were profitable enough to support their owners' and crews' families and maintain their boats and equipment. By 1893, Galora and Ambrosio each owned two boats (Galora's second boat was possibly named *Myrtle*) and gave their occupations as master divers.

The original Horn Island settlers chose to reside there for family and economic reasons: to live lives of privacy and self-sufficiency among countrymen, avoid the crowded conditions of Thursday Island, make gardens and raise fowls at a time when fresh vegetables, fruit and eggs were scarce and expensive, and facilitate the conduct of the men's businesses. Horn was close to Thursday Island but distant enough to allow the men and their families to live quietly among their kin and countrymen away from the prying eyes of the police and non-Filipino neighbours. Some descriptions of their houses and way of life survive in courthouse records and can be reconstituted in part from their descendants' stories. Each family maintained at least one small cutter not only to gather shell, trochus or bêche-de-mer, but to enable the family to row across the short passage to Thursday Island to deliver their produce, for entertainment, to attend church on Sundays and to buy provisions. Most of their food, however, except for flour, rice, salt, onions and potatoes, consisted of vegetables grown in the household gardens (tended by the wives), shellfish and crabs gathered near the shoreline by the women and children, fish every day, caught either by line by the women or by the men from their boats, and fruit from the coconut, banana, mango and pawpaw trees planted near their houses for food and privacy. They made the Filipino wine, *tuba*, from coconut blossoms 'and sometimes the village men returned from Vicente's place along the beach in the moonlight, happily intoxicated'.[73] They built small houses using the abundant local mangrove wood as supports, with iron roofs, floors of split bamboo in the Filipino fashion, one or perhaps two verandahs, usually no more than one or two bedrooms, an outside kitchen, a water tank, a fowl house and a well dug by the occupants with their neighbours' help. Lucio Jerusalem's house had 'a sort of grass humpy about 5 yards from the corner … attached to the dwelling and part of the premises' connected to the house by 'a sort of mangrove covering'.[74] Behind the village there was a large patch of bamboo, planted by Galora, 'which was used to produce all manner of things from fishing spears to building materials'.[75] There was no electricity — it did not come to Thursday Island until 1932 — and the women cooked damper and scones in a Dutch oven and washed their clothes in the creek or with well water. Written and oral sources reveal complex networks of social and family relationships: Lucio Artigoza rented his house from Pedro Galora; when Lucio built his own house, Mariano lived there; Lucio and Charlie Hodges, brother-in-law of Gregoria Assacruz, worked together on the boats; adult sons went crayfishing and shared with families who had no grown sons; families visited each other and their children played together.

A minority of the early community residents were Muslim Malays, Horn Island by 1895 having become 'a resort for all the crews of boats'.[76] Courthouse records attest the following Muslim Malay seamen as living on Horn: Etam from Java and his wife, Topsy from Seven Rivers; Jimmy Malay and his wife, Para from Cape Grenville; Sedora; and Solomon Amboyn from Borneo, who cut firewood for a living and was married to Saratha from Nagi (Mt Ernest Island) — their daughter, Martha, married the diver, Jaffa, from Singapore; their son, Massat, married Charlotte Hodges and Martha and Massat lived there until their deaths. Usop and his wife, Mona from Batavia River, lived in Lucio Artigoza's house for a time and Thomas Dorales, a friend of Lucio's, lived in Usop's house. Whatever the ethnic and religious differences between the Filipinos and Malays, they were transcended by interpersonal and kinship bonds maintained particularly by their Indigenous wives. Some of the Malay descendants married the children of Filipinos and adopted the Catholic faith. According to Monica Walton Gould, Muslims formed no part of the second-generation community she grew up in: by that time, religious attitudes had hardened and 'Catholics didn't mix with Muslims'.[77] It is significant that no Japanese, Chinese or Sri Lankans lived among them: members of these groups tended to be sojourners, not settlers, and there was some antagonism between them and 'Malays'.

According to Father Doyle, a church was built on Horn Island in the 1890s but fell into disrepair.[78] The Catholic Mission had opened a school for young New Guinea catechists in March 1896 on Thursday Island but transferred it to the more secluded environment of Horn Island a few months later.[79] The school was closed in November 1897 and the students repatriated after the Governor of New Guinea forbade the emigration of New Guineans. Nothing has survived of the former school or church building[80] and, until the opening of a new church in 1933, community members rowed over to the church on Thursday Island each Sunday for Mass.

Passage of the Aboriginals Protection and Restriction of the Sale of Opium Act in 1897 and its amendments negatively affected the business operations of members of the Horn Island Filipino community and their compatriots, as it was intended to do. Abductions by Filipinos (and others) of Cape York Aboriginal men and women by force or trickery had provoked several well-documented retaliatory attacks and murders and, to stem abuses, the Queensland Government had introduced the Native Labourers Protection Act of 1884,[81] a precursor to the 1897 act. Under the latter, the carrying of 'native' women or minors on boats became illegal and 'coloured men' were targeted by the newly appointed local Protector of Aboriginals.

Lacking alternative primary written sources or contradictory oral narratives, historians have necessarily relied on the official view of the apparently unproblematic matter of abuses.[82] However, a review of the Protector's correspondence and trial evidence shows that circumstances regarding the presence of women and minors on boats were not always as straightforward as the indignant reports of local officials, missionaries and contemporary newspaper articles suggest. In 1900, for example, the Protector reported finding Galora, Fabian and Remedio in company with others at Hannibal Island. Everything was in order except that the men

> had their wives and families with them. I saw the women on shore on the Island, and on the boats. I spoke to the men and pointed out the illegality of what they were doing and told them I would probably have to prosecute them. They all made excuse that the women were their lawful wives (as in fact they are) and that they were afraid to leave them on shore during their long absences. I told them that I would report the matter. Two of the men (Fabian and Remedio) promised to take out occupation licences for shore stations next year and the other (Pedro Galoria [Galora]) said he would probably stay on shore after Xmas and would not, in any case, take his wife with him again. The women are natives of Torres Straits Islands (Mabuiag [sic] and Murray Islds.).[83]

The Protector and police launched several successful prosecutions of 'coloured' trepangers in 1904 and 1905 for various offences, including 'harbouring an Aboriginal'. The men were convicted and fined but the trial evidence reveals more complex social relationships between Cape York people and the Horn Island Filipinos than a bare recital of the legal facts. More often than not the women concerned were relatives of the men's wives or wives of their crewmen: for example, Annie from Seven Rivers, who was accused of being harboured by Lucio Jerusalem (Hermida), was his wife's niece, who had come to pay her a visit.[84] By this time, most abuses were checked by the licensing of boats, the reduction of shipping articles from 12 to six months, more frequent police patrols and the appointment of a local Protector. Writing in 1904, the former Somerset Police Magistrate, Frank Jardine, compared the current situation with the early days of the bêche-de-mer industry:

> those times, men, and manners are long since past, the spasmodic trade being now carried on by small cutters from Thursday Island, which, owing to the difficulty and restriction placed on procuring native labour, unless for missionary purposes, are manned by two men (usually Manila-men),

and at times by one, or a man and his wife, who sail the boat along the
coast and procure local native labour, bound only by some verbal
agreement, which is apparently satisfactory to the employee, as he is
always ready and willing to 'come again' so long as the work does not take
him away from his district; and the people engaged in the trade do not
carry firearms, as by so doing they are afraid of putting weapons into the
hands of their crew.[85]

From that snapshot of the earliest community, bound by ties of
geographical origin, occupation, marriage to Indigenous women and the raising
of mixed-descent children, there is little in the historical record until after
World War I. In the 1920s and 1930s, a 'second wave' of settlers came after the
granting of a lease to Daniel Charles Hodges. Hodges was the son of an English
father, Charles Hodges, and a Torres Strait Islander mother, Dinah Walton from
Puruma (Coconut Island), who were recorded as having a house on Horn Island
and lived there for a time. Daniel Hodges' aunt had married Gregoria (Guria)
Assacruz, a member of one of the first families to settle on Horn and he knew
and worked with several of the inhabitants. He was born on Haggerston Island
in 1894 and served in the AIF in France, where he lost a leg. On 12 January,
1918, six months before his marriage, he applied to the Lands Commissioner on
Thursday Island for a lease of 20 acres on Horn Island adjoining Mining
Homestead Leases Nos. 3 and 8 'for the purpose of growing vegetables and
cocoanuts'.[86] The land in question was situated on the north-west coast,
adjoining Galora's lease. On 27 July, 1918, Daniel Hodges married Henrietta
(Etta) Lockett, born on Badu of English-Torres Strait Islander descent. The
couple would not at that time have been accepted into White society on
Thursday Island, given the prevailing caste system; nor were they 'Aboriginals'.
Hodges received official approval for an Informal Lease 412 for 10 years at £1 per
annum beginning 1 December, 1918, rent payable in advance.[87] Like previous
settlers, he planted mango, coconut and banana trees and dug a small well.

According to Monica Walton Gould, who moved with her family to
Horn Island in the early 1930s, they and other members of Hodges' extended
family followed Hodges, who encouraged them to build their houses on his land.
By then, the Horn Island community numbered 35 to 40 people: most were
Catholic and all were connected to each other and to the surviving first-
generation Filipino residents by the dense, multiple bonds of kinship and
association characteristic of rural, communally organised societies. It was now
large enough to support its own church and, on Ascension Thursday 1933, the
community welcomed visitors from Thursday and Hammond Islands to
celebrate the opening of a 'picturesque' new Catholic Church, built by the
residents, with a bamboo floor, coconut-thatch walls and an iron roof, 'nestled

away under the cocoanut trees'.[88] The photograph on p. 80 shows some of the old Filipino pearl divers present at the opening, who 'can tell some very interesting stories of their former fortunes and mishaps. Though their fortunes have long since passed away they still bear some evident signs of their mishaps.' Behind them stands the Hammond Island Mission priest, Fr McDermott, who celebrated Mass.

> He came from Hammond Island that morning, bringing with him many of his flock for the opening of the new Church. A good number went from Thursday Island, also, so it was a real gala-day at Horn Island. Crafts of various sizes and descriptions and all of them overloaded were requisitioned for the occasion. You will understand that it added to the day's enjoyment when I was able to baptise six children belonging to one family.[89]

Another glimpse of the 1930s community comes from the account by Pedro Galora's granddaughter[90] and is confirmed by fellow resident, Monica Walton Gould. By then, the community consisted of the following families: Galora (headed by Pedro's son, Ambrose, and his wife, Jacopita Savage, from Badu), Raymond, Mallie, Hodges, Lee, Walton and Seden. Only a few of the original inhabitants remained, among them the three *tiyos*, 'uncles', Bisenti (Vicente), Dualdo and Thomas, as well as Mariano the hermit, all elderly, single men, who had retired from pearling but who no longer wished to return to the Philippines.[91] *Tiyo* Thomas had a vegetable garden at the back of his house, which was made from bamboo with a 'wooden' (probably bamboo) floor — 'a real Filipino hut, not a shanty'.[92] He looked the same as the others, remembers Monica Walton Gould: 'Old, thin, short, wiry, with leathery skin after being in the sun all his life, a bald head but a little bit of grey at the sides.' *Tiyo* Dualdo used to sell firewood: 'He had a boat and would put the chopped wood into the dinghy and take it to T. I. to sell. It was blood-red mangrove wood.'[93] *Tiyo* Bisenti had made a 'wonderful' garden and kept fowls and ducks.[94] The men were visited regularly and cared for by the young families, who took cooked meals of fish and rice to share with them, gossiped about old times and listened to their reminiscences and nostalgic songs of lament. *Tiyo* Dualdo lived at the eastern shore boundary of the village, near the Jardines' old wharf; *Tiyo* Bisenti lived 'down behind the mangroves near a creek at the western end of the village';[95] and *Tiyo* Thomas lived inland towards the airport. Their cottages formed a triangular boundary around the village, the three 'uncles' symbolically enfolding the community in a Filipino embrace.

Despite an official report in January 1938 that the 'rough dwellings' along the beach belonged to 'people squatting on the island',[96] the children of the Horn Island community, growing up carefree and well fed, remember it as 'a paradise'. When war broke out, the only official lease was held by C. G. Vidgen of Thursday Island, who ran cattle and pigs to supply meat for the island,[97] and the community members were possibly unaware of their tenuous legal hold over the land. The village, with its related extended families, was typical of the second-generation Asian-Indigenous communities of Torres Strait, which were destroyed by the war. Ties of homeland and occupation had yielded to connections of friendship and family forged in the strait. The second-generation families were united by kinship and affinal connections rather than Filipino origin: Daniel Hodges was the son of Charles Hodges and Dinah Walton; his wife, Henrietta (Etta) Lockett, was related to Louisa Mallie; Daniel's sister was Charlotte, who married Massat Solomon, the son of Solomon and Saratha Amboyn, and Joseph Lee, a Badu Islander; Dinah's brother was William Walton, husband of Gregoria (Guria) Assacruz. Even when the familial connections were more tenuous, the children called each other 'cousins'. The families lived separately, screened from their neighbours but close by, sharing food and play, constantly visiting and in touch with one another, creating a 'place-based social identity'[98] based on 'notions of shared blood, food and work as well as through the recognition of a common living area or ancestral place of origin'.[99]

Malaytown on Badu (c.1890–c.1906)

Like the Filipino community of Horn Island, the Muslim Malay community of Badu (Mulgrave Island) was also self-initiated. Badu in the 1880s, like Horn Island, became 'a resort for all the crews of boats', including many Malays who had partnered local Indigenous women. Wishing to live quietly among their countrymen, observe cultural tradition and raise their children away from the crowded dwellings and official oversight of the town, they negotiated with a local clan leader for permission to build on his land. Unlike the Filipino Horn Island community, however, Badu's Malay community lasted less than a generation. Lacking any form of institutional support and removed from its home community on Thursday Island, it could not survive the loss of its economic foundations and changes in official policy and was effectively disbanded in about 1906.

The community was located at Upai at the southern end of Badu and was called 'Malaytown' (after Thursday Island's Malaytown) in recognition of its predominantly Muslim Malay population, although some Pacific Islanders also lived there.[100] Referred to as a 'Malay settlement' or 'village' or 'camp', the place is still called 'Malaytown', although the names of the original settlers are mostly forgotten save by the older inhabitants.[101] Some of its residents were single or had wives elsewhere, but the minority whose names are remembered married or partnered local women and fathered children born at Upai. Those kinship ties continue to be respected to the present day.

Badu is a large western island, 'irregularly shaped … about 6 miles in diameter and hilly in the centre'.[102] Despite its size, it had only a small Indigenous population at the turn of the 20th century and authorities rarely visited except to deal with a disturbance. The Baduans are said to have brought themselves almost to extinction by prosecuting numerous wars with their neighbours from Mua (Banks Island) and Mabuiag (Jervis Island). Badu was repopulated by Mabuiag Islanders, who were given the northern half of the island in gratitude for their assistance in warfare.[103] Laade thought that Badu was not settled before about 1800.[104]

Thursday Island Cemetery, 1927.
Courtesy of John Oxley Library, Brisbane
(Item No. 55672).

In 1872, within two years of the beginning of the pearl rush, Captain Gay had established a pearl-shell station on Mua, directly opposite Badu[105] and separated from it by a narrow channel. There may have been another station on Badu itself at that time,[106] but it is more likely that the first attempt to establish a station there in July 1878 was made by Captain Francis Cadell.[107] Members of his advance party were murdered by the Aboriginal crew, who made off with the boat. Whether Cadell or perhaps others continued with the venture, there were 'some shelling stations' on Mua and Badu in September 1878.[108] At the end of 1881, after the opening of 'the Old Ground' nearby,[109] men of every nationality were recorded as working the boats and for years they provided a lucrative market for Thursday Island traders in vegetables and liquor.[110] In 1884, Badu had two pearling stations,[111] perhaps the same two stations mentioned previously, although under different ownership,[112] and the Islanders had become dependent on them for food and clothing. In 1874, 'few natives' lived on Badu, too few to support a missionary[113] and there were likewise 'very few' in 1882.[114] The population had, however, grown to 124 in 1891[115] (enough for a missionary), 130 in 1897,[116] about 165 in 1903[117] and a little more than 200 in 1908, at that time mostly 'Aboriginals', but also 'a few South Sea Islanders and a few Malays'.[118]

The Malays were attracted to Badu by the employment opportunities afforded by the stations. Following traditional protocol, they sought permission to settle at Upai from the clan leader, Sagigi of Wakaid. According to Tanu Nona, Sagigi agreed so as to increase the size of his clan and thereby his own importance at the expense of the other two clans, Argan and Badu.[119] By 1891, Rev. James Chalmers was complaining to John Douglas about the prevalence of marriages with 'foreign natives': 'the South Sea Islanders and Malays are able to give very large prices for the girls and the girls can have anything they want afterwards.'[120] By 1898, there were seven recorded marriages between Malay men and women from Badu and Mabuiag.[121] Walter Nona, the oldest resident on Badu, recalled six families who had once resided at Badu's Malaytown: Ahwang, Binawel,[122] Binjuda, Bowie, Jia and Ketchell. Other Malays he remembered were Jimmy Sander, who is buried at Dhadhalaig, a small island near Waral, and Jimmy Coconut, buried at Graz on Badu.[123] Also attested as living at Badu for some time were Charlie Ahmat from Singapore and his wife, Flora Geata from Mua; Mahomet Abdurraman from Borneo and his wife, Kassia from Thursday Island; Pablo Ahmat from Singapore, whose Mabuiag wife, Jane Hankin, remained with her family at Mabuiag; and Ah Mat Poontiana (Ahmat Abin Abdoela or Ali Ahmat) from Borneo, who met his Badu-born wife, Anima Ahwang, on Badu. The *Somerset Register of Births and Marriages*, although not comprehensive, records 24 children born on Badu to Malay-headed families from about 1891 to about 1906 and 15 from 1907 to 1921, 12 of the latter belonging to the Bowie and Ketchell families (Table 4.3).

Table 4.3: Children born on Badu to Malay fathers, c.1891–1921

DOB	Name	Father	Father's POB	Mother	Mother's POB
c.1891	Anima	Jaffa Ahwang	Singapore	Annie Savage	Badu, TS, Q
c.1892	Abusman	Jaffa Ahwang	Singapore	Annie Savage	Badu, TS, Q
c.1893	Jenap Esther Waahape Jia	Makassar	Serai Mabua		Badu, TS, Q
c.1893	Mariam	Moy	South-East Asia	Maria	Boigu, TS, Q
c.1895	Saptu	Jaffa Ahwang	Singapore	Annie Savage	Badu, TS, Q
c.1897	Solomon	Waahape Jia	Makassar	Serai Mabua	Badu, TS, Q
3/5/1898	Atima	Jaffa Ahwang	Singapore	Annie Savage	Badu, TS, Q
c.1899	Unnamed female	Albert Bowie	Makassar	Baimat Getawan	Badu, TS, Q
c.1900	John	Waahape Jia	Makassar	Serai Mabua	Badu, TS, Q
5/8/1901	Jaffa	Jaffa Ahwang	Singapore	Annie Savage	Badu, TS, Q
c.1902	Osman Bin Japa	Mahomet Abdurraman	Borneo	Kassia	Thursday Island, TS, Q
c.1903	Doseena	Waahape Jia	Makassar	Serai Mabua	Badu, TS, Q
3/2/1903	Aaron	Chee Ketchell	Singapore	Aigarie Gainab	Badu, TS, Q
17/4/1904	Aaron	Chee Ketchell	Singapore	Aigarie Gainab	Badu, TS, Q
3/5/1904	Osman Bin Ali	Mahomet Abdurraman	Borneo	Kassia	Thursday Island, TS, Q
30/8/1904	Nelam	Jaffa Ahwang	Singapore	Annie Savage	Badu, TS, Q
12/9/1904	Jelany	Long Sambar	Singapore	Patima Abduraman	Thursday Island, TS, Q
c.1905	Drummond (Dick)	Waahape Jia	Makassar	Serai Mabua	Badu, TS, Q
25/2/1905	Patima Norma	Charlie Ahmat	Singapore	Flora Savage	Mua, TS, Q
15/11/1905	Leah	Chee Ketchell	Singapore	Aigarie Gainab	Badu, TS, Q
c.1906	Possa	Ah Mat Usop	Singapore	Maria	Boigu, TS, Q
23/2/1906	Aramina Lillian Jumula	Charlie Ahmat	Singapore	Flora Savage	Mua, TS, Q
9/6/1906	Matilda	Albert Bowie	Makassar	Baimat Getawan	Badu, TS, Q
15/8/1906	Noranee (Rocky)	Jaffa Ahwang	Singapore	Annie Savage	Badu, TS, Q
29/4/1907	Dijohn	Mahomet Abdurraman	Borneo	Kassia	Thursday Island, TS, Q
17/6/1908	Massassan	Charlie Ahmat	Singapore	Flora Savage	Mua, TS, Q
17/8/1908	Albert	Albert Bowie	Makassar	Baimat Getawan	Badu, TS, Q
17/9/1908	Alia	Chee Ketchell	Singapore	Aigarie Gainab	Badu, TS, Q
23/5/1909	Saia	Jaffa Ahwang	Singapore	Annie Savage	Badu, TS, Q

continued

Table 4.3: continued

DOB	Name	Father	Father's POB	Mother	Mother's POB
15/6/1910	Bertha	Albert Bowie	Makassar	Baimat Getawan	Badu, TS, Q
16/12/1911	Marsat	Chee Ketchell	Singapore	Aigarie Gainab	Badu, TS, Q
5/5/1913	May	Albert Bowie	Makassar	Baimat Getawan	Badu, TS, Q
25/1/1914	Samat	Chee Ketchell	Singapore	Aigarie Gainab	Badu, TS, Q
4/9/1915	Jack	Albert Bowie	Makassar	Baimat Getawan	Badu, TS, Q
23/2/1916	Ruth	Chee Ketchell	Singapore	Aigarie Gainab	Badu, TS, Q
23/1/1918	Dulcie	Albert Bowie	Makassar	Baimat Getawan	Badu, TS, Q
19/10/1918	Jane	Chee Ketchell	Singapore	Aigarie Gainab	Badu, TS, Q
24/2/1921	Nauma	Chee Ketchell	Singapore	Aigarie Gainab	Badu, TS, Q
29/7/1921	Edward	Albert Bowie	Makassar	Baimat Getawan	Badu, TS, Q

Sources: *Somerset Register of Births and Marriages*; tombstone inscriptions; information from 'Condy' Canuto, Mary Bowie Eseli, Nauma Ketchell, Walter Nona; Chief Protector of Aboriginals correspondence in QSA.

There are few contemporary references to Badu's Malay population. In one of them, the newly arrived schoolteacher wrote an enthusiastic letter to the Under Secretary, Education Department, on 12 April 1906, giving her impressions of the people of Badu and contrasting their 'well-shaped heads' and slender build with the stolidness of the local Malays. There were some Malays living on Badu, she wrote, 'but they are heavily built with big, round, bullet heads'.[124]

Shortly after this letter was sent, the Malays began to leave Badu. There is no record of their departure and the exact dates are unknown. Scattered references in official correspondence[125] and subsequent births on Thursday Island suggest that most of the families left towards the end of 1905 or the beginning of 1906, although some stayed on for another year or two. By about 1909, however, only the Bowies and Ketchells remained. Albert Bowie, of Dutch-Malay heritage, was born at Makassar in Sulawesi, then part of the Dutch East Indies; Chee Ketchell (Kitchel Mahomed) came from the British colony of Singapore and worked with pearling fleets at Broome, Port Darwin and Thursday Island before his marriage.[126] Both men were originally divers, married Badu women and lived almost all their married lives on Badu, where all their children were born and raised;[127] both were fully incorporated into Badu social networks, sharing their knowledge of European ways with their relatives.

PIL buildings, Badu, western Torres Strait, 1916.
Courtesy of John Oxley Library, Brisbane (Item No. 58234).

A combination of economic, environmental and ideological motives appears to have brought about the abandonment of Badu's Malaytown. The year 1906 was a momentous one for Badu and ushered in significant changes. With the collapse of the price of pearl shell, most of the pearling fleets and their predominantly Malay crews had departed for Aru in September 1905. Shell prices continued their decline and the four pearling stations on Badu and Mabuiag, which provided most of the paid employment, became bankrupt and ceased operations in January/February 1906, putting 115 men out of work.[128] This economic devastation was exacerbated by a region-wide drought in late 1905, with subsequent crop failures and widespread food shortages in 1906.[129] Yopelli Panuel's understanding was that the economic imperative was the most significant factor: the 'Malay people came here and made a village on the southside called Upai. When the station went away, these divers belong to station shift to Thursday Island.'[130] At the same time, Queensland policy was becoming more protectionist and segregationist. Badu and the other remote islands were to become reserves in which the Islanders, now recast as 'Aboriginals', could be 'protected' from outsiders. Asian-Indigenous families were being pressured to move to Thursday Island away from their 'Aboriginal' kinfolk on the outer islands. Ted Loban stressed the ideological factor, saying that the Malay-headed families moved from Badu and Mabuiag at the urging of their wives and this was a direct result of anxieties about the future.[131] According to

Loban, it was the wives who were most in favour of the move, citing more freedom, better job opportunities and a better education for their children.

It was a combination of these same economic, environmental and ideological conditions that provided the impetus for the bureaucracy to attempt a radical economic and social experiment. If successful, it could provide a model for the rest of the strait and possibly the mainland.[132] The death of John Douglas in mid-1904 had provided the long-sought opportunity for the policy-makers to segregate the Torres Strait Islanders from Asians and Europeans and control their labour and wages; the proposed partnership with Pacific Industries Ltd (PIL), a newly formed Christian industrial organisation with links to the London Missionary Society (LMS), provided the means. Departmental authorities had been in negotiations for some time with the former LMS missionary, Frederick William Walker, the managing director of PIL. In January 1906, the local Protector suggested that, in view of the urgency of the situation, Walker might advance the money to purchase boats for the Badu Islanders.[133] His department had already assisted some islands to buy boats to be worked collectively, but what it wanted, and what Walker undertook to provide, was an alternative to the previous labour system, which had integrated Islanders into the broader regional workforce. In February 1906, PIL and the department agreed to work together to provide a viable, self-contained economic base for local development under the ultimate control of the local Protector:

> With a view to helping the natives to help themselves and so fulfilling one of the primary objects of the Company, 15 small second-hand luggers and cutters have been purchased by the Company. These vessels are either let out to natives under an arrangement by which the proceeds are divided into three parts — one-third going to the Company, one-third to the men, and one-third for working expenses, stores and insurance; or have been sold to natives, and are being paid for by instalments out of the money they are able to earn by diving for Pearls and pearl-shell, and collecting Turtle-shell, Beche-de-mer and other produce of the Sea. Employment is thus found for a considerable number of men.[134]

In 1906, PIL, with Queensland Government support, acquired 'a freehold of 406 acres of excellent land on Badu for the Headquarters of the Company' for the construction of a number of buildings and a copra plantation.[135] The land chosen was in a sheltered shore position at Dogai, immediately opposite Mua and the site of the present village. In late October or early November, the company's stores, building and supplies arrived, to be followed on 16 November by the European staff:

Boat-building at PIL, Badu, western Torres Strait, 1916.
Courtesy of John Oxley Library, Brisbane (Item No. 58172).

Building began in December 1906: a retail store and a bulk store with a covered way between the two, and a back warehouse for produce, kerosene, coke, merchandise, stores, and other similar goods; a living house with six rooms, including a kitchen; a rough work-shed on the beach, for repairing boats; a short jetty, for landing goods; a tramway for conveying them to the stores; and an adequate water supply.[136]

The labour and trading opportunities provided by the company were to change the nature of Badu society. Having resisted missionary efforts to move from their clan lands to settle near the church,[137] they now began to shift to this new economic centre. Preference in hiring was naturally given to Christian Torres Strait Islanders (and Pacific Islanders who had settled permanently in the strait). The free Muslim Malays of Malaytown were less favoured under the new conditions. Only Bowie and Ketchell found long-term employment with PIL, but by then they were living permanently on Badu with their Christian 'Aboriginal' families. Most Malays, however, had already made the choice to leave.

'Malay Village' on Port Lihou (1939–42)

The case of the third of the communities under discussion, the small Malay community of Port Lihou, again illustrates how members of a marginalised Asian minority in Torres Strait attempted to create an independent and economically self-reliant space for themselves and their families away from Thursday Island. It began shortly before the outbreak of World War II as the continuation of a Pacific Islander community and became a temporary makeshift refuge for the residents' extended families when they were threatened with evacuation. The Pacific Islander connections have been largely forgotten: a long-time European resident explained to me a few years ago that Port Lihou is now referred to as 'Malay Village', because 'a lot of Malays lived there early [last] century'.[138] In the event, this Malay community proved to be even more transient than Malaytown on Badu and, like the Filipino community on nearby Horn Island, ended abruptly with the evacuation of its members in 1942.

Port Lihou, which, along with Muralag (Prince of Wales Island), Horn Island and Thursday Island, forms part of traditional Kaurareg land, is physically separated from Muralag by a narrow channel. About 1922, three decades after the removal of the Kaurareg to Hammond Island, it was settled by ni-Vanuatu retirees from the marine industries, who made superb gardens in the scrub above the beach and cut firewood to fuel the homes and businesses of Thursday Island.[139]

A number of Muslim Malays also held fuel licences during the 1920s and 1930s and cut wood on the surrounding islands. Among them were Assan Ah Boo (Abu Assan) from Malaysia, Doela Banda from Bolton Island, Timsir Cassina, Mahomet Drummond from Borneo, Batcho Mingo from Makassar, Sariman from Java, Assan Bin Rassip from Singapore and Assan Singapore from Java.[140] They did not live in the Port Lihou community, but all the woodcutters knew one another and marriages occurred between the locally born descendants of Malays and Pacific Islanders during the inter-war years, when ethnic origin became a less important factor for 'Coloured' people in the choice of a spouse.

The Malays who initiated their own community at Port Lihou had, like their countrymen, been drawn to Torres Strait by employment in the marine industries. Once there, they married local women of mixed descent and became aware of an opportunity for economic self-sufficiency in agricultural rather than marine activities by taking over the gardens made by the Pacific Islanders. They shared the latter's desire to 'reside where they were their own agents and did not come under the control of the Aboriginal department'.[141] The Pacific men did not want Europeans living nearby, but raised no objections to the Malays, with whom they had established good relations over the years.[142] Family bonds were created between the two groups when, in 1920, the step-daughter of one of the original Pacific Islander settlers married Saptu Ahwang, born on Badu to a Malay father. The couple briefly resided at Port Lihou in the mid-1920s.

In mid-1939, Willem Olie Dewis from Timor, Thomas Loban (Simeon Sadir) from Indonesia and Bora Bin Juda from Makassar took over the informal leases originally held by Pacific Islanders, who had either died or grown too infirm to garden. The original leases were renumbered as IL 2230 (Dewis), IL 2234 (Loban) and IL 2260 (Bin Juda), the latter not taken up until 1940.[143] Dewis was a 'free Malay' and a Christian. His wife, Noressa (Nodi), was the daughter of Ah Mat and Maria Usop, once residents of Badu's Malaytown. Tom Loban was also a 'free man', whose wife, Gertie Summers of White Australian-Mabuiag descent, was locally born, as was Bin Juda's wife, Mareja Doolah, three of whose grandparents were Malay.

The deaths of the old Pacific men and the handing over of their leases effectively signalled the end of the Pacific Islander community and the beginning of its short-lived Malay successor. Jianna Seden Richardson recalls how she and her family used to visit their cousins, the Bin Judas, on weekends and during school holidays — her mother and Bin Juda's wife were sisters:[144] 'We had our own section, we and the Dewises were in the end section. The people were all related.'[145] Other visitors to Port Lihou included the Rassip and Barba families, whose Malay-Boigu Islander mothers were sisters of Mrs Dewis.

The Malay community of Port Lihou did not endure for more than a few years. In late 1941, after the internment of the Japanese, a number of Malay-descended families from Thursday Island fled to Port Lihou to stay with one of the families in their weekend shack, hoping to hide from the authorities for the duration of the war:

> They thought: 'Oh well, we'll be safe [here]. There's lots of food. We won't be in danger.' More TI families followed. Some had inboard motors on their clinker dinghies; others rowed down Boat Channel to Endeavour Strait, taking advantage of the wind by fixing sheeting between upright oars attached to the sides of the boats.[146]

Jianna Seden Richardson and her mother stayed with the Bin Juda family. Jianna remembers that the Dewis family were there but not the Lobans, who had already been evacuated. Also present were the Ahwangs and Ahmats and the Barba family, all staying with the Bin Judas, along with Lassmintan Seden Cowley and Sogi Baruna Messa, wife of Roy Messa, the son of one of the original Pacific Islander settlers.[147] The existing dwellings became too crowded and the families constructed makeshift 'grass houses'. They managed to evade detection for some months and became among the last evacuees from Thursday Island the next year.[148] Jianna Richardson recalls being there when an army boat came with orders for their evacuation, telling the families that they had only 24–36 hours to get to Thursday Island to be sent south.

The short-lived Malay community of Port Lihou also demonstrates the characteristics that typify the communities under discussion. Like them, it was established by South-East Asian immigrants married to local Indigenous women, who wished to live peacefully and independently with their wives and children among like-minded countrymen away from the racism of Thursday Island and the constant scrutiny of local officials. The beach at Port Lihou is secluded and the bay is protected from the tides of Endeavour Strait. It was close enough to Thursday Island to reach by launch or rowboat, yet sheltered from view behind a rocky headland. The settlement had few amenities but the physical needs of the residents were met by 'plenty of "lovely, sweet" water in wells and running creeks just beyond the beach',[149] fish from the nearby reefs, fruit from the banana, coconut, mango, pawpaw and pineapple trees planted by the Pacific men, and garden produce: cassava, pumpkin, sugar cane, sweet potato, taro and yam. The families also kept fowls. Their crude dwellings, dismissed in a report as 'rough shacks … of little value',[150] were constructed from local materials and hidden from immediate view among lush vegetation. The members were bound together through actual and imagined kinship ties, they lived separately but maintained daily contact. For adults and children, surrounded by their extended families, it was a secure and happy place.

Conclusion

The three autonomous, self-sufficient Filipino and Malay 'outstation' communities of Torres Strait demonstrate the adaptations made by economically and politically subordinated South-East Asian immigrants and their locally born families, whose individual life paths and collective history were profoundly influenced by social and political events. These little-known communities are interesting in themselves and as examples of the ways marginalised people have always sought to counter power through solidarity. Finding their choices restricted by official policies of segregation, some Filipinos and Malays took matters into their own hands and established communities in which they could pursue their own economic and family interests, freely express aspects of their personal and group identity and find refuge from the racism and restriction that blighted interpersonal relations between Whites and non-Whites on Thursday Island. They were shielded from direct surveillance by authorities, with whom they always cooperated when circumstances demanded, although the authorities knew little about 'what went on underneath'.

All the communities discussed in this chapter were self-organising and self-reliant, materially poor but socially and culturally rich and diverse. Although initiated by the people themselves, they depended for survival on the vagaries of the marine industries and the good will of government or clan authorities. And, while each community arose independently and had a different composition, there are intriguing interconnections, continuities and discontinuities among these more transient communities and between them and the larger and more ethnically self-conscious Filipino and Malay 'home' communities of Thursday Island, on which the outstations depended for the provision of services and the celebration of culturally and religiously significant events.

It is significant that only the Filipinos and Malays established such 'outstation' communities. A motivating factor in their creation was the desire of their members, almost all of whom had married local Indigenous women with ancestral ties to land and sea, to raise their locally born children in safe, healthy communities as far as possible from the racism and crowding of Thursday Island. This motivation was not shared to the same degree by members of the other Asian communities, who tended to be sojourners rather than settlers and who, for various legal, administrative and cultural reasons, contracted few marriages with local Indigenous women.

In the process of creating their new communities, the immigrants and their children also created a rich and unique hybrid culture, much of which was destroyed by the upheavals of World War II. The children were to create a new place-based social identity — as 'Thursday Islanders' or 'Thursday Island half-castes' — the focus shifting from place of origin to a shared ethos that privileged community and fellowship and the reciprocal responsibilities of family and friends above ethnic and religious differences. In time, the interpersonal relationships they forged through the multiple connections of daily life were to bind the families of Asian descent to each other and to a majority of Torres Strait families through marriage, descent and adoption, bequeathing a lasting pan-Asian/Indigenous cultural legacy to all Torres Strait Islanders.

Acknowledgements

Many thanks to Mary Galora Bowie, 'Condy' Canuto, Fr Anthony Caruana, M. S. C., Peter Elder, Barbara Erskine, Mary Bowie Eseli, Betty Ah Boo Foster, Stephen Foster, Monica Walton Gould, Anne Gray, Jeremy Hodes, Herbert Hofer, Reynaldo Ileto, Nauma Ketchell, Ted Loban (now deceased), Vic McGrath, Walter Nona, Yopelli Panuel (now deceased), Eva Salam (Mingo) Peacock, Guy Ramsay, Jenny Rich, Jianna Seden Richardson, John Scott, Rod Sullivan, Phyllis Spain Travis.

Footnotes

[1]   'They write from the top. They don't know what went on underneath.' Comment by an anonymous Palm Island woman about an academic account of Palm Island events. Interview dated 1982, OHC 182/1, Oral History Collection of James Cook University of North Queensland.

[2]   The reference term 'Thursday Islander' and its synonyms 'Thursday Island half-caste' and 'Malay' were coined during the inter-war years and demonstrate the recognition of a new category of individual and the impossibility of working within the racial guidelines and classifications that underpinned Queensland legislation at that time. They indicate the emergence in Torres Strait of a new 'placed-based social identity' (for discussion, see Schug, D. M. 1995. 'The marine realm and a sense of place among Papua New Guinean communities of Torres Strait.' PhD thesis, University of Hawai'i. p. 7).

[3]   Osborne, E. 1997. *Torres Strait Islander Women and the Pacific War*. Canberra: Aboriginal Studies Press. Perdon, R. 1998. *Brown Americans of Asia*. Sydney: Manila Prints.

[4]   Information on the Horn Island community can be found in Bowie, M. and J. Singe, 'The Galora family of Horn Island', *Torres News*, 14–20 May, 1993. p. 12. And Doyle, F. J. 'Thursday Island' *Annals of Our Lady of the Sacred Heart*. 1 September, 1933. p. 569. However, as unofficial, independent settlements, whose residents were exempt from the Queensland Aboriginal Protection Acts, they do not appear in the annual reports of the Government Resident of Thursday Island, Northern Protector of Aboriginals, Queensland Native Affairs Department, Queensland Department of Public Lands, or the *Queensland Government Gazette*.

[5]   When quoting primary sources, I have kept the original spelling; the modern spelling is 'Manila'.

[6]   These include the sole occupants of smaller islands, such as the Dorante family of Nipin, the Francis family of Auridh and the Salam/Mingo family of Wednesday Island; as well as residents of more populated islands, such as the Ahmat, Carabello, Guivarra, Jardine and Kanak families of Erub, the Cloudy family of Ugar, the Doolah family of Mer, the Ahmat, Ahwang, Bowie, Jia and Ketchell families of Badu, the Ahmat family of Mabuiag and the Sabatino and Cadauas families of Yam.

[7]   Nor is it necessarily possible to tell an individual's origins from his name, e.g., William Andrew and William Francis, 'native[s] of Manilla', in 'Charlie vs Joe Reis and Francis, 17 February 1885', and Thomas Larkins, 'native of Borneo', in 'Longley vs Ah Mat, 31 December 1885', CPS13D/P1, Queensland State Archives (hereafter QSA). Others, such as Anthony Spain (Antonio Puerte) and Matthew Rodericks (Matteo Rodriguez), two long-term Filipino residents of Thursday Island, anglicised their names.

[8]   Manderson, L. 1988. 'Malays.' In J. Jupp (ed.), *The Australian people: an encyclopedia of the nation, its people and their origins*. North Ryde: Angus and Robertson. pp. 691–3, at pp. 691–2.

[9]   Martinez, J. 1999. 'The "Malay" community in pre-war Darwin.' In R. Ganter (ed.), *Asians in Australian history, Queensland Review*, Vol. 6, No. 2. pp. 44–57, at p. 45.

[10]   Before Federation, Great Britain had responsibility for the external affairs of the Australian colonies.

[11]   'Chambers Bruce McNab to Under Secretary, Home Secretary's Department, 17 May 1897.' HOM/A30, QSA.

[12]   Writing to his son on 28 September, 1897, Thursday Island's Government Resident, Hon. John Douglas, expressed surprise at Zarcal's naturalisation, when the equally successful and prominent Japanese businessmen, Torajiro Sato and Kametsu Taguchi, were refused: 'Zarkal [sic] has been nationalised, how I don't know, for he is not legally qualified for naturalisation, not being married, while Satow [sic] and Taguchi have been refused being qualified. Great indignation is proposed, but like most of our agitations it is a storm in a teacup and will soon blow over.' John Douglas to Edward Douglas, OM89-3/B/2(2)/15, John Oxley Library (hereafter JOL). My thanks to Jeremy Hodes for making his transcription of the Douglas letters available to me. Zarcal married Emma Esther Beach, the daughter of the Thursday Island postmaster, on 12 May, 1900, on Thursday Island. For the business implications of Zarcal's naturalisation see Reynaldo Ileto's Chapter Five, this volume, and Perdon, R., *Brown Americans of Asia*, pp. 126–7.

13 'Chambers Bruce McNab to Under Secretary, Home Secretary's Department, 10 May 1897.'
    HOM/A30, QSA.
14 Ellis, A. F. 1936. *Adventuring in Coral Seas*. Sydney: Angus and Robertson. p. 76. Later, visiting
    Mornington Island, he writes on p. 118 that '[t]he leading Malay with me was known as "Big
    Alik"; a native of one of the North African countries and fine type of fellow'.
15 Coppinger, R. W. 1885. *Cruise of the 'Alert': four years in Patagonian, Polynesian, and Mascarene
    waters (1878–82)*. London: Swan Sonnenschein. p. 196.
16 Shnukal, A. 1995. '"Manilamen": the first Filipino migrants in Australia.' *Australia New Zealand
    Provincial Bulletin (Society of the Sacred Heart)*, No. 27, May. pp. 11–14.
17 *Annual Report* of the Government Resident of Thursday Island for 1902: 'Of the Filipinos also a
    few are married women, for it is the custom of the Manila man, when he is sufficiently well off,
    to order a wife from the conventual schools at Mecao [sic]. In addition to these there are a few
    aboriginal women who are married, chiefly to Manila men.'
18 *Torres Straits Pilot*, 14 December, 1901. p. 1. My thanks to Karl Neuenfeldt for providing this
    reference.
19 See, for example, 'Charlie vs Joe Reis and Francis [Manila men], 17 February 1885.' CPS13D/P1,
    QSA.
20 The first was between Pedro de la Cruz and Eliza Hinkley on 26 July, 1887.
21 Comment by Chief Protector of Aboriginals, 19 June, 1914, at bottom of telegram from 'Riley,
    Thursday Island, to Home Secretary, 17 June 1914.' A/58761 (Restricted), QSA.
22 The brig, *Freak* (master William Walton), which was wrecked in Torres Strait on 27 November,
    1870, carried among its sailors three Filipinos, Peter Minas, Domingo Rossa and Salvador Glass;
    and two Malays, Simon and Cassim. 'Department of Ports and Harbours, Brisbane, to Marquis of
    Normanby, 28 November 1871.' GOV/A4, p. 419, QSA. They were given passage to Sydney,
    arriving on 19 January, 1871. *Colonial Secretary In-letters, Somerset 1871*, Margaret Lawrie
    Collection, MLC 1791-37/2, JOL.
23 'Police Magistrate, Somerset, to Port Master, Brisbane, 26 May 1873.' *Records of Somerset, Cape
    York 1872–77*, MS.Q 589, Mitchell Library (hereafter ML). See also 'Portmaster, Department
    of Ports and Harbours, Brisbane, to the Colonial Treasurer re. the shipment of Polynesians and
    Asiatics in NSW to the marine industries in northern Queensland, 29 August 1877.' The writer
    complains that there has been no satisfactory result of letters written by the Marine Board dated
    19 March and 12 May, 1873, and communications with the Government of NSW. He continues:
    'The imposition practised upon these Islanders and Asiatics by the practice in vogue in Sydney
    of allowing them to be shipped elsewhere than at the shipping office and independently of and
    without the supervision of the Shipping Master is a matter which should not be allowed to
    continue. For although these practices originate in NSW the discredit attached to them
    practically falls on this colony.' TRE/A18/1883, QSA.
24 In the early 1790s, sugar from the Philippines was shipped to the new settlement at Sydney, part
    of a triangular pattern of trade between Sydney, Canton and Manila. Coal was sent from
    Newcastle to Manila from 1871 to 1923 and from Melbourne to Manila between 1874 and 1895;
    sugar was brought from Manila for Queensland refineries from 1875. For an overview of early
    Australian-Philippine trade links, see Battersby, P. 1993. 'Influential circles: the Philippines in
    Australian trade and tourism, 1840 to 1926.' In R. C. Ileto and R. Sullivan (eds), *Discovering
    Australasia: essays on Philippine-Australian interactions*, Townsville: James Cook University,
    Department of History and Politics. pp. 47–69. And Perdon, R., *Brown Americans of Asia*, pp.
    105–12.
25 'T. De Hoghton, Lieutenant-Commanding HMS *Beagle*, Thursday Island, to Commodore J. C.
    Wilson, RN, HMS *Wolverine*, Sydney, 22 September 1879.' p. 3. Reporting on the Pearl-Shell
    Fisheries of Torres Straits, *Queensland Votes and Proceedings* (hereafter QVP), 1880.
26 See Perdon's reference to Filipino divers in 1874 in Perdon, R., *Brown Americans of Asia*, p. 115,
    and Sissons' remarks that, by 1876, there were already several Malays and Filipinos engaged in

the pearling industry in Sissons, D. C. S., 1979, 'The Japanese in the Australian pearling industry', *Queensland Heritage*, Vol. 3, No. 10. pp. 8–27, at p. 8. One of these was Maximo Gomez, designated as both 'Manilla man' and 'Malay', who was responsible for the death in 1879 of the young Londoner, William Clarke, and was subsequently hanged. See Perdon, op. cit. and *Somerset Register of Deaths* entry for 26 December, 1879.

27 'Mr Bissex, Master of the *Sri Singapura*, applied for a piece of land [at the settlement of Victoria, Port Essington, northern Australia] and then went to China to get labourers and two small ships to start up an enterprise for trepang fishing. He also hoped to grow cotton on his piece of land.' 'McArthur to Colonial Secretary, Despatch of 27 March 1846', quoted in Spillett, P. G. 1972. *Forsaken settlement: an illustrated history of the settlement of Victoria, Port Essington, North Australia 1838–1849*. Melbourne: Lansdowne. p. 129. There had already been several attempts to persuade the visiting Macassans to settle permanently at the settlement and, in 1845, the British Government decided 'to encourage the immigration of a limited number of Chinese and Malays who may feel disposed to adventure there'. Ibid., p. 116.

28 On 26 November, 1879, Sanie, Julius Conception and Aboo successfully sued W. R. Mogg, manager for Francis Cadell, for unpaid wages. CPS/13D P1, QSA.

29 'Police Magistrate, Thursday Island, to Colonial Secretary, 2 June 1879.' *Somerset Letterbooks* 84–79, ML.

30 T. De Hoghton, Reporting on the Pearl-Shell Fisheries, p. 3.

31 'Report on Pearl Fisheries by H. M. Chester to Colonial Secretary, 4 June 1880.' COL/A295/3587, QSA.

32 The charge was 'continued wilful disobedience to the lawful commands of William Summers, master of the cutter *Sylph* 17 & 18 Vic. S.104.' 11 September, 1877, CPS13D/P1, QSA.

33 'W. R. Mogg vs Joseph Tucker for wilfully harboring a seaman who has neglected to join his ship, 18 October 1881.' CPS13D/P1, QSA.

34 This practice was continued by the first annual report of the Government Resident for 1885, which also enumerated the Javanese as a separate category.

35 Dupeyrat, A. 1935. *Papouasie: histoire de la mission (1885–1935)*. Paris: Dillen. p. 68.

36 In some instances, the pearlers refused to pay for their repatriation and were sued in the Thursday Island court. See, e.g., 'John Francis, Sambo Amadu and Charley Johnny vs William Thomas Kirkpatrick, master and owner of the lugger *Viking*, 28 September 1883.' CPS13D/P1. The men, whose period of service was 18 months from 30 August, 1883, said they were promised that the master would pay their passages to Sydney when their time was finished. This was denied by Kirkpatrick: 'The articles state that "any port in Queensland or Sydney shall be the final port of discharge".' See also 'George Pearson vs Abdul Japar, Nani, Mahomet Alli, Warsema Omar for wilful disobedience of lawful commands, 10 August 1885.' CPS13D/P1, QSA.

37 Much later, when extremely stringent regulations governed indenture, individual permits to remain could still be extended at the discretion of local customs officials. 'Protector of Aboriginals, Thursday Island, to Chief Protector of Aboriginals, 20 February 1922.' A/58771, QSA.

38 'Police Magistrate, Thursday Island, to Colonial Secretary, 3 March 1879.' COL A/272/932, QSA.

39 'Police Magistrate, Thursday Island, to Colonial Secretary, 4 June 1879.' COL/A284/3725, QSA.

40 Although of unsound mind and discharged after a month, his countrymen kept him for almost two years, finally asking the court whether he could be treated in a hospital.

41 'Thomas vs Walton as Agent for W. Walton for claim for £20 wages as hired servant, 5 February 1885.' CPS13D/P1, QSA.

42 The exception was John Thomas, an Englishman, who, on his release from prison for deserting his ship at Singapore, took the place of one of the men.

43 'Bowden vs Abdel Rahman for refusing to fulfil his hired service, 5 June 1883.' CPS13D/P1, QSA.

44 'Police vs Rahmoon (Manilla) for having no lawful visible means of support and suspected to be of unsound mind, 20 September 1884.' CPS13D/P1, QSA.

45 'George Pearson vs Abdul Japar, Nani, Mahomet Alli, Warsema Omar for wilful disobedience of lawful commands, 10 August 1885.' CPS13D/P1, QSA.

46 'Anticipated riots at Thursday Island.' *The Queensland Figaro*, 25 April, 1885. p. 515.
47 'The Torres Straits Pearl Shell Fishers Association vs Ah Mat for refusing to perform work after obtaining an advance of wages, 2 October 1885.' CPS13D/P1, QSA.
48 *Annual Report* of Department of Harbours and Marine for 1934–35.
49 Between 1887 and 1914, 35 marriages between Filipino men and Aboriginal and Torres Strait Islander women were celebrated in the Thursday Island Catholic church. Women generally married young, and there was often a considerable age difference between husband and wife, so that from the turn of the century the brides were themselves almost all the daughters of Filipino or other foreign seamen.
50 The Queensland Government, aware of planned legislation, refused all applications for naturalisation shortly before Federation.
51 'Report of the Government Resident at Thursday Island for 1896 and 1897.' p. 4, *QVP*, 1898.
52 Thomas Eykyn, the Church of England priest who visited the islands of the Prince of Wales Group between 1885 and 1895 as part of his parish, noted that 'these islands, grouped closely together, are covered with low wooded hills, with clusters of houses near the beach in every direction. These are the homes of the pearl-shellers; for the industry of the place is diving for mother-of-pearl shells; and fleets of shelling-boats are seen everywhere.' Eykyn, T. 1896. *Parts of the Pacific*. London: Swan Sonnenschein. p. 96.
53 'E. McKeown, National Parks Ranger, Forests Office, Tully, to Forestry Sub-Department of the Queensland Department of Public Lands, re Islands along the Coast, Cape York Peninsular [sic] and in the vicinity of Thursday Island (225/38), 4 January 1938.' TR1817/1, Box 16, IL 598, QSA.
54 Today, Horn Island is the site of the regional airport, and is the first island encountered by visitors arriving by air. Its 'Horned Hill', which gave the island its English name, rises to about 102 metres.
55 Bowie and Singe, who have written the fullest account of the Horn Island Filipino community, state that Kaurareg from Kubin began to arrive in the late 1950s, some of them camping on Galora land. Pedro Galora's son, Ambrose, wrote to them on 14 November, 1960, 'pointing out that they were on his land without permission and had no right to build houses there. Consequently these Kubin families moved further back to the present village site where land was provided for them by the Queensland Government.'
56 *Annual Report* of Under Secretary for Mines for 1901.
57 *Torres Straits Daily Pilot*, 3 April, 1897.
58 According to Babbage, R., 1990, *The Strategic Significance of Torres Strait*, Canberra: Strategic and Defence Studies Centre, Research School of Pacific Studies, The Australian National University, p. 21, this mine during its short life was producing gold, silver and lead-zinc worth about $20 million annually.
59 Burchill, E. 1972. *Thursday Island Nurse*. Adelaide: Rigby. p. 29.
60 Bowie, M. and J. Singe, 'The Galora family of Horn Island'.
61 'Charles Savage vs Thomas F. McEwen for neglect of duty as a Police Constable, Police Court, Port Kennedy, 29 July 1889.' A/40083/AF/1254, QSA.
62 'Police vs Lasses for drunkenness, 2 October 1889.' CPS 13D/P2, QSA.
63 *Register of Thursday Island Baptisms, Marriages, Burials*, October 1884–January 1894, Box 0566, Order of the Sacred Heart Archives, Kensington, NSW.
64 *Register of Special Leases*, July 1887–January 1898, Nos. 349–548, Queensland Department of Public Lands (hereafter QDPL), LAN/U3, QSA. The lease was written off on 1 February, 1897, but Galora continued to live there until he moved to Bloomfield, where he died in 1920. Anne Gray, pers. comm., July 2000.
65 'Horn Island c.18 sq.m. (exclusive of 3 acres on western side under lease [to Galora]) opened for Occupation Licence, under Par V. of *The Crown Lands Act* of 1884, at Thursday Island Land Office, on and after 22 December 1890 at annual rental of £1 per square mile.' *Government Gazette*, 22 November, 1890.
66 *Register of Special Leases*, July 1887–January 1898, Nos. 349–548, QDPL, LAN/U3, QSA.

67 Ibid. By 1932, it had become Gold Mining Lease No. 3 and was held by Ambrose Galora, Pedro's son. After Ambrose's death in 1961, his daughter, Mary Galora Bowie, inherited the land, which in 1984 was converted from Miners' Homestead Lease to freehold. TR1818/1/595, OL46: Horn Island, QSA, and Bowie, M. and J. Singe, 'The Galora family of Horn Island'.

68 Anthony Jenkins, Clerk of the Court of Petty Sessions on Thursday Island, producing the *Register of Timber Licenses* as evidence in the case of 'Police vs Dayman, Osen, Bendara, Solomon, Nariga, 19 July 1902.' CPS 13D/S2, QSA.

69 'Police vs Charley Omar for having no visible lawful means of support, 14 March 1904.' CPS13D/P11, QSA.

70 'Police vs Dayman, Osen, Bendara, Solomon, Nariga, 19 July 1902.' CPS 13D/S2, QSA.

71 *Annual Reports* of the Government Resident of Thursday Island for 1894–95 to 1906.

72 Betty Ah Boo Foster, pers. comm., May 2003.

73 Bowie, M. and J. Singe, 'The Galora family of Horn Island'.

74 'Police vs Lucio Jerusalem, 6 May 1904.' CPS 13D/P11, QSA.

75 Mary Galora Bowie, pers. comm., May 2003; Bowie, M. and J. Singe, 'The Galora family of Horn Island'.

76 Evidence from Malcolm Smith, Coxswain, Water Police, in 'Police vs Horatio Sammayer for vagrancy, 19 April 1895.' CPS13D/P6, QSA.

77 Monica Walton Gould, pers. comm., March 2003. Relations were apparently closer during the first generation. Judging from the names and birthplaces of many of the Cape York Aboriginal wives, many of these men were affines.

78 Doyle, F. J., 'Thursday Island'.

79 Dupeyrat, A., *Papouasie*, pp. 434–5.

80 Doyle, F. J., 'Thursday Island'.

81 Loos, N. A. 1980. 'Queensland's kidnapping act: The Native Labourers Protection Act of 1884.' *Aboriginal History*, Vol. 4, No. 2. pp. 150–73.

82 See, for example: Bolton, G. C. 1963. *A Thousand Miles Away: a history of north Queensland to 1920.* Brisbane: Jacaranda Press. Loos, N. A. 1982. *Invasion and Resistance: Aboriginal–European relations on the North Queensland frontier 1861–1897.* Canberra: Australian National University Press. Evans, R., K. Saunders and K. Cronin. 1988. *Race Relations in Colonial Queensland: a history of exclusion, exploitation and extermination.* St Lucia: University of Queensland Press. The anthropologist, Chase, is more even-handed, citing the accommodations made between the Asian trepangers and Aboriginal people of the mainland and their long period of mutual interdependence. See Chase, A. K. 1981. 'All kind of nation: Aborigines and Asians in Cape York Peninsula.' *Aboriginal History*, Vol. 1, No. 5. pp. 6–15.

83 'Protector of Aboriginals, Thursday Island, to Northern Protector of Aborigines, 27 November 1900.' A/69491, QSA.

84 'Lucio Jerusalem for harbouring an Aboriginal to wit "Annie", 20 April 1904.' CPS13D/P11, QSA.

85 Jardine, F. L. 1904. 'The nutmeg (Torres Strait) pigeon.' *Emu*, Vol. 3, No. 7. pp. 181–5, at p. 183.

86 Correspondence regarding Informal Lease 412, TR1817/1, Box 12, QSA.

87 *Register of Informal Leases* Nos. 294–574, IL 412, QDPL, LAN/67, QSA.

88 Doyle, F. J., 'Thursday Island'. The church was located just in front of the present hotel on Horn Island, says Mary Galora Bowie, pers. comm., May 2003.

89 Doyle, F. J., 'Thursday Island'.

90 Bowie, M. and J. Singe, 'The Galora family of Horn Island'. Mary Galora Bowie was the only prewar resident to return to live on Horn Island after the war.

91 Rey Ileto, pers. comm., May 2003, suspects that Dualdo is a short form of Clodualdo, a common Filipino personal name in the past. I have been unable to identify these men with certainty, although Tiyo Bisenti was probably Vicente Camposano. According to Mary Galora Bowie, pers. comm., May 2003, Bisenti and Dualdo died before the war and were buried in the Horn Island cemetery; Mariano also died on Horn Island; Thomas was the last one to die — he was sent to Merauke during the war but returned afterwards, stayed with the Galora family for a while, then got sick and went to hospital, where he died. *Tiyo* Thomas is therefore not Thomas Dorales, who died in 1902.

92 Monica Walton Gould, pers. comm., March 2003.

93 Ibid.

94 Betty Ah Boo Foster and Mary Galora Bowie, pers. comm., May 2003.

95 Bowie, M. and J. Singe, 'The Galora family of Horn Island'.

96 'E. McKeown, National Parks Ranger, Forests Office, Tully, to Forestry Sub-Department of QDPL, re Islands along the Coast, Cape York Peninsular [sic] and in the vicinity of Thursday Island (225/38), 4 January 1938.' TR1817/1, Box 16, IL 598, QSA.

97 Vidgen had taken over Occupation Lease 46 from A. T. Sullivan in December 1938 and it was written off in December 1942. Occupation licences: Torres 11–86, QDPL, A/47743, QSA. The only other non-mining lease recorded on prewar Horn Island was Informal Lease 430 over an acre of land on the northern foreshore, granted to E. J. Hennessey in August 1919, cancelled in August 1937. *Register of Informal Leases* Nos. 294–574, QDPL, LAN/66, QSA.

98 Schug, D. M., 'The marine realm and a sense of place among Papua New Guinean communities of Torres Strait', p. 7.

99 These are the ways that the Mandok, a coastal New Guinea community, reckon kinship, according to Pomponio, cited by Schug, D. M., ibid., p. 87.

100 Yopelli Panuel, pers. comm., June 1982. Walter Nona, pers. comm., February 2001. John Scott, pers. comm., September 2002.

101 Vic McGrath, pers. comm., May 2003, adds that there is now a crayfish factory there owned by William Bowie, but Jack Ahmat has just taken over the lease.

102 Haddon, A. C. 1890. 'The ethnography of the western tribe of Torres Straits.' *Journal of the Royal Anthropological Institute*, Vol. 19, No. 3. pp. 297–440, at p. 407.

103 Lawrie, M. 1970. *Myths and legends of Torres Strait*. St Lucia: University of Queensland Press. p. 79: 'The people of Badu showed their gratitude to the people of Mabuiag for their help in avenging Pitai by giving them half of their island. From that day, all the land on Badu north of a line drawn from Kulkai on the east coast to Wam on the west coast belonged to Mabuiag.'

104 Laade, W. 1968. 'The Torres Strait Islanders own traditions on their origins.' *Ethnos*, No. 33. pp. 141–58, at pp. 148–9.

105 'A. W. Murray, Letter to Rev Dr Mullens, 9 December 1872.' London Missionary Society (hereafter LMS), *Papuan Letters 1872*, LMS Reel M91, State Library of Queensland (hereafter SLQ).

106 'Police Magistrate, Somerset, to The Port Master, Brisbane, 6 October 1872.' *Somerset Letterbooks* 66–72, ML.

107 Cadell sent out an advance party consisting of 'Mr James Price in Charge, with one Manilla Man, one South Sea Islander, one Chinaman as Gardener, nine Northern Territory Aboriginals' and their wives. 'Pro Sub-Collector of Customs, Thursday Island, to Colonial Secretary, 1 August 1878.' COL/A262/2974, QSA.

108 Letter from Samuel White to his wife headed, 'Somerset, September 25, 1878', quoted in White, S. A. 1920. *The life of Samuel White: soldier, naturalist, sailor*. Adelaide: W. K. Thomas. p. 30.

109 'A very extensive patch of shell has been lately found about 15 miles to leeward of Mulgrave Island which is likely to double the annual produce of the fishery. Boats which last year only averaged about 4 tons for the whole year are now getting 3 tons per month! It can only be worked, however, during fine weather.' 'Police Magistrate Chester to Colonial Secretary, 13 January 1882.' COL A/330/307, QSA.

110 'Police vs Doolah Mustapha, 12 October 1904'; 'Police vs Florence Ming Lee, 13 October 1904.' CPS13D/P12, QSA.

111 Beckett, J. R. 1987. *Torres Strait Islanders: custom and colonialism*. Cambridge University Press. p. 152.

112 Ibid.

113 'S. McFarlane, Report of the sixth voyage of the *Ellengowan*, 10 May 1875.' LMS *Papuan Letters 1875*, LMS Reel M91, SLQ.

114 'C. Pennefather, Report re duties performed since arrival of *Pearl* in Torres Straits, 31 October 1882.' Attached to COL/A348/5560, QSA.

115 'J. Chalmers, Report from Motumotu, 28 November 1891.' LMS *Papuan Letters 1891*, SLQ.

116 *Annual Report* of the Government Resident of Thursday Island for 1897.

117 *London Missionary Society Chronicle*, 1904, p. 16.

118 'Frederick William Walker, Managing Director of PIL, Badu, to Royal Pearl-shell and Bêche-de-mer Commission, 23 June 1908.' *Queensland Parliamentary Papers*, 1908. p. 206.

119 'Tanu Nona to Margaret Lawrie.' *Notebook II*, 1 December 1973, p. 12, MLC 1791–277, JOL.

120 'J. Chalmers, Report from Motumotu, 28 November 1891.' LMS *Papuan Letters 1891*, SLQ.

121 W. H. R. Rivers recorded three marriages between Malays and Mabuiag women: Mary Gonelai to Ahmat Singapore (Table 1), Aigiwak to Peter (Table 2), Buku to Ketchell (Table 2); and four with Badu women: Annie Savage to Jaffa Ahwang (Table 3A), Serai Mabua to Waahape Jia (Table 8), Baimad Gainab to Albert Bowie (Table 9), Maythaway Baut to Sedin Amber (Table 11). See Haddon, A. C. 1904. 'Reports of the Cambridge Expedition to Torres Strait.' *Sociology, magic and religion of the Western Islanders*, Vol. 5. Cambridge University Press.

122 Hassan Binawel from Ambon married Saia Ahwang from Badu. The couple may have visited Badu, but they made their home on Thursday Island, where all their children were born.

123 These are Jimmy Sander, born c.1889 on Burke Island, Torres Strait, to a Malay father and Torres Strait Islander or Aboriginal mother, husband of Luna Maikuik from Badu; and George Coconut, born c.1872 in the Malay Straits, died 1922 on Badu, husband of Maima from Dauan (Cornwallis Island). *Somerset Registers of Marriages and Deaths*.

124 'L. C. Weston to Under Secretary, Education Department, 12 April 1906.' A/15993, QSA.

125 Various official correspondence during the 1920s puts the approximate years as 1904–05. See, for example, 'Protector of Aboriginals, Thursday Island, to Chief Protector of Aboriginals, 24 June 1921', A/58761; 'Protector of Aboriginals, Thursday Island, on the status of Noalum Ah Wong, 1923', A/58761/23/5899; 'Protector of Aboriginals, Thursday Island, to Chief Protector of Aboriginals, 20 July 1925', A/58773, QSA.

126 Nauma Ketchell, pers. comm., June 1997.

127 These are respectively the 'Macassan' and 'Malay' referred to by Beckett, J. R., *Torres Strait Islanders*, p. 153. And Ganter, R. 1994. *The pearlshellers of Torres Strait*. Melbourne University Press. p. 65. Beckett implies that the two men were attracted to Badu by the opportunity for employment with PIL, but both had already settled there permanently — Bowie about 1887, Ketchell about 1902.

128 'Protector of Aboriginals, Thursday Island, to Chief Protector of Aboriginals, 25 January 1906.' A/58755, QSA. See also 'B. Butcher, Report from Daru, 7 December 1908.' LMS *Papuan Letters*, p. 2, SLQ.

129 'Protector of Aboriginals, Thursday Island, to Chief Protector of Aboriginals, 25 January 1906 and 29 March 1906.' A/58755, QSA. See also 'H. M. Dauncey, Report from Delena, 28 March 1906.' LMS *Papuan Letters*, p. 7, SLQ.

130 Yopelli Panuel, pers. comm., June 1982.

131 Ted Loban, pers. comm., October 1981: 'Thursday Island was the base for mixed married couples. For example, my parents couldn't live on Mabuiag, it was against the law. Mabuiag was a reserve for indentured labour and their families. There was also work on Thursday Island.'

132 Several years later, on 2 May, 1911, the Governor of Queensland paid a visit to Badu and praised the PIL's 'interesting experiment'. Walker, he wrote, 'has established a central station that is a model in every way'.

133 'Protector of Aboriginals, Thursday Island, to Chief Protector of Aboriginals, 25 January 1906.' A/58755, QSA.

134 Walker, F. W. *Industrial Missions: The Papuan Industries Limited: its progress and aims*. pp. 11–12. A/58755, QSA.

135 This was in addition to the two acres acquired as leasehold (SL 956) on 1 June, 1906, by the LMS for its mission station. The lease was surrendered in 1912 to the Australian Board of Missions on behalf of the Church of England, to which the LMS was about to cede responsibility for the evangelisation and spiritual care of the Torres Strait Islanders. *Register of Special Leases*, July 1902 January 1907, Nos. 740–903, QPDL, LAN/UJ, QSA.

136 Plans for the undertaking were revealed to the public in February 1904 and, in the pamphlet that
sets out the goals of the company, it is implied that Badu, although not named, had already been
selected as the Torres Strait headquarters. See 'A new departure in missionary enterprise: "Papuan
Industries, Ltd." Interview with Rev F. W. Walker, reprinted by permission from *Examiner* of
11 February, 1904.' This and the following material, which is found in A/58755, QSA, strongly
implies that the Queensland Government had given a commitment in principle to the enterprise
and its location.
The company was registered in November 1904 with the aim of encouraging local industry
through agriculture and trade and more than £21,000 of capital was raised in the next two
months. See Walker, F. W. 1908. *Industrial missions: The Papuan Industries Limited: its progress and
aims*. pp. 4–6. According to Walker, who had resigned from the LMS in 1903 to found the
company, 'The idea of our enterprise originated in a transaction ... some ten years ago when with
the hearty co-operation of the late Hon. John Douglas I secured a boat for the natives of Mabuiag,
from which most satisfactory results were obtained.' F. W. Walker, Managing Director, PIL, to
Chief Protector of Aboriginals, 2 February 1906.' This may be the source for Beckett's incorrect
assertion that PIL began its activities on Badu in the late 1890s. See Beckett, J. R., *Torres Strait
Islanders*, p. 152.
Towards the end of January 1906, the local Protector, with the support of his department,
approached PIL to consider financially assisting the purchase of boats for the people of Badu and
Darnley Islands. Walker accepted on behalf of the company, stating that 'if the Government will
find half the money required we shall be pleased to find the other half, all payments from the
natives in reduction of the liability for the boats to be equally divided between the Government
and the Company'. 'F. W. Walker, Managing Director, PIL, to Chief Protector of Aboriginals,
2 February 1906.' For various reasons, the venture ultimately proved financially unsuccessful. It was
bought by the Queensland Government in 1929 and, in 1930, was renamed Aboriginal Industries.

137 'S. McFarlane, Report of a missionary voyage in the *Ellengowan* amongst the islands in Torres
Straits made in October 1874, 26 October 1874.' LMS *Papuan Letters*, SLQ.

138 Hubert Hofer, pers. comm., April 1995.

139 For an account of the Pacific Islanders at Port Lihou, see Shnukal, A. 2001. 'The interwar Pacific
Islander community at Port Lihou, Torres Strait.' *Journal of the Royal Historical Society of
Queensland*, Vol. 17, No. 10. pp. 433–60.

140 *Thursday Island Courthouse Cash Record Books 1924–29, 1929–32, 1932–36, 1936–41*. Notes
were taken at Thursday Island Courthouse, July–August 1996, and the books sent to QSA.

141 'Bishop of Carpentaria to the Acting Land Agent, Thursday Island, 8 September 1947.' File
on Prince of Wales Island, Batch 895/21, QDPL.

142 Ibid.

143 Informal Lease Register Sheets 2201–2500, QDPL, A/50851, QSA.

144 Jianna Seden Richardson, pers. comm., July 1999.

145 Jianna Seden Richardson, pers. comm., March 2003.

146 Osborne, E., *Torres Strait Islander Women and the Pacific War*, p. 19.

147 Jianna Seden Richardson, pers. comm., July 1999.

148 Osborne, E., *Torres Strait Islander Women and the Pacific War*, p. 22.

149 Ibid., p. 19.

150 'E. McKeown, National Parks Ranger, Forests Office, Tully, to Forestry Sub-Department of QDPL,
re Islands along the Coast, Cape York Peninsular [sic] and in the vicinity of Thursday Island
(225/38), 4 January 1938.' TR1817/1, Box 16, IL 598, QSA.

Thursday Island boat slips, 1908.
Courtesy of John Oxley Library, Brisbane (Item No. 177595).

CHAPTER FIVE

Heriberto Zarcal

The first Filipino-Australian[1]

Reynaldo C. Ileto

Australia's proximity to the Philippines on the map has led me to wonder sometimes why there has to be such a void separating the two nations and peoples. Historically, of course, it is clear that the lines were drawn by Spain and Britain. The Philippines was defined by the claims of the Spanish Church and Crown; Australia was a collection of colonies attached to the British Crown. Filipinos looked to Manila and thence to Madrid as their centres; Queenslanders looked to Brisbane and thence to London. Policies such as Australia's Immigration Restriction Act of 1901 further deepened the void between the two.

Historically, however, it is also clear that individuals have a way of stumbling across lines and upsetting boundaries. In the second half of the 19th century, some Australians made Manila their home; they had drifted in as sailors, businessmen, tourists, prostitutes and entertainers (yes, White Australian prostitutes and entertainers). There weren't many of them; after all, in 1899, Manila and its suburbs had only 300 White foreigners other than Spanish in a population of 300,000. Far more Filipinos, hundreds of them in fact, went in the other direction to work as pearl divers and seamen in the northern parts of Australia.

The image of such movements of people across borders, bleaching those imperial reds and yellows or creating blotches of grey on the map, inspired me to title a book Rod Sullivan and I edited in 1993 *Discovering Austral-Asia: Essays on Philippine-Australian Interactions*. To my horror, however, I discovered on my return from sabbatical leave that my colleagues had removed that all-important hyphen, and so the book was published under the rather puzzling title *Discovering Australasia*. I have since seen it cited in even more garbled fashion as *Discovering Australia*. Why? Because, I think, of the sheer difficulty in imagining such an indeterminate entity, an Austral-hyphen-Asia, a crossing of two fictions.

One of the characters I uncovered in my research on Austral-Asia was Heriberto Zarcal, a resident of Queensland, a naturalised British citizen, yet also a significant figure in the Philippine revolution. Zarcal is mentioned fleetingly in Philippine history textbooks as the 1898 Revolutionary Government's 'diplomatic agent' in Australia.[2] At the turn of the century, many Australians would have come across the name 'H. Zarcal', but in a very different context. In the 1899 edition of *Pugh's Almanac*, which was a compendium of current information about Queensland, there was an advertisement for a Thursday Island business that said: 'H. Zarcal Jeweller and Pearl Merchant, Wholesale and Retail, Licensed Dealer and Provision Merchant.' The skills on offer included: 'Lapidary and Optician, Goldsmith, Watchmaker, and Pearl Cleaner.'

More impressive even than the range of skills and claims advertised was the accompanying photograph of Zarcal's premises, which, with its airy two storeys and its cast-iron-fringed upper verandah, was typical of a successful northern Australian hotel. But where the sign 'Royal Hotel' or 'Commonwealth Hotel' should have been, there was a Latin inscription, '*Noli Me Tangere*' ('Touch Me Not').[3] These are the words Christ used to Mary Magdalene after His resurrection, and they constitute the title of José Rizal's 1887 novel.[4] Apart from its renowned literary merits, *Noli Me Tangere* was also a political document that had a shattering effect on the Philippine society of its day because it vividly communicated the corruption of the Spanish colonial regime, and a sense of the Filipinos as a national community.[5] For this, Rizal was executed on 30 December, 1896. Few, if any, Australian readers of *Pugh's Almanac* would have realised this, but *Noli Me Tangere*, displayed in large script on his business premises, signified Zarcal's empathy with the martyred Rizal and all that he stood for.

What was Zarcal doing up there on the northern tip of Australia? Writing in 1902, John Douglas, Government Resident on Thursday Island, anticipated present-day concerns when he observed that 'this question of Asia and Australia is one of the great questions of the present and of the future for Australia'. From his experience in the Torres Strait, Douglas knew that northern Australia was not and could never be an exclusively European domain; it was set on a different course demographically from southern Australia. Douglas advocated a 'White Australia' but defined it in *institutional* rather than racial terms. He maintained that Thursday Island, where Europeans constituted but one in three of the population, was nonetheless still 'White Australia' because

> we have the same all-pervading British law, applicable to Asian and Australian alike, the same English language, and the same forms of social intercourse which prevail in Southern Australia; our churches and schools are an exact counterpart on a small scale of what they are in Melbourne or in Brisbane.[6]

Heriberto Zarcal would not have disputed Douglas's views. What Filipinos moving up the socioeconomic scale found particularly odious about Spanish rule was that, at some point, race *did* matter and worked to block their progress. Spanish institutions in the friar-dominated colony were not what they were in liberalised Spain. Spanish law was not applicable to Indio and Spaniard alike. But Filipinos who moved or escaped to the British Crown colonies of Hong Kong and Singapore found the sociopolitical environments there quite liberating, with good prospects as well for economic gain. Quite likely, Thursday Island in the 19th century offered similar attractions.

Then, as now, skilled Filipino seamen and workers could be found wherever they were needed and welcomed. For the majority of them, going to sea and working overseas offered an opportunity to accumulate some savings, which would be remitted to, or invested in, the Philippines. For example, a Filipino crew-member of the Confederate raider, *Alabama*, which visited Cape Town, South Africa, in 1863, decided to settle there and was so successful that other Filipino seamen joined him to form a colony. Filipinos were usually the steersmen or quartermasters on American ships in the Pacific and had early colonies in New Orleans, Philadelphia and Boston.[7] It is not surprising then, that soon after pearl-shelling began in Torres Strait in 1870, Filipinos were working there as 'swimming divers' and, later, as dress divers.[8] They were recruited in Singapore and brought to northern Australia by the steamers that plied the Singapore-Brisbane route.[9] Over the years their numbers grew steadily. By 1896, there were 212 Filipinos employed fishing for pearls and bêche-de-mer.[10] In March of that year, there were 119 Filipinos, including six women and 58 children, resident on Thursday Island, now the pearling centre of Torres Strait.[11]

Percival Outridge, who had worked in the northern pearling industry for some 10 years, told the 1897 Queensland Commission of Inquiry into the pearl-shell and bêche-de-mer industries that the '[M]anilla men … make excellent divers and excellent citizens. They marry and settle down here.'[12] Douglas observed that the Filipinos on Thursday Island were generally married and had families, and were regarded as 'amongst the most settled of our Asiatic population'. In fact, these married and settled 'Manila men' showed great eagerness to become naturalised citizens.[13] Such willingness and ability to integrate into the local community was a feature that distinguished Filipinos from other Asian settlers, especially the Japanese. Being for the most part Catholics helped. In 1895, Douglas described how some of the naturalised Filipinos had 'married wives selected for them by the Roman Catholic Fraternity, from their own country'.[14] Commonality of religion would have eliminated one hindrance to relations with White Australians.

It should be noted that for Filipinos in the late 19th century, taking out British-Australian citizenship meant merely transferring affiliation from one European empire to another. The Philippines was not yet a nation-state that demanded the unswerving loyalties of its citizens. The term 'Filipino', in fact, still technically applied to Spaniards in the Philippines; the people from whose ranks came the 'Manila men' were still demanding recognition as 'Filipinos' in their own homeland. It is not, therefore, surprising that there was a great demand for naturalisation among the settled Filipinos in northern Australia.

Lest we forget, however, there were just as many who returned to their homeland, much as overseas contract workers do today. Two Filipinos working in Australia were lucky enough to win a lottery and went straight back home with their prize. Candido Iban and Francisco del Castillo, however, did something unusual, which earned them an honoured place in Philippine history. On returning to Manila in 1894 or 1895, they joined the radical Katipunan secret society[15] and donated 400 pesos of their 1,000-pesos Australian lottery prize for the purchase of a printing press. This was used to put out the Katipunan's journal, *Kalayaan* (*Liberty*), the first issue of which appeared in March 1896. They then returned to their home island of Capiz 'to spread the doctrines of the Katipunan'.[16] In March 1897, Candido Iban and his brother Benito were executed by the Spanish authorities and are remembered as two of the 'Nineteen Martyrs of Capiz'.[17]

Zarcal arrived on Thursday Island in May 1892.[18] Where he came from is a bit of a mystery, but there are suggestions that he had escaped from exile in the Marianas, one of many who eventually found his way to Hong Kong, Singapore and (or so it seems) Thursday Island. By 1897, Zarcal surfaces as a big man on the island. He is mentioned as one of only five men on the island licensed to deal in pearls.[19] Moreover, he had just acquired his own fleet of pearling vessels.[20] And, about this time, he was also establishing himself in the capital cities of Brisbane and Melbourne.[21] He was assisted by a nephew and adopted son, Manuel Anastacio, who served as treasurer of the pearling business and apparently did some schooling in Melbourne.[22] By January 1898, Zarcal would be expanding his pearling operations to the Northern Territory.[23]

In May 1897, Zarcal became a naturalised British subject, taking the Oath of Allegiance before the Supreme Court of Queensland in Brisbane.[24] From the heated discussions that took place in the pages of the local newspaper during the months after Zarcal's naturalisation, we get some idea of the scale of his success in business after five years of residence on Thursday Island, and why becoming a British subject was a natural recourse for him.

A European Thursday Islander, calling himself 'Torres Straits for the Whites', wrote complaining about Zarcal as 'a naturalised Manilla man ... reported to be importing several luggers and a schooner to work on the pearling grounds'. The success of Zarcal and other Asians was deemed 'to exceed reasonable limits'. The angry writer summed up his frustration with the question, 'Shall we suffer the men who ought to be our servants to become our masters?'[25]

The abovementioned letter attracted a response from James Clark, one of the most successful European pearl-shellers in northern Australia and a leading campaigner against the acquisition of pearling licences by Japanese.[26] Clark had earlier protested to the 1897 Queensland Commission of Inquiry that, Queensland being a British colony, 'the profits should belong to the white men instead of the Japanese'. Clearly, he was in favour of Japanese labour in the pearl-shelling industry, but he objected to them becoming boat-owners and therefore competitors: 'By all means, pay them a fair wage for their labour, but let them remain labourers and not owners.'[27] In responding to 'Torres Straits for the Whites', Clark widened his anti-Japanese campaign to include Zarcal. He was particularly incensed by Zarcal's newly won citizenship, which enabled him to operate a pearling fleet regardless of prohibitions on aliens. Clark appeared to regard 'whiteness' as a prerequisite of citizenship, and the naturalisation process as an unwelcome source of Asian competitors:

> Naturalisation is a farce, and all naturalisation papers of Asiatics should be cancelled. Take Mr Zarcal's case for example. He gets naturalised here, but will anyone take him for an Englishman in Manilla, where anyway his Australian naturalisation does not give him the protection of a Britisher? Therefore he is a Manillaman in Manilla and an Australian here. If Mr Zarcal wishes to carry on his business of pearl buyer and sheller let him go back to his own country; he can get both pearls and shell there; we want ours for our own people.[28]

Clark's attack did not pass unchallenged. Robert Cremer, who spoke for European labour on Thursday Island, accused him of hypocrisy since he happily employed Asian labour while campaigning to exclude Asians from boat-ownership.[29] Clark's credibility suffered further when it emerged that he had sponsored Zarcal in his application for citizenship. Moreover, Zarcal had rebuffed an overture from Clark to join 'a combination of pearl buyers' in the interests of price maintenance.[30]

Zarcal survived the racist diatribe. By 1897, he was too well established to be displaced from a major role in the Torres Strait pearl-shelling industry. Besides, he had roots in the community. He was married to a woman born in Queensland of Irish descent, Esther Emma Beach, and had close ties with the Catholic missionaries on the island.[31] In any case, he had the foresight to adopt British citizenship before restrictive legislation against non-Whites in the pearl-shelling industry set in.

Adopting British citizenship was a wise move in more ways than one. Clearly, it provided protection against the spectre of a 'White Australia'. But, also, it would have facilitated Zarcal's travel to and from business dealings in British Hong Kong, and provided some personal security for a task he had embarked on by 1897: to materially support the Philippine revolutionary forces. While Zarcal was in Hong Kong that year to look after the construction of his pearling vessels, he was in close contact with the Central Junta of the Philippine Revolutionary Government based there. About October, under instructions from Hong Kong, he organised an Australian committee in support of the nationalist cause.[32]

Overseas Nationalists

Zarcal's involvement in the revolution should be viewed in the context of a Filipino diaspora after 1872. The execution, in February of that year, of three Filipino priests for alleged complicity in a mutiny of native troops was accompanied by deportations of Filipinos suspected of involvement in the affair. In the years after, more Filipinos were deported for student activities, while many others left the repressive atmosphere of Manila to seek higher education in Europe. These Filipinos eventually grouped together to organise reform movements based in Hong Kong, Singapore, London, Paris, Barcelona, Madrid and other cities.

Manila itself became the centre of a movement calling itself La Propaganda. On 1 March, 1888, Manila witnessed a massive demonstration of reformists, who marched through the streets to the residence of the civil Governor of Manila Province, Jose Centeno, a Spaniard of liberal and anti-friar sentiments. Centeno was handed a petition addressed to the Governor-General, titled 'Long Live Spain! Long Live the Queen! Long Live the Army! Away with the Friars!' It demanded the expulsion of all friars and the secularisation of all parishes. In the wake of the demonstration, many prominent Filipinos in

Manila and its suburbs were arrested and jailed. Among them was Doroteo Jose, the *gobernadorcillo* ('petty governor', mayor) of Santa Cruz, Zarcal's home district. Although the detainees were released owing to lack of evidence, they suffered persistent harassment afterwards. Many fled the country.[33]

Hong Kong Haven

For most of those who left the Philippines, British Hong Kong was the favoured destination. Since the 1870s, Hong Kong had been a haven for exiles. Some of them had escaped from exile in the Spanish Marianas and Guam. Persecutions in the 1890s of freemasons and suspected members of the reformist movement, La Liga Filipina, further swelled the ranks of

Advertisements for Chinese, European, Filipino, Indian and Sri Lankan merchants, Thursday Island, 1897.
Queensland Post Office Directory 1896–97, p. 483.

the Filipino expatriate community in Hong Kong. This made inevitable its crucial supporting role in the 1896 revolution and thereafter. In December 1896, the Hong Kong Filipinos organised a revolutionary committee in support of the cause. It became the conduit for the Revolutionary Government's communications with the rest of the world. Its political climate was, furthermore, congenial. According to Galicano Apacible, who chaired the Hong Kong committee and junta from 1899 to 1903, political refugees from many countries residing in the colony were protected by the same English laws and 'English spirit of equity'. We can appreciate the value of Zarcal's British passport in the light of Apacible's glowing observations:

In our conflicts with some agents of the American secret service the British Government helped and protected us promptly, its official declaring that so long as we complied with the laws of the colony and did not violate the avowed neutrality of England in that conflict (ie., the Spanish-American War), we could rest assured that we would receive protection of the British Government.[34]

The Revolutionary Committee was able to send to the revolutionists food, clothing and medicine donated by Filipino residents in the colony. What the revolutionists needed, above all, however, were war materials. Hong Kong was the place to contact other foreign agents and close deals for the purchase of guns and ammunition. In late 1897, the Central Junta, successor to the Revolutionary Committee, was successful in smuggling arms into the Philippines with the help of the American consul.[35]

Australian Support Committee

Hong Kong was the nerve centre for a worldwide network of support committees which, by late 1897, included one in Australia. In October 1897, Mariano Ponce, a veteran Hong Kong exile who would become Aguinaldo's emissary to Japan, wrote to a group of Filipinos in Australia reminding them that 'the same causes' had led them to emigrate all over the world. Physical distance, however, was 'not enough to separate our hearts, united by common sympathies'. Now was the time 'to collect all our energies, to convert them into one common force'. Alluding to the victories of the Spanish forces and General Aguinaldo's consequent retreat to the hills of Biak-na-bato, Ponce emphasised that 'the setbacks of the fatherland oblige all Filipinos with dignity to become part of this movement'. Ponce sought to mobilise the sizeable Filipino community in Australia, and to link it with others into 'one common force'. Thus he announced that a branch committee of the Hong Kong Central Junta was being organised in Australia under the leadership of Zarcal.[36]

Meanwhile, events were moving quickly in the Philippines. In early December 1897, formal hostilities between Spanish and Filipino forces ended with the signing of the 'Pact of Biak-na-bato'. Aguinaldo and other top military commanders then went into exile in Hong Kong, taking with them some $US200,000 given to them by Spain. This they intended to spend on guns and preparations for a resumption of the struggle. Zarcal, a frequent visitor to Hong Kong, was among the many expatriate nationalists who consulted with Aguinaldo. An issue of the *Overland China Mail*, which appeared in late March 1898, reported that Zarcal had commissioned the construction of three pearling schooners and named them the *Aguinaldo*, the *Llanera* and the *Natividad* — in honour of three Filipino generals who had won victories against Spanish forces.[37] This must have been a well-publicised event because the Spanish Governor-General in the Philippines, Fernando Primo de Rivera, took offence at the names of Zarcal's boats and protested to Aguinaldo that they be changed to honour pioneers of Spanish settlement in the Philippines: Magellan, Legaspi and Salcedo.[38] Zarcal, it seems, did not heed the protest. In fact, his other boats bore names that alluded to Philippine history, nationalism, the revolution and Zarcal's own past; names such as *Santa Cruz* (Zarcal's birthplace), *Kavite* (the heartland of the revolution), *Sikatuna* and *Lacandola* (pre-Spanish chiefs), *Magdalo* (Aguinaldo's Katipunan name), *Kalayaan* (Liberty), *Kapayapaan* (Peace), *Justicia* (Justice), *Esperanza* (Hope), *Filipino* and *Esther* (Mrs Zarcal).[39]

Zarcal's new boats may have been intended for more than just pearling and propaganda service. After the US Navy's destruction of the Spanish fleet in Manila Bay in May 1898, Aguinaldo quickly returned to the Philippines to liberate the provinces from Spanish rule. On 12 June, he was able to proclaim Philippine independence and, on 23 June, to establish a Revolutionary Government. Despite a vague alliance with the US, however, the revolutionists still lacked the physical resources with which to completely overcome Spanish resistance. Urgent requests for help were sent to Filipinos overseas.

On 7 July, Aguinaldo wrote to two Filipinos of substance whom he personally knew — Pedro Roxas in Paris and Zarcal, somewhere in Australia — asking for 'some modern cannon and rifles with their corresponding ammunition, in quantities which your resources will allow'.[40] He assured them that this assistance would constitute a legal debt, which the Government would repay through an internal loan that was being floated, with occupied friar lands as guarantee. What is intriguing about Aguinaldo's request is that Zarcal or Roxas were to mount an expedition to land the supplies on the coast of Batangas.[41] Was Zarcal expected to use his new boats for this? A month later, a rather disappointed Aguinaldo instructed his chief envoy, Felipe Agoncillo, to tell Roxas and Zarcal 'that if they can't help with weapons I asked in my initial letter to them, they could at least send ammunition for Mauser and Remington rifles, if they have a heart (*kun sila'y may loób*)'.[42] No evidence has been unearthed thus far indicating that Zarcal even tried to smuggle arms or ammunition to the Philippines. In any case, by early 1899, such shipments would have become 'almost impossible, on account of the strict vigilance of American agents at Hong Kong and Chinese and Philippine ports'.[43]

Aguinaldo's letter of 9 July also contained an invitation for Roxas and Zarcal to act as representatives or 'correspondents' of the Revolutionary Government in their respective countries. The two must have acquiesced, for, on 10 August, Aguinaldo established the Revolutionary Committee, which included representatives in France, England, the US, Japan and Australia (Heriberto Zarcal). This was an elite group of men of education and means.[44] Their task was to 'take care of Propaganda activities outside the country', to engage in 'diplomatic negotiations with foreign governments', and to 'prepare and contract all kinds of necessary expeditions for the maintenance of the Revolution'.[45]

What transpired in the months and years after the establishment of the fledgling Filipino Government is a tragic story of Asian nationalist aspirations floundering in a hostile, imperialist world order. Foreign recognition was nowhere to be gained; the highly educated and articulate Agoncillo, for example, was consistently rebuffed in Washington. On 10 December, 1898, Spanish and American commissioners signed the Treaty of Paris, handing the Philippines over to the US — ignoring the Filipinos both as belligerent (they bore the brunt of the fighting) and as an ally of the US against Spain.[46] As soon as the treaty was ratified two months later, hostilities between Filipino and American troops broke out. The Philippine-American war was to last until May 1902.

Bearing in mind the difficulties faced by his compatriots elsewhere, how did Zarcal fare in Australia? In October 1898, the nationalist legislator, Maximo Paterno, sent him a bundle of newspapers and other documents presumably to assist him in propagating the cause.[47] But the phrase *Noli Me Tangere* displayed on his business establishment, and the revolutionary connotations of his ships' names, are the only visible evidence of his efforts.[48] Such symbolic acts may not even have been taken seriously. The *Torres Straits Pilot* scoffed at the implications of the naming of his boats, observing that 'doubtless Mr Zarcal will be amused at the naive insinuation that he is in active sympathy with the insurgents'.[49] Zarcal would have had to be extremely discreet in championing the Filipino side in the war with the US. The predominant sentiment in Australia was that a Philippines run by brown natives would either be chaotic or, if successful, threatening to a sparsely populated Australia; in either case, Philippine independence would bring instability to a region dominated by European powers.[50] There was thus no hesitation in Australian acquiescence to a US takeover of the islands. The one piece of evidence concerning Australian involvement in the Filipino side of the conflict has to do with an Australian trying to sell arms and ammunition to the revolutionists in 1899.[51]

While surely he must have contributed generously to the revolutionary coffers, Zarcal appears to have thoroughly failed to gather Australian support for, or at least recognition of, Philippine independence. But, after all, did not Ponce emphasise in his letter to Australia back in 1897 that there was a need to propagate the cause, 'but we are not obliged to do more than what is in our power to accomplish'?[52] We might point out that there is no evidence either that Zarcal campaigned *against* the cause. Owing to concerns about their personal fortunes, and the attractions of the American system (compared with Spain's), nearly half of the members of the Filipino Central Committee — successor to the Hong Kong Junta — had, by the end of 1898, turned around to support US annexation. The veteran, José Maria Basa, was among them. Pedro Roxas, while still contributing financially to the Revolutionary Government, told the Americans in Washington that Filipinos did not deserve independence, but could manage with an autonomy *like that of Australia*.[53] These sentiments did not come from Zarcal. Significantly, as late as May 1900, Aguinaldo — then leading a desperate guerrilla resistance — would be assured that Australia was one place where there continued to be a correspondent.[54]

The more we think about it, *Noli Me Tangere* — 'Touch Me Not' — so boldly displayed at the very heart of Zarcal's business operations, could not have pointed solely to the Philippines. In Rizal's novel, it clearly meant 'we want Liberty, Fraternity, and Equality'. Filipinos had 'awakened' and were asserting themselves against a Spanish regime dominated by conservative and even racist friar elements. But, to Zarcal, the struggle for recognition as equals was one to be waged in Australia as well. 'Oriental nations are awakening, their peoples are swarming out from their shores like ants whose nests have been trampled upon', declared Senator Staniforth Smith during the debates on the Immigration Restriction Bill.[55] Such awakening could mean only danger for a White Australia. The stakes were high, as Charles Pearson, an Oxford historian and former education minister of Victoria, put it as far back as 1894:

> We know that coloured and white labour cannot exist side by side … and we know that if national existence is sacrificed to the working of a few mines and sugar plantations, it is not the Englishman in Australia alone, but the whole civilised world, that will be the losers … We are guarding the last part of the world, in which the higher races can live and increase freely, for the higher civilisation. We are denying the yellow race nothing but what it can find in the home of its birth, or in countries like the Indian Archipelago, where the white man can never live except as an exotic.[56]

Pearson would have had some detractors in northern Australia where, as pointed out earlier, multiracialism was a stark reality. Nonetheless, as the *Brisbane Courier* pointed out in August 1901, 'The people of Queensland have been as strongly in favour of the exclusion of alien races as the people in the Southern States'. And the danger to a 'White Australia' came not from transient labourers such as the Kanakas, but 'from Asiatic races, which have *permanently settled* in the large cities of the South as well as in the country districts throughout Australia'.[57]

Up on distant and tiny Thursday Island, backed by Queensland citizenship, Zarcal was fairly secure from such acrimony. But, by 1902, protectionist measures were being taken to bar non-White aliens from owning pearling vessels and to prevent the issue of new licences to non-White divers.[58] Such moves were aimed primarily at the Japanese, who had come to dominate the industry; however, Zarcal's expansion to other areas would still have been hindered. In January 1898, he temporarily expanded his operations to the Northern Territory, securing licences from the Government Resident in Port Darwin over the protests of European boat-owners, who alleged that his Queensland naturalisation had no validity in South Australia — that he was, in effect, a British subject in Queensland but an alien in the Northern Territory. Perhaps these protests did have an effect, for, by January 1899, Zarcal's fleet had departed from Northern Territory waters.[59]

A major turning point in Zarcal's fortunes came on 30 April, 1905, when a massive fire destroyed 14 buildings on Thursday Island's main commercial block. Zarcal's 'fine two-storeyed' building, still sporting the inscription *Noli Me Tangere*, was the main casualty.[60]

Forced to sell his fleet to recover from the disaster, Zarcal was left with only a handful of boats for pearl-shelling.[61] In semi-retirement, he concentrated on his Thursday Island business as pearl-buyer and jeweller, augmenting his local stock of pearls with purchases from Port Darwin and the Dutch East Indies.[62] Characteristically, perhaps, the final episode in his life was an extended journey to Europe begun in 1914. Mr and Mrs Zarcal are said to have paid homage to their monarch, the Queen of England, giving her a huge pearl. Prevented from returning home by the outbreak of the Great War, the Zarcals waited it out in Europe, finally renting a flat in Paris in early 1916. There, on 9 February, 1917, Zarcal succumbed to a stomach ulcer. At his deathbed were his wife Esther and 'an old friend from Thursday Island', the Rev. Father Ferdinand Hartzer.[63]

With Heriberto Zarcal died an era of Philippine-Australian or Austral-Asian interactions. Owing to the 1901 Immigration Restriction Act, no longer would Filipinos, for a couple of decades at least, be able to filter into Australia's frontier regions in order to work or settle there. It was the relative openness of late 19th-century Australia that had enabled Zarcal to bring the world of Rizal, Aguinaldo and the Philippine revolution of 1898 right to her doorstep. But it was a move ahead of its time, which entertained no hope of success; fear of 'Asian assertion' was already in place at that time. Quite appropriately, by the end of 1905, all visible reminders of this episode had disappeared from Thursday Island. Zarcal himself died and was buried in France, the country whose history had inspired the Filipino revolutionists.

Acknowledgements

I owe a debt to Dr Isagani Medina of the Department of History, University of the Philippines, for locating the family of Heriberto Zarcal and to the Zarcal family for their generosity in sharing old photographs and correspondence relating to Heriberto and his nephew and adopted son, Manuel Anastacio. My thanks also to Rod Sullivan, my friend, colleague and co-editor.

Footnotes

1   This chapter is based largely on my 'Philippine-Australian interactions: the late nineteenth century.' In Ileto, R. C. and R. Sullivan (eds), 1993, *Discovering Australasia: essays on Philippine-Australian interactions*, Townsville: James Cook University, Department of History and Politics. pp. 10–46.

2   See Zaide, G. F. 1979. *The Pageant of Philippine History*, Vol. 2. Manila: Philippine Education Co. p. 308. Agoncillo, T. A. 1969. *Malolos: the crisis of the republic*. Quezon City. p. 312.

3   Pugh, T. P. 1899. *Pugh's Almanac*. Brisbane: T. P. Pugh. p. 108.

4   Rizal, J., translated by L. Guerrero. 1961. *Noli Me Tangere*. London: Longman.

5   Anderson, B. 1983. *Imagined Communities, Reflections on the Origin and Spread of Nationalism*. London: Verso. p. 32.

6   Douglas, J. 1902. 'Asia and Australasia.' *The Nineteenth Century and After*, Vol. 52, July–December. pp. 43–54, at p. 51.

7   Netzorg, M. annotations to R. MacMicking. 1967. *Recollections of Manilla and the Philippines*. Manila: Filipiniana Book Guild. pp. 31–2, note 4.

8   'Report by his Honour Judge Dashwood, Government Resident, Palmerston, on the Pearl-Shelling Industry (Dashwood Report).' *Commonwealth Parliamentary Papers*, Vol. 2, 1901–02. p. 9. Bach, J. P. S. 1962. 'The pearlshelling industry and the "White Australia Policy".' *Historical Studies Australia and New Zealand*, Vol. 10, No. 38. pp. 203–13, at pp. 203–4. The diving dress with mechanised air pump allowed them to work further from shore in deeper water.

9   Douglas, J., 'Asia and Australasia', pp. 47–8.

10 'Report of the Commission appointed to Inquire into the General Working of the Laws Regulating the Pearl-Shell and Bêche-de-Mer Fisheries in the Colony (Hamilton Report).' *Queensland Votes and Proceedings* (hereafter *QVP*), Vol. 2, 1897, p. xxx.

11 Ibid., p. 35.

12 Ibid., p. 19.

13 Ibid., p. 2.

14 Douglas, J. 'Asiatic aliens in Torres Straits.' 13 July, 1895, PRE/102/8767, Queensland State Archives (hereafter QSA).

15 The Katipunan secret society, which in 1896 led the first phase of the revolution against Spain, was founded by Andres Bonifacio.

16 Agoncillo, T. A. and M. C. Guerrero. 1973, 4th Ed. *History of the Filipino People*. Quezon City: R. P. Garcia. p. 183.

17 Manuel, E. A. 1955. *Dictionary of Philippine Biography*, Vol. 1. Quezon City: Filipinana Publications. p. 229.

18 Pugh, T. P., *Pugh's Almanac*, p. 154.

19 *Torres Straits Pilot*, 19 June, 1897.

20 Ibid., 25 September, 1897.

21 Ibid., 16 April, 1898. The *Pilot* was citing a write-up in a late-March 1898 issue of the Hong Kong journal, *Overland China Mail*.

22 Zarcal family interview, Manila, 18 December, 1990. The family's claim that Manuel was educated in Melbourne is plausible since his uncle owned an establishment in that city. Manuel eventually returned to Manila to become a highly successful lawyer.

23 *Northern Territory Times and Gazette*, 27 January, 1899.

24 SCJ/CF27, QSA.

25 *Torres Straits Pilot*, 18 September, 1897.

26 See Mercer, P. 1981. 'Clark, James (1857–1993).' *Australian Dictionary of Biography*, Vol. 8, 1891–1939. Melbourne University Press. pp. 9–10.

27 'Hamilton Report', *QVP*, p. 32.

28 *Torres Straits Pilot*, 25 September, 1897.

29 Ibid., 9 October, 1897.

30 Ibid., 30 October, 1897.

31 He was very close to the missionary, Rev. Father Ferdinand Hartzer. 'Esther E. Zarcal to Manuel Zarcal, Thursday Island, 9 January 1920.' Zarcal Family Papers.

32 'Mariano Ponce to D. M. Español, D. M. Reyes and D. F. Consuji [in Spanish], Hong Kong, 22 October 1897.' In M. Ponce, 1936, *Cartas Sobre la Revolución*, Manila. pp. 57–8.

33 See Zaide, G. F. 1973. *Manila During the Revolutionary Period*. Manila: National Historical Commission. pp. 33–42.

34 Alzona, E. 1971. *Galicano Apacible: profile of a Filipino patriot*. Manila. pp. 62–3.

35 Ibid. See also de Ocampo, E. A. 1970. *First Filipino Diplomat*. Manila: National Historical Institute. pp. 71–2.

36 'Ponce to D. M. Español, etc.'

37 Mariano Llanera accompanied Aguinaldo to his Hong Kong exile. Mamerto Natividad was killed in action in November 1897. It is tempting to speculate that some of the funds paid by the Spanish Government to Aguinaldo and his fellow exiles may have been used to finance the boat-building.

38 Magallanes was Ferdinand Magellan, a Portuguese who sailed for the Spanish Court and, in 1521, 'discovered' the Philippines for Spain. Miguel Lopez de Legaspi led an expedition to the Philippines in 1564–65 and proclaimed Spanish sovereignty there. Juan de Salcedo, Legaspi's grandson, played a leading part in the Spanish conquest of Luzon, 1571–72. The report in the *Overland China Mail* was reprinted in the *Torres Straits Pilot*, 16 April, 1898.

39 *Torres Straits Pilot*, 29 July and 30 September, 1905.

40 Aguinaldo, E. 'Letter sent to Sres Zarcal and Roxas [in Spanish], Bakood, 9 July 1898.' *Philippine Insurgent Records* (hereafter *PIR*), Box FA-2 'Correspondencia', pp. 6–7, Philippine National Library (hereafter PNL).

41 Ibid.

42 'E. Aguinaldo to F. Agoncillo [in Tagalog], Bakood, 7 August 1898.' In *PIR* FA-2 Tagalog, PNL. The Mausers and Remingtons had been captured from Spanish Guardia Civil and Infantry units.

43 Alzona, E., *Galicano Apacible*, p. 66.

44 Between 1910 and 1916, Faustino Lichauco, dubbed the 'Cattle King of Manila', did business in live cattle with the Western Australian pastoral firm of Conner, Doherty and Durack. See Durack, M. 1983. *Sons in the Saddle*. London: Constable.

45 Aguinaldo, E. 'Establishment of "El Comite Revolucionario" [in Spanish], Bakood, 10 August 1898.' *PIR* FA-2 'Correspondencia', pp. 20–2, PNL. See also Taylor, J. R. M. 1971. *The Philippine Insurrection Against the United States*, Vol. 3. Pasay City: Eugenio Lopez Foundation. p. 197.

46 See De Ocampo, E. A., *First Filipino Diplomat*, p. 92.

47 Invoice No. 14 in *Marina* 1898-99, B-105, Philippine National Archives (hereafter PNA).

48 A metropolitan newspaper apparently contained an advertisement in support of the Philippine Revolutionary Government, but this has not been confirmed.

49 *Torres Straits Pilot*, 16 April, 1898.

50 These views were culled from reports in the Sydney *Bulletin* and the *Brisbane Courier*. Unfortunately, the detailed citations have been lost. For an overview of the Australian reaction to the conflict see Perdon, R. 1998. *Brown Americans of Asia*. Sydney: Manila Prints. pp. 91–103.

51 Turnbull, W. 1974. 'Reminiscences of an army surgeon in Cuba and the Philippines.' *Bulletin of the American Historical Association*, No. 2, April. p. 42.

52 Ibid.

53 De Ocampo, E. A., *First Filipino Diplomat*, p. 96. My italics.

54 'I. de Santos to E. Aguinaldo, Hong Kong, 1 May 1900', PIR SD516.6, PNL.

55 *Commonwealth of Australia Parliamentary Debates*, Session 1901–02, Vol. 6, p. 7245.

56 Pearson, C. 1894. *National Life and Character: a forecast*. London: Macmillan. p. 17.

57 *Brisbane Courier*, 13 August, 1901. My italics.

58 *Dashwood Report*, Appendixes C and D, p. 1004.

59 *Northern Territory Times and Gazette*, 27 January, 1899. Two Thursday Island luggers, which continued to fish off Port Darwin, the *Daisy* and the *Electra*, were alleged to be 'notoriously owned by a Japanese syndicate' although permitted to work on the basis that they were Zarcal's property. Ibid.

60 'Thursday Island's record fire.' *Queenslander*, 20 May, 1905. I am grateful to my colleague Elizabeth Holt for her transcription of this account.

61 *Torres Straits Pilot*, 29 July and 30 September, 1905. There was another reason why the sale would have made sense. By 1905, the yield of pearl shell in the Torres Strait was down to 527 tonnes, well less than half the peak 1897 figure of 1,223 tonnes. 'Report of the Royal Commission appointed to enquire into the working of the Pearl-shell and Bêche-de-Mer Industries (Mackay Report).' *QVP*, Vol. 2, 1908, p. xlix.

62 'Mackay Report', p. 154. Moreover, at his death, he still owned 'boats for obtaining mother of pearl, black conch, tortoise shell and black pez[?]'. Memorandum attached to Heriberto Zarcal's will, Zarcal Family Papers.

63 'Manuel Zarcal to Esther E. Zarcal, Manila, 3 November 1915'; 'Esther E. Zarcal to Manuel Zarcal, Thursday Island, 9 January 1920'; both in Zarcal Family Papers. The information about the gift of a huge pearl to the Queen is from the Zarcal family interview. Esther Zarcal did not remarry. She eventually moved to Sydney, where she died in 1951.

Japanese divers in diving suits, 1928.
Courtesy of John Oxley Library, Brisbane (Item No. 177901).

CHAPTER SIX

The Japanese in Torres Strait[1]

Yuriko Nagata

Introduction

The establishment of the Japanese presence in Torres Strait from the late 19th century until the Pacific War was, in many ways, parallel to other Japanese settlements formed in other parts of the Asia-Pacific region (more popularly referred to in Japan as *Nan'yô* before the Pacific War). These Japanese settlements were formed by labourers who were predominantly single men, or men who had left their families behind and who sought better economic opportunities outside Japan to help their families. Some small merchants were accompanied by their families, but mostly they were contract labourers in various primary industries — agriculture, fishing and mining. In 1935, 88,176 Japanese emigrants were living and working in various parts of *Nan'yô*, including Australia.[2]

Some young Japanese women were among early arrivals in many parts of *Nan'yô*. They were smuggled out of Japan by traffickers and sold to brothels to work as prostitutes to support their families. They were called *Karayuki-san*[3] and were mostly from poor farming and fishing villages in the south-west of the main island of Honshû and the south island of Kyûshû. According to Yano, *Karayuki-san* and peddlers often paved the way for later Japanese commercial activities and Japanese settlements in the region.[4] Before the outbreak of the Pacific War, Japanese communities became well established, with Japanese clubs as central bodies to serve the close-knit societies, including the Japanese community in Torres Strait.

This chapter draws on existing scholarship[5] to provide an overview of the establishment and decline of the Japanese community in Torres Strait from the 1880s to the 1990s. It also seeks to integrate lives of women as wives, mothers and workers into the existing historiography of the Japanese in Torres Strait. As Bottomley argues, 'Women tend to disappear in discussion about migration, as immigrants often disappear in discussions about class and about women.'[6] In the early days, Japanese prostitutes, in particular, played a substantial role in the Japanese society on Thursday Island. Due to their small numbers and the illicit nature of their presence, they have been relegated to the periphery of the historiography of Japanese migration to Australia. This chapter will shed light on the significant role that Japanese women played in Thursday Island society, economically and socially.

Early Arrivals

Before J. A. Miller of the Australian Pearl Co. brought 37 Japanese males to Thursday Island as the first contracted labour immigrants from Japan in 1883, 95 Japanese were already among other Asians working in the then developing pearl-shell and sea-cucumber industries — 36 on Prince of Wales Island, 38 on Friday Island, 17 on Weiweer Island, three on Hammond Island and one on Goode Island.[7] The earliest Japanese arrivals in the region recorded in Hattori's report in 1894 are Kojiro Nonami of Shimane (known as Japanese Nona) in 1878, Tomiji Nakagawa of Shizuoka (known as Tommy Japan) and Yasugorô Tanaka of Tokyo in 1881, Kiryû Nakamura of Wakayama and Shunnosuke Watanabe of Hiroshima in 1882.[8] All but Tanaka became divers in the pearl-shell industry. Tanaka went into business and later became the owner of three billiard halls on the island.

The success of these early Japanese divers eventually led to the use of large numbers of Japanese in pearling operations in the region by the latter half of the 1890s. Their involvement and achievements in the marine industries in Torres Strait and elsewhere in Australia have been documented extensively by historians and anthropologists in Australia, Japan and elsewhere.

Yokohama — Japtown

The Japanese onshore settlement on Thursday Island gradually expanded as the Japanese population in the region grew. As other Japanese with commercial interests arrived, the Japanese quarter developed to provide services for Japanese labourers when they came ashore. Community leaders were keen to establish 'a semi-official administrative body as well as a centre for social activity'[9] for the fast-growing Japanese population in the region. In 1893, they established a community club called *Nihonjin-kai* (Japanese Club/Society). Foundation committee members included some of the first arrivals. Although it has not been substantiated, the

Japanese quarter had probably been named 'Yokohama' by about this time.[10] According to Hattori, in 1894 there were already 22 buildings occupied by Japanese on the island.[11] They included three Japanese shops, one boarding house (owned by Tommy Japan), three eateries, three billiard halls (owned by Yasugorô Tanaka), one laundry, one Japanese clubhouse and 10 family homes. Some of the private homes were used as brothels.[12] The buildings were wooden with tin roofs and each had a rainwater tank. The houses were used in a Western style, with polished floors, table, chairs and beds.[13] By the late 1890s, Japtown was functioning well, commercially and socially, and was self-sufficient. By the 1910s, there were three soy-sauce factories and shops selling Japanese silk, draperies and furniture.[14]

In 1900, one visitor to the island described it as being 'more a Japanese settlement than a British colony'.[15] In 1900, the onshore population on Thursday Island was recorded at 614 Europeans, 385 Japanese, 79 Filipinos, 74 Chinese, 48 Malays, 48 Ceylonese, 39 Aborigines and 40 people who were classified as belonging to 'other mixed races'.[16] There were, however, other Japanese labourers who were stationed on other islands or working at sea. They were not included in this census. The Japanese population for the entire Torres Strait was 1,091, comprising 1,030 males and 61 females.[17]

Japanese marine labourers lived on their boats. When they came ashore during the 'lay-up' season, which ran from December to April, the Japanese presence was significant and had a strong impact on the island's commercial and social life. Yokohama became a vibrant commercial, social and entertainment centre with boarding houses filled with hundreds of young men with sufficient money to entertain themselves with drink and in the gambling house and brothels. An 18-year-old male could earn as much as a Japanese high school principal,[18] but living costs were very high and it took careful budgeting to make regular remittances home.[19] Gambling and drinking caused serious problems and Japanese were frequently prosecuted. Deep-sea diving for shells was physically demanding and dangerous, causing many deaths, but other causes of death included beriberi, malaria and tuberculosis. There were also some murders.[20]

Japanese Prostitutes

Japanese prostitutes were also early arrivals in Torres Strait. According to Sissons, the first recorded female who came to Thursday Island was 12-year-old Mitsu Shigematsu, who was smuggled in by a trafficker in 1883. She spent eight years on Thursday Island and moved to the mainland of Australia, where she worked for 12 years, then returned to Japan.[21] Other early arrivals include Mary Shime, a 22-year-old Japanese woman from Nagasaki, who in 1885 married

Tommy Japan.[22] According to Sissons, by 1887, Japanese prostitutes were working in many places including Thursday Island, Darwin and Melbourne and, the next year, in Cossack and Geraldton in Western Australia.[23] According to Hattori, there were 32 Japanese women on the island and, of those, 21 were identified as prostitutes.[24]

By 1897, there were 54 Japanese prostitutes[25] offering their services to the male population on the island.[26] Their clientele were generally Japanese men, but they also served the 'Coloured' and 'White' populations.[27] Existing studies suggest that Japanese prostitutes entered Australia 'virtually without let or hindrance'.[28] In fact, only Western Australia had a 'statutory power to prevent the landing of prostitutes or persons living off them', which came into effect in 1897.[29]

By the early 1890s, the Queensland Colonial Government began to take notice of the presence of Japanese prostitutes throughout the northern regions of the colony and did have concerns about their activities, but did not restrict their entry. One reason was, according to Murakami, that the authorities could not assert how many were actually engaged in prostitution as their houses were 'not kept as brothels, but as a store, a boarding house, or a laundry'.[30] Indeed, the Government saw Japanese prostitutes as providers of 'a service essential to the economic growth of the north' and their sexual services 'made life more palatable for European and Asian men who worked in pearling, mining and pastoral industries'.[31] Because authorities considered 'sexual intercourse between White females and Coloured males as being a disgrace', the authorities accepted the Japanese brothels as a safety device, which allowed Coloured men's sexual desires to be fulfilled, not by White, but by Japanese prostitutes.'[32]

John Douglas, the Government Resident on Thursday Island, was concerned about the spread of venereal diseases among the coastal Aboriginal tribes of Cape York.[33] However, he also saw some value in the activities of Japanese prostitutes on the island. In 1893, he observed that 'the establishments were well conducted with no rows, no drinking and there was no trouble with the women in public', and he suggested that 'if they were prevented from carrying out their trade as they were at that time, it would not diminish the immorality which would exist in another and probably a more objectionable form'.[34]

In fact, one of the purposes of the establishment of the Japanese Club on the island in 1893 was to control the trade. In 1892, Sasaki Shigetoshi, a community leader, criticised their activities. But brothel owners replied:

> ... you have no grounds to point an accusing finger even if you had the authority of the Japanese government behind you. What's more, if the [Thursday] Island authorities continue to find no fault with our business, why restrain our activities? ... What you advise, we will not do.[35]

Japtown, 1938. Clockwise from top left: Susami Boarding House,
Nishi's residence, Ebisu (shop) and Oshima Boarding House.
Courtesy of John Oxley Library, Brisbane (Item No. 171750).

Japanese prostitutes also responded:

In Japan, poor people like us have sweat on our brow night and day working like beasts of burden. Far from having the wherewithal to cook our daily meals, we barely have that to rinse our mouths. Now that we are living overseas and engaged in such a profession, as for things heavy we pick up nothing more than a knife or fork. What's more, we wear gorgeous clothes and have our fill of fine food. All our wishes are respected. We have all that we desire. What could add to our happiness? We do, alas, regret most profoundly not to have been born daughters to such gentlemen as you.[36]

Douglas also reported: 'The profits are very considerable ... several Japanese women are known to have made a good deal of money and much of this has been invested in shares of shelling boats.'[37] In other parts of *Nan'yô*, Japanese prostitution also exerted a profound economic influence.[38] Japanese prostitutes in Australia earned more per capita than their counterparts in any part of *Nan'yô*: 400 yen per month in 1896, as opposed to 200 yen in India, 120 yen in Singapore and 100 yen in Hong Kong.[39] Their remittances contributed significantly to the home economy.

Leading up to Federation in 1901, however, the Queensland Government, in consultation with the Japanese Consulate in Townsville, tried to control Japanese arriving without passports.[40] After a ban was placed on the immigration of all Japanese women into the colony in 1898, some women attempted to enter Queensland by dressing as men.[41] The Japanese brothel business on Thursday Island and elsewhere in Australia peaked about 1897, while this happened during the 1910s in other places in South-East Asia.[42]

Stowaways

Thursday Island was on the regular Japanese shipping route to Australia, which began in 1896. Among the circle of Japanese brokers, hotel proprietors and traffickers based in Hong Kong and Singapore, it was known as an easier entry point into Australia as well as 'a good place to make money'.[43] The Japanese prostitutes who entered Australia were normally smuggled out of Japan and brought in through northern ports via Hong Kong or Singapore. They were hidden in cargo ships and escorted by their traffickers.[44] One Japanese woman who left Japan without a passport was advised by a Japanese boarding-house keeper in Hong Kong to go to Thursday Island as she 'could freely land there without passports [sic]'.[45] In August 1898, for example, the vessel, *Yamashiro Maru*, arrived at Thursday Island carrying 12 Japanese — eight males and four females. Two of the men were without passports, as were all the women. All of the females came through Hong Kong.[46]

The Japanese Under the Immigration Restriction Act 1901

While the other Asian communities were, in general, directly affected by the passing of the Immigration Restriction Act in 1901, the Japanese who were working in the pearl-shell and sea-cucumber fishing industries were exempted from the provisions of this act because of the heavy dependence on the Japanese and other Coloured labourers. Japanese contract labourers continued to arrive and dominate the industry until the outbreak of World War II.[47] By 1904, the Australian Government had also relaxed the act with respect to the entry of other Japanese and allowed tourists, students and merchants to enter on passports, without being subjected to the dictation test.[48] According to Evans, officials on Thursday Island quietly allowed the arrival of additional Japanese merchants and the family members of already established island residents.[49]

The act, however, specifically prohibited the entry of 'any prostitutes or person living on the prostitution of others'.[50] No new young *Karayuki-san* were to be recruited and business for Japanese brothels became less profitable. According to Sissons, however, young women continued to be smuggled into Australia until the late 1920s. One former diver who worked on Thursday Island recalled the arrival of seven or eight young girls in the 1910s:

Japtown, 1938. Left to right: Yamashita's shoyu factory,
Iyo Boarding House, Yamashita's residence, Susami Boarding House.
Courtesy of John Oxley Library, Brisbane (Item No. 171742).

The girls had their hair all done up and dressed in a Japanese hakama with black socks in black high heel shoes. They strode on the main street. Residents all came to watch them. The girls were just like movie stars or Takarazuka performers. They didn't look like they were stowaways.[51]

According to Sissons, 'No Japanese woman was ever charged as a prohibited immigrant.'[52] Some were, however, subjected to the dictation test, which was provided for under the act to control entry of undesirable immigrants. This test could be administered to anyone in the first year after arrival. The one-year period was extended to two in 1910, three in 1920 and five in 1932.[53] Some Japanese prostitutes were deported on these grounds, but generally speaking, Japanese prostitutes 'enjoyed a remarkably prosecution-free existence'.[54]

By 1920, trafficking was curtailed elsewhere in the *Nan'yô* region due to the Japanese Government's intervention. Japan had established its economic foundations in the region and the Government began to recognise the adverse effect on national prestige that the presence of Japanese prostitutes caused.[55] In 1912, when Japan signed the Convention Against Traffic in Women and Children, many women were repatriated by the Japanese Government. This resulted in a drastic reduction in the numbers of Japanese prostitutes in *Nan'yô* by 1926. In his report compiled in 1916, Tsubotani described how one petroleum factory at Balikpapan in East Borneo received special consideration from the local government and managed to keep some *Karayuki-san* so that they would not lose their labourers.[56] This special arrangement, however, was ended in 1922. Some *Karayuki-san* in *Nan'yô* were repatriated, while others married and stayed on. In Macassar, for example, 70 to 80 per cent of the women married local Japanese and the rest married local Chinese or Indonesians.[57]

Marriages and Relationships

Some of the *Karayuki-san* who came to Thursday Island also married, but this number was small. According to the author's research, they married Japanese nationals on the island. Most of the former *Karayuki-san* who stayed on, however, remained single. The only women who were able to stay on were those who had arrived before 1901. As they aged, they started other businesses that catered to the domestic needs of single men on and off the island, playing a uniquely maternal role for the Japanese community.[58]

They were not only running boarding houses and a small eatery, but were washing clothes and mending work clothes for Japanese marine labourers.[59] As a nine-year-old child, Sadako Ike (nee Yamashita) remembers them. She spoke in Japanese:

> They were getting old. Onobu Obâsan was running a bathhouse, Oyone Obâsan was running her own boarding house and others were quiet and doing odd jobs for the workers. Otomo Obâsan was living in a small house behind Kushimoto boarding house … They could hardly speak English. We didn't need English. They used to call me and ask me to pick out husks from rice grains. [60]

In 1941, when the war broke out, five single Japanese women were included among the internees from Thursday Island — Tomi Hamasaki, Nobu Ide, Chie Yukawa, Yone Nagata and Masu Kusano.[61] They were former *Karayuki-san*.[62] Chie Yukawa moved to Thursday Island from Broome just before the war and was subsequently interned.

Japanese wives also did work for the Japanese labourers while they were busy as homemakers within their own houses. The only male Japanese migrants who were able to lead married lives were either on commercial visas or resident Japanese men who married local women of either Japanese or non-Japanese descent. In 1941, there were 12 households of Japanese heritage, including three of mixed marriage.

Tame Nishi ran a little shop where she did sewing for the men and made Japanese sweet buns and lemon juice for the divers during the lay-up season.[65] Tei Yamashita did seamstress work while bringing up her eight children. Tei was born on Thursday Island in 1907 to the Shiosaki family, early Japanese settlers on the island, but when she was two years old she was taken to Japan, where she grew up. She returned at the age of 20 when it was arranged for her to marry Haruyoshi Yamashita, a resident soy-sauce factory owner and community leader on the island. It was common among Japanese immigrants in various parts of the world to send their children to Japan for education in the prewar years. Shigeno Nakata, the wife of Jirokichi Nakata, is another example from this category.

The number of Australian-born women of Japanese descent available for marriage was very small. Evans' study, which covers 1878–1914, claims that 'there was a severe shortage of non-European women apart from mainland Aborigines and Torres Strait Islanders in the community'.[66] According to the author's investigation, there were only five divers who married and became permanent residents on the island — two married Japanese and three married women of other heritage. This is surprisingly low considering the thousands of young Japanese males who worked in the region for almost half a century. The availability of sexual services on the island may have encouraged this low rate of marriage. The sexual exploitation of Aboriginal women by Japanese marine labourers was also noted by White administrators in various parts of Australia's northern coastal regions. According to Evans, prostitution and the abduction of Aboriginal women were widespread.[67]

There are only three families whose descendents are still on the island: Kyûkichi Shibasaki, who arrived in 1918 and married Jean Ah Boo, born on Horn Island of Malay and Aboriginal parents in 1930; Tomitarô Fujii, who arrived in 1925 and married Josephine Chin Soon, of Chinese, Samoan and Torres Strait Islander origin, in 1938; and Iwazô Takai, who married Sopia Barba of Malay origin and who had three children, but who became ill and returned to Japan where he died before the war. [68]

Table 6.1: Former *Karayuki-san* resident on Thursday Island in 1941[63]

Name (approximate age in 1941)	Year of Arrival in Australia	Occupation in 1941	Marital Status
Hamasaki, Tomo (56)	Unknown, but sometime before 1901	Laundry, mending clothes for marine workers	Single
Kusano, Masu (unknown, but similar age to others) died in the internment camp	As above	As above	Single
Ide, Nobu (51)	1899 at the age of 19	Bathhouse	Single
Yukawa, Chie (64)	1897 at the age of 20	Moved from Broome before the war	Single
Nagata, Yone (59)	1897 at the age of 15	Boarding house	Single

Table 6.2: Japanese families on Thursday Island in 1941[64]

Husband (approximate age in 1941) [occupation]	Birthplace/Arrival in Australia	Wife (approximate age in 1941)	Birthplace/Arrival in Australia	Children
Fujii, Tomitarô (34), diver	Wakayama, Japan, 1907	Josephine Chin Soon (24)	Torres Strait (Chinese, Samoan and Torres Strait Islander)	2
Fukushima, Shôji, Ebisu & Co.	Wakayama, 1916	Tomie	Japan, 1924	1
Mana, Tsuneichi (30), diver	Wakayama, Japan, 1932	Tanaka, Kiyo (46)	Thursday Island	0
Matsushita, Tomijirô, Miwasaki boarding house	Unknown	Uno	Unknown	Unknown
Nakata, Jirokichi (60), formerly diver	Wakayama, Japan, 1898	Shigeno (43)	Queensland, but went back to Japan and re-entered in 1927	4
Nishi, Yasubê, died in the internment camp in 1944	Unknown	Tame (64) widow	Japan, about 1898	0
Sakakibara, Isekichi, Shiojima &Co., Hiroshima boarding house	Unknown	Shigeno	Unknown	1
Shibasaki, Kyûkichi (41), diver	Wakayama, Japan, 1925	Jena Ah Boo (32)	Horn Island	6
Takemoto, Iwakichi (36), diver	Japan, 1922	Yaeno, Shiosaki (32)	Thursday Island	2
Takai, Iwazô, deceased in Japan before the war, diver	Wakayama, Japan, Unknown	Sopia Barba	Thursday Island, Malay	1
Yamashita, Haruyoshi (55), soy-sauce factory, guesthouse owner, President of Japanese Club	Ehime, Japan, 1898	Tei (40)	Thursday Island, but grew up in Japan	8
Yamamoto, Tsunejirô (66), died on a repatriation ship in 1946	Japan, 1899	Kisu (58)	Japan, 1902	0

Japanese compound leaders at the internment camp at
Tatura, Victoria, 1942–45. Mr Haruyoshi Yamashita in the centre.
Courtesy of Evelyn Suzuki.

Informal interracial unions, however, were not uncommon. Sopia Barba and her sister Leah said, 'Japanese divers were very popular amongst girls on the island and some girls were living with Japanese divers, but only a few married.'[69] The sisters did various jobs in Yokohama, including working as shop attendants in a Japanese refreshment shop and washing clothes for workers. Leah had three children from different Japanese fathers. According to Leah and Sopia, de facto relationships between Japanese men and local women were common and sometimes they produced children. Some of these men were married and had wives in Japan.

Interruption — Internment[70]

When Japan entered World War II in December 1941, almost all Japanese nationals and their descendents resident in Allied countries were interned by the various governments. Australia interned 1,141 Japanese, including second- and third-generation Japanese. Of those, 359 were from Torres Strait. Yokohama was turned into a temporary internment camp surrounded by barbed wire, with machine guns on each corner of the town. Sadako Ike, born on Thursday Island, recalled that day:

> My friend and I used to race each other home after school and I came
> running round the corner and there was a soldier standing guard there with a

rifle and bayonet. We just stopped … My friend started crying … We didn't know what was going on.[71]

Former Japanese divers recalled: 'We were not allowed out, but that wasn't any different to usual. We were only permitted within Yokohama before then anyway.'[72] Japanese onshore residents (23 adults and 24 children) and indentured labourers (312 men) were taken into custody there until they were transferred to the mainland of Australia.[73]

The Thursday Island Japanese were later interned with other Japanese on the Australian mainland in three permanent camps: marine labourers at Hay, in NSW, other unattached males at Loveday in South Australia, and women and family groups at Tatura in Victoria. Australia accepted other Japanese internees from colonies of Allied governments, including the Netherlands East Indies, New Zealand, New Hebrides and New Caledonia. When they arrived, the Japanese numbers exceeded 4,000, the largest number Australia had ever had.

In terms of national security, Thursday Island was considered to be vulnerable and the authorities were concerned that Aborigines in the region might aid the Japanese during the war. In a civilian evacuation, 280 Coloured and 20 Chinese were removed from Thursday Island.[74] Among them were the Shibasaki and Fujii families of mixed marriage. Although the wives and children were regarded as 'Japanese' under the Nationality Act of 1920 and the Alien Registration Act of 1920,[75] the non-Japanese wives were given the option of accompanying their husbands to internment camps or remaining behind. Many Chinese residents went to Cairns and the Fujii family stayed there. The Shibasaki family was included in the Coloured group and was taken to Cherbourg Aboriginal Reserve in January 1942.

In the early months of 1943, however, Jean, the wife of Kyûkichi Shibasaki, and three other Coloured evacuees from Thursday Island, including Leah Barba, were again removed from the reserve as they were thought to be 'pro-Japanese' and, therefore, were deemed a security risk. The authorities thought they might be a bad influence on the others on the reserve. They were imprisoned from March 1942 to April 1943 at the Gaythorne Prison in Brisbane.[76] In February 1943, at a Security Service hearing, Jean said, 'I am not taking any side, either the Japanese or our own Australian side. I am just on my own with my children, not thinking of anything.'[77] Jamel, the oldest son of the Shibasaki Family, was 15 years old. He recalled:

> You live on Thursday Island. You never been anywhere else. There are three hundred Japanese divers living there. They talk to you. You talk to them. Then all of a sudden, it's wartime and you're picked out as a spy or mixing with the enemy. Makes you think, I was born in this country. I don't speak Japanese. I know nothing about spying. As a young fellow, I was so confused. So we were all shipped off south. When we got there, there were other

people from T. I. There was a woman there that used to live with a Japanese bloke years and years ago. There was Leah. She wasn't married to this Japanese bloke, but her sister was, but he went back to Japan years ago and died there. They couldn't speak Japanese.[78]

Starting Anew

During the early months of 1946, everyone, except for Australian-born Japanese or Japanese nationals whose wives or children were Australian born, was repatriated or deported to Japan, regardless of their length of residency. Among them were former *Karayuki-san*. Those who were brought from other countries were also returned to Japan. Some internees died during the war, including Masu Kusano and Yasubê Nishi. They are buried in the Japanese War Cemetery at Cowra, NSW.[79]

Before repatriation, some former divers appealed to former employers to return to their prewar jobs, but their hopes were not realised. All, except for Fujii, Shibasaki and Mana, who were married to Australian-born wives, were sent back to Japan. Of the shore-based families, the Yamashita and Nakata families were the only two who remained in Australia. When the island was placed back under civilian control on 1 April, 1946, those who were allowed to remain in Australia gradually made their way back to Thursday Island.[80] During the war, Thursday Island had been used as one of the principal naval bases for the Commonwealth and much of Yokohama had been demolished to make way for the construction of military barracks. Occupying soldiers had looted the vacant homes of the Japanese as well as other evacuees' homes on the island.[81]

In spite of a general suspicion prevalent in Australia during the immediate postwar years, the Japanese who returned to Thursday Island seemed to have been well accepted by other residents. The experiences of Japanese in other parts of Australia during the same period were more difficult. The Japanese returning to Broome and Darwin, for example, received a much more antagonistic reception from their communities.[82] Although Broome and Darwin also had a long history of Japanese involvement in their pearling industries, they had been bombed during the early months of the war. Thursday Island itself was never bombed by the Japanese, although nearby Horn Island was bombed several times. The re-establishment of normal life by the Japanese does not seem to have been substantially different from the experiences of other residents, whose lives had been similarly interrupted.[83] Amira Mendis, a Sri Lankan, who went to live on the island for the first time in 1947, observed that as people came back to the island they all seemed happy to see each other again, including former internees of Japanese descent. She recalled:

> There were about 50 people on the island and there was a feeling of 'let's start all over again'. There was a small group of White people who placed themselves above others, but the rest were living in harmony.[84]

The first Japanese resident to return was Tamiya, the eldest son of the Nakata family. He was 19 years old in 1947. He said:

> I arrived on T. I. on 3 June, 1947. I was amazed at the desolation; there used to be six hotels ... I stayed with the Dewis family [of Malay-Islander origin] who I knew before the war. They welcomed me.[85]

Evelyn Suzuki, the eldest daughter of Haruyoshi and Tei Yamashita, was 19 years old in 1946. She explained how the family was assured of accommodation and a job to facilitate their release to Thursday Island. She spoke about the way a Chinese friend of her father helped him to start a shop. She said:

> My father contacted his Chinese friend who was only too pleased to assist. Before the war, my father had helped him when his father died. He [the Chinese friend] was still quite young and was left to support his mother, younger brother and sister. The 'On' [return of gratitude] is only my interpretation of the circumstances.[86]

According to the author's investigations, 38 people, comprising six families, one couple, one widow and one single man, resettled on the island after the war. More than two-thirds were *Nisei* (second generation), and many were young children. Of the 25 *Nisei*, 11 were of mixed descent. These 38 returnees were a link, albeit small and tenuous, between the pre- and postwar Japanese presence on the island. Small though this number was, it was still the largest concentration of Japanese in Australia after the war. This remained the case until the gradual easing of restrictions to allow limited entry from Japan for specific purposes after Japan's signing of the San Francisco Peace Treaty in 1951.

The *Issei* (first generation) were not only dispossessed of what they had built before the war, they lost the social and economic infrastructure on which their lives depended. The financial loss was great for some families, but they were not compensated. Under the then National Security (Enemy Property) Regulations and the Peace Treaty in 1951, the Australian Government was empowered to seize and liquidate 'enemy property' and to distribute Japanese moneys retained under the treaty to Australian POWs who had been held by the Japanese.[87] The *Issei* maintained their silence on the subject and occupied themselves with family life and avoiding potential problems. Many of the *Nisei* (second generation), too, wanted to put the war behind them. In 1999, Tomiya Nakata reflected on the time:

> I wanted to get along well with people and didn't want to stir up things. I didn't speak about it a lot myself, but people asked me what the internment camp life was like. I answered 'No ill treatment' ... diplomatically handled.[88]

Japanese residents who resettled on Thursday Island after World War II, 1958.
Left to right: Chiyomi Fujii (baby girl), Tomitaro Fujii, Shigeno Nakata, Kiyo Tanaka
Mana, Hideo Oki, Sadako Yamashita, Thomas Pryce (baby boy), Josephine Fujii,
Mr Takase (Consul-General of Japan in Brisbane) and Kenny Pryce.
Courtesy of Sadako Ike.

The *Nisei* on Thursday Island seemed to have rehabilitated themselves well into the postwar Thursday Island community. The prewar Japanese community was physically destroyed, but socially they were not completely uprooted. Unlike other *Nisei* former internees who resettled in other parts of Australia, they did not have to resort to concealing their ethnicity by changing their surnames. They were known to the Thursday Island community and their Japanese surnames were already socially established names in the community. Harumi Ahloy, the second-eldest daughter of the Yamashita family, was 16 in 1946. She said:

> People who knew us from before the war were always good to us after we came back. Old Islanders sort of protected us. They told their sons, 'Don't touch them [Japanese girls].'[89]

Newcomers

After the war, a complete ban was placed on the entry of Japanese into Australia. It was not until the San Francisco Peace Treaty was signed in 1951 that the Australian Government allowed a few categories of Japanese to enter, including wool-buyers and war brides. The arrival of war brides meant that, for the first time,

Table 6.3: Japanese residents who returned to Thursday Island

Family surname (in alphabetical order)	Husband	Wife (Widow)	Children	Single	Total
Fujii	1	1	*2		4
Mana	1	1	0		2
Nakata	1	1	5		7
Shibasaki	1	1	*6		8
Takai	dec.	(1)	0		1
Tanaka	dec.	1	*3		4
Yagura				*1	1
Yamashita	1	1	9		11
TOTAL		7 (1)	25	1	38

*Mixed descent

there was a majority of female Japanese on the mainland, although this was not the case on Thursday Island.

With the return of male workers to the pearl-shell industry, the postwar Japanese community on Thursday Island had the same demographic pattern as during the prewar years. The pearl-shell industry was eager to bring back Japanese to revive the industry[90] and, in 1958, 106 Okinawans were permitted entry. Okinawa was then an American-mandated territory. The entry of Okinawans could then, according to Ganter, 'satisfy Australian master pearlers without offending anti-Japanese sentiments'.[91] The Okinawans, however, were salvage divers, without appropriate diving skills for pearling and most of them were soon sent back.[92] Only three Okinawan men from this original recruitment remain in the region today, two on Thursday Island and one in Bamaga on Cape York. They married local Thursday Islanders, including a daughter of the Shibasaki family.

In the 1960s, the pearl-shell industry declined as a result of the use of plastic for the manufacture of buttons. During the same period, however, Japanese companies started to invest in cultured pearls.[93] With the arrival of Japanese cultured-pearl technicians in the region, the Japanese presence in Torres Strait grew again, although this time on a much smaller scale. By this time, the Federal Government had already relaxed its entry restrictions on Japanese and numbers were growing slowly on the mainland, too. The newly revived industry again declined when Japanese companies gradually withdrew from the region and pearl-farming operations declined in the 1980s. In 2003, only one small pearl-farming operation survived on Friday Island, run by Kazuyoshi Takami, who originally came to Thursday Island to work as a cultured-pearl technician in 1973.

The development of the postwar Japanese presence was again industry-specific, but the Japanese technicians who came were sent by their companies. Single men lived in their company boarding house on Friday Island and married

men commuted between Friday and Thursday Island where their families lived.
Only a few had their families with them. Shoji Takizawa had his family with him.
In 2003, Yachiyo, his wife, recalled her life on the island:

> We had two children. I was busy looking after them. There were other
> Japanese on the island, but I didn't have much in common with them.
> I sometimes went to Yamashita san's shop to buy this and that. That's about
> it. I and my children were there for three years and moved to Brisbane for
> their schooling. All the Japanese food was regularly supplied from Japan by
> the company and there was plenty of fresh fish and prawns. Vegetables were
> a bit scarce. It was a very isolated world.[94]

The men worked and socialised with their own workmates. In 1999, the late
Gwen Moloney, editor of the *Torres Strait News*, reflected: 'They didn't mix with
us. They came and went.'[95] Forming such a 'corporate boundary', in the words of
Kazuyoshi Takami of Friday Island, 'was perhaps necessary to protect industry
secrets from others'.[96] Most of them didn't speak English well and had little to do
with the wider community.

Conclusion — Japanese Thursday Islanders

With the withdrawal of Japanese companies from Torres Strait in the 1980s,
Japanese trade with the Thursday Island community greatly diminished. Today, the
region is left with no distinct Japanese ethnic presence, but fragments of Japanese
language and culture survive in various ways (see Anna Shnukal's Chapter 10, this
volume), and they are an integral part of the region's daily life. There are also some
physical reminders of the Japanese influence before and after the war. Japanese
tombstones remain as the most tangible reminder of the Japanese presence.
Because visitors to Thursday Island usually visit the cemetery to see these graves,
Islanders of Japanese descent regularly cleaned their ancestors graves to present a
tidy image, until the Torres Strait Shire Council decided to take over the cemetery
as its Community Development Project about 2001.[97] Although these graves are
seen as proof of the contribution of Japanese men to the pearling industry, not all of
the 640 tombstones belong to men, but this has tended to be left out of academic
history. Unfortunately, the burial list does not register the causes of death and,
furthermore, almost half of the 640 gravestones have not been identified. At least
12 tombstones have been identified as belonging to women, some of whom were
likely to have been *Karayuki-san*.

The *Karayuki-san* have left little reminder of their strong presence in the
community. In the historiography of the Japanese on Thursday Island, these
women existed only as occasional statistics, or as passing references in official
reports. The only permanent physical reminders are the handful of graves in the

cemetery and the Japanese bathtub (*ofuro*) excavated in 1999 at Onobu san's bathhouse in the prewar Japanese quarter. Just as with most male Japanese, most of the prostitutes intended to stay only for a short time before returning home with their hard-earned savings. Their existence was, however, socially and economically an integral part of the Japanese labour settlement in Torres Strait in the late 19th to the early 20th centuries.

Some of the current Thursday Islanders who can trace their lineage to the prewar Japanese era are descendants of the *Karayuki-san*. While some of them may not be comfortable with this fact, it is part of the reality of the early Japanese experience in the region. To give the concept of 'Japanese Thursday Islanders' its full historical integrity, it is essential to understand the links between pre- and postwar Japanese communities as well as to recognise all those who participated in making that history.

After several generations of intermarriage, the Japanese presence has become an integral part of the Thursday Islander identity. This 'localised' Japanese ethnic heritage will continue to live not only in those who identify with Japanese culture, but it will survive indefinitely in the island's hybrid community. In 1975, Sugimoto, a researcher from Japan, found 110 second- and third-generation Japanese in Torres Strait, 85 of whom lived on Thursday Island.[98] Today, all original *Issei* are long gone and only the three Okinawans remain. Some of the *Nisei* have also passed away. It is difficult to estimate what the numbers are today. According to the author's investigation, the eight *Nisei* of the Shibasaki family alone produced 26 *Sansei* (third generation), who then produced 26 *Yonsei* (fourth generation). The Yamashita family has also expanded from eight *Nisei* to 44 *Sansei* and *Yonsei* and so have the Nakata, Fujii and Takai families. The increasing number of descendents does not necessarily mean a stronger ethnic continuity in the region. While they are proud of their Japanese ancestry, they are more proud of belonging to a wider, essentially multicultural community that identifies itself as Thursday Islander.

Acknowledgements

I gratefully acknowledge all the Japanese Thursday Islanders who have provided me with information and personal stories, particularly Evelyn Suzuki, Sadako Ike and Bill Shibasaki. My special thanks to Anna Shnukal for offering me information from her Torres Strait genealogical database, and Anna Shnukal and Guy Ramsay for commenting on my drafts.

Footnotes

1 Substantial parts of this chapter have appeared in two of my published articles: 'Japanese-Australian in the Post-war Thursday Island Community',in R. Ganter (ed.), 1999, *Queensland Review*, Vol. 6, No. 2; and 'Gendering Australia-Japan Relations: Prostitutes and the Japanese Diaspora in Australia', in *Ritsumeikan Journal of Asia Pacific Studies*, Vol. 11, March 2003. I gratefully acknowledge the permission of the publishers to reproduce them here.

2 Konno, T. and Y. Fujisaki (eds). 1985. *Iminshi II*. Shinsensha. pp. 236–7.

3 The business of trafficking young Japanese women for prostitution emerged in the rapid socioeconomic changes occurring in 19th-century Japan. More than 300,000 Japanese were working overseas in 1906 and it is estimated that between 20,000 and 30,000 women were engaged in prostitution around the world. See Warren, J. 1993. *Ah Ku and Karayuki-san: Prostitution in Singapore 1870–1940*. Oxford University Press. And Kenkyukai, Sogojoseishi (ed). 1992. *Nihonjosei no Rekishi: Sei Ai Kazoku*. p. 194.

4 Yano, T. 1975. *Nanshin no Kêfu*. Tokyo: Chûkô Shinsho. p. 18.

5 Major works on the history of the Japanese in Torres Strait include: Sissons, D. C. S. 1979. 'The Japanese in the Australian Pearling Industry.' *Queensland Heritage*, Vol. 3, No. 10. pp. 8–27. Sissons, D. C. S. '*Karayuki-san*: Japanese Prostitutes in Australia, 1887–1916, Part II.' *Historical Studies*, Vol. 17, No. 69. Sissons, D. C. S. 1977. '*Karayuki-san*: Japanese Prostitutes in Australia, 1887–1916, Part II.' *Historical Studies*, Vol. 17, No. 69. pp. 474–88. Ganter, R. 1994. *The Pearl-Shellers of Torres Strait: Resource Use, Development and Decline, 1860s–1960s*. Carlton: Melbourne University Press. Ganter, R. 1999. 'Wakayama Triangle.' *Journal of Australian Studies, Imaginary Homelands*, No. 61. Ogawa, T. 1976. *Arafura Kai no Shinju*. Ayumi Shuppan. Haig, K. 1999. 'By the Bounty of the Sea: Industry, Economy and Society in Maritime Japanese Immigrant Communities in Hawaii and Australia, 1890s to World War II.' Honours thesis, Harvard University. Nagata, Y. 1996. *Unwanted Aliens: Japanese Internment in Australia During WW2*. University of Queensland Press. Other works include: Bach, J. P. S. 1962. 'The Pearlshelling Industry and the White Australia Policy.' *Historical Studies*, Vol. 10, No. 38. pp. 205–13. Armstrong, J. 1973. 'Aspects of Japanese Immigration to Queensland Before 1900.' *Queensland Heritage*, Vol. 2, No. 9. pp. 3–9. Ohshima, G. (ed.) 1983. *Toresu Kaikyō no Hitobito [People of the Torres Strait]*. Tokyo: Kokon Shoin.

6 Bottomley, G. 1984. 'Women on the move: migration and feminism.' In G. Bottomley and M. De Lepervanche (eds), *Ethnicity, Class and Gender in Australia*, Allen & Unwin. p. 98.

7 Sissons, D. C. S., 'The Japanese in the Australian Pearl Industry', endnote 39, p. 23.

8 Hattori, T. 1894. *Nankyû no Shinshokumin*. Tokyo: Hakubunsha. pp. 9–12.

9 Haig, K., 'By the Bounty of the Sea', p. 61.

10 Yokohama was and is a major international port near Tokyo and it is unknown when it was first named. The quarter was bordered by Victoria Parade and the waterfront on one side, and by Milman, John and Hargrave Streets further inland.

11 Hattori, T., *Nankyū no Shinshokumin*, p. 22.

12 Ibid., p. 28.

13 Ibid., p. 24.

14 Haig, K., 'By the Bounty of the Sea', p. 61.

15 Kyūhara, S. 1977. 'Remains of Japanese Settlers on the Torres Straits Islands.' Unpublished paper in possession of Yuriko Nagata. According to Kyûhara, in the early stage, pearling stations in Torres Strait were located at approximately 10 sites, including Somerset on Cape York Peninsula, Albany Island, Roko Island, Possession Island, Friday Island, Goode Island, Waiweer Island, Prince of Wales Island and Mabuiag Island.

16 Evans, G. 1972. 'Thursday Island 1878–1914: A Plural Society.' Honours Thesis, University of Queensland. Tables inserted between pp. 26–7.

17 Mullins, S. 1995. *Torres Strait, a History of Colonial Occupation and Culture Contact, 1864–1897*. Central Queensland University Press. p. 157.

18 Ganter, R. 1991. 'Images of Japanese Pearl-shellers in Queensland.' *Royal Historical Society of Queensland Journal*, Vol. XIV, No. 7. p. 269.

[19]   Hattori, *Nankyū no Shinshokumin*, p. 25.
[20]   Sissons, D. C. S., 'The Japanese in the Australian Pearling Industry', p. 19.
[21]   Sissons, D. C. S., '*Karayuki-san*, II', p. 478. Warren, J., *Ah Ku and Karayuki-san*, p. 86.
[22]   Kyūhara, S., 'Remains of Japanese Settlers on the Torres Straits Islands', p. 1.
[23]   Sissons, D. C. S., '*Karayuki-san*, I', p. 328. Sissons, D. C. S., '*Karayuki-san*, II', p. 488.
[24]   Hattori, T., *Nankyū no Shinshokumin*, p. 20.
[25]   'Telegraph from J. Douglas to Under Secretary, Home Office, as at 18 July 1898.' PRV 11136, Queensland State Archives (hereafter QSA).
[26]   Evans, G., 'Thursday Island 1878–1914', pp. 26–7.
[27]   Ibid., pp. 48–9.
[28]   See Sissons, D. C. S., '*Karayuki-san*, I', p. 474. Ganter, R., 'Wakayama Triangle', p. 57.
[29]   Sissons, D. C. S., '*Karayuki-san*, I', p. 474.
[30]   Murakami, Y. 1999. 'Civilised Asian: Images of Japan and the Japanese as viewed by Australians from the early 19th century to 1901.' PhD thesis, University of Queensland. p. 168.
[31]   Ibid., p. 168.
[32]   Ibid., p. 170. According to Ogawa's interviews with former divers, White prostitutes also came to work during the lay-up season. Ogawa, T., *Arafura no Shinju*, p. 175.
[33]   Evans, G., 'Thursday Island 1878–1914', p. 49.
[34]   Armstrong, J. 1970. 'The Question of Japanese Immigration to Queensland in the 19th Century.' MA qualifying thesis, University of Queensland. p. 71.
[35]   Mihalopoulos, B. 2001. 'Ousting the "Prostitute": Retelling the Story of the Karayuki-san', *Postcolonial Studies*, Vol. 4, No. 2, pp. 211–39.
[36]   Ibid.
[37]   Sissons, D. C. S., '*Karayuki-san*, II', p. 331.
[38]   Sone, S. 1990. 'The Karayuki-san of Asia 1868–1938: The Role of Prostitutes Overseas in Japanese Economies and Social Development', unpublished paper, p. 19.
[39]   Sissons, D. C. S., '*Karayuki-san*, II', p. 323.
[40]   August 1899, PRV11136, QSA.
[41]   Armstrong, J., 'Aspects of Japanese Immigration to Queensland Before 1900', p. 5.
[42]   Kenkyukai, Sogojoseishi. 1992. *Nihonjosei no Rekishi: Sei Ai Kazoku*. p. 194.
[43]   'Letter to Government Resident Thursday Island, 13 December 1897.' PRV11136, QSA.
[44]   Sissons, D. C. S., '*Karayuki-san*, II', pp. 339–40.
[45]   'Letter to Government Resident, Thursday Island, 13 December, 1897', as included in Ganter, R., 'Wakayama Triangle', p. 57.
[46]   'Telegraph memo from John Douglas, 10 August 1898.' PRV11136, QSA.
[47]   Sissons, D. C. S., 'The Japanese in the Australian Pearl Industry', p. 16. Ganter, R., 'Images of Japanese pearl-shellers in Queensland', pp. 107–9.
[48]   Frei, P. H. *Japan's Southward Advance and Australia: from the sixteenth century to World War II*. Melbourne University Press. p. 84.
[49]   Evans, G., 'Thursday Island 1878–1914', p. 145.
[50]   Immigration Restriction Act, No. 17 of 1901, Section 3(f). In A. I. Yarwood, *Asian Migration to Australia*, Appendix 1, p. 157.
[51]   Ogawa, T., *Arafura Kai no Shinju*, p. 175. *Hakama* is an ankle-length pleated skirt. *Takarazuka* is a women-only theatre company in Japan, which was established in 1913.
[52]   Sissons, D. C. S., '*Karayuki-san*, I', p. 477.
[53]   Choi, C. Y. 1975. *Chinese Migration and Settlement in Australia*. Sydney University Press. p. 39.
[54]   Frances, R. 1994. 'The History of Female Prostitution in Australia.' In R. Perkins et al. (eds), *Sex Work and Sex Workers in Australia*, University of New South Wales. p. 52.
[55]   Warren, J., *Ah Ku and Karayuki-san*, p. 86.
[56]   Tsubotani, Z. 1916. 'Nan'yo Shisatsudan.' *Saikin Ishokumin Kenkyu*. Nihon Iminkyokai. In T. Konno and Y. Fujisaki, 1996, *Iminshi II*, Shinsensha. p. 195.
[57]   S. Nakabayashi's interview included in 'Shirochôgai no Umi ni moguru', *Aruku Miru Kiku*, Vol. 237 (1988). pp. 12–13.
[58]   Haig writes that the women who occupied a unique maternal role within the Japanese community were wives, however, my investigation shows that single women who were former *Karayuki-san* were also among them.

59 Haig, K., 'By the Bounty of the Sea', p. 62. Sadako Ike, pers. comm. to Yuriko Nagata, 6 June, 2003.

60 Ike Sadako, pers. comm., June 6, 2003.

61 'Japanese Internment Action — Nominal Roll of Japanese Internees EX Thursday Island.' Q39362,
    c.1924–54, BP242, CA 753, Australian Archives.

62 I have been able to substantiate this fact with the information I gathered from many interviews
    I conducted with current and former residents of the island from the late 1980s to the 1990s. The
    interviewees included the late Toshi Nishi, the late Ted Loban, the late Mitsuru Sano, Capri and Leah
    Barba, Sadako Ike and Evelyn Suzuki.

63 'Japanese Internment Action — Nominal Roll of Japanese Internees EX Thursday Island.' Q39362,
    no date, BP242, CA 753, Australian Archives.

64 This chart has been tabulated from three information sources: Anna Shnukal's private Torres Strait
    genealogical database; 'Japanese Internment Action', Q39362, BP242/1, AA; and 'List of Japanese
    Civilian Internees', included in Repatriation File, 46/6/72, CRS A 437, AA, 4 January, 1947.

65 Haig, K., 'By the Bounty of the Sea', p. 63.

66 Evans, G, 'Thursday Island 1878–1914', p. 53.

67 Ibid.

68 Sopia Caprice, pers. comm. to Yuriko Nagata, Mackay, 6 July, 1992.

69 Lear Lam Sami, nee Barba, pers. comm. to Yuriko Nagata, 6 July, 1992.

70 See Nagata, Y., Unwanted Aliens for further details.

71 Courier-Mail, 31 July, 1995, p. 7.

72 Ogawa, T., Arafura Kai no Shinju, p. 248.

73 Nagata, Y., Unwanted Aliens, p. 68.

74 Ibid., p. 89.

75 Ibid., p. 51.

76 Ibid., p. 91.

77 Transcription of Jean Shibasaki's court hearing for release of 24 February, 1943, Q24780,
    BP242/1, CA753.

78 Staples, J. and K. O'Shea. 1995. 'Thursday Island's Asian Heritage: An Oral History.'
    Unpublished research paper in possession of Yuriko Nagata. p. 15.

79 Cowra Japanese War Cemetery burial list.

80 Thursday Island State High School (hereafter TISHS). 1987. Torres Strait at War: a recollection
    of wartime experience. p. 32.

81 Osborne, E. 1997. Torres Strait Islander Women and the Pacific War. Aboriginal Studies Press.
    p. 85; TISHS, Torres Strait at War, p. 33.

82 Nagata, Y., Unwanted Aliens, pp. 226–9.

83 TISHS, Torres Strait at War, pp. 33, 43.

84 Amira Mendis, pers. comm. to Yuriko Nagata, 6 April, 1999.

85 Nagata, Y., Unwanted Aliens, p. 230.

86 Evelyn Suzuki, pers. comm. to Yuriko Nagata, 14 August, 1992.

87 Memo of 1 August, 1956, from 'Controller of Enemy Property, Memo, to the Secretary of Department
    of External Affairs', A 1379/1, Item EPJ 1142, QSA.

88 Tamiya Nakata, pers. comm. to Yuriko Nagata, December 1999.

89 Nagata, Y., Unwanted Aliens, p. 231.

90 Nagata, Y. 1991. 'A Foot in the Door: The Evolution of Australian Policy with regard to
    Japanese Immigration post WWII.' Unpublished paper in possession of Yuriko Nagata.

91 Ganter, R., 'Images of Japanese Pearl-shellers in Queensland', pp. 280–1.

92 Sadako Ike, pers. comm., 1 April, 1999.

93 Singe, J. 1989. The Torres Strait: People and History. University of Queensland Press. p. 161.
    The companies include Kakuta Shinju, Union Shinju, Nisshin Shinju and Taiyô Gyôgyô.

94 Yachiyo Takizawa, pers. comm. to Yuriko Nagata, June 2003.

95 The late Gwen Moloney, pers. comm. to Yuriko Nagata, November 1999.

96 Kazuyoshi Takami, pers. comm. to Yuriko Nagata, December 1999.

97 Billy Shibasaki, pers. comm. to Yuriko Nagata, May 2004.

98 Kehoe-Forutan, S. 1990. 'Effectiveness of Thursday Island as an Urban Centre in Meeting the Needs
    of its Community.' PhD thesis, University of Queensland. p. 79.

Burns Philp & Co., Victoria Parade, Thursday Island, 1906.
Courtesy of John Oxley Library, Brisbane (Item No. 109141).

CHAPTER SEVEN

The Sri Lankan Settlers of Thursday Island[1]

Stanley J. Sparkes and *Anna Shnukal*

Introduction

The dismantling of the White Australia Policy in the early 1970s, allied with periodic civil strife in their homeland, brought significant numbers of Sri Lankan immigrants to Australia. Few Australians, however, are aware that, a century before, hundreds of mostly male 'Cingalese' (as Sri Lankans were then called),[2] mainly from the southern coastal districts of Galle and Matara in the British colony of Ceylon, came as labourers to the British colony of Queensland.[3] The first of these arrived independently in the 1870s to join the Torres Strait pearling fleets, but larger numbers were brought to Queensland a decade later as indentured (contract) seamen on Thursday Island and, shortly thereafter, as farm workers for the cane fields around Mackay and Bundaberg, where many of their descendants still live. The arrival of the first batch of 25 indentured Sri Lankan seamen on Thursday Island in 1882 coincided with the importation of 'Malays' and Japanese. Yet, unlike the latter, comparatively little has been published on their origins, lives and destinies, nor their contributions to the business, social and cultural life of Thursday Island.

Some of those first arrivals demonstrated a remarkable entrepreneurial flair, taking up employment as 'watermen' (boatmen), ferrying passengers and cargo from ship to shore and subsequently taking out licences as small businessmen: boarding-house keepers, billiard-room proprietors, shopkeepers, pawnbrokers, boat-owners, gem and curio hawkers and commercial fishermen. They were joined by professional jewellers, part of the Sri Lankan gem-trade diaspora into the islands of South-East Asia during the last decade of the 19th century. Although never as numerous as some other Thursday Island Asian communities, the Sri Lankans were perceived as a distinctive group and inhabited a recognised 'Cingalese quarter': a cluster of buildings — boarding house, billiard room, store and dwelling houses — located at the eastern end of Victoria Street. Religious life was centred on the Buddhist temple. Yet, after two decades, only 20 individuals remained. The decision to leave was influenced by economic difficulties in the marine industries and, it is said, increasing uneasiness among community members who feared the confiscation of their assets and either internment in or expulsion from a newly federated Australia.[4] Most of them, however, did not return to their homes in Sri Lanka but took their skills, experience and newly acquired capital to Singapore, Malaysia, Indonesia and other parts of South-East Asia.[5]

First Arrivals

Sri Lankan seamen joined hundreds of other outsiders in the Torres Strait pearl rush of the 1870s. One independent arrival was the seaman, James, who, with three others, was engaged by Police Magistrate H. M. Chester on Thursday Island on 31 May, 1879, to travel south to Brisbane and bring back the Government schooner, *Pearl*. His monthly wages were specified as £3.10 but, reliable crewmen being hard to procure at that time, Chester was obliged to give him £1 to secure the contract.[6] He may be the enterprising James Appu De Silva who, in 1885, ran the Cingalese boarding house and went on to establish several other businesses. Another independent arrival was Assan Ceylon, who told an inquiry in 1901 that he had been diving in Torres Strait since about 1879.[7]

James and Assan Ceylon may have been among the 20 Sri Lankans who, by 1882, were already living in Queensland and who found the place to be 'quite satisfactory'.[8] There are also oral accounts from Torres Strait Islanders and Papua New Guineans claiming Sri Lankan connections that predate the arrival of the first indentured seamen. One was the husband of Konai from Erub (Darnley Island). His name is forgotten, but he is said to have fathered three daughters, Morabisi, Sophie and Balo, born on Erub in the 1870s.[9] Another may have been the diver, Yusuf (known locally as John Joseph Bombay).[10]

Mass Indenture

Organised mass migration of Sri Lankans to Thursday Island began officially on 12 June, 1882, when Scottish businessman James Burns (of Burns Philp & Co.), acting as agent for the pearl-shellers, secured the services of some 25 'Cingalese' from the Galle area. Burns had recently imported 50 'Malays' on three-year contracts from Singapore and had had no difficulty in finding shellers to employ them. In his letter to the Colonial Secretary of Ceylon, dated 19 June, 1882, he expressed his intention of increasing the number of Sri Lankan indents to 100 'in a few months time'.

The 25 men James Burns initially recruited were undoubtedly eager to work in Torres Strait. They, like the Chinese, Indonesians, Filipinos, Japanese, Pacific Islanders and Europeans, were attracted by the prospect of making their fortune. Pearling was 'in full swing', new shelling stations were being established under a recently instituted system of official lease agreements, and demand for labour was at a premium at a time when the entire population of Thursday Island 'white and coloured [did] not exceed a hundred'.[11] Some of the newcomers may have gained prior experience in the pearl fields of the Gulf of Mannar and would have been anxious to try their luck in Torres Strait.

Moreover, as the historian, Swan, points out, there were economic pressures at home that 'pushed' the men to seek employment elsewhere. The Sri Lankan coffee industry had collapsed in the 1870s and 1880s due to blight and times were difficult.[12] Perhaps fearing that the Colonial Secretary might veto their plans, they went with Burns to the Police Magistrate in Galle and signed a contract, declaring that they were 'free British subjects belonging to the British Colony of Ceylon', who understood English and Sinhalese, and were desirous of proceeding to 'the British Colony of Queensland in Australia' to serve in the Torres Strait marine industries for three years. They were to be given the sum of three rupees for travelling expenses between Galle and Colombo, the cost of their steamship passages from Colombo to Thursday Island, return passage from Thursday Island to Colombo at the expiry of their term of indenture, and a month's pay in advance. Their wages were to be 'twelve rupees per month for the first twelve months, fifteen rupees per month for the second twelve months and 20 rupees per month for the third twelve months'. Each man would be supplied 'with the usual food and clothing to the extent of two shirts and two pairs of trousers every year'. There were also conditions on their transfer and possible repatriation, should they fail to give satisfaction.[13]

The Colonial Secretary in Ceylon gave his official permission on 22 June, 1882.[14] The 'Cingalese' who signed this document were eventually provided with berths on board the S.S. *Scotland* and arrived in Queensland in August of that year.[15] They were the first batch of indentured Sri Lankans to arrive in Queensland. On 30 August, all the men were transferred with their consent to the employ of Joseph Tucker, who had established a pearling station on Goode Island, 8km from Thursday Island. The new agreements were ratified and confirmed by the Police Magistrate on Thursday Island, who noted that the men had the option of remaining on Thursday Island after the termination of their contracts, if their work was satisfactory and that was their wish.[16]

This was a period of expansion for the pearling industry, which was chronically short of labour. The 1880 Pacific Island Labourers Act and its amendments had signalled to the shellers that they could not rely indefinitely on indentured Melanesians and Polynesians as their chief labour source. In 1881, two events — passage of the Pearl Shell and Beche-de-Mer Fishery Act and discovery of a vast new pearl bed to the south-west of Mabuiag — also changed the legal and social context of labour procurement. Mindful of the likely deleterious effects on the Islanders, the Government that year created several reserves for their exclusive use[17] and granted officially registered leases to selected shellers, for the first time guaranteeing them limited security of tenure. These onshore stations, consisting of houses for the manager and men and 'storehouses for shell, diving gear, provisions, kitchen, etc.', were the centre of operations, where 'all stores are kept for the men and boats, all repairs done, and the shell is received, cleaned, and packed'.[18] Men were required to erect the buildings, jetties and slipways of the new stations, dig the wells, man the diving boats and clean and pack the shell. Ancillary staff was also required to provision and cook for the men, row the whaleboats to and from the stations to Thursday Island and act as house servants for the European owners and managers. Efficiency demanded a continuing and dependable supply of workmen and, with the Pacific closed as the primary source of cheap labour, the shellers turned their attention to the possibility of mass indenture from Asia.

In October 1883, the shelling population was concentrated on the islands adjacent to Thursday Island, which, apart from six government buildings, comprised merely 'two hotels, one store and four private houses'.[19] John Douglas, who arrived as Government Resident in 1885, is credited with encouraging the shellers to move their headquarters from the nearby islands and thus increase the township's population and commercial base.[20] Among the 307 inhabitants of Thursday Island about 1885, 160 were Asians, including 20 'East Indians', mostly Sri Lankans. Five were crewmen on a British India Company vessel then in port. Of the 15 others, only one is mentioned by name, De Sylva (likely James Appu De Silva). Five were storehands working for De Silva; five were living in Tommy Japan's (Tomiji Nakagawa) lodging house and two in Ah

Sue's lodging house; one was employed by and lodged with Humphrey Davy Mills, the local boatbuilder; one was working as a storeman in Burns Philp & Co.'s Native Barracks; and one was in prison.[21] Not recorded in that census, however, were Sri Lankans living on islands of the Prince of Wales Group or on board their vessels. During 1885, of the 1,144 seamen engaged through the Shipping Office and the 980 discharged, 75 were Sri Lankans.[22]

Despite assertions that the turn-of-the-century population numbered some 100 families, historical evidence does not support this number. The most comprehensive statistics available enumerated marine workers (pearl shell, bêche-de-mer and trochus) by ethnicity, but Sri Lankans were too few to warrant a separate category. Table 2.2 (in Chapter Two, this volume) charts the decline of the Sri Lankans on Thursday Island from about 1885 to 1914, but those who resided on the nearby stations or on boats were not counted. In 1890, the Sri Lankan Thursday Island population was recorded as 22 males out of a total of 526; in 1892, it was 43 out of 1,067; by 1893, it was 32 males out of 1,441; and, in 1898, 40 out of 1,702. By April 1901, there were 54 males (52 adults and two children), a figure unchanged a year later when the total population was 1,695.[23] This was the heyday of the Thursday Island Sri Lankan community, which declined rapidly after Federation in 1901 and a major collapse of the pearling industry in 1904. By 1918, only 12 Sri Lankans were living either on Thursday Island or the neighbouring Prince of Wales Group of islands.[24]

First Settlers

Many of the early Sri Lankan indents became 'watermen' (boatmen) and appear to have had a monopoly over that occupation. The pilot station and harbour-master's office were at that time located on Goode Island, a few kilometres away from Thursday Island, and required boatmen for all transport and transhipment between the islands.[25] In 1887, the Government established a lazaret and quarantine station on Gialag (Friday Island), which, until the former's closure and the latter's transfer to Thursday Island in 1907, also required boat transport.[26] The two Thursday Island jetties were not completed until 1893 and all passengers and cargo destined for the port had to be rowed ashore in watermen's skiffs from the hulk, which lay offshore. At Federation, there was a permanent customs post on Thursday Island, which was manned at one stage by a staff of 28, most of whom were launch crew.[27] Whether the watermen worked under government contract or were self-employed, they were relatively well paid and possessed greater independence and opportunity for engaging in commercial activity than their indentured countrymen.

Thursday Island Court of Petty Sessions and Police Summons Books identify some of the first settlers and their circumstances. They fill the gap between the first arrivals and the establishment of the earliest small businesses.[28] We have tentatively identified about 60 of those early arrivals, who are recorded as being of 'Cingalese' origin in Thursday Island court and other records between 1883 and 1907:[29]

> Ahmat, L. K. Amaris, Simba K. Amadoris, Gostene Waduga Andris (George William Andris), Androsami, Allis Appu, Charles Appu (possibly K. N. Saris Appu), Dionas Appu, Don Singho Appu (John Ceylon), Arnolis, Singho Babu (S. K. Babunappu), M. W. Bastian, Peter Brown, Assan Ceylon (B. Assan), Usop Ceylon, Charley Cingalese, Conieham, Cornelius, Danolis, Denishamy, Didwan, Dionysius, Elias, P. H. Endoris, Frank Gabriel, J. Harmanis, Idroos, J. P. James, M. W. James, Billy Jetsunamy (Billy Cingalese), Henry Louis Johannes, Bob Kitchalan, Peter Kuruneru, Matho (Matthew Appu), Charles Mendis, W. V. Mendis, Menzies, Miskin, Thomas Roderick Morris, Katta Nandoris, Henry Odiris, Samuel, Charles De Silva, H. L. De Silva, James Appu De Silva (Jimmy Cingalese), S. A. De Silva, William De Silva, Simon,[30] Henry Louis Simon, L. D Simon, S. K. Simon, K. P. Appu Singho, Punchi Singho (James Cingalese), Abdula Siyadoris, Thadeus, Theodorus, L. H. Trolis, Thomas Weerasooria (who also signed as 'W. S. Thomas'), William De Silva, Bala Williams, H. Wimalaratna.

To the above list can be added the 10 Sri Lankans who were brought before the court by the pearl-sheller, Edward Morey, for breach of agreement in January 1901. The case was adjourned and then withdrawn, presumably because the men returned to work. Their names were: John Jayasuriya Gunawardene, Hatharasingha Widanage Thomis, Widane Gamage Charles, Lamahewage Johannes, Ratneweera Patabendige Andrayas, Kukunhenego Matho, Hewanamage Simon, Don Charles, Adoris, Geedrick.[31]

Most of the men were either watermen or crew; i.e., they ranked towards the middle of the hierarchy of marine workers in terms of skill level, wages and ethnic origin. The majority were Buddhists, some very devout,[32] although a small number were Muslim, such as Assan Ceylon and Ahmat, and possibly — judging by his name — Usop Ceylon.[33] Many were literate in Sinhalese, could read Buddhist texts and signed their names in Sinhalese script (more rarely in English) to their witness statements. When giving evidence in court, they swore to tell the truth on their 'sacred volume the Cingalese bible'. During their time ashore, they lived at the 'Cingalese' lodging house on Victoria Parade or in houses close by, bought provisions at the Sri Lankan store, drank with countrymen and other workmates in the local hotels,[34] played billiards in the

Victoria Parade, Thursday Island, 1895.
Courtesy of John Oxley Library, Brisbane (Item No. 121658).

Sri Lankan billiard room, visited their countrymen at home or in the boarding house, and gambled in the Chinese-run establishments. They probably also visited the Yokohama brothels. No Sri Lankan women are mentioned and only a few of the men are recorded as being married, although some are known to have lived with local Indigenous women and/or had families in Sri Lanka.[35]

At the apex of the marine-worker hierarchy were the divers, who were the best paid and most highly respected. They captained their boats, being solely responsible for each trip and answerable only to the owners or managers.[36] Sri Lankans were rarely employed as divers, but we have found evidence of two: Assan Ceylon and Thomas Morris.

Assan Ceylon began diving for pearl shell about 1879 and worked as a diver for more than 20 years. In 1901, he was employed by the Filipino pearl-sheller and businessman, Heriberto Zarcal, as diver and captain of his ketch *Lacandola*. Although generally known as Assan Ceylon, he was registered on articles of the schooner *Ethel* and other boats as B. Assan, No. 179. He was found to be partly responsible for the death of Cypriano Trinidad, one of the Filipino crew of the *Lacandola*, in that he had allowed Trinidad to dive without a diver's licence, and was fined the large sum of £10.15.6.[37] Two years later, perhaps because of his conviction or because he had sustained an injury to his hand, he was working as a commercial fisherman in partnership with Henry Louis Simon.[38] Thomas Roderick Morris, born in Badulla, Ceylon, about 1863, may have been of European-Asian descent. His parents are recorded as James Morris, a coffee planter, and Caroline. In 1890, he was working as a diver for the pearl-sheller, John Tolman;[39] and, on 31 January, 1891, he gave his occupation as diver when he married a mainland Aboriginal woman from Cape Grenville named Kate Paremah.[40] Another putative Sri Lankan diver was Yusuf (a Muslim known locally as John Joseph Bombay), who was in charge of the *Lily* in 1885.[41]

With few exceptions, little is known about the fate of most of these early seamen. Simon Silva, a man 'of an excitable nature', was likely the coxswain of the first transport between Thursday and Goode Island in 1884.[42] At the outbreak of World War I, Simon was listed as the only 'Coloured' man on Thursday Island possessing a service rifle.[43] He survived to become the oldest man on the island.[44] According to Amara and Mahendra Mendis, who knew him towards the end of his life, he used to live behind the Saranealis family, who cooked his meals as he grew older and more infirm and gave him fish after their fishing trips. His last years were spent in hospital, where his friend, the doctor, provided him with a glass of whisky after their evening walk together.[45] Three long-term residents died intestate on Thursday Island: Allis Appu in 1891, leaving the sum of £103.3.4;[46] Gostene Waduga Andris in 1900, leaving an estate of £60;[47] and M. V. Mendis in 1913, leaving assets of £5.12.6.[48] James De Silva and Simon Silva appear to have become indigent in old age. The waterman, Miskin, who was often in trouble with the law, was born about 1853 and may have been one of the original indents. He died on Thursday Island on 31 July, 1908.[49] At least three Sri Lankans required hospitalisation due to temporary mental illness.[50]

The 'Cingalese Quarter' of Thursday Island

To cater for the needs of the growing Sri Lankan workforce, a 'Cingalese boarding house' was established, probably during the second half of 1885. It was run by James Appu De Silva.[51] James De Silva was the proprietor, not only of the boarding house but of a billiard room that was under the same roof and was joined to the boarding house by a verandah.[52] He employed his countryman, a former waterman named Andris, as a billiard marker. By April 1886, he also ran a 'Cingalese store' on the same allotment.[53] Close by was the house which the Sri Lankans used as a place of worship before the construction and dedication of 'a tiny tin Buddhist temple'. For many years, the temple, 'an equally small

Chinese Joss house' and two Christian churches were the only places of worship on the island.[54]

The section of Thursday Island where the Sri Lankans congregated was referred to as the 'Cingalese quarter'. It consisted of a cluster of buildings on Allotments 1 and 2 of Section 5 of the town plan towards the eastern end of Victoria Parade near the Post Office, separate from the Asian quarters (see Map C).[55] This was the locus of their community, a predominantly masculine world of work, recreation and prayer. It was centred on their lodging house, billiard room, store and Buddhist temple and included at least three houses, two located in a passage from Victoria Parade to Douglas Street and the other fronting on to Victoria Parade.[56] However, neither the Sri Lankans (nor other 'Coloured aliens') owned the buildings or land they occupied. Property on Thursday Island at the time was exclusively in the hands of Europeans: the boarding house, billiard room, store and houses belonged to Burns Philp & Co. Once a Sri Lankan house tenant left, however, he generally found a countryman to take his place.[57]

The tendency of the Sri Lankans to work and live together, to exploit a specialised economic niche in the local economy and to behave as a cohesive ethnic group in the event of disturbances conforms to the general pattern of the Thursday Island Asian communities during their early formation. To these factors can be added the Sri Lankans' 'exotic' (to European eyes) appearance, apparel and general demeanour. Although they kept largely to themselves, there were occasional fights with their main economic competitors, the Malays,[58] and later the Japanese.[59] Each side accused the other of being the instigator of these affrays, but the police considered them equally to blame.[60]

More covert was Sri Lankan participation in the shadowy world of Malaytown's gambling and opium dens and brothels. These semi-legal establishments were frequented by seamen of all ethnicities during the lay-up season and remained largely free from official supervision and control provided there were no disturbances. From time to time, however, the police would conduct raids, usually with the help of informers. In 1899, the seaman, Siyadoris, was one of a group of Sir Lankans gambling with Malays and Chinese in Hop Sing's back shop in Douglas Street;[61] in 1901, H. L. Simon was arrested in a police raid against William Sam Hee's gambling room on Douglas Street. He had been one of a 'crowd' of about 25 men, including Europeans, Japanese, Chinese, Malays and three of his countrymen — one was the waterman, Bala Williams, another the hawker, Weerasooria Thomas.[62] This world was depicted by novelist Colin Simpson, who based his fictionalised hero's adventures on his own experiences on Thursday Island during the early 1890s. Recalling his impressions of a Chinese-run gambling room, he wrote:

A few of the men there he knew. The big Dane was Ewald, who had a beche-de-mer fishery. The West Indian with thin gold rings in his ears was the bosun of Pymont's luggers. Kono, the 'king' Jap diver who had brought in the biggest shell-take the previous season, was at the table ... De Silva, the little Cingalese storekeeper, was at the gaming table between an old Chinese and a red-bearded engineer named McGowan, who was working on the construction of the new jetty.[63]

Refugees from Normanton

The early community gained an unknown number of new members in July 1888 as a result of the influx of 84 refugees from anti-Asian riots in the remote township of Normanton on the Gulf of Carpentaria. The riots had broken out in response to three murders by a 'Malay' named Sedin, but they brought to a head several years of tension between the Asian newcomers and the predominantly European townspeople, which was fanned by articles in the local press.[64] The majority of those involved were 'Malays', a general term for 'Coloured' people, but Sri Lankans were included among those who fled to Thursday Island in the vessel, *Birksgate*.[65] In an article headed 'The Normanton disturbances', the *Queenslander* of 7 July, 1888, reported that:

> Sedin, a Malay, was charged yesterday week at Normanton for the murder of John Fitzgerald and Christian Muynga. He insisted on describing how the murders were committed. He was committed to stand trial for wilful murder. He was also charged with the murder of J. P. O. Davis.

The 'Malays' and Sri Lankans had reportedly 'dribbled down in twos and threes' from Thursday Island over a number of years, hence the decision to send them back there. On a lagoon near the town they had constructed their own village and some had gone into service as cooks and house servants. Their presence was increasingly resented and the climax came with the murder by Sedin of three Europeans, two of whom may have gone to the Malay village to cause trouble, but one, a ship's carpenter, seeking to make peace.

> Immediately the townspeople decided on direct action. With strong ropes they pulled down every structure in Malaytown. The terrified Malays fled to the bush, but about one hundred of them were captured and put on board the sailing ship Rapido.[66]

Reports of the happenings in Normanton eventually filtered through to Ceylon and evoked a storm of indignation, which found an echo in Queensland. The 12 October, 1888, issue of the *Queenslander* contained the following article, datelined Thursday Island and headed 'The deported [sic] Cingalese':

> A letter from Louis Mendis, a leading Cingalese resident of Colombo, has been received by a Cingalese man here, who came away from Normanton with the other coloured deportees in June last year. Mendis says he will spare no pains to get justice done for the men through the Ceylon Government; he will get all the papers necessary to back him in his efforts; he will get the Cingalese representatives in the Legislative Council to move in the matter in the Council, and he will do all in his power to obtain redress. Mendis asks to be supplied with full information concerning the case, and also newspapers containing the narrative or comments thereon; and he offers to be responsible personally for all expenses incurred in keeping up the correspondence, which he says will have to be pursued until something is done for his countrymen.

Whether Louis Mendis's efforts bore any fruit is not known, since the newspapers remained silent on the subject.

Contemporary Observations

Despite their relatively small numbers, the Sri Lankans were singled out for comment from the beginning. In an 1883 petition to the Colonial Secretary of Queensland, the Torres Strait pearl-shellers wrote that 'Arabs, Egyptians, Malays and Macassar men, Javanese, Cingalese, West Indies, and natives from almost every island in the South Pacific' were employed in the marine industries.[67] At the end of the next year, they complained that they were 'continually engaging men from Sydney, Brisbane, Singapore, Batavia, Ceylon and Japan for various terms; and at the highest port wages; paying all expenses, and passage here, and frequently home again', only to see their employees fleeced by others at no profit to themselves.[68]

The Church of England priest, Thomas Eykyn, who began visiting Thursday Island in 1885, specifically mentioned 'Hindoos, Cingalese, Malays, Siamese, Javanese, Japanese, Poles, Irish, Scotch, and a few English and Germans' among its '32 different nationalities'.[69] The Moravian missionaries established Mapoon Mission as a refuge for Cape York Aboriginal people in 1891 to protect the men and women from abduction by 'Whites, Malays, Cingalese, Japanese, and Manilla men'.[70] Visiting Thursday Island in 1892, the painter, Ellis Rowan, was struck by the 'medley of tongues and faces' belonging to 'Britons, Italians, Spaniards, Maltese, Hindus, Cingalese, Negroes, Malays, Kanakas';[71] and, according to a visiting Sydney journalist, who attended a local theatrical production in 1899, the audience included 'Cingalese … mostly in cool garb of singlet and dungaree trousers'.[72] The growing commercial success of the Sri Lankans and other non-Europeans infuriated their Anglo-Australian business competitors, one of whom penned the following verses about 1900:

> *Up in regions equatorial,*
> *Blest with scenery pictorial,*
> *Pursuits mainly piscatorial,*
> > *Lies an island known to fame.*
> *Pearling lives and pearling thrives there,*
> *Coloured races live in hives there,*
> *White men risk their lives there*
> > *Thursday Island is its name.*
> *Every race it opes its gates to,*
> *Every country it relates to,*
> *Key to Hell and Torres Straits too,*
> > *Though a speck upon the map.*
> *What though whites first trod upon it!*
> *What though Anglo-Saxons won it!*
> *Chows and Cingalese now run it,*
> > *Aided by the wily Jap.*[73]

From Indents to Entrepreneurs

The beginnings of commercial activity among the Sri Lankans occurred soon after the arrival of the first indentured workers. The earliest entrepreneurs were two watermen, James De Silva and Henry Louis Simon. By 1885, the energetic De Silva was the proprietor of a newly constructed lodging house, to which, by 1888, he had added a billiard room and general store. He advertised his various services in the first issue of the *Torres Straits Pilot and New Guinea Gazette* on 2 January, 1888: 'James Silva, General Storekeeper, Boarding House Keeper and Waterman, Victoria Parade, Thursday Island.' Silva offered 'good accommodation for boarders at lowest rates' and 'boats for hire at all hours'. In the same issue was an advertisement for De Silva's business competitor, H. L. Simon of Victoria Parade, who, in addition to his stock of 'Ceylon Curios', also kept 'boats for hire at any time of day or night'. Other licensed watermen followed their example in hiring out their boats and services: M. W. Bastian in 1889;[74] J. Harmanis from 1889–99;[75] Saris Appu and J. Hermanis in 1898;[76] Ahmat from 1892–99;[77] and J. P. James, who, in January 1902, had a boatshed near the Grand Hotel.[78] All had lived for some time on Thursday Island; some may have been among the original indents. Becoming boat-owners was a

Saranealis family graves, Thursday Island.
Courtesy of Stanley J. Sparkes.

natural progression for thrifty boatmen, who had saved enough out of their wages to start their own boat-hire businesses.

Buoyed by their successes, De Silva and Simon expanded into other commercial ventures, notably the burgeoning tourist trade in jewellery and curios.[79] In 1888, James de Silva was one of several Sri Lankans recorded as having been granted a hawker's licence. In his application, he listed as his sureties Henry Dubbins (a European pearl-sheller then Chairman of the Torres Divisional Board and a Justice of the Peace) and Moyden (a Muslim Indian waterman from Madras).[80] This suggests he had begun to establish personal and business contacts beyond the confines of the Sri Lankan community. In 1890, he married May Scott Mosa, a local shopkeeper, and with her help continued to expand his business interests. That same year he advertised himself as a blacksmith[81] and, in August 1891, he kept at least two shops, one of which he sub-leased to a Greek storekeeper, George Machal.[82] By May 1892, he had become a pearl-sheller, purchasing the lugger, *Mobiag*, and employing as his agent the European, Patrick Joseph Doyle. On 20 July, 1892, he successfully sued William Price for refusing to go to sea in his boat, despite the latter's having signed on articles and received an advance of £5. De Silva testified that not only had he lost the money he had advanced to Price, but two or three days' time, the cost of which he estimated at 'about one pound per day'.[82] It was during this difficult time that he was brought before the court, convicted of obscene language, required to provide sureties of the peace for six months at a total of £50 and fined £6.10.6. Despite this setback, he continued as a pearl-sheller until at least January 1895.[84] He had, however, withdrawn from pearling by September 1900 when he gave his occupation as fisherman during his trial for disorderly conduct. He had gone to Esteban Filomeno's house to get money owing to him for fish, had been roughly treated by a group of Filipinos, Filomeno's countrymen, and reacted by shouting and throwing stones.[85] The next month he was charged with being mentally unsound, but was released almost immediately.[86] De Silva remained on Thursday Island at least into the 1920s: in 1927, he was twice convicted of refusing to vacate premises he occupied on Arthur Filewood's property.[87]

Henry Louis Simon's career followed a similar trajectory. On 15 January, 1885, he married a European woman, Annie May Holmes, and they rented a house close to Odiris and Theodorus.[88] On 12 May, 1888, Annie complained to the court about the actions of James De Silva, her husband's business rival.[89] Both men advertised boats for hire from 1888 and, in 1888–89, both held billiard licences for one table each, located in premises on Victoria Parade (presumably the billiard room run by James De Silva until 1896).[90] Simon did not renew his billiard licence after 1889, the year he advertised a jewellery partnership with P. H. Endoris.[91] In 1892, he was granted a licence to deal in pearls (one of two held by Sri Lankans and which he held until at least 1896), a hawker's licence and a pawnbroker's licence.[92] In 1893 and 1894, he advertised his services as a jeweller and watchmaker.[93] In October 1901, however, Simon was arrested and fined for gambling illegally with a group of his countrymen in William Sam Hee's room on Douglas Street.[94] Since only men of the highest probity were permitted to hold licences to deal in pearls, his gambling conviction may have precluded him from renewing his licence. By 1903, he, like De Silva, was working as a licensed commercial fisherman in partnership with the ex-diver, Assan Ceylon,[95] and thereafter disappears from the historical record.

James De Silva may have been the first Sri Lankan to have been granted a hawker's licence (in 1888), but he was followed shortly thereafter by H. L. De Silva in 1889 and K. M. Saris Appu in 1890. The next year, Odiris gave evidence that he, too, was a licensed hawker with 'money and jewels'; and H. L. Simon followed in 1892.[96] They may have been among the Sri Lankans who rowed out to visiting passenger steamships and were described by Boothby during his visit to Thursday Island in December 1892:

No sooner are we at anchor than our decks are covered with strangers of all descriptions. Arabs, Chinese, Cinghalese, Japanese etc. clamber over the side, everyone with something to sell, and everyone with a tremendous amount to say.[97]

Boothby cast a cynical eye over the sale of 'pearls' to unwary tourists:

For even this self-same tourist, so ignorant in other matters, knows that it is not wise to buy pearls from the smooth-spoken Cinghalese who crowd the ship's deck. To this end these simple children of fair Ceylon manufacture pearls that would deceive even the mother oyster herself and dispose of them on advantageous terms to their darker skinned brethren.[98]

From the mid-1890s, coinciding with a general downturn in the Torres Strait marine industries, the completion of the Thursday Island jetty, the ageing of the original watermen and the community's fears about the consequences of Federation, we see a greater range of occupations embraced by the remaining members of the Sri Lankan community. For example, in 1895, George William Andris was working as a carpenter; and, in 1899, Simba K. Amadoris (who was to become a jeweller and business rival of Y. B. Saranealis) was employed at Brown Campbells store on Thursday Island; in 1906, Henry Louis Johannes was a general labourer.[99] Shortly after Federation, a few of the older men, former watermen who had chosen to remain on the island, took out commercial fishermen's licences from the Shipping Inspector. Demand for their previous services had all but ceased and, with declining physical strength, they no doubt sought to take advantage of their long experience of local currents and conditions, selling their catch from Thursday Island. Among ex-watermen and ex-seamen recorded as licensed fishermen carrying on business on Thursday Island were Matthew Appu, Assan Ceylon, Miskin, James De Silva, S. K. Simon and Henry Louis Simon.

Leaving aside the gem traders discussed below, various other small entrepreneurs appeared from time to time on Thursday Island, some setting up on their own and others buying established businesses. On 27 June, 1901, H. Fernando put the following advertisement in the *Pilot*: 'I, the undersigned, have this day disposed of my business as a laundryman carried on in Douglas Street to P. H. James on whose behalf I solicit the patronage of the public of Thursday Island.' The advertisement was repeated for some weeks. A few years later, the Queensland Oriental Trading Co., General Merchants, Douglas Street, began to advertise 'Sinha Tea' among a list of other groceries. They stated they were 'importers of Best Ceylon Tea, Hand-made Ceylon Lace, Curios etc'.[100] A mail-order entrepreneur appeared briefly on the scene in 1907. The following advertisement appeared in the *Pilot* on 14 February, 1907, and was repeated on 14 March:

Ceylon Precious Stones. Direct from the Gemming District to Jewellery Manufacturers. Sample packet of 100 Cut Stones, Rubies, Sapphires, Etc., £5.0.0. Send P.O. Money Order to J. Wickramanayaka & Co., Kalutara, Ceylon, and try a packet, it will lead to good business. Best references. What other goods do you require from Ceylon?

The Gem-Trading Enterprises

All local memory of the first Sri Lankan settlers has been lost, but the gem-trading enterprises, established during the closing years of the 19th century, remain part of the island's historical record. Commerce in pearls (genuine and manufactured) became the main stimulus for a 'second wave' of Sri Lankan migrants to Thursday Island. The first indents, some of whom had already entered the gem trade as hawkers and pearl dealers, were joined by the professional jewellers and gem dealers who are remembered today. They were part of a move by Sri Lankan jewellers to seek outlets in ports abroad, which were visited regularly by passenger vessels. The new arrivals exploited the profitable middleman trade in jewellery, particularly pearls, pearl blisters and items manufactured from pearl shell for which Thursday Island was famous. It was a natural commercial target for Sri Lankan jewellers whose expertise already embraced pearls from the beds of the Gulf of Mannar. According to Swan, several of these men were sponsored by Mudaliyar B. P. De Silva, 'a well-known entrepreneur in the gem trade in Ceylon'.[101] Moreover, those who could afford to returned home periodically and their success stories encouraged others to try their luck on the same turf.[102] This 'second wave' contributed to the more complex ethnic specialisation that was emerging within the marine industries. By the 1920s, observers noted that there were 'Japanese agents for trochus shell, Chinese agents for bêche-de-mer and Cingalese who specialise in tortoiseshell'.[103]

Most of the stores were mixed businesses, offering services as watch and clock repairers and jewellery manufacturers, along with all manner of imported and locally fabricated curios made from pearl shell and tortoise shell — spoons, pen handles, paper knives, necklaces, pendants, bracelets and watch cases — as well as Ceylon tea, Parker pens, gas lighters and lottery tickets.

The first of these stores to be recorded was opened on Victoria Parade during the late 1880s by the enterprising waterman and boat owner, Henry Louis Simon. In January 1888, he advertised a second trade as 'Practical Jeweller and Goldsmith' and 'Dealer in Ceylon Curios and Jewellery'. He formed a partnership with P. H. Endoris, which was advertised between 1889 and 1893.[104] By 1890, Simon and W. E. Wimalasundera operated jewellery stores on Victoria Parade.[105] Two years later, Simon was so well established, professionally and personally, that he had obtained one of the seven licences to deal in pearls — licences that were issued at the discretion of the Police Magistrate of Thursday Island only to 'reputable persons'.[106] Also in 1892, S. A. De Silva advertised himself as a jeweller and watchmaker with an establishment in Normanby Street. He continued to advertise his services, which grew to include a 'manufacturing department' for customers wishing to design or alter their own jewellery, until 1897.[107]

H. L. De Silva, the second licence holder in 1892, became successful enough to employ a second jeweller, his countryman Deeris, who was possibly, like many others throughout that period, brought out under indenture.[108] L. D. Simon also briefly advertised himself as a jeweller and goldsmith from 1895–96;[109] and Y. B. Saranealis carried on a jewellery business in Normanby Street from 1896–1919.[110] Towards the end of 1900, J. C. Amadoris opened a similar business, also in Normanby Street, under the name, James Charles; and, about the same time, Simba K. Amadoris (who had been employed at Brown Campbells store on Thursday Island in 1899) set up in business as a jeweller and watchmaker. He purchased the business of Y. B. Saranealis in 1900 after the latter's bankruptcy, but they later became rivals. Amadoris was periodically in trouble with the law and, in 1900, was convicted of manslaughter. After serving his jail sentence, he returned to Thursday Island and went into partnership with H. L. Mowlis. On 13 October, 1906, Amadoris described himself as a pearl dealer and jeweller with a shop in Douglas Street; in 1908, he appears to have transferred his pearl dealer's licence to Mowlis, but nothing is recorded about that association after 1915.

The Major Gem Traders: Saranealis, Charles, Mowlis and Mendis

In 1896, the young Yanandaygoda Buddalegay De Costa Saranealis arrived on Thursday Island and immediately set himself up as a jeweller and watchmaker in premises in Normanby Street.[111] Announcing that he had commenced business, Saranealis advertised himself as a 'Pearl Merchant and Buyer, Watchmaker and Manufacturing Jeweller … prepared to execute every description of work entrusted to him'. He added that he kept a 'large stock of all kinds of precious stones and jewellery', manufactured every description of jewellery to order and repaired watches and clocks.[112] On 31 March, 1897, he was fined 5/- for a minor breach of local by-laws, probably in connection with his business.[113] In the 7 January, 1899, issue of the *Pilot*, Saranealis advertised that he was now a licensed pearl dealer and court records reveal that in April of that year he was sworn in as court interpreter, a sign of his high standing in the general community.[114] His advertisements continued throughout 1899, but he was declared bankrupt on 6 December, 1899, with debts of £374.11.10 and assets of only £231.6.[115] He sold his business to his countryman, S. K. Amadoris, in 1900 but was soon back in business. On 10 December, 1903, he advertised the availability of 'Ceylon Lace and Precious Stones, Watches and Jewellery' for sale. On 26 December, 1903, he advertised again, stating 'New and Expensive Machinery for Electroplating and Gilding has been received and all orders can be completed equal to the best English and Continental work'. After the disastrous fire, which, in April 1905, destroyed 14 buildings on Thursday Island's main commercial block, most of the Sri Lankan shopkeepers, Saranealis among them, moved to Douglas Street. By 30 September, 1905, he was back in business: in addition to his normal weekly advertisement on the front page of the *Pilot*, he advertised that he was still prepared to buy and clean pearls as usual. On 13 October, 1906, just four days before an assault by Amadoris, Saranealis advertised the arrival of a consignment of Ceylon lace. In 1909, in the issue of 26 June, Saranealis added to his regular advertisement with an Australian coat-of-arms and the words 'Under the Patronage of His Excellency the Governor-General of the Commonwealth of Australia, Lord Northcote'. He kept Lord Northcote's patronage until at least 1913.[116] Saranealis continued as a pearl buyer and cleaner, watchmaker and jeweller until his death in 1919, when his widow and sons took over the business.[117]

On 29 December, 1900, James Charles (formerly James Charles Amadoris) advertised his services as watchmaker, jeweller and engraver with a shop in Normanby Street, which he may have taken over from S. K. Amadoris during his term of imprisonment.[118] He claimed to be well known in many places in Australia. On 12 January, 1901, Charles's regular advertisement began appearing on the front page of the *Pilot* and continued to do so for some years. He married Florence Elizabeth Murton on 6 July, 1902, and, by 1903, had moved his jewellery establishment to Douglas Street.[119] He and Y. B. Saranealis were the only Sri Lankans to hold any of the nine pearl dealer's licences issued for 1907.[120] He ceased advertising in 1909 after an attempt on his life and may have left Thursday Island.

Hikkadawa Leana Mowlis, also from Galle, arrived on Thursday Island in the early 1900s. He established a jewellery business in partnership with S. K. Amadoris, after the latter's release from jail, and, in 1908, held a coveted licence to deal in pearls. On 19 June, 1909, the following advertisement appeared in the *Pilot*: 'Amadoris and Mowlis, Pearl Dealers and Manufacturing Jewellers. Splendid Assortment of Ceylon Lace Received.' On 1 February, 1913, Mowlis advertised in *The Parish Gazette* without mentioning Amadoris and again failed to mention Amadoris in his advertisement in the *Pilot* of 24 January, 1914:

H. L. Mowlis. Pearl Merchant & Manufacturer of Mother-of-Pearl Goods, Thursday Island. Having acquired from Mr. H[eriberto] Zarcal his business with stock-in-trade etc., at Thursday Island, H. L. Mowlis will now continue the business in his own name. The fine selection of pearl and pearl-shell goods, jewellery, watches and other time-pieces, electroplate ware etc., will be kept up to the present high standard; and my usual fine stocks of Ceylon Lace will be added to, and satisfaction to all patrons so guaranteed, prices also being most moderate.

Punchi Hewa Mendis, c.1950s.
Courtesy of Mahendra Mendis.

In 1915, however, Amadoris and Mowlis advertised together as pearl cleaners, an indication that the partnership had been reconstituted at least for that year.[121] That is the last year in which Amadoris's name appears. Mowlis, however, continued to advertise annually in *Pugh's Almanac* as a pearl buyer, watchmaker and jeweller until 1923.

The most successful of all the gem traders was Mendis Punchihewa, known in Australia as P. H. (Punchi Hewa) Mendis. Mendis came to Thursday Island in 1898 as a 15-year-old boy, sponsored by his father's cousin, Mendis De Silva, who had apparently lived there for a time.[122] Mendis found employment with the *Pilot* as a compositor and part-time reporter — later in life, he recalled delivering the newspaper to Hon. John Douglas and sometimes receiving an apple in return. Beginning as a retailer in small rented premises, by good luck he made a large profit from the sale of an exceptionally beautiful pearl. This gave him the start-up capital to purchase a larger shop on Douglas Street opposite the Metropole Hotel in 1905 from the Chinese businessman, See Kee. There he opened a jewellery and general store and, within a few years, had established himself as an importer and retailer and a leading businessman in the town.[123]

On 24 January, 1914, Mendis, describing himself as a licensed pearl merchant, advertised in the *Pilot* 'to purchase Pearl Blisters in the rough in any quantity for cash. Highest prices given. Pearlshellers please note.' He placed another, larger advertisement in the same issue, enumerating a wide range of goods for sale:

> Oriental Embroidery Work … also Silk and Crepe Kimonos, Silk and Emboidered Jackets, Silk, Gauze and Muslin Blouse Lengths … Silk Stockings. Hand-painted velvet Cushion Covers, Silk Fans, etc. A large variety of Antimony Picture Frames, Hair Brushes, Mirrors, Shaving Sets, Trinket Boxes, Inkstands, etc., and a quantity of Damasceine, Cloisonne and Satsum, Hatpins, Buckles, Tiepins, Sleeve Links, Vest and Coat Buttons, Cigarette Cases … Painted Postcards, Visiting Cards.

Mendis was quick to see business opportunities and astute and courageous enough to seize them. Alexander Corran, whose father had been a printer, taught him the printer's craft[124] and, during the 1920s, he and Corran's wife (the owner of the *Pilot*) operated the only printery on the island, running off not only the *Pilot*, *The Carpentarian* and *The Parish Gazette* for the Diocese of Carpentaria, but community announcements and items of local interest.[125] He claimed to have pioneered the trochus export trade from Thursday Island. In response to a request from his brother-in-law, then living in Japan, he sent a shipment of trochus and they began to organise the trade on a regular and systematic basis: it was soon taken over by the Japanese. As he expanded his various enterprises, Mendis brought several members of his extended family to work for him in his various businesses on Thursday Island and, later in Darwin and Brisbane, continuing a long-established practice in the Sri Lankan gem trade. The family also conducted a wholesale and retail business, Galle Stores Ltd, in Sri Lanka.[126] In 1940, Mendis left for Darwin to set up another store, later moving to Brisbane for the duration of the war. Returning to Thursday Island at war's end, he re-established his business on the same street but closer to the Post Office and, by the end of 1949, he owned jewellery stores on Thursday Island, in Darwin and Brisbane. His gem and pearl buying operations on behalf of American interests alone were 'said to run to £100,000 per annum'.[127] By the early 1950s, he was reported to own most of the Douglas Street business centre, and operated 'two cafes, one radio-shop, a jewellery-shop and pearl-shell packing houses'. The business was to pass into other hands in 1978 and, soon afterwards, the death of Donsiman Saranealis, who ran the only other jewellery store on the island, brought to an end the era of the Sri Lankan gem-trading enterprises of Thursday Island.[128]

Sri Lankans and the Law

Our corpus of legal data is inherently biased, dealing as it does with instances of law-breaking. However, it contains much incidental detail that allows us to present a more nuanced account than previously of the lives and dealings of particular individuals and their interaction with the wider community. It attests to a number of convictions for assault and petty theft by a minority of Sri Lankans, usually against their countrymen and usually as a result of personal and commercial rivalries. Disputes about money figure prominently as a source of conflict, as does drunkenness, disorderly conduct and abusive language. Yet this should not surprise us: like other Asian communities on Thursday Island, self-preservation and even survival required the Sri Lankans to cultivate reciprocal relationships with their countrymen. As members of an 'exotic' minority, the Sri Lankans were tolerated rather than accepted, despite their contribution to the local economic, social and cultural life.

Our overall impression is that the Sri Lankan community was no more and no less law-abiding than others. Certainly, it was never singled out by the authorities as particularly violent or uncontrollable (as others were on occasion). Indeed, despite its frontier reputation, Thursday Island's prisoners consisted almost entirely of men sentenced for offences such as drunkenness, obscene language and otherwise disturbing the peace, petty theft and 'continued wilful disobedience', i.e., refusal to obey an employer's 'lawful commands'. The offences committed were generally minor and intra-ethnic, the result of tensions among men living in close proximity to one another on a small island. A few involved inter-ethnic assaults, usually fights between rival groups of seamen during the monsoon lay-up times, when the water was too 'dirty' for diving and the men returned to Thursday Island to drink, gamble and visit the brothels.[129]

Criminal cases were rare. One involved three Sri Lankans, who, in October 1885, were charged with robbery with violence against an elderly Singaporean, Mehemet Ali, who 'was left a cripple, almost blind, and very feeble' and was repatriated to Singapore. The men were held in custody for three months, but discharged due to lack of substantial proof.[130] Five years later, the *Pilot* of 21 July, 1900, reported that Aboo Bacca, an Indian migrant from Simla, had been murdered by gunshot and two Sri Lankans had been arrested in connection with the murder. The men, S. K. Amadoris and Peter Kuruneru, were tried in Cooktown on 5 October, 1900, and found guilty of manslaughter. Each received a sentence of seven years' imprisonment.[131]

Four early immigrants account for a disproportionate number of court cases: Miskin, Billy Jetsunamy, Simon Silva and S. K. Amadoris. The waterman, Miskin, was often the instigator and ringleader of fights with Malays and served various prison terms between 1890 and 1903 for fighting and petty theft.[132] The seaman, Billy Jetsunamy, was charged with increasingly serious felonies between 1901 and 1903 and was said to 'all the time make row' (be very quarrelsome). On 13 July, 1901, he was found guilty of refusing to join his ship and sentenced to four weeks' imprisonment. On 21 September, he was charged with being armed with an offensive weapon with intent to commit a felony. Evidence was given that he had come to Kate Samuels' house and used abusive language. He was found guilty and sentenced to six months' imprisonment with hard labour. Two years later, on 27 October, 1903, Billy pleaded guilty to 'being armed with axe intent to commit a felony' against his countryman, waterman Punchi Singho, and served another prison term.[133] The 'excitable' Simon Silva was convicted on a number of disorderly conduct offences and for selling alcohol to 'Aboriginals'; and S. K. Amadoris was charged with several assaults before his conviction for manslaughter.

The court data confirm the existence of a social status distinction between the watermen and seamen, who committed most of the minor offences, and the small businessmen, who served as interpreters during the 1880s and 1890s. Interpreters were rarely needed after that: the jewellers who comprised the 'second wave' of Sri Lankan immigrants were not only more temperate in their behaviour but spoke and wrote good English, the medium of education in Ceylon. They were also required by law to keep their books in English for inspection by local authorities.[134]

Most of the lawsuits during the early years of the 20th century involved members of the gem-trading fraternity and sprang from interlaced personal and commercial rivalries. In February 1902, J. P. James, a jeweller living in Douglas Street, was called on to show cause why he should not be bound over to keep the peace towards K. P. Appu Singho.[135] J. P. Charles was bound over to keep the peace towards H. Wimalaratna and, on the next Friday, H. L. Simon was similarly bound over.[136] The next year, on 14 December, 1903, Charles was arrested and taken to prison. The next day he pleaded guilty to a charge of disorderly conduct in Douglas Street.[137] Four days later, Florence Charles appeared in court demanding sureties of the peace against H. L. Simon for threatening her. She gave evidence that on the night of her husband's arrest, H. L. Simon had knocked on the door of their house in Douglas Street saying that he wanted

> to take care of the jewellery as a relation of my husband. He wanted to come into the shop and said if I did not give him the jewellery he would force me to. He persisted in trying to get into the shop. He said he would force his way into the shop if I didn't let him come. I was frightened as I was alone. I was afraid he might do something to me or injure the premises.

Simon returned with four of his countrymen at 3am and tried the back door, but Florence threatened to shoot him if he came in.[138]

A little more than a year later, on 21 March, 1905, Y. B. Saranealis brought a successful action against Charles De Silva for sureties of the peace. The dispute involved two (presumably threatening) letters written by De Silva asking for the return of the pound he had either lent to Saranealis or given to him for safekeeping.[139] Some time later, on 5 October, 1906, James Charles instituted court proceedings against Saris Appu for using threatening words. He must have thought better of it, because he failed to appear in court and the case was dismissed.[140]

A more serious business lawsuit occurred soon afterwards between Y. B. Saranealis, now occupying his new premises on Douglas Street, and S. K. Amadoris, who had completed his term of imprisonment and returned to Thursday Island. The *Pilot* in its issue of Saturday 20 October, 1906, carried the following story:

> On Wednesday evening about a quarter past five, the police were called to Y. B. Saranealis' shop in Douglas Street, where a disturbance had been made, it is alleged by S. K. Amadoris, a fellow-countryman and a rival in business as pearl-dealer, etc. Amadoris was taken in charge and locked up; and on Thursday morning was brought up at the Police Court, before Mr. C. D. O'Brien, Acting Police Magistrate, charged with being armed with a lethal weapon.

Evidence was given that Amadoris had gone into Saranealis's office holding a knife behind his back and attempted to stab him. He was prevented by Johannes, a Sri Lankan in Saranealis's employ, and a carpenter named Pryke. The police were immediately summoned and charged Amadoris with being armed with an offensive weapon. According to Amadoris, he had purchased a pearl from a Japanese, which Saranealis had offered to purchase from him for £45, but, the money not being forthcoming, he came twice to the shop to ask for it. On both occasions Saranealis was out. On the third visit, when he saw Saranealis go into the shop, he followed him, asked for his money and was hit on the neck by Johannes. 'While the police were there, [Amadoris] offered Saranealis the pearl and £50 if he would withdraw the charge, but Saranealis would not; he wanted satisfaction for what happened six or seven years ago.' Amadoris made the same offer at the lockup, but it was refused. The zeal and meticulousness with which the editor of the *Pilot* reported the first day's hearing of the case were not repeated when it came to the second day's hearing. The magistrate delivered his verdict in favour of Amadoris, who was discharged forthwith.[141] Y. B. Saranealis was the target of at least two other attacks: on

7 July, 1913, he complained successfully against Charlie Saris (possibly K. N. Saris) for assault and sureties of the peace; and he was apparently stabbed in late 1918, although he laid no complaint on that occasion.

A far more serious case involved James Charles. In September 1908, he was the victim of attempted murder by Charlie Madras, either an Indian from Madras or another Sri Lankan.[142] Madras was brought before the court on 2 September, remanded and recommitted to the next Criminal Sittings of the Circuit Court to be held in Cairns on Monday 21 September, 1908.

The Sri Lankan business community, which had not yet assumed its relatively settled inter-war character, was clearly in ferment. We can only speculate as to whether these cases, which occurred during a period of economic contraction, were the result of personality clashes, personal grievances or business rivalries; whether they arose from the struggle to survive in an intensely competitive commercial environment; or indicate attempts by certain individuals to dominate the lucrative local gem trade by forcing out competitors.

Social Integration

Vital registration data, court records and gravestones on Thursday Island reveal something of the personal lives of the Sri Lankans who made the place their long-term home. Despite hysterical reports in the *Bulletin* that, on Thursday Island, 'Chinaman, Cingalese, Manila natives, aliens of all sorts soon discover resting places for themselves upon [female immigrant] British bosoms',[143] the majority of 'first wave' immigrants survived on Thursday Island without the comfort and support of legitimate family. Even those who were married were prevented by government policy from bringing their foreign-born wives with them to live in Australia and were discouraged from associating with local Indigenous women. Naturally, there were 'irregular' unions that resulted in the births of children who took either the maiden or married name of their mother. Since the natural fathers are not officially recorded in such cases, we have relied on information passed down through families who claim some measure of Sri Lankan heritage, among them: Ahmat, Barba, Cowley, Dan, Doolah, Dorante, Dubbins, Gagai, Mills, Mingo, Randolph, Sabatino, Salam, Walters and Ware (from Torres Strait); Albaniel, Bon, Conboy, Fabila, Natera, Rautoka and Silva (from PNG).

Some of the early settlers did contract legal marriages. James de Silva, who was born about 1875 in Galle, married the widow, May Scott Mosa, on 21 May, 1890, in Cooktown. May was a shopkeeper on Thursday Island at the time of her marriage and was three years older than her husband. She was born in

Samoa to a European father and possibly a Samoan mother. Interestingly, in the light of race relations at the time, the witnesses to their marriage were the Filipino-English couple, Antonio Puerte and Elizabeth Massey Spain.

De Silva's rival, Henry Louis Simon, had married Annie May Holmes in 1885. There were tensions in the marriage and some years later she complained to police that her husband had used threatening language to her. Elizabeth Massey Spain testified that he had accused his wife of sleeping with his nephew and she had been present in their house when:

Joe Warnakulasuriya as a young man, c.1950s.
Courtesy of Mahendra Mendis.

> He upset the chair his wife was sitting on and punched her over against the rail and said, go and put me in gaol again — she said I will go and get a separation. He said go. She went and as she was going he said, Come back or I will shoot you. I thought he would take her life and followed her in. She gave him a lot of papers. He tore them all up. He was growling at her all the time.[144]

Two other early arrivals who are attested as being married were the divers, Assan Ceylon, who was living with his unnamed wife in John Street in 1900, and Thomas Morris, who married an Aboriginal woman on Thursday Island in 1891 — the only marriage of a Sri Lankan recorded on Thursday Island before Federation.

Despite cultural differences, marriages to European or 'half-caste' Australian-born women conferred personal, social and commercial benefits, and others besides James de Silva, Henry Louis Simon and Thomas Morris made such marriages.[145] James Charles (Amadoris), the jeweller living in Douglas Street, had a European wife, Florence Elizabeth Charles, who, like Annie May Simon, helped in her husband's business and was also subject to abuse.[146] On 20 January, 1905, Florence took her husband to court for using threatening language.[147]

The later marriages between Y. B. Saranealis and English-born Alice Stewart, and between H. L. Mowlis and the young widow, Clara Fabian Santos, the locally born daughter of a Filipino father and Torres Strait Islander mother, appear to have been less volatile. Y. B. Saranealis was born about 1876 in Galle to Yanandaygoda Buddalegay Donsiman and Beuter Anohamy.[148] The young Saranealis arrived on Thursday Island aged about 20 and rapidly immersed himself in mainstream community life. On 30 October, 1897, the *Pilot*, reporting on forthcoming festivities in honour of the Prince of Wales' birthday on 9 November, mentioned that the Wybenia Cycle Club had organised a series of cycle races. Saranealis had entered five races in all and was placed fairly high up on the handicap list. When the races were run, he was able to secure third place in one race. The newspaper also revealed that he was a contributor to the Thursday Island Hospital.

Saranealis married Alice Stewart on 24 September, 1900, on Thursday Island. Alice was a year older, born in London of Scottish descent. Saranealis was naturalised on 26 March, 1902, soon after the birth of his first child.[149] He is said to have been mysteriously stabbed one night in about 1918, although nobody was charged with the assault.[150] Weakened by the wound, he died shortly afterwards during the influenza epidemic on Thursday Island on 30 January, 1919. Alice died on 3 January, 1955. They lie in the same grave along with four of their six children, three boys and three girls, all born on Thursday Island.[151]

Of the Saranealis boys, it was Eddie who was the best known. Despite his lack of formal qualifications, Y. B. Saranealis had successfully practised dentistry from at least 1900, having studied by correspondence course, and, after his death, Eddie continued to practice from the new premises on Douglas Street, not far from the Metropole Hotel.[152] He is said to have treated the Governor of Queensland, Sir Leslie Wilson, during his visit in October 1933. When the Queensland Home Secretary passed a new act enabling practising but unqualified practitioners to sit for a qualifying examination, Eddie Saranealis left Thursday Island for the first time in his life for Brisbane, where he 'passed the examination with flying colours, and returned to Thursday Island a diplomaed dentist'.[153] According to Y. B. Saranealis's grandson, the brothers, despite their contributions to the commercial and cultural life of the island, 'suffered from a great deal of racial prejudice' and, with the exception of Buddy, became recluses. All the children were 'gifted artists and musicians', the daughters were also talented painters, and Ruby 'made the most exquisite carvings from mother-of-pearl and tortoise shell using what I must assume are traditional Sinhalese handcraft methods'.[154] Some of her pieces are held in private collections throughout Australia.

Hikkadawa Leana Mowlis, another immigrant from Galle, was born about 1886, the son of a merchant, Hikkadawa Leana Singho Appu, and his wife, Gegarabamak Balo Hanney. Mowlis, a man of recognised probity, became a naturalised Australian on 19 April, 1911.[155] Mowlis married the widow, Clara Fabian Santos, on 2 June, 1915, on Thursday Island after the murder of her first husband and an unwittingly bigamous second marriage. Clara and Mowlis began living together 'some time' before their marriage, possibly about the time of his naturalisation, which was also the time of the discovery of the bigamous marriage. The legal difficulties were resolved after advice from the Queensland Crown Solicitor. Mowlis, wrote the Protector of Aboriginals on Thursday Island, was in business there 'as a jeweller and pearl dealer' and had 'a good reputation'.[156] The couple had no children and Clara died on 28 June, 1917, at Thursday Island. Mowlis continued to advertise his services as a pearl buyer, watchmaker and jeweller until 1923, after which he disappears from the Thursday Island records.[157]

Another family that figures prominently in the Thursday Island cemetery is the Warnakulasuriya/Ahmat family. Punchi Appu (Peter) Warnakulasuriya was born in Tangalla, Ceylon, in 1888 and died on 15 April, 1981. He was a relative of Punchi Hewa Mendis, who brought him to Thursday Island under indenture 'in the early part of 1918'. Warnakulasuriya was educated at St Thomas's College, Mt Lavinia (between Colombo and Galle), and had previously lived in Burma and Singapore. He became a highly proficient pearl cleaner and spent the rest of his long life on Thursday Island.[158] Warnakulasuriya reputedly fathered six children by Amcia Usop Ahmat, the Thursday Island-born daughter of a Muslim fisherman from Borneo and his Cape York Aboriginal wife.[159] After Ahmat's death from tuberculosis, Peter and Amcia lived together, effectively regularising their long-lasting union.[160] Their second son, Joseph (Joe), born on 12 February, 1927, was legally adopted and took his father's name. According to Nissanka Mendis, son of Punchi Hewa Mendis, his father took Joe to Sri Lanka at the age of seven and educated him at Mahinda College, Galle, hoping that he would become a Buddhist monk. However, he returned to Thursday Island in 1949. He died of a heart attack on 4 October, 1973, while closing up Mendis's shop one afternoon, and he is buried on Thursday Island.[161]

Warnakulasuriya's sponsor, patron and relative was Punchi Hewa Mendis, who was born on 12 September, 1883, in Galle and arrived on Thursday Island on 23 October, 1898, on the S.S. *Duke of Westminster*. He died there on 8 September, 1965. In 1915, he married Mercy De Silva, a niece of Singapore's famed jeweller and sponsor of jewellers, Mudaliyar B. P. De Silva. Under the immigration restrictions of the time, he was not permitted to bring his wife to Australia but visited her every few years and their union produced two sons.[162] Extremely respected, he and later his family held an ambiguous position in the racial hierarchy of Thursday Island (as did the families of mixed Sri Lankan heritage). His business acumen, personal charm and evident integrity led to social acceptance by a wide cross-section of the community; he also privately assisted other local businessmen in adversity, such as Chinese merchant Tsing See Kee, from whom he had purchased his shop on Douglas Street and to whom he lent money on the strength of their long relationship and a handshake.[163] The family counted a range of Thursday Island residents among their friends: these included not only members of the European and Coloured business elite, but the families of the old 'Malays', whom Mendis had met soon after his arrival, such as the Ahmats, Bindorahos, Jias and Lobans. Some of these were among the more than 200 guests who attended Amara Mendis's 76th birthday celebration in Brisbane in March 2004.

What emerges from the biographies of these men, apart from their entrepreneurial success, is the manner of their 'recruitment' to Thursday Island — being sponsored by extended family members and sponsoring others in turn — their continued adherence to Buddhist principles and practice, sometimes turbulent commercial partnerships with countrymen, and cultivation of a wide-ranging network of personal and business connections throughout Australia and Asia. People of all ethnic backgrounds and religious affiliations were included among their Thursday Island friends. Indeed, crucial to their success was the extent to which they gained the support of non-Sri Lankan residents of Thursday Island. James De Silva's sureties when he took out his hawker's licence were the European sheller, Henry Dubbins, and Moyden, a Muslim Indian waterman; and the witnesses to his marriage were a Filipino-English couple, Antonio Puerte Spain and Elizabeth Massey. Mowlis acquired the business and stock of the prominent Filipino businessman, Heriberto Zarcal; and his marriage witnesses were Thomas Toulasik, a Timorese pearl shell cleaner and member of the Dutch Reformed Church, and Johanna Mayor, the Catholic daughter of a Filipino diver and Torres Strait Islander mother. Saranealis named his second son for Zarcal, who, like him, had married a European wife. Mendis owed his business beginnings to the confidence placed in him by English-born Alexander Corran, the editor of the *Pilot*, who treated him like a son; the local European bank manager; and the Chinese businessman, See Kee.

The 'second wave' of Sri Lankan immigrants, who came with the intention of participating in the gem trade, put down deeper roots on Thursday Island than their predecessors. However, they immigrated during a period of intense racism and suffered its emotional consequences. Their children, who were born in Australia to mothers of Indigenous descent, were generally accepted by their mothers' community. The ethnic status of those born locally to European mothers was more problematical: they, in fact, belonged neither to the White nor local 'Coloured' communities. While technically 'Coloured', i.e., not of entirely northern European origin, their parents were prominent, wealthy and well-educated businesspeople, spoke excellent English, were British subjects, entertained a wide range of local people in their homes, provided essential services to the whole community without distinction as to ethnic origin, and their behaviour and aspirations were essentially those of the surrounding Europeans. However, dominant European racial attitudes towards the children of Sri Lankan-European descent were paradoxical, as indicated by the Acting Principal of the State School (not quite correctly) just before the outbreak of the Pacific War:

> The races represented on the Island, in addition to Europeans, are: Chinese, Japanese, Torres Strait islanders and mainland Aboriginals … In addition there are a couple of families, white predominating, containing Southern European or Cingalese blood. These live as white people and are accepted in white society …[164]

Cultural Contribution

Business was the main arena in which Sri Lankans interacted with and were known to the Thursday Island community —

> In the distilled sunlight of the streets, with their avenues of almond and weeping fig and light green cocoanuts, are the shaded shops of Cingalese jewellers and Japanese and Chinese merchants selling all that is quaint and delightful, from deftly carved trifles of Australian pearl and tortoiseshell to dugong steak and long soup[165]

— but they also shared their cultural heritage in the spheres of religion, sport, music, dance and philanthropy. Even before the construction of the Buddhist temple, between 10 and 12 devout Sri Lankan Buddhists came to Alis Appu's house to pray together on the verandah almost every evening. They called the house a 'temple', since it served that function, but the court insisted that 'temple' be crossed out and 'house' inserted. Evidence was taken in court from Alis Appu in 1890 that 'every day except when steamer in', he prayed in the temple between 6 and 7.30pm. Saris, too, came regularly to pray. Alis Appu described the manner of their devotion as follows:

We sit down when we pray. We no use book at that time. All pray. All
people say prayer together. There was not lamp in the room. Every body
was outside in the verandah. Nobody get up before the finish.[166]

The prewar Buddhist temple was located about four doors down from the
Post Office at the end of Douglas Street and near the Chinese quarter. A sacred
tree was planted nearby.[167] A Buddhist monk was brought from Sri Lanka to
inaugurate the temple and it was visited from time to time by a Sri Lankan
priest.[168] Every full moon there was a procession with lighted candles, Chinese
lanterns, flags and a drummer; and *Wesak*, the most significant Sri Lankan
Buddhist festival, was celebrated annually with a long procession, 'fervour and
festivity'.[169] Sri Lankans may have planted the cluster of vivid pink frangipani
trees near the entrance to the Church of England Quetta Memorial Cathedral
in memory of their compatriots who died in the wreck of the S. S. *Quetta*.[170] A
visitor to Thursday Island remarked that this particular variety of frangipani 'is
found in profusion in Ceylon and is known as the "temple flower". When we
visited any of the rock temples in that country we saw the Singalese placing the
vivid blossoms before the shrine of Buddha.'[171]

Buddhism, which was symbolised by the monthly processions and
construction of the temple, was not the only major projection of Sri Lankan
culture on Thursday Island. Moreover, while the majority of the Sri Lankans
were Buddhist, some were Muslim and there were Buddhists among the
Japanese.[172] Despite their vigorous religious and cultural independence,
revealed by the absence on gravestones of any Christian associations,[173]
members of the community made many contributions to civic life in their
adopted home. Of particular importance was their contribution through
performance — in sport, music and dance — to the vibrant, syncretic
'Coloured' culture that was evolving at the time. As Neuenfeldt points out
(Chapter 11, this volume), the Asian seamen 'brought their musicianship,
music and performance cultures with them' to Torres Strait, the Sri Lankans
contributing their drums and drumming style to the dance band interpretations
of popular music.

On 18 May, 1901, the *Pilot* carried a review of a brilliant display of Sri
Lankan musical and literary culture at the local School of Arts. Members of the
community pooled their resources to present two performances of *Prince Ramlan
and Princess Pewlina*, a musical drama based on a traditional story, in English and
Sinhalese. The enthusiastic reviewer commented that 'the whole of the
performers did their work with credit to themselves greater than could in many
other instances be accorded to amateurs, or some professionals'. This was not
the only performance given by the community during its heyday. In early 1902,

some Sri Lankans, who were upset by the noise made during rehearsals for a play and concert at J. P. James's house on Victoria Parade, took the offenders to court. Charles Mendis, who was not one of the performers, told the magistrate: 'They make a great noise every night getting ready for a play.' Those complained of were members of the Sinhalese Opera Club and, at the end of January 1902, they performed a series of operas at the School of Arts, one of which was *Prince Manora and Princess Emlin*. The *Pilot* of 1 February, 1902, commented on the 'curiously oriental' character of the operas and on the fact that few Europeans attended. The Sri Lankans were great supporters of the local hospital and contributed to various charitable funds:[174] on this occasion, the club donated one evening's takings of £1.15 to the hospital.[175]

The 'Coloured' culture of music and dance, to which each Thursday Island Asian community contributed, flowered most brilliantly during the inter-war years. Various commentators remarked on its vitality and richness, including the novelist, Ernestine Hill, who wrote favourably of the Sri Lankan contribution during her 1933 visit:

> The impression that all is well would be heightened by listening to the Thursday Island Town Band, polychromatic, but full of harmony and vigour, playing upon the jetty on Sunday evenings. Its members, in dapper uniform, are under the baton of a half-caste Cingalese conductor, and the strains of 'Dixie' and other melodies are wafted across the Straits ...[176]

The conductor was probably Edward Saranealis, who was also an excellent violinist and composer of violin music.[177] He and his brother Donsiman belonged to the town band,[178] which sometimes accompanied the silent films shown at the local cinema,[179] and both contributed to the Thursday Island Silver Jubilee Celebration of King George V in 1935. On that occasion, at the height of prewar racism, all the officials named were Europeans and only two items were performed by non-Whites: Item 1, the National Anthem, performed by 'Mrs Sullivan and Mr E[dward] Saranealis'; and Item 13, 'a cornet solo entitled *True Love Polka* performed by Mr D[onsiman] H[eriberto] Saranealis, with piano accompaniment by Mrs Sullivan'.[180]

Conclusion

Individual Sri Lankans ('Cingalese') joined other foreign seamen in the 1870s Torres Strait pearl rush but a distinctive Sri Lankan community came into existence only after 1882 with the arrival on Thursday Island of 25 indentured seamen. Some became the first watermen who, before the construction of the jetties in 1893, provided a crucial service to the regional economy by ferrying passengers and cargo to and from visiting ships. The shift of most commercial activity to the township from the mid-1880s led to the establishment of a 'Cingalese quarter' and, for most of its 60-year history, the Sri Lankan community was associated with that section of Thursday Island. The once flourishing community declined precipitously soon after Federation with the departure of most of its members amid widespread prejudice against Asians, fears for what the future might hold and the collapse of the pearling industry.

While their exact numbers are unknown, the Sri Lankans remained a salient group until the outbreak of World War II, distinctive enough to be singled out by contemporary observers. Some of the early immigrants became commercial fishermen and owners of boats for hire; others took out hawkers' licences to sell jewellery and other curios made from tortoise shell, pearl shell and pearls to tourists and visitors. By the early 1900s, the original watermen, known for their quarrelsome behaviour, had declined in actual numbers and as a proportion of the general population, and had been replaced by a 'second wave' of immigrants. More sedate than their predecessors, these small-shopkeepers and businessmen occupied a specialised and profitable niche in the gem trade as cleaners, polishers, manufacturers, valuers and dealers in pearls, pearl shell and tortoise shell. As Swan remarks, 'These middlemen were among the best rewarded although not among the more colourful of the pearling hierarchy.'[181]

For more than six decades, the Sri Lankan community made significant contributions to the economic, religious, social and cultural life of Thursday Island. All of them have left, the Mendis and Saranealis families being the last to end their association. Little physical trace of their presence remains, but the prominent business families are still remembered. Not only did they provide goods and services not available elsewhere, but, through their acts of generosity and willingness to share their heritage with the entire community, they formed enduring relationships with their fellow residents, regardless of ethnic origin or religious affiliation.

Notes

1   This is a revised and expanded version of Chapter Eight of Sparkes, S. J., 1988, *Sri Lankan Migrants in Queensland in the Nineteenth Century*, Brisbane. pp. 75–85. Additional information was provided by the second author from archival and vital registration data and the chapter also draws on Swan, B., 'Sinhalese emigration to Queensland in the nineteenth century: a note', *Journal of the Royal Australian Historical Society*, Vol. 67, No. 1. pp. 55–63. Also Weerasooria, W. S. 1988. *Links Between Sri Lanka and Australia: a book about the Sri Lankans (Ceylonese) in Australia*. Colombo: Government Press. Pinnawala, S. 1988. 'Sri Lankans.' In James Jupp (ed.), *The Australian People: an encyclopedia of the nation, its people and their origins*, North Ryde: Angus and Robertson. pp. 805–8. Sparkes, S. J. 2001. 'Sri Lankans.' In M. Brandle (ed.), *Multicultural Queensland 2001*, Brisbane: Multicultural Affairs Queensland. pp. 330–2.
     Court records, which provide most of the new data, generally specify an individual's Sri Lankan origin and are therefore more accurate regarding origin than the mainland sources examined by Sparkes (*Sri*

Lankan Migrants in Queensland in the Nineteenth Century, p. 86), who found that death records were compromised by spelling errors and errors of ethnic identification. Difficulties also arise because of the widespread use of the omnibus term 'Malay' for 'men from all over the Malay Archipelago, from Ceylon and parts of India' (Ellis, A. F. 1936. *Adventuring in Coral Seas*. Sydney: Angus and Robertson. p. 76.), and the different categorisation procedures employed by official agencies. For example, Queensland departure statistics for 'Coloured Persons from the Commonwealth' conflate 'Cingalese and Hindoos' as a single category. 'Departures of Coloured Persons from the Commonwealth', NAA/CRS/A/38, National Archives of Australia (hereafter NAA).

We wish to express our special gratitude to Amara and Mahendra Mendis for their contribution to this chapter and gratefully acknowledge the assistance of Joan Humphreys, of the Sydney Burns Philp Archives; Jeremy Hodes, Siripala Mendis, Yuriko Nagata, Rodney Sullivan, Colin Sheehan and Michael Stubbins, former Registrar of the Magistrates Court, Thursday Island.

2   The term 'Cingalese' is not entirely synonymous with the present-day form of the word 'Sinhalese', since a small number of the immigrants may have been Tamils or Ceylon Moors.

3   Ceylon gained its independence from Great Britain in 1948 and became Sri Lanka in 1972.

4   'Punchi Hewa Mendis to Amara Mendis.' Amara Mendis, pers. comm., 20 February, 2004.

5   Amara Mendis, pers. comm., 21 March, 2004.

6   'H. M. Chester, Police Magistrate, Thursday Island, to Colonial Secretary, Brisbane, 4 June 1879.' COL/A284/3725, Queensland State Archives (hereafter QSA).

7   'Inquiry into death of Cypriano Trinidad held 3 April 1901.' JUS/N295/01/183, QSA.

8   Letter from James Burns to the Colonial Secretary in Ceylon, dated 19 June, 1882, seeking approval for the recruitment of 'Cingalese', reproduced in Sparkes, S. J., *Sri Lankan Migrants in Queensland in the Nineteenth Century*, pp. 3–4.

9   Eva Mingo Peacock, granddaughter of Balo and the Danish pearl-sheller, Thomas Randolph, pers. comm., 10 August, 2000.

10   Bombay was the father of Rosie, who married Nicholas Albaniel, a Filipino catechist. Both became early Catholic missionaries in PNG (Jeanette Fabila, great-granddaughter of Rosie Albaniel, pers. comm., 1 April, 2004). One branch of the family believes he may have been Sri Lankan.

11   Coppinger, R. W. 1883. *Cruise of the 'Alert': four years in the Patagonian, Polynesian, and Mascarene waters (1878–1882)*. London: Swan Sonnenschein. p. 194.

12   Swan, B., 'Sinhalese emigration to Queensland in the nineteenth century', p. 55.

13   For the full text of the contract, signed by the men before J. D. Mason, Police Magistrate, in Galle on 12 June, 1882, see Sparkes, S. J., *Sri Lankan Migrants in Queensland in the Nineteenth Century*, pp. 75–6.

14   Weerasooria, W. S., *Links Between Sri Lanka and Australia*, p. 139.

15   'Governor of Ceylon to the Secretary of State for the Colonies in London, despatch dated 12 August 1882'; 'H. M. Chester, Police Magistrate, Thursday Island, to Colonial Secretary, Brisbane, 31 August 1882', COL A/346/4742, QSA.

16   'H. M. Chester, Police Magistrate, Thursday Island, to Colonial Secretary, Brisbane, 5 September 1882.' COL A/346, QSA.

17   See, for example, the letter from 'Acting Secretary, Land Administration Board, to Under Secretary, Department of Health and Home Affairs, Brisbane', dated 7 July, 1937, regarding the creation of the Hammond Island reserve. TR1794 Box 142 SL6614, QSA.

18   'T. De Hoghton, Lieutenant-Commanding HMS *Beagle*, to Colonial Secretary, Brisbane, 22 September 1879, Reporting on the Pearl-shell Fisheries of Torres Straits.' *Queensland Votes and Proceedings* (hereafter *QVP*), 1880, p. 1163.

19   'Thomas McNulty, Thursday Island, to Attorney-General, 13 October 1883.' COL/A370/5183, QSA.

20   '[T]he original policy discouraged pearl shellers to [sic] settle there. So at first the population did not increase rapidly. There was no appreciable increase until 1885, which coincided with the

arrival of the Hon. John Douglas … as Government Resident.' Lock, A. C. C. 1955. *Destination Barrier Reef*. Melbourne: Georgian House. p. 75.

21   Thursday Island census c.1885, A/18963, QSA.

22   'Report from John Douglas, Thursday Island, 1 July 1886.' COL/A457/1583, QSA.

23   'Thursday Island: Return of population collected by police on 1st April 1901' and again 'on March 1st 1902', *Fort Record Book, Green Hill, Thursday Island, 1899–1912*, AWM 1/12/2. Canberra: Australian War Memorial Library.

24   'Return of population of Thursday Island and the Prince of Wales group of islands on the 24th day of April 1918.' *Fort Record Book, Green Hill, Thursday Island, 1898–1927*, AWM 1/12/1. Canberra: Australian War Memorial Library.

25   The correct name is 'Goods Island' but, probably because of a misreading of the final 's' as an 'e', it has been called 'Goode Island' since at least the 1880s. The island was named by Matthew Flinders in November 1802 for the botanical gardener, Peter Good, who accompanied him on his surveying mission. Good, Peter. 1981. *The Journal of Peter Good: gardener on Matthew Flinders voyage to Terra Australia 1801–03*. London: British Museum (Natural History). p. 28.

26   At least one Sri Lankan, Jimmy Cook, was a patient of the lazaret. He was the cook on a station west of Townsville and was admitted on 11 August, 1894. 'Report of the Medical Officer of the Lazaret, Friday Island, 31 August 1898.' QVP (4), p. 633.

27   *Torres News*, No. 32, 19 August, 1986.

28   The latter can be traced through advertisements in the local newspaper, *The Torres Straits Pilot and New Guinea Gazette* (hereafter the *Pilot*), which first appeared on 2 January, 1888, and entries in *Pugh's Almanac and General Directory* (hereafter *Pugh's Almanac*), *Queensland Post Office Directory* (hereafter *Post Office*) and *Willmett's North Queensland Almanac Directory*.

29   The variant spellings and sometimes illegible handwriting of court records, the similarity of names and the absence of oral evidence make unique identification impossible except in a few cases. An additional problem concerns the Anglicised variants of names: James Charles Amadoris, for example, adopted James Charles as his business name; Gostene Waduga Andris also signed George William Andris. We have regularised the spellings for consistency: thus, Amadoris for Amadorus, Amodoris; Harmanis for Armenis, Hermanes, Hermanus, Hermonious; Siyadoris for Sedoris, Sedorus, Seedoris, Sidorus, etc. Despite the appellation of 'Cingalese' for their owners, some names are not recognisably Sri Lankan, e.g., Danolis, Didwan, Jetsunamy and its variants, Jetuan, Jetuharry, Jetsuany, Jetsunany.

30   Probably Simon Silva from Galle, who is said to have been responsible for establishing the Buddhist temple on Thursday Island.

31   'Edward Morey vs Ten Singalese for breach of agreement, 8–9 January 1901.' CPS13D/P8, QSA.

32   According to Pinnawala ('Sri Lankans', p. 805), this was in contrast with the majority of recent Sri Lankan immigrants to Australia, who have been Christians.

33   They may have been the descendants of Indonesians brought to Ceylon by the Dutch to man their garrisons.

34   Most of the brawls started after drinking bouts in the local hotels and a minority of the men became alcoholics. One was the fisherman, S. K. Simon, who 'gets drunk every day'. 'H. L. Simon vs S. K. Simon for using threatening language to one H. L. Simon, 17 July 1903.' CPS13D/P11, QSA.

35   It would seem that Henry Reynolds' reference to 'Cingalese' women (*North of Capricorn: the untold story of Australia's north*. 2003. Crows Nest, NSW: Allen and Unwin. p. 89) is not supported by the cited source.

36   '[T]he management of the boats, the locality of the fishing, the times of fishing, besides the actual gathering of the shell, is entirely left to the divers.' 'T. De Hoghton, Lieutenant-Commanding HMS *Beagle*, to Colonial Secretary, Brisbane, 22 September 1879: Reporting on the Pearl-shell Fisheries of Torres Straits.' QVP, 1880.

37   'G. H. Bennett (Inspector of Pearlshell Fisheries) vs Assan Ceylon for permitting an unlicensed person to be employed as diver, 12 April 1901.' CPS13D/P9, QSA.

38 'H. L. Simon vs S. K. Simon for using threatening language to one H.L. Simon, 17 July 1903.' CPS13D/P11, QSA.

39 'Frank Vassou vs John Tolman for claim wages, 21 and 23 July 1890.' CPS 13D/P3, QSA.

40 *Somerset Register of Marriages*, 31 January, 1891.

41 'Martin vs Johnny Bombay for assault, 18 and 24 February 1885.' CPS13D/P1, QSA. Some of Bombay's descendants claim he was Sri Lankan but there is no direct proof of his origins. He may have died in February 1889 in Cygnet Bay, King Sound, Western Australia. Photograph of death notice taken by Val Burton at Cygnet Bay, WA, in Malay/Koepanger vertical file, Broome Historical Society, Broome, WA.

42 Swan, B., 'Sinhalese emigration to Queensland in the nineteenth century', p. 59.

43 'List of male inhabitants of Thursday Island having had military service and/or possessing service rifles', [n.d. c.1914], *Fort Record Book, Green Hill, Thursday Island, 1898–1927*, AWM 1/12/1. Canberra: Australian War Memorial Library.

44 Simon is thought to have died in the early 1960s, aged in his 90s. There is a photograph of him in Burchill, E. 1972. *Thursday Island Nurse*. Adelaide: Rigby. opp. p. 23., with the caption: 'Photo of Simon, reputedly the oldest man on Thursday Island and probably of the whole Torres Straits. He is a permanent resident of the General Hospital.'

45 Amara and Mahendra Mendis, pers. comm., 20 February, 2004.

46 'Annual Return of Curator of Intestate Estates, 1 January 1891–31 December 1891.' *QVP*, 1892.

47 'Annual Return of Curator of Intestate Estates, 1 January 1900–31 December 1900.' *QVP*, 1901.

48 'Annual Return of Curator of Intestate Estates, 1 July 1913–31 December 1913.' *QVP*, 1914.

49 *Somerset Register of Deaths*, 31 July, 1908.

50 They were Don Singho Appu (John Ceylon), James De Silva and P. Singho (James Cingalese). 'Police vs Singho Appu for unsound mind, 11 April 1892', CPS13D/P5; 'Police vs John Ceylon for protection, 12 April 1892', CPS13D/P5; 'James de Silva on suspicion of being of unsound mind, remanded, 20 September 1900', CPS13D/P8; 'James De Silva on remand charged with lunacy, 11 October 1900', CPS13D/P8; 'James Cingalese for being of unsound mind, 22 February 1905', CPS13D/P12, QSA. Arthur Graham, of Sri Lankan and European heritage, who was living in the South Sea Home in April 1915, was said to be 'half cracked'. *Notes of the Diocese of Carpentaria*, April 1915, back of p. 41, OM.AV/113/1, John Oxley Library.

51 'Police vs Andrew Johnston, 1 August 1885', CPS13D/P1; 'Police vs Benjamin Raymondo, 30 June 1888', CPS13D/P2, QSA.

52 'Police vs Baboon [S. K. Babunappu], 7 November 1889', CPS13D/P2; 'Police vs Walady, 9 December 1889', CPS 13D/P3; 'Police vs Thomas, 28 January 1891', CPS 13D/P4, QSA.

53 'Valuation by E. L. Brown, Valuer, for the Division of Torres, of the ratable properties in the Division of Torres, 22 April 1886.' COL/077, QSA.

54 Jones, E. 1921. *Florence Buchanan: the little Deaconess of the South Seas*. Sydney: Australian Board of Missions. p. 18. Since Geil does not list it with the other places of worship on the island, we infer that it was built after his visit in 1901. Geil, W. E. 1902. *Ocean and Isle*. Melbourne: Pater. p. 199.

55 'Police vs Tommy Japanese for disorderly conduct on Victoria Parade, 26 December 1888.' CPS13D/P2, QSA.

56 At various times the houses were rented by Amadoris, Allis Appu, Singho Babu, Charles Mendis, H. L. Simon and his wife, and S. K. Simon. 'Police vs Odiris for drunk and disorderly, 8 and 9 December 1891.' CPS 13D/P4, QSA.

57 The boatman, Amadoris, took over from Allis Appu the tenancy of the house situated on Section 5/Allotment 2 in the township of Port Kennedy, which the latter had occupied before his death in 1891. He in turn shared the house with the billiard-marker, Andris, and possibly other countrymen and all paid rent to Herbert Bowden, manager for Burns Philp & Co. The house, along with two others, fronted on to a passage which led from Douglas Street to Victoria Parade. 'Police vs Odiris on bail for disorderly conduct in Douglas Street, 8 December 1891.' CPS 13D/P4, QSA. There appears to have been a particularly close association between the Sri Lankans and Burns Philp & Co.: Burns organised the first mass indenture in 1882; the firm employed mainly

Sri Lankan watermen on its hulk, *Star of Peace*; and it also rented its property for use as the 'Cingalese' boarding house, billiard room and store.

58 'Police vs Miskin for disorderly conduct in Victoria Parade, 7 January 1890.' CPS 13D/P3, QSA. Miskin was arrested for fighting with a Malay before a crowd of about 70 men, threatening 'a general engagement between the Cingalese and the Malays'.

59 'Police vs Kicumato for assaulting one Saris Appu, 21 July 1902.' CPS13D/P10, QSA.

60 'Police vs Miskin and Woo Lin for disorderly conduct, 7 January 1890.' CPS 13D/P3, QSA.

61 'Abdula alias Siyadoris on warrant charged with assaulting one Hop Sing, 12 January 1899.' CPS13D/P7, QSA.

62 'Police vs William Sam Hee for keeping a common gaming house, 18 October 1901.' CPS13D/P9, QSA.

63 Simpson, C. 1952. *Come Away, Pearler*. Sydney: Angus and Robertson. pp. 14–15.

64 See Evans, R., K. Saunders and K. Cronin. 1975. *Exclusion, Exploitation and Extermination: race relations in colonial Queensland*. Sydney: Australia and New Zealand Book Co. pp. 2–4.

65 Sedin was found guilty and sentenced to death in Normanton on 15 October, 1888.

66 'Viator', 'The Gulf country'. *Cummins & Campbell's Monthly Magazine*, Vol. 4, No. 44 (December 1930). pp. 73, 75.

67 Petition from owners and managers of pearl-shelling stations in Torres Strait, October 1883, attached to letter from 'H. M. Chester, Thursday Island, to Colonial Secretary, Brisbane', COL/370/5183, QSA.

68 Report of a meeting of the Torres Straits Pearl Shellers Mutual Association, held 19 December, 1884, and sent to Colonial Treasurer by T. O. Stanton, Hon. Secretary, 29 January 1885, TRE/A30/648, QSA.

69 Eykyn, T. 1896. *Parts of the Pacific*. London: Swan Sonnenschein. p. 96.

70 Ward, A. *The Miracle of Mapoon*. London: Partridge. p. 65.

71 Rowan, E. 1991. *The Flower Hunter: the adventures, in northern Australia and New Zealand, of flower painter Ellis Rowan*. North Ryde: Collins Angus and Robertson. p. 109.

72 *Pilot*, 23 and 30 September, 1899, cited in Reynolds, H., *North of Capricorn*, p. 89.

73 Quoted in Geil, W. E., *Ocean and Isle*, p. 192.

74 'Bastian vs Mendis for sureties of the peace, 22 November 1899.' CPS13D/P8, QSA.

75 *Post Office*, 1889, 1892, 1892–93, 1893, 1895–96, 1897–99.

76 *Willmett's North Queensland Almanac Directory for 1898*, Willmett, 1898.

77 *Post Office*, 1892, 1893, 1895–96, 1897–99.

78 'K. P. Appu Singho vs J. P. James for sureties of the peace, 24 January 1902.' CPS13D/P10, QSA.

79 At that time, Thursday Island lay on the main sea route between Australia and the Far East as well as Europe and was an important port of call. By 1886, it was visited regularly by ocean steamers of the British India Co., Eastern and Australian Steamship Co., China Steamship Navigation Co. and Gibb, Livingstone and Co.; and, by the turn of the century, the Eastern and Australian Steamship Co., China Navigation Co., Australasian United Steam Navigation Co., Japan Mail Steamship Co. (Nippon Yusen Kaisha) and Queensland Line. *Pugh's Almanac*, 1886, p. 511. *Pilot*, 6 January, 1900.

80 'Police vs Humphrey Davy Mills for assaulting one Henry Dubbins in the bar of the Thursday Island Hotel on 10 July 1888, 12 July 1888.' CPS13D/P2. 'Application of H. L. James Appu de Silva for a Hawkers Licence, sureties Henry Dubbins, Thursday Island, and Moyden, Thursday Island, 27 November 1888.' PS13D/P2, QSA.

81 *Post Office*, 1890.

82 'James De Silva vs George Machal for sureties of the peace, 28 August 1891.' CPS 13D/P4, QSA. De Silva is listed as waterman and storekeeper from 1890–99 in *Post Office*, 1890, 1891, 1892, 1893, 1895–96, 1897–99.

83 'J. Silva vs William Price for refusing to proceed to sea in lugger *Mobiag*, 20 July 1892.' CPS13D/P5, QSA.

84 'Punchi Singho vs Samuel for assault, 10 January 1895.' CPS13D/P6, QSA.

85 'Police vs James De Silva for disorderly conduct, 15 September 1900.' CPS13D/P8, QSA.

86 'James De Silva on remand charged with lunacy, 11 October 1900.' CPS13D/P8, QSA.

87 'Arthur Clarence Filewood vs Jimmy De Silva for trespass under the *Enclosed Land Act*, 11 and 18 July 1927, 15 August 1927.' QS787/1/3, QSA.

88 'Police vs Simon for indecent language in the vicinity of persons passing in Milman Street, 21 September 1885.' CPS13D/P1, QSA.

89 'Annie Simon vs James De Silva for sureties of the peace, 14 May 1888.' CPS13D/P2, QSA.

90 'Application of Henry L. Simon for a Billiard Licence, one table for premises situated at Victoria Parade, Thursday Island, 26 November 1888', CPS13D/P2; 'Henry L. Simon for renewal of Billiard Licence, one table, Billiard Room, Victoria Parade, Thursday Island, 3 April 1889', CPS13D/P2; 'Application of James De Silva of Victoria Parade, Thursday Island, for a Billiard Licence for one table, 1 February 1889', CPS 13D/P2; 'Application by James De Silva for Billiard Licence, Victoria Parade, 2 April 1891', CPS 13D/P4; 'Application by James De Silva for renewal of Billiard Licence, one table, 6 April 1892', CPS13D/P5, QSA; *Post Office*, 1891, 1892, 1893, 1895–96.

91 *Post Office*, 1889, 1892–93. The partnership may have lasted five years and appears to have been the earliest of the gem trade enterprises.

92 'Application for Hawker's Licence by H. L. Simon granted, 29 December 1891', CPS 13D/P4; 'Application for Pawnbroker's Licence by Henry L. Simon of Victoria Parade, 24 March 1892', CPS13D/P5, QSA; *Post Office*, 1893, 1895–96.

93 *Pugh's Almanac*, 1893, p. 166; 1894, p. 162.

94 'Police vs William Sam Hee for keeping a common gaming house, 18 October 1901.' CPS13D/P9, QSA.

95 'H. L. Simon vs S. K. Simon for using threatening language to one H. L. Simon, 17 July 1903.' CPS13D/P11, QSA.

96 'Ah Wang vs O. McLaverty, 16 September 1891', CPS 13D/P4; 'Application for Hawker's Licence by H. L. Simon granted, 29 December 1891', CPS 13D/P4. Another licensed hawker was Thomas Weerasooria, who gave evidence in 'Police vs Ah Bow and Tommy Low Chong for unlawfully conducting an unlawful game in a common gaming house, 24 October 1901', CPS13D/P9, QSA. While there was a considerable amount of money to be made from selling jewellery and curios to tourists, the penalty for hawking without a licence was severe. In 1888, William De Silva was convicted of this offence and fined £2 with 3/6 costs, in default one week's imprisonment. 'William De Silva for hawking without a licence, 14 November 1888.' CPS 13D/S1, QSA.

97 Boothby, G. 1894. *On the Wallaby or Through the East and Across Australia*. London: Longmans. p. 110.

98 Ibid., pp. 114–15.

99 'Matho vs Amadoris for common assault, 14 April 1899', CPS13D/P7; 'Upon Y. B. Saranealis swearing on information against Simba K. Amadoris for threatening words, 26 October 1906', CPS13D/P13, QSA.

100 There was no indication of the name of the proprietor, but the wording of the advertisement and the nature of the merchandise offered suggest a Sri Lankan.

101 Swan, B., 'Sinhalese emigration to Queensland in the nineteenth century', p. 59. Some of the men were related: Henry Louis Simon and James Charles Amadoris, for example; and possibly the latter and Simba K. Amadoris. Simon's nephew is also attested as living on Thursday Island in 1885.

102 This 'chain migration' of immigrants is a familiar motif in Torres Strait history and prehistory, beginning with the arrival of the earliest inhabitants from the southern coasts of New Guinea.

103 Yonge, C. M. 1930. *A Year on the Great Barrier Reef: the story of corals and of the greatest of their creations*. London: Putnam. p. 172.

104 In *Post Office*, 1889, 1892–93.

105 'W. D. Wimalasundera vs Saris, 24 October 1890', QSA. Wimalasundera's shop was next to that of Francis De Bracey, a waterman, possibly also a Sri Lankan.

106 'Inspector of Fisheries vs Thomas Fleming for dealing in pearls without having obtained a licence, 7 December 1892.' CPS13D/P5, QSA. H. L. Simon and H. L. De Silva were the only Sri Lankans to hold licences that year.

107 *Pilot*, 3 July, 1897; *Post Office*, 1894–95, 1896–97. The trades of jeweller and watchmaker, a euphemism for 'watch repairer', were allied in Ceylon in those days.

108 'H. L. Silva vs Siyadoris for assault, 15 July 1892.' CPS13D/P5, QSA.

109 *Post Office*, 1895–96.

110 *Pilot*, 7 January, 1899. 'Y. B. Saranealis vs Charles De Silva for sureties of the peace, 21 March 1905.' CPS13D/P12, QSA. *Post Office*, 1918–19. Saranealis died on Thursday Island in 1919 (see below).

111 'Police vs Kicumato for assaulting one Saris Appu, 21 July 1902.' CPS13D/P10. Y. B. Saranealis may have been related to the Saranealis who appeared as a witness for the jeweller, W. D. Wimalasundera, in 'W. D. Wimalasundera vs Saris for sureties of the peace, 24 October 1890', CPS 13D/P3, QSA.

112 Photograph of Saranealis's store, Normanby Street, Thursday Island, Plate 17, in G. Cocks, and J. Grace, 1990, 'Queensland manufacturing and working jewellers — 1850–1900', *Australiana*, Vol. 12, No. 4, November. pp. 89–95, at p. 95.

113 'David Dietrichson (clerk to the Torres Divisional Board) vs Saranealis and others, 31 March 1897.' CPS 13D/S2, QSA.

114 'Matho vs Amadorus for common assault, 14 April 1899.' CPS13D/P7, QSA.

115 'Report of the Official Trustee in Insolvency, Townsville, for the year 1899.' QVP, 1900, p. 19.

116 *The Parish Gazette*, 1 February, 1913.

117 *Pugh's Almanac*, 1915–19; 1926–27.

118 Weerasooria, W. S., *Links Between Sri Lanka and Australia*, p. 171.

119 He occupied Allotment 7.7.6. 'Valuation Appeal Court held 17 April 1905.' CPS13D/P12, QSA.

120 'List of Licences to Deal in Pearls Issued in Pursuance of Section 14 of *The Pearl-shell and Beche-de-Mer Fishery Act Amendment Act* of 1891 during 1907' ... Royal Pearl-shell and Bêche-de-mer Commission, Appendix VI, p. 268, *Queensland Parliamentary Papers*, 1908.

121 *Pugh's Almanac*, 1915, p. 758.

122 Apparently, it was his older brother, Marshall Punchihewa, who was given the boat ticket. He was reluctant to leave home but Mendis, having the same initial, decided, much against his parents' wishes, to use the ticket himself and seek his fortune in Australia. Marshall Punchihewa later went to Japan. Amara Mendis, pers. comm., 29 April, 2004.

123 Material on P. H. Mendis's life and business career comes from Weerasooria, W. S., *Links Between Sri Lanka and Australia*, pp. 191–209; Lock, A. C. C., *Destination Barrier Reef*, pp. 130–4; 'The pearly way to riches', *People Magazine*, 9 April, 1952, pp. 30–1; Arun, K. C., 'Pearl-shell facade for new Wynnum store of pearl industry pioneer', *Courier-Mail* (Brisbane), 13 September, 1960. And from archival files, interviews and family documents kindly made available by Amara and Mahendra Mendis.

124 Mrs Mary Ann Corran bought the business in June 1896 from Frederick Charles Hodel and she and her husband published their first issue on 4 July, 1896. Typewritten notes [unsigned, probably by Rev. W. H. MacFarlane, and undated], MS3373, National Library of Australia.

125 Siripala Mendis to Weerasooria, W. S., *Links Between Sri Lanka and Australia*, p. 193. *Pugh's Almanac*, 1920–27. In the *Pilot* of 19 September, 1927, Mendis advertised that he would take orders for personalised greeting cards, 'with Name and Address printed thereon'.

126 Letter dated 16 October, 1962, J25/190/1972/66, NAA. In possession of Amara and Mahendra Mendis.

127 'Communist Party of Australia activity and interest in Thursday Island, 11 December 1949.' A6122/40/273, p. 11, NAA.

128 Swan, B., 'Sinhalese emigration to Queensland in the nineteenth century', p. 60. Mahendra Mendis, pers. comm., 29 April, 2004.

129 Bands of Sri Lankans occasionally fought with their economic rivals, the Malays and Japanese,

and there are examples of inter-ethnic assaults against individuals. The latter may have been occasioned by ethnically charged or personal grievances or both, e.g., 'Abdula alias Siyadoris on warrant charged with assaulting one Hop Sing, 12 January 1899', CPS13D/P7, QSA.

130 'John Douglas, Government Resident, Thursday Island, to Colonial Secretary, 26 October 1885.' A/443/8337, QSA. Our thanks to Jeremy Hodes for providing a transcription of this letter.

131 Rama Soopaya, a prominent Indian trader in the town, and his wife were reportedly assaulted at the same time by some Sri Lankans who used slingshots against them. Soopaya was the Sri Lankans' main competitor, selling many of the same lines at very low prices and purchasing tortoise shell, then a virtual Sri Lankan monopoly. *Pilot*, 27 February, 1897.

132 'Police vs Miskin for disorderly conduct in Victoria Parade, 7 January 1890', CPS 13D/P3, QSA; *Queensland Police Gazette*, No. 73 (12 December, 1903). p. 560.

133 'Police vs Billy Jetsunamy for being armed with axe intent to commit a felony, 27 October 1903.' CPS13D/P11, QSA.

134 'Inspector of Fisheries vs Thomas Fleming for dealing in pearls without having obtained a licence, 7 December 1892.' CPS13D/P5, QSA.

135 Appu Singho and H. L. Simon gave evidence for the prosecution, while J. P. James, Charles Mendis and Saris Appu gave evidence for the defence. James was bound over for a period of six months and was required to provide security in the sum of £10 plus two sureties of £5 each.

136 *Pilot*, 1 February, 1902.

137 'Police vs James Charles for disorderly conduct in Douglas Street, 15 December 1903.' CPS13D/P11, QSA.

138 She told the court that she bore 'no ill will or malice towards the defendant'. She had instituted proceedings because she was afraid of him. Simon was bound over to keep the peace for six months and ordered to pay a fine of £25 plus other costs. 'Police (F. Charles) vs H. L. Simon for sureties of the peace, 15 December 1903.' CPS13D/P11, QSA.

139 'Y. B. Saranealis vs C. De Silva for sureties of the peace, 21 March 1905.' CPS13D/P12, QSA.

140 'James Charles vs Saris Appo for threatening words and required sureties, 5, 15 and 26 October 1906.' CPS13D/P13, QSA.

141 The case was continued on 20 October and its outcome reported in a brief paragraph. *Pilot*, 27 October',1906.

142 'Rex vs Charlie Madras for attempting to kill one John Charles, 2 and 7 September 1908.' CPS13D/P13, QSA.

143 Quoted in Evans, R. et al., *Exclusion, Exploitation and Extermination*, p. 357.

144 'Police vs Henry L. Simon for using threatening language to one Annie Simon at Thursday Island, 29 September 1888.' CPS13D/P2, QSA.

145 For discussion of the benefits of such marriages for Chinese settlers on Thursday Island, see Ramsay, G. and A. Shnukal. 2003. '"Aspirational" Chinese: achieving community prominence on Thursday Island, northeast Australia.' *Asian and Pacific Migration Journal*, Vol. 12, No. 3. pp. 337–59.

146 'F. Charles vs H. L. Simon (on remand) for using threatening language to one Florence Charles, 18 December 1903.' CPS13D/P11, QSA.

147 'Florence Charles vs James Charles for threatening language, 20 January 1905', CPS13D/P12, QSA.

148 Donsiman, the spelling that appears in Australian official records, may have originated as a scribal error for 'Don Simon'.

149 *Registers of Aliens Naturalized* 1901–03, SCT/CF/39, QSA.

150 Letter from Walter J. Woods, grandson of Y. B. Saranealis to W. S. Weerasooria, dated 2 October, 1987, and quoted in *Links Between Sri Lanka and Australia*, p. 165.

151 The children buried there are: Edward William (Eddie) Saranealis L. D. G., born 2 February, 1902, and died 2 October, 1971; Donsiman Heriverto (Hubby) Saranealis, born 20 May, 1903, and died 3 December, 1978; Stephen Buddalegay (Buddy) Saranealis, born 25 June, 1904, and died 16 February, 1969; Dotchihamy Emma (Dotchie) Saranealis, who died 20 December, 1987. Hubby

was likely named for Heriberto Zarcal, who sold his business to Mowlis (see Reynaldo Ileto, Chapter Five, this volume). Buddy, who was a well-known boxer, was married briefly, but none of the Saranealis sons, as far as is known, produced children. Two of the three daughters, Ruby Mango and Dotchihamy Emma (Dotchie), never married, but Anohamy Esther married Walter Thomas Woods on 29 November, 1928. The couple moved to Cairns and Anohamy died there on the same day as her eldest brother, Eddie. Weerasooria, W. S., *Links Between Sri Lanka and Australia*, p. 163. *Pilot*, 25 September, 1935.

152 Eva Mingo Peacock, pers. comm., 10 August, 2000. Weerasooria, W. S., *Links Between Sri Lanka and Australia*, p. 164. The alternative was to wait for the visits of a mainland dentist every four months. *Pilot*, 12 September, 1928.

153 "Curate's Egg", 'Thursday Island's dentist', *Smith's Weekly*, 31 October, 1936. Eddie Saranealis changed his official occupation from 'jeweller' to 'dentist' during the 1938–39 financial year. *56th Annual Balance Returns*, Thursday Island Branch, Burns Philp & Co., 31 March, 1939, Burns Philp Archive.

154 Letter from Walter J. Woods, grandson of Y. B. Saranealis to W. S. Weerasooria, dated 2 October, 1987, and quoted in *Links Between Sri Lanka and Australia*, p. 166.

155 'H. L. Mowlis Commonwealth Naturalisation: Oath taken this 19th April 1911, before Hugh Milman, P. M., 19 April 1911.' QS787/1/2, QSA. This was unusual for an unmarried man, but necessary in order to own property. Mowlis's naturalisation was no doubt facilitated by his being legally a British subject, as was Heriberto Zarcal's on the grounds of being a Spanish subject (see Anna Shnukal, Chapter Four, this volume).

156 'Protector of Aboriginals, Thursday Island, to Chief Protector of Aboriginals, Brisbane, 24 February 1915.' A/58768 (restricted), QSA.

157 He may have left the state permanently, as there is no record of his death in Queensland.

158 Lock, A. C. C., *Destination Barrier Reef*, pp. 134–5. Swan, B., 'Sinhalese emigration to Queensland in the nineteenth century.' Swan, B., 'Sinhala settlers of Thursday Island.' *Ceylon Observer*, 3 September, 1978, quoted in Weerasooria, W. S., *Links Between Sri Lanka and Australia*, p. 169.

159 Amara Mendis, pers. comm., 6 April, 1999.

160 Amcia already had two sons, Arthur and Peter (Petrie) Ahmat, born to her husband before 1919. All the children were raised together and the girls — Mercia (Mercy), named for Punchi Hewa Mendis's wife, Evelyn, Juliet (Julie), and Portia — signed Ahmat. The couple's first son, Paul, was born on 18 September, 1923, but died tragically young on 4 January, 1926.

161 Weerasooria, W. S., *Links Between Sri Lanka and Australia*, p. 168.

162 Siripala and Nissanka, born in Galle on 29 August, 1919, and 2 April, 1924, respectively. Both sons subsequently married into families associated with jewellery in South-East Asia and each pursued a successful career in Australia. See also Weerasooria, W. S., *Links Between Sri Lanka and Australia*, p. 192.

163 Amara Mendis, pers. comm., 1 November, 2001. Amara remembers that every week See Kee, who grew vegetables such as Chinese cabbage and lettuce, would send vegetables to her father-in-law 'as a mark of respect and gratitude'.

164 'Albert Edward Kelly, Acting Head Teacher, State School, Thursday Island, to Director of Education, Department of Public Instruction, 9 March 1942, re Admission of Coloured Children.' EDU/Z2676, QSA. The full text reads: 'The races represented on the Island, in addition to Europeans, are: Chinese, Japanese, Torres Strait islanders and mainland Aboriginals while the crosses comprise: China-White, Islander-White, Japanese-Islander, Japanese-Malay, Malay-Islander, Malay-Aboriginal in varying proportions while many are of doubtful origin. In addition there are a couple of families, white predominating, containing Southern European or Cingalese blood. These live as white people and are accepted in white society together with Chinese and caste [sic] Chinese-White and to a lesser degree the Japanese whose children are not yet matured.' Despite the authorities' desire to assign each resident of Thursday Island to a rigid 'racial' category, many decisions were ad hoc and mutable. With decisions rarely based entirely on descent or community acceptance, it is the unclear cases that permit a more nuanced explanation than heretofore (see Regina Ganter, Chapter Nine, this volume).

165 Hill, E. 'Vignettes of Thursday Island's picturesque scenes: where a happy polyglot people seek for pearlshell.' *The Queensland Times*, 17 June, 1933.

166 'W. D. Wimalasundera vs Saris, 24 October 1890.' CPS 13D/P3, QSA.

167 Information about the temple location from Punchi Hewa Mendis to Amara Mendis. Amara was shown the tree when she arrived on Thursday Island after World War II, but it had been stripped of its leaves and died shortly afterwards. It had once been quite tall. Amara Mendis, pers. comm., 1 November, 2001, 21 February, 2004. According to Siri Mendis, pers. comm., 31 October, 2001, the Buddhist temple had disappeared by the time of his arrival on Thursday Island in 1937. Its date of construction is unknown but it may have been the first Buddhist centre in Australia.

168 Swan, B., 'Sinhalese emigration to Queensland in the nineteenth century', p. 59.

169 Ibid.

170 The *Quetta*, on a voyage from Brisbane to London via Colombo, sank on the night of 28 February, 1890, off Muri (Mt Adolphus Island) not far from Thursday Island after having struck a submerged rock. Singe, J. 1989. *The Torres Strait: people and history*. St Lucia: University of Queensland Press. p. 94; Foley, J. C. H. 1990. *The Quetta: Queensland's worst disaster: the story of the wreck of RMS Quetta in Torres Strait in 1890*. Aspley: Nairana.

171 England, A. 'Thursday Island has memorial Cathedral to the Quetta.' *Telegraph* (Brisbane), 29 February, 1940. p. 11.

172 M. Sasaki, presumably a Japanese, served as the Buddhist priest on Thursday Island in 1900. *Post Office*, 1900, p. 540.

173 This in itself was atypical of the Sri Lankan migrations to other parts of Queensland. Those 'who settled down on the mainland were soon lost to sight in the cultures that surrounded them, but on Thursday Island they established a community which long retained its identity.' Swan, B., 'Sinhalese emigration to Queensland in the nineteenth century', p. 58.

174 In 1897, for example, Saris and De Silva donated money to the Jubilee Benevolent Fund; and, in 1903, the Sri Lankans made the attractive bamboo screens and other decorations for an Arcadian Fête lucky dip to raise money for fencing the Anglican Church grounds. *Pilot*, 3 July, 1897, and 24 January, 1903.

175 *Torres Strait Pilot*, 1 February, 1902. p. 1.

176 Hill, E., 'Vignettes of Thursday Island's picturesque scenes'.

177 Amara Mendis, pers. comm., 16 April, 2004.

178 Weerasooria, W. S., *Links Between Sri Lanka and Australia*, p. 164.

179 *Pilot*, 8 December, 1928.

180 *Souvenir Program* dated 24 May, 1935, 'Federal Hotel Register 10 June 1901–c.1956.' p. 258. Royal Historical Society of Queensland Library.

181 Swan, B., 'Sinhalese emigration to Queensland in the nineteenth century', p. 59.

Government Residence, 1897.
Courtesy of John Oxley Library, Brisbane (Item No. 49817).

CHAPTER EIGHT

John Douglas and the Asian Presence on Thursday Island: 1885–1904

Jeremy Hodes

Torres Strait during the colonial era was synonymous with the name of John Douglas, who, as its Government Resident, ruled this remote and far-flung administration. Here was the last great Australian imperialist — devising, implementing and maintaining an administrative apparatus for the region and its people that was paternalistic, benevolent and autocratic. In this task, he was guided by the principles of 'providential duty, the destiny of race, and the other lofty abstractions of late Victorian imperialism'.[1]

That he was able to rule Torres Strait as a sort of 'constitutional sovereign'[2] for the benefit of its inhabitants, according to his own liberal beliefs, tenets and values, possessing unbounded moral and statutory authority,[3] was without parallel in Queensland colonial history. While he was aided and abetted in this by the geographical remoteness of Torres Strait, it was also due in large part to his undoubted administrative ability, coupled with his extensive political connections and experience. Douglas brooked no interference in his domain and indeed encountered little, being left largely to his own benevolent devices by his grateful political masters in far-off Brisbane. This chapter will examine his interaction with Asian peoples on Thursday Island, particularly the Japanese, his attitudes towards them, and his impact on their lives. In order to better understand his role and influence, it is necessary to briefly examine his life and career prior to his arrival in the region.

Hon. John Douglas: his formation and early career

John Douglas was born in London on 6 March, 1828, a nephew of the Marquess of Queensberry. Educated at Rugby and Durham University, he came to NSW in 1851, working as a sub-commissioner of crown lands and magistrate on the goldfields, before purchasing *Talgai* on the Darling Downs. He represented the Downs and Camden districts in the NSW Parliament before purchasing the property, *Tooloombah*, in the Rockhampton district. Elected to the Queensland Parliament as the Member for Port Curtis in 1863, he first entered the ministry in 1866 as Postmaster General. In 1869, he was appointed to the post of Agent-General for Emigration to the Colony of Queensland in England. He returned to Queensland in 1871, re-entered parliament in 1875, becoming Minister for Lands in 1876 and Premier from 1877 to 1879, before retiring from parliament and becoming a leader writer for the leading Queensland newspaper, the *Brisbane Courier*.

His role in the genesis of European settlement and administration in Torres Strait was profound, beginning in 1866, when, on his recommendation as Postmaster General, the Torres Strait mail service first began. In 1877, under his premiership and on his initiative, the Queensland Government established the administrative settlement of Thursday Island,[4] Douglas travelling to Torres Strait later that year on an official visit of inspection.[5] In 1879, at his insistence, the maritime boundary of Queensland was extended to include all islands of Torres Strait and, on 13 April, 1885, he was appointed as the first Government Resident for Thursday Island. He held this position until his death, nearly 20 years later, aged 76, on 21 July, 1904. From 27 December, 1885, to 3 September, 1888, he also served as Special Commissioner for the protectorate of British New Guinea, administering the territory preparatory to it being formally proclaimed a crown colony.

At the time of his appointment, Thursday Island was a small, isolated settlement, the population of which consisted of a few Europeans, with pearling the main industry, employing Europeans, Filipinos, Malays and Pacific Islanders.

By the end of the century, it had become a multiracial, multi-ethnic, cosmopolitan outpost, the commercial and administrative centre for Torres Strait, with the pearling industry dominated numerically by Japanese. An 1899 visitor to this 'Insular Babel' found:

> Europeans, about half a dozen nationalities, Chinese, Japanese, Javanese, New Guinea men, South Sea Islanders, including Rotuma boys, who are much esteemed, and Tanna boys, who are esteemed less, Manilamen, Mauritius blacks, Hindoos from British India, from Goa, from Pondicherry, Australian mainland blackfellows (here called Binghis), Australian island blacks from places like Prince of Wales Island, Goode Island, and Jervis Island or Mabuac [sic], and American and West Indian Negroes.[6]

Douglas, already 56 years of age when he settled on the island, cut a commanding presence as the benevolent older statesman:

> Bearded like winter, and his plentiful white hair covers the large area of his head in wavy undulations, almost to be described as ringlets. He is … a large man, and his keen eyes scintillate with that immense sagacity regarding men and things which is the characteristic of veteran politicians. His voice is deep and clear. His utterances come forth in well mannered periods, the concluding word of each one of which was strongly emphasised, as if he were clinching every point in an argument against some redoubtable oratorical opponent. But with it all was the mellowing which comes with age.[7]

Like many Victorians, Douglas had strong views on race and class. A lifelong adherent to the concept of liberalism, he supported the underdog and those trying to improve their status. He consistently opposed the importation of Pacific Islanders to the sugar industry in Queensland, considering it to be little better than slavery. Under his premiership, Polynesian immigration was restricted. As Government Resident, he was particularly concerned for the welfare of Torres Strait Islanders, and it was mainly due to his efforts that they did not come under the Aboriginals Protection and Restriction of the Sale of Opium Act of 1897, but were considered a group separate from Aborigines and were better treated. That they held a special place in his heart is evident from this impassioned plea in 1900:

> The native-born population are British subjects. They are civilised people; they are being educated, and they are entitled, and I say, should be treated as British subjects. Still they are not enumerated even in the census. I hope that in any future census notice will be taken of them … They are human beings; they are our own flesh and blood; they are born under our

jurisdiction; and they are entitled, I maintain, to the privileges we enjoy
… The natives of the islands of Torres Strait are capable of exercising all
the rights of British citizens, and they aught to be regarded as such.[8]

Douglas had no antipathy to individual Asians. He counted the Chinese
mandarin, Quong Tart, among his friends,[9] he helped a destitute Malay return
home to Singapore,[10] and was the sole European attending a reception put on
by the Japanese Brethren Society for the Townsville-based honorary Japanese
consul, K. Iijima.[11] When it came to groups that were deemed to threaten the
British way of life in colonial Queensland, however, Douglas had a very
different response. As premier, he halted Chinese immigration into Queensland
in 1877, to popular acclaim; in the 1890s, he played a major part in restricting
and regulating Japanese immigration into Torres Strait. In doing this, he was
not motivated primarily by considerations of race, but rather by a desire to keep
Queensland a colony in which British values and the British way of life were
paramount. Douglas had no desire to see his adopted land go the way of Hong
Kong or Singapore. Although a proud 'White Australian' and a devout
Anglican who strived to do his best for all, he, like many 19th-century liberals,
maintained that 'the distinction of colour or creed should not exist for us, so
long as we secure the rightful ascendency of our race'.[12]

Douglas and the Japanese

Douglas's main interaction with Asians was with the Japanese, who, through
their overwhelming numbers, dominated the fishing industry in Torres Strait.
His early years were devoted to restricting Japanese immigration and influence,
his later years to ensuring that they abided by the regulations and legislation
governing the pearl-shelling industry. As a police magistrate, he was involved in
upholding the peace and meting out justice, and this he did without fear or
favour.

One celebrated instance of Douglas's impartiality in dispensing justice
concerned the arrest of a Japanese diver, Nakane, for indecency and resisting
arrest on Thursday Island in January 1898. The arrest was made under what
appeared to be difficult circumstances, with 200 of his countrymen present. The
case was heard before Douglas over four days, with several hundred Japanese
attending. Douglas found that Nakane was indeed guilty of indecent exposure,
for urinating in public on a Saturday afternoon in the main thoroughfare while
under the influence of liquor. He called, however, for discretion on the part of
police, noting that not only were there no urinals there, but that 'I have also
myself urinated in a public street, though of course in a quiet corner, and never
felt that I had committed an act of indecency'.[13]

Government buildings, Thursday Island, 1897.
Courtesy of John Oxley Library, Brisbane (Item No. 11962).

While agreeing that Nakane resisted arrest, Douglas refused to record a conviction on this count, instead criticising the police for their excessive use of force, the constable having 'downed him [Nakane] a second time in a rather inhuman manner, and knocked him senseless'.[14]

This verdict caused a storm throughout the colony, the local paper saying it all in its choice of subheadings when reporting the case:

> A charge of Indecency: Extraordinary decisions: The police snubbed: The lawbreakers complimented.[15]

A contemporary, writing under the nom de plume 'Old Colonist', went much further, using this case as an illustration of how Thursday Island had fallen into the 'hand of the Japs'.

> In a recent riot case in which the Japanese had been the delinquents, legal proceedings were taken by the police. The case was heard in the local court before the government resident, who is also police magistrate. This functionary is reported as being so overawed by the overwhelming number of Japanese, in and around the court, interested in the case, that he was unable to administer strict justice through lack of power to enforce his decision and uphold the authority of the court, and to prevent a possible outbreak a paltry fine of 20s. was imposed, instead of a sentence of six months' imprisonment.[16]

The first Japanese came to Torres Strait in the 1870s, seeking work in the pearling industry.[17] They were employed as divers, performing so well that employers preferred them to other groups. From 1891, Japanese merchants facilitated worker migration, resulting in increased numbers coming to Torres Strait.[18] On Thursday Island, the Japanese population grew from 22 in 1890 to a peak of 619 in 1898, when, for the first time, they outnumbered the European population.

This rapid growth and dominance greatly concerned Douglas and other like-minded Queenslanders, who saw Japanese as a threat to their livelihood and to their British way of life.[19] Douglas's remarks in 1895 about Japanese residing on Thursday Island are illustrative of this concern:

> They have their own shops, their own boat building slip, and they are trying, they say, to establish a public house of their own it will very soon be a case, I fear, of the survival of the fittest, and if things go on as they are doing, the Caucasian will be played out.[20]

Although Douglas had nothing against Japanese personally, he believed they posed a danger to the European way of life on the island: 'I have really a great respect for the Japanese and a great admiration for their physical and mental capacities; all the same, I think we shall have to look out.'[21] As a group, he regarded them as 'a positive menace to the White population' residing there,[22] outlining his reasons as follows:

> If there is one conviction, one passion, I may almost say, which is more deeply rooted in the Australian character, than another, it is that of maintaining the idiosyncrasy of the races from which we derive our origin — We must, through the length and breadth of Australia, be commandingly European. That is my conviction still, and here am I living in one of the most cosmopolitan communities in the world. This conviction arises not from any particular pride in one country, though that is not a bad thing in itself. It arises, I believe, from a fixed assurance that the best interests of Australians as a whole are bound up in the integrity and homogeneity of the people.[23]

So when Japanese began entrenching themselves in the pearling industry in Torres Strait in the mid-1890s, Douglas and others became alarmed.

> They very soon began to evince a greater aptitude for independent enterprise than any of the other Asiatic races, and they have shown their capacity not only as seaman and divers, but also as artificers and tradesman.[24]

At every turn, Douglas warned the Government as to what was happening — the numbers of Japanese arriving and the impact their presence was having — consistently demanding action.[25] He complained that Japanese women were being brought to the island for prostitution and that the number of Japanese men arriving was too great to be absorbed into the local fishing industry.[26] His concerns, however, were ameliorated by his belief that, being fishermen, they would not settle permanently on Thursday Island, while his strong belief in liberalism admired them as 'hardworking people, tractable, inoffensive, and reasonable'.[27] Douglas also believed it unfair that aliens, who would never settle permanently in Torres Strait, should be allowed to exploit the fisheries.

> I hardly think that British fishermen, with all their pluck and indomitable love of freedom, would as cheerfully invite their French or Dutch neighbours to share in the privileges of their home fisheries as we do when we license Japanese or Malays to fish within the limits of our maritime boundary.[28]

The Queensland Government was receptive to Douglas's concerns and acted quickly, voicing opposition to the flow of migration from Japan, and appointing a commission of inquiry in March 1897, which resulted in the act being amended so that Japanese could not rent boats or be issued with boat licences.[29] These restrictions, allied with the active involvement of the Japanese Government in restricting immigration to Queensland[30] and the Commonwealth Government's Immigration Restriction Act of 1901, were effective in stemming the tide of Japanese to Torres Strait.

Nevertheless, resentment towards the Japanese 'invasion' took time to abate, as this 1899 observation attests:

> The Japanese, despite his industry and his cleverness, is not liked and is not trusted. The race are personally agreeable, but they get everything into their own hands, both by underselling, mysterious, and unfathomable systems of combination. Japanese were first brought to Thursday Island as divers. Then they got to win boats and then combined in the ownership of boats subsequently they took to building boats, and very good boats, from schooners downwards, they do build. The 30 or 40 White men who formerly worked at boat-building and repairing work are no more.[31]

Douglas was satisfied that the threat had been seen off. He observed in 1901 that Japanese arrivals to the island had ceased almost entirely, resulting in the 'Japanese problem' being 'solved'.[32] Despite the White Australia Policy now in force, Japanese and other non-Europeans were still needed in the pearling industry. Douglas knew that while 'White men can do well as divers', they refused to do this sort of dangerous work, and he therefore recognised the industry's need for Japanese, but only as 'auxiliaries'.[33] For Douglas, the solution was obvious: employ Torres Strait Islanders and Papua New Guineans.[34]

Douglas and the Chinese

The discovery of gold on the Palmer River led to large numbers of Chinese flocking to north Queensland. In a three-week period in April 1875, 3,272 Chinese disembarked at Cooktown, the port of entry to the Palmer.[35] By 1877, there were an estimated 17,000 Chinese on the field, about 10 per cent of the entire European population of Queensland.[36] As premier at this time, Douglas took action to stop the flow of Chinese miners into the colony by insisting they be quarantined, and then legislating the imposition of a £10 head tax. His attitude, and that of his compatriots, was fully in accord with the belief of the time that not only were Asian and Western values irreconcilable, but it was their duty to ensure that Queensland remained a colony true to British values and ideals.

Douglas was concerned that the Asians would dominate the north of the colony. Queenslanders were well aware of what was occurring in America, where many Chinese goldminers had settled after the California gold rushes, and were afraid that would also happen here.[37] The following comment, by explorer and bushman Christie Palmerston, articulated the thoughts and fears of many colonists:

> When once the Chinese swarm a goldfield, they overrun it as a horde of locusts do a wheat crop. They are of no earthly use to Queensland, which they rob annually of much wealth, without yielding any reciprocal revenue or helping to develop the productive resources of the colony.[38]

Queenslanders had a stake in the future of their colony, demanding the right to settle and develop the vast, sparsely populated colony as they saw fit. Above all, they wanted it peopled by men who subscribed to British values and who embraced the British way of life. As the *Brisbane Courier* insisted, 'Australia cannot be both Chinese and British; it must be one or the other.'[39] The determination of Queenslanders to reject Chinese immigration was compared with the actions of an earlier generation of Australian colonists who refused to receive convicts.[40] Not only did they believe the comparison with convict labour was apt, they believed that this was the gravest issue to have arisen in Australia since the abolition of convict transportation in 1868.[41]

In putting a halt to continued Chinese immigration to Queensland, Douglas had shown to what lengths he would go in order to achieve what he

Opening of All Souls' Quetta Memorial Cathedral, Thursday Island, 29 June, 1913.
Courtesy of John Oxley Library, Brisbane (Item No. 167655).

considered a just outcome for Queensland. He passionately believed in the superiority of British civilisation, British values and British institutions, and he was not prepared to have them subsumed by what he considered an alien culture.[42]

It is difficult to analyse this strong antipathy to Chinese using only contemporary constructions of race and racism. What to us appears as outright racism would not have been recognised as such by Queenslanders in the 1870s. Rather, there was a complex mix of racial superiority, patriotism,[43] a clash of civilisations, the right to determine what sort of country Queensland would become, social Darwinism,[44] and especially fear — the fear of disease,[45] fear of miscegenation,[46] fear of lowered living standards, fear of opium,[47] and, above all, the fear of invasion. Queenslanders were strongly resolved that northern Australia would not become another Hong Kong or Singapore. They would prevent what happened in California happening here.

Douglas's attitude to Chinese on Thursday Island was very different. Being fewer in number, they were never going to threaten the European way of life on the island in the same way the Japanese did. Nevertheless, that did not mean that they were liked or respected, as attested by this 1899 Thursday Island description:

John Chinaman is represented by about a hundred depressed and inscrutable looking persons, principally hawkers and small shopkeepers, and the keepers of boarding houses for pearlers — frowsy-looking establishments with flyblown and blood-curdling advertisements of 'ham and eggs' in the windows. Looking at the awful entrances and the glimpses afforded of the interiors, also remembering the Chinese prejudice in favour of eggs of a certain antiquity, one can judge of the quality of the provisions. But despite his subdued air and the unsubduable nature of his eggs, John on Thursday Island, as elsewhere, always gets on. He will take a little shop and display a few pennyworth of speckled fruit in his window, of which no one will be ever seen to enter and purchase, and from this mysterious trade he will rise to the boarding-house and ham and eggs business, or to the keeping of a small general store, in which no customers are ever seen either, or even to the running of a game of a much more complicated nature than Pak Ah-puh or Fan-tan, of a game (with an unpronounceable name) the principles of which are so recondite that the collective wisdom of the Thursday Island police has never yet been able to ascertain whether it be a game of chance or not and so there is no ground for a prosecution.[48]

Wishing to create a community on Thursday Island that would impart a civilising influence on all those who lived there, Douglas abhorred what he perceived as the pernicious effects of drink, gambling and opium, constantly preaching the need for restraint or abstinence. For Douglas, the major problem with Chinese was their opium-smoking: he considered this vice far worse than alcohol.[49] He also disapproved of gambling, condemning Chinese as 'insatiate gamblers'.[50] By 1899, there were two wholesale and eight retail opium dealers on the island, the regulars at the island's opium dens now including Malays and some Europeans.[51]

Douglas and the Filipinos and Malays

Filipinos and Malays were the other major Asian groups living and working in Torres Strait. Filipinos were known as 'Manila men', and, like Malays, were brought to Torres Strait from Singapore on three-year work agreements.[52] By 1885, there were 147 Filipinos in Torres Strait, but there were rarely more than 100 of them in subsequent years. Some of them settled permanently on Thursday Island, marrying women selected for them in the Philippines, and acquiring boats of their own.[53] Becoming naturalised, they were seen to be the 'only fully integrated Asians' on the island.[54] Nevertheless, being identified as Asian subjected them to racial hostility and misunderstanding: the *Newcastle Morning Herald and Miners Advocate* expressed alarm over 'hordes of Asiatic aliens'[55] when an additional 150 Filipinos arrived on the island in 1899.

Douglas, however, viewed Filipinos in a different light, considering them the most settled of the Asians, 'good residents who circulated their money on the island'.[56]

Filipinos, who were devout Catholics, took their religious celebrations very seriously, while borrowing elements from the other groups on the island, something Thomas Eykyn observed on a visit to Thursday Island about 1890:

> On Christmas Eve, after dinner at the residency, numbers of Manilamen labourers came to give their Christmas performance. Chinese lanterns swung from the flagstaff on the lawn, beneath which, with the aid of the moon, they danced and sang. The band consisted of a concertina, a penny whistle, and a lovely Japanese drum.[57]

Douglas was impressed also with Malays, considering them to 'have furnished both good crews and good divers'. Unlike Filipinos, however, most Malays returned home at the end of their agreements.[58] Douglas's views of the Malay and Filipino populations on the island were atypical of the period. Malays were widely believed to be capable of running amuck at any time, while Manila men were routinely seen as dangerous, carrying sharp knives and forever tainted with the murder of Senior Constable William Conroy by one of their number, Frank Tinyana, in 1896.[59] Douglas was particularly moved by the plight of a Malay leper, consigned to the leprosarium on Dayman Island, remarking that he was 'an intelligent man, who, in spite of his troubles, contemplates life with equanimity'.[60]

Douglas did his best to keep the peace on the island. In 1892, he was able to observe, with some satisfaction, 'that among this motley population very fair order is maintained', with no serious crimes recorded in the previous five years.[61] This state of affairs could not last forever. Early in 1901, an organised fracas occurred between the Pacific Islanders and Manila men, leaving one person dead, several seriously injured, and the shop of the leading Filipino on the island, Heriberto Zarcal, extensively damaged (see Reynaldo Ileto's Chapter Five, this volume).[62] Douglas took immediate steps to prevent any further outbreak of violence, swearing in special constables and imposing a curfew, during which the police and military patrolled the streets.[63]

This melee was atypical: there was a surprising degree of tolerance and harmony, considering the small size of the island, its tropical climate and isolated location. Economic interdependence required a degree of cooperation between all sectors of the community, leading to the development of a cosmopolitan and relatively stable society. As Douglas proudly observed of his beloved island in 1902:

> We have all the essentials which may be regarded as appertaining to a white Australia: we have the same all-pervading British law, applicable to Asian and Australian alike, the same English language, and the same forms of social intercourse which prevail in southern Australia: our churches and schools are an exact counterpart on a small scale of what they are in Melbourne or in Brisbane.[64]

Conclusion

Douglas was Government Resident during the formative stages of the development of Thursday Island as a thriving multiracial community. The introduction of the Immigration Restriction Act of 1901 after Federation would forever change the nature of the fisheries in Torres Strait, changes that would inevitably affect the composition of the Thursday Island community. By the time of Douglas's death in 1904, aliens, as authorised under this act, were being brought in as indentured labour under articles and were allowed to set foot ashore for a short period only twice a year.[65]

The White Australia Policy, coupled with the diminished authority of his successors, ensured that never again would they achieve their previous dominance or influence.

Footnotes

[1]   These words were used by James Morris, the distinguished British historian, of the annexation of the Punjab by the Raj. See Morris, J. 1979. *Heaven's Command: an imperial progress.* Harmondsworth: Penguin. p. 181.

[2]   'As others see us'. *Torres Straits Pilot and New Guinea Gazette*, 30 September, 1898. p. 2.

[3]   Ibid.

[4]   'J. Douglas to the Under Secretary, Home Office, 24 January 1902.' HOM/A39/01610, Queensland State Archives (hereafter QSA).

[5]   For an account of this voyage, see 'Our northern outposts.' *Brisbane Courier*, 8 December, 1877. p. 6.

[6]   'As others see us'. *Torres Straits Pilots and New Guinea Gazette*, 23 September, 1899. p. 2.

[7]   'A new view of Federation: address by the Hon. John Douglas.' *Telegraph*, 2 October, 1896. John Douglas papers, OM89-3/Series C, news clippings and postcards, John Oxley Library, State Library of Queensland.

[8]   Douglas, J. 1899–1900. 'The Islands and inhabitants of Torres Strait.' *Queensland Geographical Journal*, 15th session. p. 35.

[9]   J. Douglas to his children, 19 May, 1894, copy in possession of the author.

[10] 'J. Douglas to Colonial Secretary, 26 October 1885.' A/443/8337, QSA.

[11] 'The Futami Maru.' *Torres Straits Pilot and New Guinea Gazette*, 14 October, 1899.

[12] 'J. Douglas, Report of the Government Resident at Thursday Island for 1896 and 1897.' p. 4.
      'J. Douglas, Report of the Government Resident at Thursday Island for 1898.' p. 3.

[13] 'A charge of indecency.' *Torres Strait Pilot and New Guinea Gazette*, 29 January, 1898.

[14] Ibid.

[15] Ibid.

16 Old Colonist. 1898. *Reminiscences of Half a Century and Present-Day Politics*. Rockhampton: Record Printing Company. pp. 66–7.

17 Ganter, R. 1994. *The Pearl-Shellers of Torres Strait: resource use, development and decline, 1860s–1960s*. Melbourne University Press. p. 100.

18 Ibid., pp. 102–4.

19 'J. Douglas, Report of the Government Resident at Thursday Island for 1892–93.' p. 3. For a reaction to the influx of Japanese, see Armstrong, J. B. 1970. 'The question of Japanese immigration to Queensland in the nineteenth century.' MA Qual. thesis, University of Queensland. pp. 63–70.

20 Douglas, J. 'Thursday Island and the Japanese.' 5 June, 1895, AD 39, Dixson Library, State Library of New South Wales.

21 Ibid.

22 'The Japanese question.' *Brisbane Courier*, 12 May, 1897. p. 4.

23 Ibid.

24 Douglas, J. 'Asiatic aliens in Torres Straits.' 13 July, 1895, p. 2. PRE/105, QSA.

25 Précis of papers dealing with the necessity for restricting Japanese immigration, PRE/105, QSA.

26 Ibid. He had not originally opposed the Japanese prostitutes on the grounds that they were 'clean and honest and less troublesome than the white women who had preceded them'. He soon changed his mind, however, considering them to be a corrupting and demoralising influence without which Thursday Island would be better off, and that the respectable inhabitants of Thursday Island, European and Japanese, found their antics at the Yokohama Brothel to be disgusting. He was also in no doubt that they 'are bought and sold like so many sheep and cattle'. See Armstrong, J. B. 1973. 'Aspects of Japanese immigration to Queensland before 1900.' *Queensland Heritage*, Vol. 2, No. 9, November. p. 5. 'J. Douglas, Report of the Government Resident at Thursday Island for 1894–95.' p. 2. 'J. Douglas, Report of the Government Resident at Thursday Island for 1896 and 1897.' p. 4.

27 Douglas, J. 'Asiatic aliens in Torres Straits.' p. 3. PRE/105, QSA.

28 'J. Douglas, Report of the Government Resident at Thursday Island for 1892–93.' p. 4. 'J. Douglas, Report of the Government Resident at Thursday Island for 1900.' p. 2.

29 'Report of the Departmental Commission on Pearl-Shell and Bêche-de-Mer Fisheries.' *Queensland Votes and Proceedings*, 1897, Vol. 2. pp. 1301–52.

30 See Murakami, Y. 1999. 'Civilised Asian: images of Japan and the Japanese as viewed by Australians from the early nineteenth century to 1901.' PhD thesis, University of Queensland, Chapter 5. And Willard, M. 1967. 2nd ed. *History of the White Australia Policy to 1920*. Melbourne University Press. pp. 116–18.

31 *Torres Straits Pilot and New Guinea Gazette*, 30 September, 1899. p. 2.

32 'Colour at Thursday Island.' *Brisbane Courier*, 3 May, 1901. p. 4. 'J. Douglas, Report of the Government Resident at Thursday Island for 1899.' p. 3. 'J. Douglas, Report of the Government Resident at Thursday Island for 1900.' p. 1. *Sydney Morning Herald*, 2 May, 1901. p. 4.

33 *The Age*, 6 September, 1902. p. 10. Douglas, J., 'Asiatic aliens in Torres Straits', p. 3.

34 'J. Douglas, Report of the Government Resident at Thursday Island for 1900.' pp. 3, 4.

35 Evans, R., K. Saunders and K. Cronin. 1988. *Race Relations in Colonial Queensland: a history of exclusion, exploitation and extermination*. St Lucia: University of Queensland Press. p. 255.

36 Willard, M., *History of the White Australia Policy to 1920*, p. 40.

37 Ibid., pp. 41–2. A United States Federal Commission inquiry into this matter had concluded that Chinese immigration to the US had been 'ruinous to our labouring classes, promotive of caste, and dangerous to free institutions'. C. S. Mein had brought this report to the attention of the Queensland Parliament, observing, 'I have read this report as testimony of the result to a civilised community of the same race as ourselves, possessing similar institutions to our own, from the coming among them of a large Chinese population, and from the unrestricted invasion of the country by an inferior race. That is what this country will arrive at, unless we take steps to protect ourselves against this invasion.'

38 *Queensland Figaro*, 5 February, 1877.
39 *Brisbane Courier*, 31 March, 1877. p. 4.
40 *Brisbane Courier*, 25 April, 1877. p. 2.
41 *Brisbane Courier*, 8 May, 1877. p. 2.
42 Under social Darwinism, which posited that human history was progressive and full of competition, the 'yellow races' were thought to be at a lower level than that of the 'white man'. Their civilisation and culture, instead of being recognised and celebrated, was instead considered a liability, resulting in them being 'exhausted and overborne by an ancient and different civilization'. Mills, W. 1904. *The Struggle for Existence*. Chicago: International School of Social Economy. p. 545. These ideas were widely subscribed to in Queensland at this time (see Evans, R. et al., *Race Relations in Colonial Queensland*, pp. 256–7).
43 Patriotism had a somewhat different meaning in the late nineteenth century than it does now, as can be seen from this definition: 'A person's love of the social body of which he is himself a member, and which is attached to the territory he calls his country. It involves a desire to promote its welfare, a wish that it may prosper for the time being and for the future. This desire is the outcome of a variety of sentiments; of men's affection for the people among whom they live, of attachment to the places where they have grown up or spent part of their lives, of devotion to their race and language, and to the traditions, customs, laws, and institutions of the society in which they were born and to which they belong.' Westermarck, E. 2nd ed. 1917. *The Origin and Development of Moral Ideas*. London: MacMillan. p. 167.
44 See Evans, R. et al., *Race Relations in Colonial Queensland*, pp. 241–5.
45 Smallpox had recently been encountered aboard ships plying the China route, leading to mandatory 16-day quarantine for these vessels.
46 See Evans, R. et al., *Race Relations in Colonial Queensland*, pp. 293–9. As the *Northern Miner* noted on 26 May, 1877, 'There is no affinity between them and men of the Caucasian race, and miscegenation of races so physically antagonism must inevitably degrade the higher race.' Quoted in Evans, R., op. cit., p. 261.
47 Douglas considered the scourge of opium to be 'A terrible curse to a nation … Worse even than whisky. Worse than gin or rum or brandy or any other spirits.' John Douglas to his son, Robert Douglas, 19 May, 1894, copy in possession of the author.
48 *Torres Straits Pilot and New Guinea Gazette*, 23 September, 1899. p. 3.
49 J. Douglas to his children, 7 September, 1893, copy in possession of the author. 'J. Douglas, Report of the Government Resident at Thursday Island for 1898.' p. 6.
50 J. Douglas to Edward Douglas, 7 October, 1894, copy in possession of the author.
51 'J. Douglas, Report of the Government Resident at Thursday Island for 1898.' p. 6.
52 Douglas, J., 'Asiatic aliens in Torres Straits', p. 1.
53 Ibid., p. 2; Douglas, J. 1902. 'Asia and Australasia.' *The Nineteenth Century and After*, July. p. 51.
54 Perdon, R. 1998. *Brown Americans of Asia*. Sydney: Manila Prints. p. 116. 'J. Douglas, Report of the Government Resident at Thursday Island for 1894–95.' p. 2. Douglas was a strong supporter of naturalisation, see 'Report of the Government Resident at Thursday Island for 1896 and 1897', p. 4.
55 Quoted in Perdon, R., *Brown Americans of Asia*, p. 121.
56 Douglas, J. 'Minutes of Evidence taken before the Pearl-Shell and Bêche-de-Mer Fisheries Commission.' 'Report, together with Minutes of Evidence and Proceedings, of the Commission Appointed to Inquire into the General Working of the Laws Regulating the Pearl-Shell and Bêche-de-Mer Fisheries in the Colony, 1897.' p. 2.

57 Eykyn, T. 1896. *Parts of the Pacific*. London: Swan Sonnenschein. p. 99.

58 Douglas, J, 'Asiatic aliens in Torres Straits', p. 2.

59 Ibid., pp. 6–7. 'F. Urquhart to J. Douglas, 24 July 1895.' PRE/105, QSA. For details on the murder of Conroy, see 'Police Commissioner's staff files', file 300 AF [re William Conroy], A/38748, QSA. I am indebted to Anna Shnukal for alerting me to the file's existence.

60 'J. Douglas, Annual Report of the Government Resident at Thursday Island, 1890.' p. 6.

61 'J. Douglas, Annual Report of the Government Resident at Thursday Island, 1892.' p. 2.

62 'Brown and Black.' *Torres Straits Pilot and New Guinea Gazette*, 19 January, 1901. p. 2.

63 Ibid.; 'The pearl shelling industry.' *Sydney Morning Herald*, 2 May, 1901. p. 4.

64 Douglas, J., 'Asia and Australasia', p. 51.

65 'H. Milman, Report of the Government Resident at Thursday Island for 1904.' p. 6. Ganter, R., *The pearl-shellers of Torres Strait*, p. 107.

Thursday Island personalities, 1935.
Courtesy of John Oxley Library, Brisbane (Item No. 42823).

CHAPTER NINE

Coloured People

A challenge to racial stereotypes[1]

Regina Ganter

The Asian diaspora is so deeply embedded in Australian history that its most profound consequence has been the emergence of large Coloured populations in the north. Nevertheless, the public memory of race in Australia is neatly constructed around binaries (Black/White, Asian/Anglo) where Whiteness is the central reference point. National anxieties over Asian immigration and Indigenous rights are steeped in a sense of national history where such binaries were taken to be empirically validated. Looking at the history of the northern half of the continent, however, seriously disrupts most of the central premises of Australian national history. This paper examines the historical phenomenon of Australian people beyond the racial binaries, using a case study from Thursday Island to make the point that vast populations in northern Australia were beyond the scope of such binary thinking.

Being 'Coloured' means being positioned beyond neat categories. It is not so much an individual ascription as an expression of community. Coloured communities typically include descendants of Asians, Pacific Islanders and Indigenous Australians. The very usefulness of this ascription was and continues to be its defiance of all the categories of people who have historically been the subject of legislation such as 'alien', 'naturalised', 'Aboriginal' and 'Asian'. Aboriginal protection bureaucracies were extremely concerned about Coloured populations. They invested much effort in stretching the limits of their reach, even resorting to illegal measures. Just as strenuously, the Coloured populations resisted being drawn under the powers of Aboriginal protection, with the result that they played a strong role in the assertion of Aboriginal rights.

There still are vast populations in northern Australia who refer to themselves as 'Coloured'. Since access to citizenship for Indigenous Australians has been linked to Indigenous identity — an identity that previously debarred them from citizenship — it has become difficult to remain 'Coloured', and many of these families are beset by intense conflicts over identity, uncertain whether their forebears were, or were not, considered Aboriginal people, and what impact this may have on their access to citizenship rights. Occasionally, such instances reach the courts and people who may have lived all their lives as Aborigines may be told that they have fraudulently claimed Aboriginality and certain citizenship benefits attached to that identity.[2] Uncertainty arises not only from a legacy of massive displacements from traditional land, removals from families, and unreliable records, but because the legislative boundaries that have been drawn around Indigenous Australians have been empirically fluid.

Aboriginal Protection: maintaining racial boundaries

Under the countenance of protecting them from extermination and abuse, Aboriginal people have been subject to highly paternalistic legislation. In Queensland, the first comprehensive 'Black Act' (Aboriginals Protection and Restriction of the Sale of Opium Act 1897) set in motion a vast bureaucracy with powers to remove Aborigines to reserves, to declare children of mixed descent wards of the state, to oversee all employment of Aborigines and, eventually, to channel the whole gamut of government services such as health, education, welfare and housing. It was a holistic approach to the 'Aboriginal problem'.

It was also a clear expression of anti-Chinese sentiments, its major target of intervention being the supply of charcoal opium to Aborigines by Chinese. One-third of the act dealt exclusively with the possession and distribution of opium (to anyone). Asian-Aboriginal children were specially targeted for removal as neglected children and the discussions surrounding the introduction of the 1897 act were very much focused on the experience of far north Queensland, where the marine industries, conducted almost exclusively by Asian and other Coloured men, were subject to particular government attention.[3]

Chinese had been the first target of xenophobic legislation in Australia (1850s to 1880s), responding to Chinese numerical predominance on the goldfields. By the 1890s, the more inclusive category of 'Asian' had become the target of concern, in response to the many Japanese, Filipinos and Malays

(Indonesians) who participated in the northern pearling industry, as well as Sindhis (Afghans and Indians) and Sri Lankans who had settled in northern Australia in large numbers. In Queensland, each major policy step in Aboriginal protection legislation was deeply imprinted by the meeting of Asian and Aboriginal populations in the far north, who, in many cases, shared the customs of polygyny and promised marriage, as well as a common experience of disempowerment.

The moral universe of the patriarchal state clearly defined the role of women in the maintenance of family, class and race. Coloured women, then, were an essentially intractable, morally suspicious phenomenon, an administrative and ethical problem. This 'problem' quickly moved to the core of Aboriginal administration, so that Asians in Australian history are strongly implicated in the 'Stolen Generation', which has lately become a rallying point of Indigenous politics.

The challenge Coloured women posed to a White Australia during the first half of the 20th century is intricately linked to predominant attitudes towards Asians. That Aboriginal policy must be read against the presence of Asian men in the north is demonstrated here with reference to legislation in Queensland to the 1930s.

The interactions of Asian men with Indigenous Australian women were always viewed with suspicion and considered tendentially immoral, not least since Asian men were themselves considered tendentially immoral.[4] Since very few Asian, Pacific and other 'Coloured' women were permitted entry (to discourage the formation of Coloured families in Australia), those who were in Queensland were either suspected of engaging in, or they were the offspring of, what were considered 'pernicious associations', sexual relations across racial boundaries. Coloured women therefore threatened the race/class distinctions between Black and White. Their legal existence was in the interstices between protective legislation extended over Indigenous Australians, and restrictive legislation extended over aliens, particularly Asians.

By 1901, significant advances had been made in Aboriginal administration by means of an impressively efficient network of reporting through 10 local protectors, the powers to remove Aboriginal people to missions and reserves, and the supervision of employment by means of a permit (which was refused to Chinese, again, as a matter of policy until it became law in 1902). The Southern Protector, Archibald Meston, confidently predicted that Aborigines would be extinct by the 1950s,[5] but the Northern Protector, Dr Walter Roth, became concerned about the increasing 'half-caste' population.[6] At his instigation, the 1897 act was amended to furnish further powers to the Protector of Aborigines over interracial unions. Much of the inspiration for this amendment again came from the marine industries of the far north,[7] and a close reading of the discussions surrounding this amending legislation reveals that the bureaucracy was concerned not merely about mixed descendants generally, but quite specifically about 'coloured half-castes'.

Pernicious Associations and Moral Rectitude

In January 1901, Roth brought the increase of marriages between Aboriginal women and non-Aboriginal men to the special attention of the Home Department, asking that 'some check should be placed' on this development with the parenthesised specification '(especially in the case of Asiatics and Kanakas)'.[8] While the amendment bill was being debated in parliament (July to October 1901), Roth commented several times on 'the evils to which the promiscuous marriage of aboriginal women with coloured aliens may lead' and on 'the frequency of marriages which have been solemnised of late between Kanakas and Aboriginal women'.[9] He felt certain that 'the new Aboriginals Amending Act will however easily cope with the evil'.[10]

Roth's opinion was highly esteemed by the Home Secretary, to whom he was responsible. His various reports were also the authoritative source around which the parliamentary debate was structured. The amendment bill was very much Roth's bill, the Southern Protector complaining that he had not been consulted.[11]

Roth suggested that all ministers of religion and others appointed to celebrate marriages should be instructed not to sanction any unions between Aboriginal women and Coloured aliens without seeking his advice. A circular memo was sent to all ministers of religion and marrying justices in Queensland urging them to 'use every endeavour to prevent the marriage ceremony becoming the harbour of refuge for those men who (under the Aboriginal Protection Act 1897) are deemed unfit to employ natives'.[12] The reference to Asians was implicit in these instructions.

During the debate of the amendment bill, strong concerns were expressed about the wide powers it bestowed on protectors.[13] The honorable gentlemen were concerned about the balance of power between the bureaucracy and White employers. The Home Secretary, however, assured them that the bill was framed with a view to Asian men:

> The reason why legislation is asked for is that an Asiatic, who is known to
> have been convicted of offences against the Act — for supplying blacks
> with opium, for instance — upon a prosecution being attempted against
> him for a breach of the Act with regard to harbouring a gin and her family,
> perhaps portion of that family being his own children, does this: He goes

through a form of marriage with that gin, and defies the law … If he wants to sever it he packs up his traps and goes elsewhere. But he is able, by going through that form of marriage, to defy the protector … these men are absolutely unfit to be entrusted with the care of aboriginals … The permission referred to in the Bill would never be refused in the case of any man who desired to marry an aboriginal or half-caste woman, provided he was a respectable man and was not suspected of supplying opium to Asians or aboriginals.[14]

An attempt to pass such a bill had failed in 1899. It had included a provision to bar all Asians from employing Aborigines and the Japanese Government had lodged a formal protest against this discriminatory provision. There was much support for inserting a similar clause in the 1901 amendment to bar, if possible, all Asians from employing Aborigines. Various members toyed with this amendment, seeking to exclude also Melanesians, Polynesians and Africans, but this was strenuously opposed by the Home Secretary, who feared that royal assent would be withheld as a result. After much debate, the upper and lower houses settled on excluding only Chinese: 'A permit to employ an aboriginal or half-caste shall not be granted to any alien of the Chinese race' (Section 5 clause 2), because, it was stated, China was on its knees and would not lodge a protest.[15]

Roth had tried to head off such a provision, which might jeopardise the amendment act, by arguing that Chinese could be better employers than Whites:

Chinese farmers who employ aboriginals treat them very much better than most of the white people who employ them … The Chinese offer better wages, and, what is more, pay the aboriginals their wages when due; they also house and feed them well … I cannot instruct the local protector to prevent Chinese employing them (as was urged by the Atherton Progress Association some two and a-half years ago).[16]

This does not mean that Roth viewed Asian employers favourably, only that he was politically astute. Elsewhere he stated that he was 'personally averse' to Chinese employing Aborigines.[17]

To strengthen his argument for the amendment bill, Roth made special inquiries among regional protectors about Aboriginal women living with Coloured men, and he forwarded the response received from Mossman in coastal north Queensland as a 'further illustration of the evils which the promiscuous marriage of aboriginal women with coloured aliens has led to'. The label 'promiscuous' is interesting, since the Mossman report refers to couples living in sanctioned matrimony:

> There are nine aboriginal women living in this district at present who either live with Kanakas or Chinamen but they mostly all hold a marriage certificate as most of them went through a form of marriage with the Kanakas in the English and Methodist churches here about last January … Some of these married gins are almost constantly working about the Hotels in the township and appear to be able to procure for themselves and the Kanakas a goodly supply of spirituous liquor.[18]

After the amendment bill was passed, Roth was vested with the powers to authorise mixed marriages,[19] and the policy was to disallow marriages with Coloured men. To a request by a Japanese resident of Thursday Island to marry a girl from Murray Island, the Chief Protector replied that 'such marriages are much deprecated and it is not considered advisable to allow Japanese to inter-marry with aboriginals'.[20] Local protectors and missionaries shared the Chief Protector's views that associations with Coloured men were especially pernicious.[21]

With the 1901 amendment, the Aboriginal protection bureaucracy set itself up quite explicitly as a moral arbiter. Having the power to sanction mixed marriages, it came under a barrage of requests for permission to marry, and made it its task to decide in each case whether this marriage was morally desirable. Ros Kidd has characterised the ethic of this bureaucracy, which gradually transformed itself into a fully fledged department, as a 'medical/moral policing rationale'.[22]

Moral rectitude as a guide for action is clearly reflected in the annotations that appear in the *Removals Register* as justification for removals. Next to annotations referring to destitution and disease, the recurring annotations were 'frequenting Chinese dens', 'loafer', 'quarrelsome', 'drunkard', 'immoral'. The relatively large number of case files where written objections were raised to removals, so that cases are discussed in greater detail, demonstrates that these were convenient labels to trigger and justify intervention which did not normally need to be further substantiated.

Moreover, judgments about the morality of Indigenous Australians did not need to be made on a case-by-case basis. In 1915, 159 people were removed in one sweep from Hull River in north Queensland with the explanation 'loafing class, are a hindrance and annoyance to better class of aboriginals'. One must wonder how many were left behind to whom these 159 might have been an annoyance. Administrative convenience presents itself as a much more credible explanation for this mass removal at a time when a new reserve was being established in the area. A random perusal of the *Removals Register*, which is far from comprehensive, shows that, in 1935, a group of 23 was removed from

Turn-Off Lagoon (near Burketown in the northern Gulf country), to Mornington Island for 'immoral associations'. Association with Asians was often a sufficient expression of immorality to warrant removal.

To compound the difficulties for the paternalistic state, which sought to maintain a clear distinction between White and Black, or desirable and protected populations, a numerous Coloured population emerged in the north, which challenged such distinctions. The emergence of this Coloured population owed much to the marine industries centred on Broome in Western Australia, Darwin in the Northern Territory and Thursday Island in Queensland.

The Protection Act of 1897 made provision for 'half-castes' as well as Aborigines. By 'half-castes' were meant not any mixed Aboriginal descendents, but quite specifically 'the offspring of an Aboriginal mother and other than an Aboriginal father'.[23] By the 1920s, the mixed population no longer conformed to this definition, and administrative labels were devised to gain a leverage on the emerging Coloured populations. The notion of 'quadroons' (and 'octoroons' — carrying one-eighth Aboriginal blood) emerged as an administrative category. This category was tested in the case of a young woman, Atima Ahwang, who twice served as a test case for the powers of protectors over the Coloured population of Thursday Island. This young woman became so trapped in bureaucratic machinery that it is possible to trace the extension of departmental powers through the personal story of Atima and her family, a family that was a phenomenon of the pearling industry in the north.

A Dynamic Industry and the Response of the State

From the 1880s to the turn of the century, the Torres Strait was at the edge of international opportunity, fired by a growing and modern industry that used diving apparatus to access depths of the sea never reached before, and which used all its colonial connections to assemble teams of fit and daring young men from Asia and the Pacific to staff the diving boats on the one hand and, on the other hand, to sell the mother-of-pearl raised by them on the Continent and in the US, and market bêche-de-mer into Asia.

The emergence of this industry in Torres Strait was as swift as the arrival of microchips a century later. The more or less accidental, but certainly spectacular discovery of precious pearl shell at Warrior Island in 1869 by Pacific trading connections transformed the Torres Strait and brought it to the attention of a keen government and traders. As a result of this commercial interest, the Torres Strait became part of Australia. By 1879, Pacific trading companies from Australia, Britain and Germany were running 109 vessels in the strait. In that year, Queensland responded to this new income-earning activity by extending its jurisdiction over the whole Torres Strait. The government outpost established at Albany Island in 1862 had been shifted to Somerset (March 1863) and then to Thursday Island (1876–77) in an attempt to move closer to the industry, and Queensland had extended its jurisdiction to 60 miles from Cape York in 1872 to regulate the industry. The London Missionary Society established an outpost in Torres Strait in 1871 and it and the traders brought thousands of Melanesians and Polynesians into Torres Strait. Well entrenched in the Pacific, the traders used their blackbirding connections to supply labour to the pearl-shell stations.

The trade in Pacific Island labour came under national and international criticism from the anti-slavery movement, and some measure of protection was afforded to Pacific Islanders through the Pacific Islanders Protection Act of 1872 (an imperial act, referred to as the Kidnapping Act), and Queensland's own Pacific Islanders Protection Act of 1880 (which, however, exempted the marine industries). Possibly as a result of this, Asians began to be imported as workers through Singapore and Hong Kong during the 1880s.

One of these Asians was Ahwang, or Ahwang Dai, (c.1860–1935), a Dayak, the son of a boatbuilder in the Singapore Strait settlement. In 1891, he married Annie (c.1873–1956), a woman from Badu Island in Torres Strait.[24]

The Emergence of Legal Distinctions

At the time when Annie married Ahwang, the legislative distinctions between Torres Strait Islanders (Annie's mother), Pacific Islanders (Annie's father) and Malays (classed as Asians) resident in Queensland were only just emerging, just as the genetic and cultural differences between them were becoming blurred. ('Malay' was a term used for the peoples of Malaysia, Indonesia and Singapore, including the then Dutch East Indies. See Anna Shnukal's Chapter Four, this volume.) By 1908, an estimated 200 out of 230 residents of Darnley Island in Torres Strait were South Sea Islanders and their descendants. All Torres Strait Islanders were legally Pacific Islanders ('not under the influence of any civilised power') until 1872, and those north of 10th degree latitude were so classed until 1879. The first legal distinction was made between Australian Indigenes and other Pacific Islanders with the introduction of the Native Labourers' Protection Act of 1884, which regulated the employment of Indigenes of Australia and Papua in the marine industries. When the 1897 Aborigines Protection Act was introduced, Torres Strait Islanders were exempted from its provisions until 1904.[25]

When Annie Ahwang's first three children were born, between 1891 and 1895, being a native of Torres Strait, or of the Pacific, or of the Singapore Strait settlement, made little difference to one's status as a subject vis-a-vis the State. As British subjects, Malays from Singapore were able to lease land and to become naturalised. When she was having Atima in 1898 and another three babies by 1904, Annie and her husband may have had some news about new legislation affecting Queensland Aboriginal people, though the mainland was far away, and life at Badu was vastly different from the life of camp Aborigines.[26]

In 1904, a new Government Resident and a new Protector of Aborigines were appointed to Thursday Island,[27] and both agreed that all Australian Indigenes, including those of Torres Strait, were to be protected by the new bureaucracy, and their employment and wages would be supervised and regulated. All settled Torres Strait islands were declared reserves. Torres Strait Islanders were to be brought under the act and there was to be no further distinction between Aborigines and Torres Strait Islanders.[28] This meant that part-Torres Strait descendants of Malays, Pacific Islanders and others were to be classed as 'half-caste' if they were either married to, or habitually lived or associated with Aborigines (including Torres Strait Islanders).

Like many others who felt threatened by this new policy, Ahwang promptly gathered up his now substantial family of nine children and moved to Thursday Island at some time in 1904 or 1905 so that it could not be said that his children (and perhaps his wife) 'habitually associated' with Aborigines and to protect them from the 'half-caste' label and the intrusion of the State:

> That's why my father brought the children from Badu. They left from Badu to TI. You had to be certain miles away so you don't come under the Act. Badu was in the limits. My father had to take the children to Thursday Island. But we not supposed to be under the Act, my father come from a different country. Shouldn't be under the Act.[29]

A Coloured Population

Thursday Island, the commercial centre of Torres Strait and the pearling industry, was meant to be a White administrative settlement. 'Natives' were prohibited from staying overnight and most Asians were accommodated in special guesthouses but, except during the lay-up season, crews usually stayed on the luggers.

As in the other northern townships, however, Thursday Island's supposed White predominance was always under siege. By the 1890s, the shops were owned mainly by Asians, including Japanese, Chinese and Sri Lankans, there was a 'Malaytown' and a 'Japtown' with boarding houses, a public bath, stores and a brothel. The Japanese had become deeply entrenched in the pearling industry, owning most of the boat slips and building all the boats. In 1894, there were 700 Japanese, far more than Europeans, on Thursday Island; in 1897, they numbered double the European population, which was further dwarfed by considerable numbers of other Asian residents. 'Outnumbered' is part of the standard lexicon of north Australian histories.

Queensland enacted its own Asian immigration restrictions before the Federal White Australia Policy was implemented.[30] The pearl-shell industry, however, remained exempted from the provisions of the Federal Immigration Restriction Act (1901) to enable the further importation of Asians under indenture contracts, but barring them from ownership of boats, businesses or land, and from naturalisation. Thursday Island continued to be decidedly un-British and non-White in atmosphere and population: 'You don't wear trousers, you wear sarong all the time. And *tabi*, Japanese boot.'[31]

While people on Thursday Island (as in Broome and Darwin) generally coped very well with their multi-ethnic surrounds, such developments were viewed with suspicion further south. The Hansard records the following vitriol from the Member for Clermont, who felt that:

> The presence of coloured aliens on Thursday Island was a distinct menace to the white population, not only of the island but of Australia generally. Queensland had long been recognised as the open door through which were permitted to enter not only this State but eventually the whole of Australia hundreds of thousands of coloured persons coming from the east, bringing with them their barbarous systems, the curious codes of morals which were peculiar to those peoples, and making of Thursday Island a regular little Chinese, Cingalese, or Japanese principality. The presence of those persons was undoubtedly a danger to the people of Australia who at the federal elections had declared emphatically for a white Australia. The island, he maintained, should be peopled by white races.[32]

As in the other pearling centres, a cosmopolitan, native-born population emerged on Thursday Island in addition to the 'coloured aliens' through intermarriage, a population that was not strictly Asian, not strictly Indigenous, nor 'White' enough to escape comment and which, in fact, defied all description except to call it 'Coloured'. 'Coloured' became a semi-official category for non-White Australians who were not necessarily subject to any particular set of legislation (such as that aimed at 'Asiatic aliens', Indigenous Australians, Pacific Islanders, etc.). Australian-born Coloured people could enjoy full formal citizenship, but the label itself sidestepped all such legal distinctions. Being Coloured was what united families and neighbourhoods across the various legal positions it was possible to have. A Thursday Island census of 1914 counted 1,650 Coloured men (including those engaged in the pearling fleets) and 137 Coloured women. Having close family links to Indigenous families, to Asian families, and yet mostly unfettered by restrictive and protective legislation, this population was an administrative problem.

The Ahwang family on Thursday Island was considered part of this growing administrative problem. Local Protectors of Aborigines had a special brief to supervise Indigenous and 'half-caste' women and children with a view to presiding over moral rectitude according to British legal and religious traditions. They were often faced with requests from 'half-caste' women to marry Asian men and knew that such marriages with non-British, non-Christian men did not always concur with British legal and Christian moral principles. Having placed itself in the position to adjudicate over such marriages, the bureaucracy needed frequently to ponder whether these ought to be sanctioned.

Permission to Marry

In March 1914, the Thursday Island Protector of Aborigines, Government Resident and Police Magistrate, William Lee-Bryce, was faced with a request for permission for the marriage of an Asian[33] and a 16-year-old Asian-Aboriginal woman, Saya.[34] The woman was expecting a child, and her father strongly approved of the marriage. The young woman stated that 'she was promised to him long ago'. The promise system of marriage was recognised by Australian Aborigines (the girl's mother), Filipinos (the girl's father), Muslim Indians (the prospective spouse according to oral history) and Malays (the prospective spouse according to Lee-Bryce). It was not recognised by the British legal tradition of the 19th century, although it had been practised in Britain in earlier centuries. The family, steeped in non-British traditions, sought to obtain official sanction for the marriage shortly before the child was born in order to satisfy the requirements of the current British legal-moral universe as well. Lee-Bryce speculated that the girl's father 'probably received some valuable consideration for his consent' (also a custom widely recognised among the cultures referred to) and could not avoid touching on the subject of her mother's 'intemperate habits', although the mother had been removed and was not living with the girl. He withheld approval.

The girl was working as a domestic in a White household and the child had a White father. Although the 1901 amendment act gave clear powers to discover the paternity of mixed descendants, the identity of this man was not known to or sought by the department. By the time Lee-Bryce reported on the case, the baby had been born and therefore he was able to refer to the girl's 'immoral habits', and recommended that she be removed 'to a southern settlement for a short period and then hired out to some person who will be strict with her'.[35]

At the same time, he referred to two other cases, which appeared to him to be of a similar nature. One was the Aboriginal (or part-Aboriginal) wife of a Filipino bêche-de-mer fisherman, who 'frequently lives for long periods with men engaged in the bêche-de-mer fishery'. She ought to be returned to Mapoon with her baby, and her older children should be sent to the Roman Catholic priest and Sisters of the Sacred Heart on Thursday Island, suggested the Protector.

The other, apparently similar case was that of 'Atima Awong' (Ahwang), age 17, 'the daughter of a Malay and a half-caste Torres Strait Islander'. Lee-Bryce hastened to admit that 'strictly speaking she does not come under the Aboriginal Act but she and others similarly situated have been treated as being under the control of the Protector'. Atima was about to marry a Malay engaged by a pearling company when Lee-Bryce informed her and her father that permission was required. Ahwang, evidently in favour of his daughter's marriage to a compatriot, and keen on steering his family away from the paternalistic infringements of the State, ignored this instruction and proceeded with a 'Malay fashion' wedding. Lee-Bryce speculated, 'I strongly suspect she has been married "Malay fashion" on more than one occasion.'[36] Relying on official documentation, it is difficult to ascertain what a 'Malay fashion' marriage was, except that it clearly was not an officially sanctioned wedding. The wedding was backed by the spouse's employer, Reg Hocking, a pearling master in Australia and Dutch New Guinea, who was also the Honorary Dutch Consul, and who is very likely to have had some familiarity with Malay customs. About Lee-Bryce's familiarity with or tolerance of Malay customs, we can only speculate. Certainly, the Chief Protectors in Queensland after Roth were administrators and not ethnographers, and to refer to a 'Malay fashion' marriage was clearly an expression of disapproval for unsanctioned cohabitation.

Atima and her spouse, now living as man and wife, had undermined the Protector's authority, and Lee-Bryce put his foot down. He resolved that the marriage was not to be sanctioned or recognised, and the couple should be torn apart. Knowing that Atima was not actually within his domain of powers, Lee-Bryce recommended that 'the Minister will strain the interpretations of the Act and order the removal of Atima to a southern settlement — it will be for the girl's good and serve as an example to others'.[37]

The entry in the *Removals Register*, recording the removal of Saya and Atima from Thursday Island to Barambah, reads: 'For their own protection. Living immoral lives.'[38] Both young women were sent into exile for several years for wanting to marry the men who met with the approval of their fathers.

The third woman was also removed with her baby for 'living an immoral life'. What was the thread of logic that united these three women's lives? One had a child out of wedlock, the other was suspected of prostitution, the other was in a de-facto relationship. Summarising the three cases, Lee-Bryce wrote:

> Unless some strong stand is taken with girls like Saya and Atima, numerous other cases of similar description will occur: the consent to the marriage would be accepted by the coloured population as a sign of weakness, and immorality would become a lever to procure the necessary permission to marry.[39]

The Protector had no legal powers over this population and sought to affirm his moral authority. Though the key indictments of these women's morality were by way of speculation ('I strongly *suspect* she has been married "Malay fashion" on more than one occasion', '*probably* the father received some valuable consideration for his consent', 'frequently *lives with* men engaged in the bêche-de-mer fishery'), the Chief Protector supported Lee-Bryce. The ensuing distortion of protective powers exemplifies the legal existence of Coloured people in the interstices of protective legislation at the time.

Saya was permitted to return after three years and married her promised husband, an Indian fishmonger, with whom she proceeded to have eight children. Whereas Saya's official file ends with her removal, Atima's file begins there. It contains, apart from the original copy of a personal love letter from her promised husband, no less than seven pleas for her release — from her employers, from her father, from herself, and from John Douglas MP on Thursday Island. All of these pleas fell on deaf ears. Together with the replies to these letters, they unravel the story of Atima's entirely illegal removal.

Illegal Removal

According to her employer, Atima was a highly regarded and well-protected domestic. She had worked for several respected White families on Thursday Island. Her employer, Mrs Riley, wrote:

> this girl Atima has been the best servant I have ever had including white and black and during the whole term of service with me I have not one black mark against her. She was industrious, faithful and most trustworthy and why such an extreme action has been taken I fail to see. People here who have employed her such as Mrs K. O. Mackenzie, Mrs Allan (shipping master) and others are like ourselves very incensed at the action as they all know what an extremely good girl she has been.[40]

Mrs Riley explained that Atima lived with her parents, and one of her family waited for her in the Rileys' kitchen every evening to walk her home. On the afternoon of 16 June, 1914, she had taken her employer's children for a walk to her parents' house when two plain-clothes policemen appeared to arrest her, walked her to the watch-house by a back way, kept her locked up all night and placed her the next morning on the ship to Brisbane. She had been given no warning of her arrest, no opportunity to pack a suitcase or to 'purchase one solitary warm stitch of clothing, consequently she has been freezing ever since she left here'.[41] (Barambah, now Cherbourg, near Brisbane, would have been very chilly in June/July.) Nor were her employers warned of her impending arrest, nor any arrangements made for the children who were in Atima's charge at the time. When the policemen appeared at her employer's home at 4pm, her employer protested against her removal, and promptly telexed the Home Secretary, A. G. Appel, before the close of business on the same day, arguing that Atima was under legal agreement until October and that her removal was 'unjustifiable and drastic'. Mr Riley was under the clear impression that the removal order had been signed by Appel.[42]

In response to this pressure, the police were asked to explain the 'drastic action', and the constable in charge declared that he had received the minister's order for Atima's deportation per steamer *Changsha* on 16 June, only a day before its departure. Two things are amiss with this explanation. The *Changsha* was only one of the three monthly steamer services connecting Thursday Island with Hong Kong, Manila, Japan, Singapore and the southern ports of Australia. Transportation to Brisbane could not have been very difficult in almost any week of the year. Moreover, the minister's orders for the removal of Atima and Saya were not signed until 28 September, 1914, long after the removals were effected.[43] It is possible, but undocumented, that an order for Atima's removal was issued previously by the Acting Home Secretary, A. H. Barlow, on 2 May, 1914, as Chief Protector Bleakley later claimed,[44] but it is not clear why in that case a second order had to be issued retrospectively in September.

Being under a legal agreement to an employer placed Atima outside the ambit of protectors' powers for removal according to Section 10a of the 1897 act (even if it had been agreed that she was included under this act at all). To stifle possible embarrassment in the face of the inquiries instigated by Riley, the entire administration, including the Under Secretary of the Home Department, considered that 'the matter can be best adjusted by allowing Mr Riley to engage another girl'.[45] The Rileys, however, argued that they had no need for another domestic. They entertained close links with the Ahwang family and wished Atima to be returned to their service, and for several months Mrs Riley refused to employ another domestic. In her correspondence and exchange of parcels with Atima, she claimed that 'we still do all our own work and no one to help us'.[46]

Atima became the subject of a personal consultation between the Home Secretary and Chief Protector Bleakley, with the result that the administration rallied behind the local Protector's stance because

> the removal of Atima and Saya had a great moral effect, but if they are not detained for a few years my influence with the coloured population will be seriously affected.[47]

This removal was clearly ultra vires, and the bureaucracy was fully aware of this. The Chief Protector informed the Home Department:

> From the facts that the girl was a quadroon Malay and legally under agreement at the time she was really exempt from removal, but the Protector apparently acted in the interests of discipline and morality and it is certainly expedient that this action, though perhaps not entirely correct, should be upheld.[48]

The more pressure was placed on the administration, the more determined it became to stand its ground. To the intervention by Douglas, the local Protector replied:

> it is quite evident Mr Riley has decided to ignore me and endeavour to obtain what he desires through other channels … It has been well known here for some time that Mr Riley was using every influence at his command to secure the object he has in view and if his request is granted my position will be considerably weakened in the eyes of both the white and the coloured population.[49]

In this entire correspondence, no shadow of doubt was cast on Riley's good character that would justify the action taken. The 'object he had in view' was Atima's return into his wife's employment. Riley fell foul of the administration because he challenged the bureaucracy. The Protector strongly advised that Atima should not be allowed to return.

Despite all efforts on her behalf, Atima was now fully in the grip of the act. When she asked for 10 shillings out of her earnings to send to her ailing father, the Brisbane protectress passed on the request to the Chief Protector. The Chief Protector, also unable to reach a decision by himself, consulted the local Protector on Thursday Island, who considered that 'The father is not in need and could probably do light work if he cared to'.[50]

Much doubt was cast on the character of Atima's father in this correspondence, referring to his gambling habit. He engaged in the very popular Thursday Island pastimes of *chiffa*, 'luk-luk pat', and other games. His fortunes rose and fell and he may in times of need have leaned on his children. According to his two surviving sons, he amassed the wealth to buy a house on Thursday Island through gambling, and lost it in the same manner.[51] With the removal of Atima, the whole family became subject to the paternalistic rhetoric that was part of the discursive culture of the department, where it was quite common to make unsubstantiated detrimental comments about people's lifestyles. (One of the protectors, steeped in this rhetoric, had to be reminded by another department with which he was corresponding after World War II that his incriminating comments about the living conditions of an Aboriginal/Japanese/Chinese family were 'irrelevant for the decision to be made'.[52])

After Lee-Bryce's death in December 1916, Mrs Riley resumed her lobbying efforts. The acting Protector supported Atima's release, but Bleakley insisted that she serve out her current contract as a domestic in Brisbane. He argued that 'The girl appears very happy and well looked after in her present place', that Mrs Riley was placing unwarranted pressure on her, and that

> Atima informs me she wishes to visit Thursday Island, but only for a holiday, in about six months time, after the wet season, and when she has saved sufficient to pay for her trip.[53]

Atima's own letter to the Chief Protector the next month put the lie to this interpretation:

> Dear Mr Bleakly, just a few lines to let you know that I made up my mind to go back to Mrs Riley again when my times up. I think she done her best to get me back since I been away from her place and I like her very much. I was quite happy with her. Also Mrs Cameron. And I think I been here long enough with Mrs Cameron. So I would like to know if you let me go back to Mrs Riley for good. I rote to her and told her that I was going to ask you to let me go back. So I have nothing more to say. Your faithfull Atima Ahwang.[54]

This is likely to be as determined as a 19-year-old dared to be with the Chief Protector. Atima returned to Thursday Island after more than three and a half years of exile, but she was unable to shake off the shadow of the bureaucracy's watchful eye over her personal affairs.

A Matter of Definition

At some time in 1919, Atima had a baby and it appears that she came under some pressure to enter into a marriage. In June 1919 and in March 1920, applications were made for the marriage of Atima by two different candidates, both of whom the bureaucracy would have considered 'suitable matches'. Both marriages were approved, but neither of them took place. Atima seemed quite keen now to escape the arm of the department. In her first marriage application, she claimed to have been born on Thursday Island. Forwarding this application, the new Protector pondered:

> It is questionable whether either of the applicants come under the Aboriginal Act — the former [Atima] having been signed on under the Act for some years I think it better to be on the safe side, and obtain your consent.[55]

The department remained 'on the safe side' and held vigil over this woman. In September 1920, the local Protector questioned her about her intended marriage and, within a few weeks, Atima, very likely now tired of this moral persecution and following her older brother's example, evidently decided to clear her status once and for all and applied for formal exemption from the act. Although the department had always been of the opinion that she was not 'strictly speaking' under the act, her application was refused. Subscribing to the 'safe side' logic, the refusal was justified as follows:

> it does not appear that being under Departmental control inflicts any hardships upon the girl and on the other hand apparently no additional benefit would accrue to her from being exempt from supervision.[56]

No hardship, indeed! She had been exiled for more than three years, barred from marrying, had her wages banked by the department, had been questioned by officials about her romantic involvements and had been cast as immoral.

Atima's application for exemption was supported by letters from Walter Filewood, the union representative, addressed personally to Home Secretary McCormack ('trusting this finds the labour party a successful term of office'), to Chief Protector Bleakley ('regards to you and your brother Charles'), and to the local member, Ryan ('I conduct his election business').[57]

Going over the head of the local Protector was a direct affront to the bureaucracy. The department responded by proceeding against Filewood, who was possibly having an affair with Atima, for 'harbouring a female half-caste'. To be successful, however, the department needed to first ascertain that Atima was a 'half-caste' under the act. This question was not settled in response to Atima's application for exemption, but in order to proceed against Filewood for harbouring.

The current legal definition of 'half-caste' was the offspring of an Aboriginal mother and other than an Aboriginal father (Section 3 of the 1897 act). Section 4 of the act, however, made three further provisions by which 'half-castes' could be considered Aboriginal. This was the case if they had been living with an Aboriginal spouse at the passing of the act (Clause b), if they otherwise habitually associated with Aboriginals (Clause c) or if, in the Protector's opinion, their age did not exceed 16 years (Clause d). Consequently, if it could be argued that Atima's mother Annie was not a 'half-caste', but an Aboriginal, then Atima would be a 'half-caste' under the act. Bleakley referred this question to the Home Secretary, already suggesting which decision ought to be reached on the question:

> A question has arisen in regard to the position of a crossbreed girl … It is extremely important that the Protector should, if possible, have the power to deal with this case to maintain discipline amongst the numerous crossbreeds under his charge.[58]

The Crown Solicitor was now asked for the first time to consider the status of quadroons under the act. He determined, and a circular (No. 21/6) was sent to all protectors stating that:

> A female quadroon comes within Section 14 of the A. P. Acts of 1897 if it can be established that the mother is the offspring of an aboriginal mother and other than an aboriginal father and that she (the mother) otherwise than as wife, habitually lived or associated with Aboriginals.[59]

This meant that such a female could not be harboured without penalty. This did not, however, fully answer the case because of the complicating temporal dimension of the definition. The local Protector now formulated the following questions about Atima for consideration by the Crown Law Office: Atima's mother Annie was the daughter of a native of Madagascar[60] and a full-blood native of Badu, and married to a Malay. She lived at Badu Island at the passing of the 1897 act and until 1904 or 1905, but had not since then habitually lived or associated with Aborigines. Was Annie an Aboriginal within Clause c Section 4? It was determined that Annie was Aboriginal from the time of her birth until she left Badu Island in Torres Strait.

The second question complicated the way in which the 1897 act made provision for people to 'become' Aboriginal and to 'become' 'half-caste': 'Would Annin Savage Ah Wang remain an aboriginal within the meaning of the Act after she left Badu, or would she automatically become a "half-caste" on ceasing to habitually live or associate with aboriginals?' The Crown Solicitor considered that, on ceasing to habitually live or associate with Aborigines, Annie ceased to be Aboriginal and became a 'half-caste'.

The third question was whether Annie's offspring born on Badu were 'half-caste', and this was also answered in the affirmative. Of course, the children could be considered 'half-caste' only on the strength of their mother being deemed Aboriginal. The mother was now retrospectively classed as having been an Aborigine until 1905.

The fourth question was whether Section 4 in fact provided a feedback loop for endless generations of mixed descendants to be drawn back into the act. If the 'half-caste' mother was 'deemed' Aboriginal, could the children also be 'deemed' Aboriginal under the same provisions? To which the Crown Solicitor replied:

> Each of them until in the opinion of a protector he or she was over sixteen years of age, or until he or she ceased to live or associate habitually with aboriginals, was deemed to be an aboriginal under Section 4. On attaining sixteen, or ceasing so to live or associate, he or she ceased to be deemed an aboriginal, and came within the definition of half-caste.[61]

The Protector also inquired about the status of the last two children born on Thursday Island. The Crown Solicitor determined that these were neither 'half-caste' nor Aboriginal.

All these determinations depended on Annie having lived on Badu Island, which meant that she 'must of necessity have habitually associated with aboriginals'.[62] On further inquiry, however, Protector Holmes realised that living on Badu did not necessarily mean associating with Aborigines:

> When at Badu I inquired fully into the question of Atima Ah Wang and found that she did not at any time, nor did her mother, habitually live or associate with aboriginals. It appears that the girl's grandmother lived with her husband, a native of Madagascar, at the South Sea Settlement, so that her daughter Annin Savage, Atima's mother did not from the time of her birth or at any time habitually live or associate with aboriginals. Her mother is a half-caste female within the meaning of the Act, so that her children are all exempt from its provisions.[63]

This should have been the last we heard of this family in the department's files. In November 1922, however, an ambitious young protector was appointed to Thursday Island: Cornelius O'Leary, who was to become Chief Protector from 1943 to 1963.

Greater Powers

After only half a year on the island, O'Leary gingerly raised the question of the protection of quadroon females. Atima, having been told by a previous protector that she was exempt from the act, evidently disavowed any power of the department over her. O'Leary felt that this was a bad example, and that the act should be amended to grant him powers to oversee such women:

Ever since taking over the position of Protector of Aboriginals here, an outstanding phase of aboriginal life on Thursday Island has been the prevalence of temptation to half-caste or aboriginal girls, who are domestically employed, to go the wrong road. Opportunities for such unfortunates are no doubt great, and I have come to the definite opinion that the temptation is accentuated by the example of many quadroon females who see fit to lead an unhindered and immoral life. There are some half dozen or so of those persons here, probably more who are the unhappy plaything of all and sundry. Even the survey ship 'Fantome' supplies small quotas of men who on their periodical visits here promiscuously associate with these females. This phase of the question is officially no concern of mine in that I have no jurisdiction over these females or interests in their welfare ... Mr Holmes had one such girl signed on, during his regime, as a half-caste, which was a good move, but the position has now reacted upon me in that an interested person, her present employer, schooled her to the position with the result that both the parties refused to recognise this office after the expiry of the agreement, and she now preaches her doctrine of defiance and immorality to her associates. I have had, on several occasions, to have female and male aboriginals before me for associating with those avowed immoralists, but while they are permitted to live the loose life, the position is difficult in the extreme.[64]

A strong stance is taken here, but as far as factual information goes, this report is sadly lacking. The factual allegation against Atima is that, with the support of her employer, she refused to recognise any authority of the Protector over her. From everything we read about Atima, this position is entirely justified. She appears to have had the consistent support of Whites on Thursday Island to defend her against departmental infringements. O'Leary's conclusion was that she was defiant and immoral — she and the Whites advocating for her being 'avowed immoralists'. Of the 'many' loose women who allegedly characterised Indigenous life on Thursday Island, there were about six known cases, though the Protector did not really wish to count them, since the 'half a dozen or so' were instrumental in arguing for an extension of legal powers. The purpose of O'Leary's report was to recommend an amendment of the act furnishing protectors with discretionary powers to bring quadroons under the act. O'Leary argued that 'the result of this amendment is apparent', allowing for stricter surveillance, and

> [f]urthermore, their mistaken idea that they are of equal intellect to the white would be rudely dispelled. There is no doubt that the average female half-caste is quite as intelligent as the Thursday Island quadroon whose associates are solely half-caste quadroon or cosmopolitan.[65]

O'Leary professed to be unaware of whether the question of quadroons had been raised before and asked to be informed of 'the reasons for their sole exemption from the provisions of the act'. The Chief Protector replied by forwarding a copy of circular 21/6, the Crown Solicitor's opinion that had been formulated in response to Atima's case, and regretted that this was 'apparently the only hope at present of exercising official control of such women' — by means of 'deeming' their mothers Aboriginal.[66]

Chief Protector Bleakley finally asserted his authority with a further amendment of the Protection Act in 1934, which specifically targeted, by his own admission, the Coloured population of north Queensland.[67] Defining 'half-castes' now became a tricky mathematical exercise in counting parts of 'blood' as well as retaining the social dimension of the earlier definition (habitually associating). The department's powers now extended over all 'such women' whose status under the act had been indeterminate:

> the illegitimate children of half-caste mothers, the children of parents both half-castes, and the crossbreed element of aboriginal or Pacific Island strain.[68]

The new act allowed mixed descendants to the fourth generation to be pulled into the ambit of the Protector of Aborigines as 'half-caste'.[69] The age of 'half-castes' 'deemed to be Aboriginal' was raised from 16 to 21, and all exemptions from the act were initially revoked with the effect of disenfranchising all those who had held exemptions and had been able to vote in state elections.

At the zenith of the department's powers, a resistance movement developed, fuelled by Coloured populations. A highly public campaign on Thursday Island protested against disenfranchisement, alleging that Whites had been turned into Blacks. Of 384 registered voters on Thursday Island in 1936, an estimated 70 to 85 were 'half-castes'. Closely following the objections raised by the Coloured People's Progressive Association, whose spokesmen were Whites married to Coloured women and three men referred to as 'half-castes' (T. Loban, W. H. Dubbins and D. Hodges, a returned soldier), a State Public Service Commissioner's inquiry contested the propriety of the arbitrary powers assumed by the new amendment act ('in the opinion of the protector').[70]

All over Queensland, associations were formed demanding citizenship and, in areas where there were large Coloured populations, strikes were staged against the departmental control of wages in 1936 and 1937.[71] In an attempt to stem the tide of protest from the far north, the 1897 Act with its amendments was replaced in 1939 with two separate pieces of parallel legislation, one for Aborigines and one for Torres Strait Islanders, which granted some measure of self-government to the island communities.

Conclusions: asserting hybridity

The 'medical/moral policing rationale' of Queensland's Aboriginal administration bureaucracy had always prescribed a holistic approach, taking into its brief the whole range of government services such as education, health, training, employment, welfare, housing and infrastructure. Having defined the whole Indigenous population as an administrative problem that had perennially to be solved, the bureaucracy attempted to formulate a singular and encompassing vision and to marshall the powers to implement it. Its powers could never be commensurate with the level of responsibility the department paternalistically sought to take for Indigenous Australians.

On Thursday Island, where a significant Coloured population strenuously resisted being drawn under its protection, the department's authority was constantly under siege, and much of the policy outcomes, and the justifications given for them, bespeak a siege mentality. The response to this contestation was an ever-widening ambit of powers for the department as it sought to control the blurring of distinctions between definable populations.

Coloured women therefore became a particular target for departmental concern, and this concern was much wider than with merely Indigenous populations: the cultural pluralism of a polyethnic society was contested and reined in with reference to the morality of these women. Under the spotlight of administrative reason, normal behaviour became circumspect. It was difficult for Coloured women to stay safely outside the department's ambit, because living with Asians was practically tantamount with living immoral lives and requiring protection.

The concern about the moral conduct of the Australian-born Coloured population of mixed Indigenous descent emanated as if naturally from the xenophobic attitudes towards Asians, many of whom shared with Indigenous Australians the customs of polygyny and promised marriages.[72] Associations between Indigenous women and Asian men, which often followed such customs, were considered pernicious and immoral. The result was that much of the Aboriginal protection legislation was framed with Asians firmly in mind.

Through successive administrative periods, 'Coloured' was never a neatly encompassed category. Shifting policies, coupled with vast discretionary powers vested in protectors, cast a long shadow of uncertainty over large populations in the grey areas of its ambit of powers. In the scramble for defining boundaries, it was possible to be informed that one had been an Aborigine in the past. It was possible for siblings of identical parentage to include Aborigines, 'half-castes' and people who were neither. Indigenous life experiences were tailored to available administrative categories.

Uncertainty is still part and parcel of the life experience of many Indigenous descendants, who travel paths of self-discovery similar to that described in Sally Morgan's best-selling novel *My Place*. While the vast numbers of Aboriginal descendants who have opted out of an Indigenous identity escape public comment, considerable cynicism is directed at people who commit to an Indigenous identity late in life. Under the impact of native title rights, there is a sense that one ought to be either Indigenous or not Indigenous. This quite recent idea does not stand up well to the racial history of the polyethnic north.

Indeed, a vast range of cultural productions from north Australia remembers, celebrates and affirms cultural hybridity. In Broome, the annual Shinju Festival — a Japanese celebration of pearls — has lately been organised by the Aboriginal community. Jimmy Chi's musicals, *Bran Nue Dae* and *Corrugation Road*, deal with mixed lineages, the latter professedly an autobiographical journey through the schizophrenia Chi suffered as a result of his mixed Aboriginal/Chinese/Japanese/Scottish heritage.[73] From Darwin in the Northern Territory comes a play by Gary Lee called *Keep Him My Heart* with its subtitle, 'A Filipino-Larrakia Love Story', speaking volumes about acknowledging the mixed descent of a family encompassing members who are involved in a native title land claim. Arnhem Land's Yothu Yindi, Maningrida's Sunrize Band and the Wrirrnga Band from Milingimbi have released titles celebrating local historical connections to Sulawesi. On Queensland's Thursday Island, Malayan dances were part of local festivals long before the arrival of 'multiculturalism', and the repertoire of Seaman Dan, a cultural icon recently discovered by the Brisbane music industry, includes '*Terang Bulan*' (*Shining Moon*), a Malayan song also perfectly rendered by one of the surviving sons of Ahwang Dai. Others in the Ahwang family have embraced Islam, an important religion next to Christianity in the Torres Strait region, or travelled overseas, to reconnect with a severed patrilineage.

These are some of the most celebrated heartlands of Indigenous Australia: the Kimberley region with Broome at its centre, the Northern Territory and Arnhem Land, and the Torres Strait centred on Thursday Island. From precisely these regions emanate cultural productions that celebrate hybridity, mixed relations and shared histories. These are repressed histories, once documented in moralised language, but now finding vibrant expression as a way of coming to terms with historical change. They undermine the very idea of cultural purity that props up Anglo-Celtic claims to cultural dominance. Thursday Island is, therefore, not so much unique, but quintessentially representative of these northern histories, which call into question dominant modes of representation of Australian history.

Footnotes

1 Substantial parts of this paper were published as 'Being Coloured — An Australian History' in *Margins*, February 2001, pp. 76–102. The permission of the publishers in Calcutta is gratefully acknowledged. I am indebted to Ros Kidd, Anna Shnukal and Patima Malone for comments on this paper, to living descendants for interviews and permission to access restricted files, to Jonathan Richards for research assistance and to the Australian Research Council for financial support of this research. A more extended argument about the importance of northern polyethnic history is made in Regina Ganter, *Mixed Relations*, forthcoming with UWA Press.

2 See, for example, Koch, Tony, 'Aboriginal blood feud.' *The Courier Mail*, 16 December, 2000. p. 1.

3 Ganter, Regina. 1994. *The Pearl-Shellers of Torres Strait: Resource Use, Development and Decline, 1860s–1960s*. Melbourne University Press. Figures that are not referenced in the following are extensively documented in this source.

4 The morally suspicious status of Asian women in Australia did not require substantiation. In 1897, the Commissioner of Police confidently stated about Japanese women in the colony that 'with the exception of the wife of the Japanese consul at Townsville the whole of these women, numbering 115, gain their living by prostitution', an exception that had to be made for evident diplomatic reasons ('Commissioner of Police to Under Secretary, Home Department, 14 September 1897', PRE/103, Queensland State Archives [hereafter QSA]). Histories of Japanese-Australian relations have, on the whole, accepted this sweeping statement as an expression of tested fact. An 1895 statistical return from Thursday Island, however, listed nine prostitutes among a total of 23 Japanese females, specifying that of the female Japanese, nine were single, 12 married, one widowed and one a minor. ('F. Urquhart, Sub-inspector of Police, TI, to Gov. Res., 24 July 1895', PRE/105, QSA.) The implication here is that single (Japanese) women were prostitutes and, in reports less grounded in detail, this implication became generalised for all Japanese women.

5 'Examination of Archibald Meston by the Legislative Council.' 8 October, 1901. *Queensland Parliamentary Papers* (hereafter QPP), Vol. LXXXVII (1901). p. 1142.

6 Since this paper deals with legal terminology and its interpretation, it is not possible to substitute this term for a less offensive one. Regretting any offence it may cause, it will be used in the remainder where necessary, otherwise 'mixed descendants' is used. The term 'Coloured' is not intended as a synonym, because many Coloured people were not 'half-castes' under the Protection Acts. In quotations, the terminology and capitalisation used in the originals has been retained according to standard practice of citation.

7 Prefacing his evidence, Roth stated that 'A large portion of my time is devoted to the interests of aboriginals on boats' ('Examination of Walter Roth by the Legislative Council.' 8 October 1901. QPP, Vol. LXXXVII [1901]. p. 1136), and the Home Secretary, who introduced the bill, explained that some of its provisions were particularly 'designed to meet the case of Binghis employed in swimming diving' (3 September, 1901. QPP, Vol. LXXXVII [1901]. p. 597).

8 'Roth to Under Secretary, Home Department, 21 January 1901.' A/58764, QSA.

9 'Roth Progress Report.' August 1901, A/44679, QSA.

10 'Roth Progress Report.' October 1901, A/44679, QSA.

11 'Examination of Archibald Meston by the Legislative Council.' 8 October, 1901. QPP, Vol. LXXXVII (1901). p. 1143.

12 4 March, 1901, and 26 September, 1901, A/58764, QSA.

13 The Hon. Norton observed that the 'bill is giving very drastic powers to the protectors'; Taylor argued that too much power was in the hands of any protector, and Reid felt that 'everything seemed to be left to the protector'. 15 October, 16 October and 3 September, 1901. QPP, Vol. LXXXVII (1901). pp. 1260, 1291, 597.

14 31 July, 1901. QPP, Vol. LXXXVII (1901). p. 323.

15 'The Hon. Mr Givens.' 3 September, 1901. QPP, Vol. LXXXVII (1901). p. 609.

16 Roth report, cited in 3 September, 1901, QPP, Vol. LXXXVII (1901). p. 596.

17 'Examination of Walter Roth by the Legislative Council.' 8 October, 1901. *QPP*, Vol. LXXXVII (1901). p. 1141.

18 'Const. McKenna, Mossman Police Station, to CPA, 23 August 1901.' A/58764, QSA.

19 1 June, 1902, Roth's request for authorisation under Sect. 9/1901, prepared for Minister's signature in August 1902. A/58764, QSA.

20 CPA to (a female at Murray Island), 19 February, 1913. A/58767, QSA.

21 For example, the Normanton Protector reported, with reference to an application for marriage between a Chinese man and an Aboriginal woman, that he was 'personally opposed to all such unions especially aliens to gins' (8 January, 1906, A/44680, QSA), and the Cairns Protector stated that he had 'received applications from Kanakas for leave to marry aboriginal gins but in all cases I have refused to recommend such marriages' (23 March, 1905, A/44680, QSA). The Rev. E. R. Gribble sought to consult with Roth on 'the numerous waifs and strays in the Chinese-infested districts around Redlynche and Kuranda' (Roth Progress Report, October 1902, A/44679, QSA).

22 Kidd, Rosalind. 1997. *The Way We Civilise*. St. Lucia: University of Queensland Press. In 1939, the Chief Protector became Director of Native Affairs. Thereafter, the department changed its name from Department of Native Affairs to Department of Aboriginal and Islander Affairs, then Department of Aboriginal and Islander Advancement and, later, though with much reduced responsibilities for Indigenous Australians, Department of Community Services, Department of Community Services and Ethnic Affairs, Department of Family Services and Aboriginal and Islander Affairs, and is currently known as the Department of Family, Youth and Community Care.

23 This definition excluded the children of an Aboriginal father and a non-Aboriginal mother. Prior to the 1897 act, 'half-caste' had referred to any part-White people; for example, of African/Irish descent (example in Col/A576 89/03138, QSA).

24 There is some uncertainty about the origin of Annie's father. According to the family's oral history, he was from Niue in the Pacific, and this is supported by the name given on her 1891 marriage certificate, but Annie herself declared to the police on 1 April, 1921, that her father was a native of Madagascar, and this reference is consistently made in the files used here, where Annie is referred to as 'Annin'. Annie's mother was Zarazar, the daughter of Mauno (or Mano). This name became Sarah Manahou on Annie's marriage certificate.

25 For a discussion of the rationale underwriting this exemption, cf. Ganter, Regina and Ros Kidd. 1993. 'The powers of protectors: conflicts surrounding Queensland's 1897 Aboriginal legislation.' *Australian Historical Studies*, Vol. 25, No. 101. pp. 536–54.

26 Anna Shnukal ('Contact and "Cultural Creolisation" in Torres Strait.' *Australian Aboriginal Studies*, Vol. 2 (1995). pp. 52–7) refers to 'Pacific Pidgin English' as the language, which is also referred to as 'sandalwood English' (Shineberg, Dorothy. 1967. *They Came for Sandalwood*. Melbourne University Press) or colloquially as beach-la-mar (from bêche-de-mer, the sea cucumber sought by Pacific traders).

27 Hugh Milman took over from John Douglas as Government Resident, and Charles O'Brien replaced George Bennett as local Protector.

28 This distinction reappeared only in 1939, when separate acts were passed for the administration of Aborigines and Torres Strait Islanders.

29 Interview with Starchy Ahwang, Mackay, 26 June, 1997.

30 Ganter, R., op. cit.

31 Interview with Starchy Ahwang, Mackay, 26 June, 1997.

32 Mr Lesina, Member for Clermont, Legislative Assembly, 8 October, 1901. *QPP*, Vol. LXXXVII (1901). p. 1150.

33 Lee-Bryce referred to this man as a Malay. According to family history, he was a Muslim from Delhi, had travelled widely as a sailor before settling on Thursday Island and was referred to as Ah Mat India. The young woman was the daughter of an Aboriginal woman from Pennefather River, who had been moved to Mapoon, and a Filipino from Sulu Island.

34 This name has been changed to protect the anonymity of living descendants. The woman is from a different family, unrelated to Ahwang.

35 'Lee-Bryce, Protector at TI to CPA, 14 March 1914.' A/58761, QSA.

36 Ibid.

37 Ibid.

38 *Removals Register*. 1914, pp. 65–6. Z2688, QSA.

39 'Lee-Bryce, Protector at TI to CPA, 14 March 1914.' A/58761, QSA.

40 'Clara Riley to CPA, 11 July 1914'. A/58761, QSA.

41 Ibid.

42 'Douglas Riley to Home Secretary [letter], 17 June 1914.' A/58761, QSA.

43 'Order for Removal of Aboriginal under Section 9/1897 and Section 3/1901, 28 September 1914.' A/58761, QSA.

44 'CPA to Under Secretary, Home Department, 22 July 1914.' A/58761, QSA.

45 'CPA to Lee Bryce, 21 July 1914'. A/58761, QSA.

46 'Clara Riley to Atima Awang at Barambah, 4 October 1914.' A/58761, QSA.

47 'Lee Bryce to CPA, 14 August 1914'. A/58761, QSA.

48 'CPA to Under Secretary, Home Department, 22 July 1914.' A/58761, QSA. This letter was annotated 'Bleakley to see me'.

49 'Lee Bryce to CPA, 16 February 1915.' A/58761, QSA.

50 'Atima Ahwang c/o Mrs Cameron, Toowong, to Mrs Beesten, 19 August 1915', and 'Lee Bryce, Protector TI to CPA, 4 October 1915', A/58800, QSA.

51 Interviews with Rocky Ahwang, Hervey Bay, and Starchy Ahwang, Mackay, 1997.

52 Australian Archives Queensland, BP 242/1 #Q24780.

53 'CPA to Protector, TI, 23 October 1917.' A/58761, QSA.

54 'Atima Ahwang, South Toowong, to Bleakley, 9 November 1917.' A/58761, QSA.

55 'Protector, TI to CPA, 16 June 1919.' A/58761, QSA.

56 'CPA to Filewood, 29 October 1920.' A/58761, QSA.

57 'Filewood to CPA, 20 October 1920.' 'Filewood to Home Secretary, 14 October 1920.' A/58761, QSA.

58 'CPA to Home Secretary, 18 May 1921.' A/58761, QSA.

59 'CPA to all Protectors and Superintendents [Circular 21/6], 31 May 1921.' A/58761, QSA.

60 There is some uncertainty about Annie's father. He may have been from Madagascar, Niue or Barbados.

61 'Crown Solicitor to Under Secretary, Home Secretary's Office, 26 July 1921.' A/58761, QSA.

62 'Protector Holmes, TI to CPA, 7 April 1921.' A/58761, QSA.

63 'Protector Holmes to CPA, 10 August 1921.' The reference to Madagascar stems from a statement by 'Annin Savage Ah Wong' to the police on 1 April, 1921, A/58761, QSA.

64 'Protector O'Leary to CPA, 1 June 1923.' A/58761, QSA.

65 Ibid.

66 'CPA to Protector, TI, 6 August 1923.' A/58761, QSA.

67 Kidd, R., op. cit., p. 109.

68 'CPA to Under Secretary, Home Dept., 23 August 1934.' A/58856, QSA.

69 Section 4(b) of the new act defined 'half-caste' as:

(i) Any person being the offspring of parents one of whom is an aboriginal, or both of whom are half-castes; or

(ii) Any person being the grandchild of grandparents one of whom is an aboriginal, or both of whom are half-castes, who lives or associates with aboriginals, or who lives as an aboriginal, or who in the opinion of the Chief Protector is in need of the control or protection of this Act; or

(iii) Any person of aboriginal or Pacific Island extraction who lives or associates with aboriginals, or who lives as an aboriginal or who in the opinion of the Chief Protector is in need of the control or protection of this Act.

70 A/58640, QSA.

71 Cf. Kidd, R., op. cit., p. 138. Sharp, Nonie. 1981-82. 'Culture clash in the Torres Strait islands — the maritime strike of 1936.' *Journal of the Royal Historical Society of Queensland*, Vol. 11, No. 3. pp. 107–26. And Walker, Faith. 'A very different mission: Myora Aboriginal Mission on Stradbroke Island, 1892–1940.' In Regina Ganter (ed.), *Stradbroke Island: Facilitating Change*, Brisbane: Queensland Studies Centre. pp. 9–20.

72 Cf. Ganter, Regina. 1999. 'Letters from Mapoon: colonising Aboriginal gender.' *Australian Historical Studies*, Vol. 30, No. 113, October. pp. 267–85.

73 Yu, Sarah. 1999. 'Broome creole — Aboriginal and Asian partnerships along the Kimberley coast.' In R. Ganter (ed.), *Asians in Australian History — Queensland Review*, Vol. 6, No. 2. p. 70.

Grave of Bargo Bin Ahmat, Thursday Island Cemetery, 1997.
Courtesy of Guy Ramsay.

CHAPTER 10

Confluence

Asian cultural contributions to *ailan pasin*[1]

Anna Shnukal

Introduction

Ailan pasin ('island custom') is a potent symbol of pan-Torres Strait Islander identity; it is also a cultural hybrid. Its core consists of a cluster of 'traditional' Melanesian cultural elements filtered through 19th-century Pacific Islander Christian sensibility and practice, with accretions from Europe and Asia. That *ailan pasin* is not restricted entirely to pre-contact custom is evident from the inclusion of two symbolic unifiers brought by European-influenced Pacific Islanders during the last half of the 19th century: Christianity and Torres Strait Creole, a nativised variety of Pacific Pidgin English, which has become the regional lingua franca. The other significant, though often overlooked, contribution made by Asian immigrants is the subject of this chapter.[2]

The preconditions for extensive cultural interchange with Asians, Pacific Islanders and Europeans existed in Torres Strait long before contact. The region was a locus of west-east and north-south migration and trade and the island economies were underpinned by widespread exchange complexes, maintained by interrelationships with neighbours based on shifting alliances, warfare and intermarriage. Inter-island and coastal trade provided essential objects of material culture — canoes, vegetable food, ochre, cassowary feathers, stone for the *gabagaba* 'club', pearl shell for the *dibidi* 'breast ornament' — as well as less tangible elements, such as innovative technology, myth and cosmology.[3] Traditional

Islanders, like their contemporary descendants, were pragmatic and eager to adopt, adapt and elaborate cultural elements generated elsewhere for sustenance, performance and display. Moreover, the island peoples of Torres Strait, Asia and the Pacific shared social and cultural affinities, which predisposed them to cultural exchange. The development of bonds between the Torres Strait Islanders and the Chinese, Filipino, 'Malay', Japanese and Sri Lankan sojourners and immigrants provided fertile new areas for cultural crosspollination, the results of which can be observed in contemporary Torres Strait religion, food, cooking practices, plants, gardening techniques, clothing, architecture, household implements and cooking utensils, mortuary rites, music and dance, as well as vocabulary borrowed into the Torres Strait languages from Malay, Japanese, Tagalog and Chinese. Some early borrowings left little trace and are dealt with only briefly here. Others endured and became 'nativised', i.e., were integrated into pan-Islander custom, changed to some degree to conform to existing local custom and generally recognised as part of contemporary *ailan pasin*.

I note in passing that, in addition to the material and ideological elements that were incorporated into *ailan pasin*, early Asian immigrants brought significant changes to the created environment of the islands of Torres Strait: the destruction of *wangai* stands to fuel the ships and trepang smokehouses; the cutting down of mangroves as fuel and timber; the introduction to outer island gardens and plantations of tropical plants native to their islands of origin (most notably sisal hemp, known in the strait as 'Manila rope'); the digging of wells; the planting of market gardens on Thursday, Prince of Wales and Hammond Islands with Chinese cabbage, lettuce, lombok, silver beet, string and butter beans, watermelon and sugar cane; the building of graves and headstones for deceased countrymen on Thursday Island and elsewhere; the erection of dwellings and religious buildings in Malaytown and Yokohama on Thursday Island; the building of galvanised iron housing, outbuildings and tramways on pearling stations scattered around the strait; the construction by the Filipinos of the Catholic church, hospital and school on Thursday Island and the various buildings of Hammond Island Roman Catholic Mission.

The Structural Context of Cultural Borrowing

Linguists have long observed that a genetic relationship between languages facilitates lexical (and syntactic) borrowing, whereas unrelated languages are less likely to borrow one from another: that is, other things being equal, the more fundamentally similar the languages, the more rapid, thorough and extensive the linguistic borrowing when speakers are in contact. If this abstract principle can be extended to the cultural sphere, then Torres Strait Islanders might be expected to borrow more readily from cultures that more closely approximate their own than from 'unrelated' cultures (leaving aside the vexed question of how we might measure 'cultural difference' and 'degree of borrowing').[4]

Given the socio-cultural affinities among the Indigenous communities of the wider region (noted in the Introduction), their similar maritime traditions and their shared working circumstances as non-White marine industry employees in remote colonial outposts of European empires, it is not surprising that friendships, alliances and family links were rapidly established. It was those links that provided the context for the liberal exchange of objects, practices and ideas between Asian and Torres Strait communities.

Asian Cultural Borrowings into Contemporary *Ailan Pasin*

The test for true incorporation of cultural borrowings into contemporary *ailan pasin* is their 'nativisation' and widespread distribution. The following originally Asian items have been modified in form and context of use through their appropriation by Islanders into Torres Strait custom. A review of the data suggests that most nativised borrowings fall into four cultural domains: food (ingredients, condiments, recipes, preparation and cooking methods, utensils); mortuary rites; the lexicon of the local languages; and music/dance.

Food: ingredients, condiments, recipes, preparation and cooking methods, utensils

Each Asian ethnic group sought to maintain its traditional diet as far as possible: the Chinese market gardeners on Thursday Island and neighbouring islands grew Asian green vegetables, including cabbage, lombok, lettuces and beans, and Chinese shopkeepers sold all manner of tinned Chinese delicacies in their shops: bamboo shoots, mushrooms, dried prawns, prawn paste (*ha-ma*) and long soup. The Filipino, Juan Francisco Garcia, planted more than 200 coconut trees on several islands, before settling permanently on Auridh (Skull Island), where he harvested the coconuts to make *tuba*, his Torres Strait Islander wife using the fermented drink as a rising agent when making bread.[5] Green ginger root, garlic, lemon grass, chillies, cloves and cinnamon bark, curry powder and soy sauce were introduced; there was sufficient local demand for Haruyoshi Yamashita to establish a successful soy-sauce factory on Thursday Island.[6] According to Gwen Clark Moloney, born in 1918 of European-Samoan-Filipino-Chinese descent and raised on Thursday Island,

> there were Japanese shops, boarding houses, drapery stores, where you could buy silks and Japanese novelties, souvenirs, carved trunks and Japanese food. In the morning you could buy tofu floating in water in green-painted kerosene tins as well as Japanese cakes called *manju*,

a steam bun full of sweet beans, which were carried on trays. The men
would go out early in the morning carrying the trays of tofu on a bamboo
rod with the drums hanging off. They would call out in Japanese … They
carried steam buns on wooden trays on their shoulder. You had to order.
They had big pinewood trays with rows of steam buns.[7]

Islanders, introduced to these new foods either by family connection or
in the family-like contexts of the boats,[8] began to plant *zinza* ('ginger') and
tigras ('lemon grass') in their own gardens on the outer islands and incorporate
them along with seasonings such as *pas*, a local variety of basil, into their
traditional dishes of turtle and dugong, yam and sweet potato, which were slow-
cooked in sand ovens.

The main foodstuff imported for the Asian crews was their dietary staple,
rice, although this did not become common on the outer islands until about
1912. In 1881, a single ship from Hong Kong brought 200 bags of rice to
Thursday Island[9] and Kyuuhara quotes from a letter by a Japanese indent,
Sannosuke Masuda, who arrived in 1883: 'We loaded Chinese rice of sixty pyo
[1 pyo is equal to 64kg] as our food which we carried from Hongkong', as well as
other cooking utensils, which they transported to the pearling station on
Muralag (Prince of Wales Island).[10] By 1885, the Government Resident
informed the Colonial Secretary: 'As regards rice, I can only say that for every
one, whether European or Asiatic, who lives in the Tropics, rice is a necessity of
life.'[11] The European and Pacific Islander staple starch was flour, not rice, but,
by 1917, the Church of England mission was providing its theological students
and lay workers with an allowance of rice, as well as flour, tea, sugar, baking
powder and jam.[12] Flour and rice have today become staples of the 'traditional'
Torres Strait diet, rice being served at almost every midday and evening meal
and invariably at feasts. A local variant is *sabi rais*, rice cooked in coconut milk
and often flavoured with saffron or turmeric.[13]

More than half the 76 dishes in Edwards' traditional Torres Strait Islander
cookbook are Asian-inspired.[14] Nasi Rice and Company Rice are among the
recipes and the Islanders have also adopted vermicelli, which they call 'Chinese
Macaroni', and the tamarind.[15] Vermicelli is the basis for *simur siken*, a Malay
dish locally called 'Chinese Chicken' (chicken, Chinese noodles, mushrooms,
bamboo shoots and soy sauce).[16] A local dish called 'Choppy', probably Malay,
consists of strips of beef and shredded cabbage tossed and lightly fried. The
Malays also introduced various condiments and spices, such as curry powder,
which is now used in traditional Torres Strait Islander *sabisabi* dishes (meat, fish
or root vegetables cooked in coconut cream). Any meat, dugong, turtle, fish or
vegetable dish may be curried. Jamel Shibasaki, born on Thursday Island in 1927
of Japanese-Malay-Torres Strait Islander descent, recalled that

our meals consisted of rice, fish, meat, chickens that we raised, which was made into curries, 'simured' which was chicken, Chinese noodles, mushrooms, bamboo shoots and soya sauce. We were able to get Japanese soy sauce in those days ... We also made a lot of sambal with prawn paste and chillies. We liked our spicy foods. Other things were cucumber cooked in coconut milk and other spices. We used to prepare deer meat, sliced thin, marinated in curry powder, sugar and salt and lemon juice. Let it stand over night, then sun dry them. They can be eaten as is, roasted over coals or cooked in peanut oil with fresh ginger and garlic. The salted fish can also be cooked this way. We used tamarinds soaked in hot water, then squeezed and used for cooking. Tamarinds coated with a mixture of sugar and salt make a nice sweet.[17]

Rice, ginger, garlic, curry powder and soy sauce are known by their English names; but *blasan* ('blachan') and *sambal* ('sambal'), from Malay, demonstrate their Asian provenance (as they do in English). According to one writer, sambals have been

changed and modified to suit the available ingredients, but are basically a hot spicy dish built on a foundation of onion, garlic, ginger and bird's eye chillies, plus a choice of some savoury pieces of meat, fowl or fish. The Island influence can be seen in some of the ingredients: pearl shell meat and mud clams for instance.[18]

The author notes that some Islanders now use the two terms interchangeably, a sure proof of linguistic nativisation, and gives 11 different Torres Strait recipes for blachans and sambals.

Asian crewmen also introduced new methods of food preparation. Islanders adopted the Chinese method of chopping up fowl for the pot[19] and, according to Ohshima,

the method of cooking rice was adopted from the Japanese fishermen. Islanders use the absorption method, the Japanese way. They use their index finger to measure the amount of water. The rice that is eaten in Torres Strait is prepared in a way similar to the Japanese style and different from Southeast Asia, which is dry.[20]

Japanese skippers also showed their Islander crews how to salt-cure fish and how to make *namas* (from the Japanese *namasu*, but now seen as an Islander dish) by thinly slicing raw fish and marinating it in vinegar, ginger, garlic and chilli. Islanders further elaborated *namas* by adding a small quantity of coconut milk before serving and called it *sabi namas*.[21] A variant of *namas*, called *namas kenilau*, came via the Philippines[22] and the Filipinos also introduced *dinagwan* ('blood pig', the Pacific Islander *pwakablad*).

Along with their foodstuffs, Asian immigrants imported various cooking implements and eating utensils. Excavating the remains of a 19th-century pearling station near Heath Point on Muralag (Prince of Wales Island), Kyuuhara and his colleagues found

> a big iron cooking pot for rice (93cm in inner diameter and 70cm in depth) lacking its lid, concealing itself in luxuriantly growing grass. This iron cooking pot would have been brought all the way from Yokohama with 37 emigrants in 1883.[23]

Chinese containers and crockery were also imported, sold in the shops of Thursday Island and taken to the outer islands: Gina Whap Baira informs me that an abandoned Chinese or Malay camp was discovered some time ago close to Wagadagam on Mabuiag, with Chinese crockery found in the scrub above the shore.[24] Islanders initially perceived the decorated crockery, mainly plates, bowls and mugs, as luxury items and women would place them in their homes for show as well as utility. Today's crockery dishes and enamel cups, used for everyday meals and at feasts on the islands, are almost always imports from China.

Lexical borrowing

The three Torres Strait Islander languages and Torres Strait English have all been enriched by the introduction of vocabulary from Chinese, Japanese, Malay and Tagalog. The largest components of this borrowing are family, personal and boat names, but a small number of place names, address terms, food terms and a few Japanese commands or expressions have also been borrowed. That they have become nativised is shown by their altered form ('Assan' for 'Hassan', 'Ilario' for 'Hilario', 'Zosapina' or 'Pina' for 'Josephina', 'Rapaila' for 'Raphaela', 'blasan' for 'blachan') and the extension of their contexts of use. The following are some well-known contemporary Torres Strait surnames of Asian provenance. Given the degree of intermarriage and adoption that has occurred since World War II, however, Asian names are now not necessarily restricted to individuals of Asian descent.

Surnames

Malay	Adams (from Adam Musinip), Ah Boo, Ahmat (eight different families so named), Ahwang, Assan, Barba, Binawel, Bindoraho, Bingarage, Binhamed, Binhoosen, Binjuda, Binsiar, Bintahel, Bowie, Dewis, Doolah, Drummond, Jia, Kaprisi, Kitchell, Loban, Malay, Salaam, Seden, Solomon, Tatipata, Titasey.

Grave of Miyako Mary Seden, Thursday Island Cemetery, 1997.
Courtesy of Guy Ramsay.

Filipino	Alcala, Assacruz, Blanco, Bullio, Canendo, Canuto, Carabello, Cloudy (Claudio), Conanan, Delacruz, Dorante, Elarde, Fabian, Francis, Galora, Garcia, Garr, Guivarra, Irlandes, Jose, Kanak, Lanzarote, Lasica, Lohada, Lopez, Macbire, Manantan, Mayor, Pelayo, Rapol, Raymond (from Ramon Roas), Remedio, Sabatino, Santos, Sim.
Sri Lankan	Mendis, Mowlis, Saranealis.
Japanese	Fujii, Fukumura, Ikeda, Hirakawa, Nakata, Shibasaki, Takai, Tanaka, Yamashita.
Chinese	Ahfat, Ahloy, Asange, Chinsoon, Laifoo, Seekee, Sing.

Personal names

Personal names form the second-largest group of lexical borrowings. The following is indicative, but by no means a complete list, of common contemporary Torres Strait Islander personal names of Asian origin.

Malay	Abdul, Abdullah, Ali, Hassan (Assan), Hismyal (Hismile), Ibrahim, Karim, Jamal, Mohammad (Mohamet, Mohamat, Muhammad), Omar, Rahman, Wahap, Wahid; Hagiga, Napsia, Noranee, Patimah, Raimah, Rasma, Saia, Salemah, Zillah.

Filipino	Antonio, Aurelio, Basil (from Basilio), Casimero, Celestino (Tinoi), Cornelio, Faustino, Francisco, Hislo, Ilario (from Hilario), Lucio, Pedro, Seriaco, Seto (from Inisceto), Stanislaus; Ambrosia, Camilla, Evelina, Francesca, Isabella (Bella), Johanna, Josephina (Pina), Laura, Lucia, Luneta, Magdalena, Marcellina, Maria, Monica, Raphaela, Scholastica, Teresa, Thecla, Veronica, Victorina.[25]
Japanese	Hideo, Iwazu, Kazu, Kenji, Kyozo, Kyu (Kew); Ayako, Harumi, Kazuko, Misako, Miyako, Sadako, Utako, Yoshiko.[26]

Boat names

A subsection of personal names consists of boat names of Asian provenance, all the Filipino-named being owned by Heriberto Zarcal of Thursday Island (see Rey Ileto's Chapter Five, this volume):

Filipino	Aguinaldo, Esperanza, Fortales, Justicia, Kalayaan, Kapayapaan, Katipunan, Kavite, Lacandola, Llanera, Magdalo, Manila, Maria Eusebia, Natividad, Santa Cruz, Sikatuna, Tagalog, Templanza.[27]
Japanese	Banzai,[28] Enodi, Mikado.

Reference and address terms

There is a small number of reference and address terms:

Malay	*bibi* 'sister, auntie': Ellie Loban Gaffney, for example, the daughter of a Malay father and European-Islander mother, is generally referred to as Bibi Ellie, although her husband, a European, is called 'Uncle Tony'.
	patsi 'uncle'
	nene 'grandmother'
	dato 'grandfather'
Japanese	*kuksang* 'cook'[29]
	nisang 'skipper'[30]
Tagalog	*tiyo* 'uncle'
Chinese	*pana* 'friend'[31]

This list includes at least two Japanese nicknames, bestowed on Islanders by their Japanese boat captains:

Kosi	(given to Timothy Tamwoy, born 1919). According to a nephew, he was given the name 'Kosaka' by a Japanese man, and called 'Kosi' as a pun on 'Koztrabel' (trouble-maker).
Sobo	(given to Tom Lowah, born 1914). According to Lowah, on his first voyage out on the boats at the age of 14, 'The three other Japs addressed me as "Sobo" [little one] and some address me so to this day.'[32]

Place names

As expected, few place names in Torres Strait are of Asian origin and no traditional locations were renamed. I know of only two place names of Asian origin:

Yokohama	the Asian quarter on Thursday Island.
Enodi	a place at St Paul's community on Mua (Banks Island) belonging to the Morrison family. The family says that it means 'sunset' in Japanese and was probably named for the Burns Philp boat on which a member of the Morrison family crewed under a Japanese captain.[33]

Other borrowings

The following words of Asian-language origin are also found in the Indigenous languages:

Malay	*blasan* 'blachan'
	makan 'to eat'
	sambal 'sambal'
	samasama 'equal'
Japanese	*itayo* 'it hurts' (from *itai* 'painful' + *yo* 'I tell you')
	Kura Kura 'Japanese (language)' (from *kura!* 'Watch it!', a disapproving phrase in Japanese)
	namas 'raw fish' (from *namasu* 'marinated raw fish')
	oisanyo 'hoist 'im up' (from hoist + *san* 'Mister' + *yo* 'I tell you')
Tagalog	*dinagwan* 'pig blood'
	tuba 'fermented coconut milk'
	namas kenilau 'Filipino-style rawfish'
Chinese	*zangsi* 'Chinese rice noodles' (from Jiangxi Province)

Lexical borrowing provides an analogue to cultural borrowing and these Asian-language lexical borrowings cluster in three semantic domains: family relationships, food and boat terms. That is, linguistic borrowing was promoted in the context of extended, close personal interaction, such as occurred within the family and on the boats. The majority of family-related words are of Malay origin, but Japanese supplied the bulk of non-family vocabulary, demonstrating a coincidence of linguistic, historical and cultural evidence.

Mortuary Rites: funerals, burials and tombstone unveilings

Torres Strait Islander mortuary rites are sometimes said to have been influenced by South-East Asian customs, although there is no direct historical evidence of this. At Malay funerals, however, some of which carried the requirement of feasting, participants were given white envelopes in which to contribute money to help pay for the feast. Others contributed food. These practices, which form part of the conduct of contemporary Islander funerals, may be the result of Malay influence.

As for burials, a study of the Thursday Island cemetery found that in all non-European sections offerings of food, toys or items reflecting the character or habits of the deceased had been placed on the graves. This was regardless of ethnic origin or religion and reflects both Muslim and Shinto practice. The Shinto graves often had a bottle of spirits (or Japanese beer) and cigarettes placed on them in the large Japanese memorial in the Thursday Island cemetery.[34] Tom Lowah, a Torres Strait Islander born in 1914, tells us that, when someone died, the Buddhist Chinese, like the Muslims, put out 'food or drink … at night in the house for the dead to use, and also on the graves'.[35] This practice of placing on graves 'cups, empty wine glasses, forks and spoons' and well-loved objects belonging to the deceased was adopted by Torres Strait Islanders.[36]

Less certain is the South-East Asian influence on the secondary mortuary rites, tombstone unveilings (also called tombstone openings), the origins of which are obscure, but which are now integral to *ailan pasin*.[37] The tombstone is swathed in fabric and unveiled at least a year after burial during a special Christian service to mark the final departure of the deceased's spirit. Fitzpatrick-Nietschmann characterises the practice as 'not a ceremony of grief but a celebration; a rebirth for the living, as well as for the deceased. Obligations have been fulfilled; the total passage from one world to the next has transpired — for both the living and the dead.'[38] She notes that similar rites occur in many parts of South-East Asia and hypothesises that '[a]ncestors of the Torres Strait Islanders could well have brought parts of a belief system from the west'. However, since Muslim families wrapped the body of the deceased in white cloth before burial and tombstone unveilings are not recorded in Torres Strait until the 1930s,[39] it is possible that there was some cultural merger between Islander and South-East Asian Muslim rites.

> When Nene [grandma] died, because I was 16–17, I had to stand and watch, but I was not allowed to do it. Wipe all the body down and dress her in white calico [cloth] and no clothes, wrapping only. Make like a scarf out of the same material. Had to use all the material. If got 10 yards, had to use it all on the body. Whatever was left was cut up and tied round our wrists. We had to wear it until it fell off by itself. Usually lasted over a hundred days.[40]

Additional evidence comes from the 100-day feast after death celebrated by Muslim Malays on Thursday Island to mark the end of mourning, which sometimes coincides today with Muslim tombstone openings.[41]

Music

There exists a recent body of scholarly work that examines various Asian influences on Torres Strait Islander musical traditions (see Karl Neuenfeldt's Chapter 11, this volume). Traceable Asian influences came directly from the songs of Asian seamen working on luggers in Torres Strait or in the form of artefacts: the phonograph records and musical instruments brought to Thursday Island or purchased with the men's earnings. Attested among the latter are Chinese fiddles, Filipino mandolins, guitars and banjos, Sri Lankan drums and Japanese *shamisen* and *shakuhachi* (a bamboo flute).[42] According to Karl Neuenfeldt, however, direct influences are often difficult to document beyond oral history data, which can still identify a song as having 'Indonesian', 'Timorese' or 'Filipino' influences. Another layer of complexity comes from the fact that some Filipino music is Spanish/Mexican in origin: the Philippines was a Spanish colony until 1898 and the dominant external cultural influence was Spanish; Indonesian music has a discernable Portuguese influence.[43] During the inter-war years, the Thursday Islanders formed dance bands that played popular music, including Asian influenced or derived songs. Some of these songs remain in the Torres Strait Islander musical repertoire.

Transient Borrowings

In addition to the borrowings into *ailan pasin*, scores of other Asian cultural practices and items of material culture (the easiest to track) are attested. Most of them were ephemeral, leaving no enduring imprint: they arose swiftly as a response to otherness and the desire to incorporate it, however briefly, as an elaboration of existing traditional forms and were just as rapidly abandoned. This is not to say that they were unimportant, since they provide the researcher with snapshots that brilliantly evoke the nature and social context of Asian-Torres Strait interaction.[44] This section introduces a few of these transient borrowings, which were for a time incorporated into Torres Strait cultural practice, but which did not become part of *ailan pasin*: the imbibing of opium and *tuba*; the wearing of the *hachimaki* and silk; and various games and sports.

Soporifics and Stimulants

The Islanders, as far as we know, traditionally used only two mood-altering substances: *suguba* (tobacco) and *gamadha* (a kind of *kava*), both thought to have been introduced from New Guinea. The latter was drunk at the male ceremonial ground before battle.[45] To these were added opium, introduced by the Chinese, and *tuba* ('fermented coconut milk', said to be as powerful as gin), introduced by the Filipinos. Under the Protection Acts, the Islanders were forbidden any intoxicant but tobacco. The Chinese and some Malays, however, continued to smoke opium in designated opium rooms on Thursday Island until World War II[46] and made it available to their Islander friends. And *tuba* was produced and consumed on the outer islands until the 1980s.[47]

Alcohol was prohibited on islands designated as 'Aboriginal reserves' as part of the Queensland Government's system of protection and segregation. European superintendent-teachers, appointed to oversee local affairs, forbade the making of *tuba*. They disapproved of its intoxicating effects and feared that the method of its manufacture would create a shortage of coconuts on the islands. Islanders, however, continued making *tuba* in secret and consuming it away from the eyes of the island superintendents. William Walton used to make *tuba* on (non-reserve) Horn Island in the 1930s. His daughter remembers seeing him take a hanging bunch of coconut blossoms, tying them all together and bending them over an earthenware pot. 'The juice dripped into the pot and, when it was fermented enough, they drank it. Dad used to be very happy some evenings.' Her mother used to ask him to keep some of it for her to ferment further to make vinegar.[48]

The writer and journalist, Colin Simpson, visited the islands in 1933 and described the local method of making *tuba*.

> Tuba is made by cutting off the bearing stem of the coconut palm, catching the sap that drips out of the tree and putting it aside to ferment. On the first day the liquid is merely yeast; in about 24 hours it is like light beer in strength … It has a rather refreshing taste under its sour, sweet smell, and a few minutes after it is taken the stomach begins to glow with a pleasant warmth. But week-old tuba is more than warming, and it goes right to the head.[49]

He also noted a local innovation, evidence of the 'nativisation' of the process, in the addition of a piece of mangrove bark to make a more potent variety.

Adornments, Games and Sports

Asian adornments, along with various games and sports, were at times co-opted into island ritual. According to Ohshima, the Islanders adopted the Japanese custom of wearing *hachimaki* when working, although the word itself was not borrowed.[50] Yuriko Nagata informs me that the cloth is thin and absorbent, roughly 90cm long and 24cm wide. It is usually tied around the forehead at the front and, in Japan, it is a symbol of determination. Some older Islander men, who crewed with Japanese skippers, still wear it when they embark on a strenuous task and a variant is sometimes worn by male dancers.

The beauty and lustre of imported Chinese silk was a revelation to Torres Strait Islanders. They were accustomed to clothes made of heavy cotton, coarse serge and even canvas. The Chinese and Japanese shops on Thursday Island sold silk, but Islanders could not afford to buy this luxury item until after World War II. For a time, it became the custom at eastern island weddings 'before the evening dance begins, for the groom's sisters-in-law to wrap both husband and wife with a very expensive material, mainly silk'.[51]

In May 1898, the anthropologist, Haddon, then living on Murray Island, attended a *segur* ('play') in one of the villages.[52] He described how one group of young women, singing Japanese and other songs, 'had covered their faces with white, and had painted a dab of red pigment on each cheek, perhaps in imitation of the Japanese women of the settlement in Thursday Island which goes by the name of "Yokohama"'. Few of the women who painted their faces would have seen the Japanese *karayuki-san* of Thursday Island and their men would be unlikely to have been their clients. As a striking visual phenomenon, however, it would have resonated with a people accustomed to painting their faces for war and dance.

When human geographer George Ohshima visited Masig (Yorke Island) in the 1970s, he was invited to attend a sports festival. To honour the visit, the Islanders included various games they had been taught by Japanese divers during their short stays on shore more than 40 years before, when they participated in Islander feasts and celebrations. The games included a spoon race, a local variant of a dunking race and a tug of war.[53] Islanders also incorporated into their leisure activities some of the Asian games of chance they had learned on the boats and through frequenting the gambling rooms of Malaytown on Thursday Island. Some of the games attested are mahjong, fan-tan, *che fa* and dominoes.

Concluding Discussion

Contact with outsiders introduced the Islanders of Torres Strait to European food and tobacco, as well as to the varied garden produce planted by Pacific Islanders. Under the tutelage of the Filipinos, they manufactured and drank *tuba* 'coconut liquor'; the Indonesians brought rice and blachan; the Japanese rice, *namas* and soy sauce. Islanders incorporated the more sophisticated gardening practices of the newcomers and copied and elaborated their clothing, utensils, recipes, dances, songs and crafts. New patterns of living, speaking and thinking arose as the physical character of the islands altered subtly.

Exposure to outside cultural elements is, it almost goes without saying, a necessary condition for borrowing to occur, but it is not sufficient for borrowing to endure and become integrated into a given cultural system. The duration of contact and its level of intimacy emerge as the two factors necessary for nativisation of cultural borrowing. The most enduring Asian influences on Torres Strait *ailan pasin* originated within the domestic sphere. They emerged from the daily activities of the blended families of Asian-Indigenous heritage or the 'family-like' environment of the boats, principally the reciprocal sharing of food and recreational activities, and are summations of myriad cultural accommodations and interpersonal negotiations. Of more than 1,000 pre-World War II Torres Strait families, slightly fewer than 15 per cent were headed by Asian immigrants and almost all of these lived on the islands of the Prince of Wales Group: 70 were headed by 'Malays' (mostly from present-day Indonesia, Singapore and Malaysia), 53 by Filipinos, seven by Japanese, six by Chinese, and five by Sri Lankans. These do not include 'irregular' unions, which, despite the stability and longevity of many of them, were not officially recognised.[54] In some families, there was explicit teaching of Asian culture and values; in others, the teaching was indirect, gained through childhood and adolescent exposure to community practices.

We can observe three main historical phases in the adoption of Asian cultural elements by Torres Strait Islanders. The original 'carriers' of Asian custom were the male immigrants, who formed discrete but cooperative communities of 'countrymen' on Thursday and Horn Islands and were free to follow their own customs. Their contact with the Islanders was virtually unrestricted until the latter became subject to the Protection Acts. Many early immigrants married local women, who 'adopted the culture of their husbands' and whose children, brought up in 'families practising a predominantly Asian culture', intermarried.[55] Between the wars, when Asian contacts with the outer islands were stringently regulated and Asian-Indigenous marriages largely prohibited, Asian custom was transmitted primarily through the existing mixed-descent or 'Coloured' population centred on Thursday Island. During this period, however, despite official disapproval, enduring friendships continued to be formed between Asians and Islanders. Japanese boat crews visited Masig during the inter-war years, for example, where 'they taught us how to dive, mend nets, cook rice, prepare *namasu*'.[56] The two groups also exchanged songs. After World War II, Asian influence was filtered through families, which, while celebrating their Asian heritage, had lost almost all personal connection with their communities of origin and in which the Asian connection was muted by mainstream custom and religion. All Torres Strait Islanders today, however, regardless of their ethnic heritage, are the beneficiaries of this unique confluence of Asian and Indigenous traditions.

Acknowledgements

I am indebted to Yuriko Nagata for her translation of Ohshima's research findings and to Yuriko Nagata, Karl Neuenfeldt and Guy Ramsay for information and comments. My deepest thanks also to Imam Uzair Akbar, Georgina Whap Baira, Maria Johnson Gebadi, Monica Walton Gould, Minoru Hokari, Kemuel Kiwat, Ted Loban (now deceased), Tom Lowah, Amira Mendis, Rod Mitchell, Gwen Clark Moloney (now deceased), Angela Ware Morrison, Eva Salam Peacock, Jianna Seden Richardson, Joan Staples, Titom Tamwoy, Ada Ware Tillett, Celestino (Tinoi) Williams and Ken O'Shea (Woodhead).

Footnotes

1 This chapter is based on a paper, 'Asian influences on "traditional" Torres Strait Islander custom', presented at the conference, 'Transforming Cultures/Shifting Boundaries: Asian Diasporas and Identities in Australia and Beyond', University of Queensland, 30 November, 2001.

2 Published research on Asian cultural influence in Torres Strait has focused on the music of the region, for example: Hayward, P. and J. Konishi. 2001. 'Mokuyo-to no ongaku: music and the Japanese community in the Torres Strait (1890–1941).' *Perfect Beat*, Vol. 5, No. 3. pp. 46–65. And Neuenfeldt, K. Chapter 11, this volume. The research by G. Ohshima and his team, some of it published as Ohshima, G. 1977, 'Yooku-too yuuki [Yorke Island travel diary],' *Chiri*, Vol. 22, No. 9, pp. 56–62, and under Ohshima's editorship as *Toresu Kaikyo no hitobito: people of the Torres Strait*, Tokyo, 1983, Kokon Shoin, is in Japanese, although preliminary reports in English are held by the Australian Institute of Aboriginal and Torres Strait Islander Studies (hereafter AIATSIS) in Canberra. Kyuuhara, S., 'Remains of Japanese on Torres Strait islands', March 1977, is a typescript held in the John Oxley Library (hereafter JOL) as MLC 1791–132; and the 1995 unpublished report compiled by J. Staples and K. O'Shea, 'Thursday Island's Asian heritage: an oral history', in the possession of the author.

3 For a comprehensive discussion of the complex trade routes linking Torres Strait with its neighbours, see Lawrence, D. 1994. 'Customary exchange across Torres Strait.' *Memoirs of the Queensland Museum*, Vol. 34, No. 2. pp. 241–446.

4 One could argue that cultural distance, which characterised relations at every level between the Islanders and Europeans, might be expected to impede cultural borrowing, yet we know that Islanders borrowed freely European items of material culture, religious ideology and myriad other influences. In this case, however, other things were not equal. The differential prestige and the authorities' deliberate moulding of post-contact Torres Strait Islander society in accordance with British cultural norms and values encouraged European influence. Moreover, a close examination of European borrowing demonstrates that, at least initially, elements were mediated through European-influenced Pacific Islanders. Direct observation of Europeans by Islanders was rare and circumscribed, the two groups being separated for more than a century by ideological, socioeconomic, administrative, legislative and political barriers.

5 Maria Johnson Gebadi, pers. comm., August 2000.

6 Nagata, Y. 1996. *Unwanted Aliens: Japanese internment in Australia*. St Lucia: University of Queensland Press. p. 20.

7 Gwen Moloney, pers. comm., January 2001.

8 I owe this insight to Minoru Hokari, pers. comm., November 2001.

9 Copy of letter from 'E. L. Brown, Thursday Island to Colonial Secretary, 22 June 1881', attached to report from 'Inspector J. A. Peterson, Thursday Island, to Colonial Secretary on complaints against Mr Chester, 28 July 1881.' COL/A321/3879, Queensland State Archives (hereafter QSA).

10 Kyuuhara, S., 'Remains of Japanese on Torres Strait islands', p. 12.

11 'Report from John Douglas, Thursday Island, to Colonial Secretary, 1 July 1886.' COL/A457/1583, QSA.

12 'Bishop of Carpentaria to Rev Jones, 14 February 1917', Bishop's correspondence, OM.AV 61/2; and to Rev. Cole, 13 December 1917, Bishop's correspondence, OM.AV 61/3, JOL.

13 Ted Loban, pers. comm., October 1981.

14 Edwards, R. 1988. *Traditional Torres Strait Island Cooking*. Kuranda: Rams Skull Press.

15 Ibid. Another name for Chinese Macaroni is Yancy Chicken. For Eva Peacock, 'macaroni' is the generic term and includes the colourless bean thread. Chinese Macaroni, which her mother used to cook, is made with chicken and colourless bean thread, dried mushrooms and ginger. Her mother used to cook it. Eva Peacock, pers. comm., December 2001.

16 The printed leaflet accompanying the Requiem Mass conducted in 1997 for Ella Relo Mills, daughter of Bora Bin Juda from Indonesia and Marijah Dulah Bin Juda from Darnley Island, contains the following: 'Ella was a devoted Catholic and would always cook her famous *semur chicken* for the Catholic Fetes.' MLC 1791–263, JOL.

17 Staples, J. and K. O'Shea, 'Thursday Island's Asian heritage', pp. 6–7.

18 Edwards, R., *Traditional Torres Strait Island Cooking*, p. 57.

19 According to Edwards, R., ibid., p. 37, Islanders use the Chinese method of chopping up fowl for the pot.

20 Ohshima, G., *Toresu Kaikyo no hitobito*, p. 285.

21 Ibid. Edwards, R., *Traditional Torres Strait Island Cooking*, p. 44.

22 Ibid., p. 45.

23 Kyuuhara, S., 'Remains of Japanese on Torres Strait islands', p. 12.

24 Georgina Whap Baira, pers. comm., November 2001.

25 During the period of Spanish colonial rule, Filipinos were given Spanish names at registration or baptism.

26 Some Japanese-born immigrants anglicised their Japanese names, e.g., Tomitaro (Tommy) Fujii. Their Torres Strait-born children tended to be given two names, one Japanese and one English.

27 Pugh, T. P. 1904. *Pugh's Almanac*. Brisbane. Facing p. 770. According to Ileto, the following boats in Zarcal's fleet allude to Philippine history, nationalism, the revolution and his own past: *Santa Cruz* (Zarcal's birthplace), *Kavite* (the heartland of the revolution), *Sikatuna* and *Lacandola* (pre-Spanish chiefs), *Magdalo* (Aguinaldo's Katipunan name), *Kalayaan* (Liberty), *Kapayapaan* (Peace), *Justicia* (Justice), *Esperanza* (Hope) and *Filipino*.

28 *Banzai*, meaning 'long live', was the name of the cutter (single-masted sailboat) based at St Paul's Anglican Mission from c.1909, which used to travel between the mission and Thursday Island with mail, produce, stores, etc. Rev. W. H. M. MacFarlane, AIATSIS MS 2616/1/3, Book 2. Jones, E. 1921. *Florence Buchanan: the little Deaconess of the South Seas*. Sydney: Australian Board of Missions. p. 51.

29 From English 'cook' plus Japanese *san*, 'Mister'.

30 According to Tom Lowah, pers. comm., 1981, crews called their Japanese skippers '*nisang*' as a title of respect. The word in Japanese is *niisan* [ni:sā] 'older brother', says Yuriko Nagata, pers. comm., May 2003.

31 Kemuel Kiwat, pers. comm., July 2000, told me that the Japanese men on the boats used to say: 'Hey, pana!' The Chinese word is *pangga* 'friend'.

32 Lowah, T. 1988. *Eded Mer: my life*. Kuranda: Rams Skull Press. p. 43. *Sobo* means 'small man' in English, says Yuriko Nagata.

33 According to Yuriko Nagata, the word is probably *hinode*, *hi* meaning 'the sun', *de* 'to come out' and *no* a connective meaning something like 'of'. 'Sunset' would be *hinoiri*.

34 Ayscough, H. 1914. *Priests in Carpentaria*. London: Lincoln and Southwell Branch of the Carpentarian Association. p. 18.

35 Lowah, T., *Eded Mer*, p. 65.

36 Burchill, E. 1972. *Thursday Island Nurse*. Adelaide: Rigby. p. 42. This was also the view of Ken O'Shea, pers. comm., July 1992, whose mother was raised partly in the Muslim family of Assan and Lass Ah Boo. The plates, ashtrays, cups and glasses on the graves are sometimes left there after visits by the family, who take food for themselves and the deceased as one might do 'for a family member in hospital'.

37 See Fitzpatrick-Nietschmann, J. M. 1981. 'Tombstone openings: cultural change and death ceremonies in Torres Strait, Australia.' *Kabar Seberang*, Vol. 8, No. 9. pp. 115. Lui, A. L. 1988. 'The Last Farewell: maintaining customary practice in Torres Strait Islander society.' Grad. Dip. of Material Anthropology thesis, James Cook University of North Queensland.

38 Fitzpatrick-Nietschmann, J. M., 'Tombstone openings', p. 13.

39 Sharp, N. 1993. *Stars of Tagai: the Torres Strait Islanders*. Canberra: Aboriginal Studies Press. p. 116.

40 Seriba Shibasaki quoted in Staples, J. and K. O'Shea, 'Thursday Island's Asian heritage', pp. 11–12.

41 This was the view expressed by Jamel Shibasaki in ibid, p. 13. Imam Uzair Akbar from Brisbane explains that the Muslim religion does not teach that a feast should be held 100 days after death, but suggests the Thursday Island custom may be a syncretic practice influenced by pre-Islamic cultural traditions in the Malay Archipelago and brought by the immigrants into Torres Strait. Seriba Shibasaki also comments 'that the Malay Muslim practice is different in many ways from that of the Arabian' (p. 11). In her family, 'the Malay rites include a tea three days after death, and feasts at 7, 40 and 100 days'. Jianna Seden Richardson, pers. comm., June 2003, says that in her family burials were very low-key affairs, with just the family and friends present. At the burial, the relatives drank tea, then again on the third and seventh days; on the 40th day, the family had chicken meat. There was a feast on the 100th day after burial to end the period of mourning, but it was not a celebration and, again, only the family and friends were invited.

42 Hayward, P. and J. Konishi, 'Mokuyo-to no ongaku', p. 55.

43 Karl Neuenfeldt, pers. comm., November 2001 and May 2003.

44 As Hayward, P. and J. Konishi, 'Mokuyo-to no ongaku', p. 59, point out, judgments about the significance of cultural phenomena based solely on their continuing influence are historically biased in privileging 'the [incidental] present'.

45 Rod Mitchell, pers. comm., 1998.

46 Staples J. and K. O'Shea, 'Thursday Island's Asian heritage', p. 9.

47 Kemuel Kiwat, pers. comm., August 1982.

48 Monica Walton Gould, pers. comm., March 2003.

49 Simpson, C. 1933. 'Island "hooch": no liquor of the white man.' *The Sun*, 27 November, 1933.

50 Ohshima, G., *Toresu Kaikyo no hitobito*, p. 285.

51 Autobiography by Catherine Martha Cook, dated 1989, typed manuscript in possession of the author.

52 Haddon, A. C. 1901. *Head hunters: black, white and brown*. London: Methuen. pp. 36–7.

53 Ohshima, G., 'Yooku-too yuuki', p. 60.

54 Some of the children of these unions claim that non-Christians were not permitted to marry legally on Thursday Island.

55 Staples, J. and K. O'Shea, 'Thursday Island's Asian heritage', p. 1.

56 Ohshima, G., *Toresu Kaikyo no hitobito*, p. 79.

Thursday Island festivities, 1925.
Courtesy of John Oxley Library, Brisbane (Item No. 185118).

Some Historical and Contemporary Asian Elements in the Music and Performance Culture of Torres Strait

Karl Neuenfeldt

The Torres Strait region of northern Queensland has been significantly influenced by cultures originating in Asia. Along with other cultural artefacts and social practices, migrants from Japan, the Philippines, present-day Indonesia, Sri Lanka and elsewhere brought their musicianship, music and performance cultures with them. The rich musical culture of the Torres Strait region today is the result of these diverse Asian influences combining with the equally diverse heritage of the region's Aboriginal, European, Melanesian and Polynesian peoples.

This chapter examines some of the Asian elements in particular performance events. It also examines songs in the historical and contemporary Torres Strait musical repertoire. The examples are from the *Torres Straits Pilot and New Guinea Gazette* (hereafter *Torres Straits Pilot*), published on Thursday Island. The songs are remembered and sung primarily by the current oldest generation with Asian connections who lived in Torres Strait before World War

II. After World War II, large-scale emigration from Torres Strait,[1] the eventual demise of maritime industries and the decrease in Asian immigrants[2] contributed to a decline in musical and cultural influences from Asia and Asians. Recent recordings, however, by Torres Strait Islanders are reintroducing Asian-influenced songs into the contemporary musical repertoire.[3]

The archival record of Asian musical influences in Torres Strait is limited, as are contemporary examples of the Asian-influenced musical repertoire. The historical record shows a very diverse migrant maritime workforce in Torres Strait. For example, 16 nationalities, 11 from Asia, were represented among the partial early death toll from the 1899 cyclone, which sank 66 luggers and seven tenders of the pearling fleet at Princess Charlotte Bay on the east coast of Queensland.[4]

Historical Context

Reportage of Asian involvement in Torres Strait performance culture needs to be appreciated in the context of the racial attitudes of the colonial and Federation eras. Anti-Asian sentiments were an integral part of the White Australia Policy, but were played out in Torres Strait in complex ways because of the importance of Asian labour for the maritime industries.[5] Public culture was one forum in which the Anglo-European elite tolerated a degree of inclusiveness, in particular within musical, theatrical and civic events.

The historical record demonstrates clearly that Anglo-Europeans on Thursday Island held ambivalent racial attitudes towards the Asian and other non-White migrants who lived and worked among them. On one level, they were a key component of the society and commerce of Torres Strait; yet, at another level, they were a threat to the tenets of the White Australia Policy. The following examples show how musical performances, especially in connection with civic events such as Queen Victoria's Diamond Jubilee, became opportunities for the immigrants to present accessible, although often exoticised and patronisingly reported aspects of Asian performance culture.

Examples of Historic Asian Elements in Performance Culture and Musical Repertoire

An account of Christmas Eve celebrations on Thursday Island in 1897 provides a glimpse of colonial era performance culture there and its Asian elements. Thomas Eykyn, a visiting Church of England minister, relates how 'Manilamen labourers came to give their Christmas performance' with a band made up of 'a concertina, a penny whistle, and a lovely Japanese drum played with vigour, and without cessation'.[6] The songs performed included *La Marseillaise*, *The Spanish Anthem*, *Grandfather Clock* and *Rule Britannia*, examples of the eclectic and transnational repertoire already circulating on Thursday Island. A year later, in 1889, the anthropologist, Alfred Cort Haddon, documented the circulation of Asian music and cultural practices to other islands of Torres Strait. On Mer (Murray) Island during a local performance he attended, girls 'sang Japanese and other songs'. Moreover, some of the girls' faces were painted white with a bit of red pigment on each cheek. Haddon suggested this was 'perhaps in imitation of the Japanese women of the settlement in Thursday Island, which goes by the name of "Yokohama"'.[7]

Asian decorations at Anglo-European social events are sometimes the only historically documented indication of a sizeable Asian presence of domestic workers. At an evening's entertainment at his home in November 1903, Bishop White met parishioners while '[t]he grounds looked quite fairy like with festoons of Chinese and Japanese lanterns; and the attendance of the band enlivened, most appreciatively, the course of an enjoyable evening'.[8] Along with different decorations, musical performances were a way of making such occasions special.

It is important to note that, because Thursday Island was adjacent to an important international waterway and was also a coaling station, numerous professional entertainment troupes visited either while on tour in Australia and New Zealand or in transit to Asia and Europe, often performing at the local School of Arts.[9] One example was the Beresford Variety Company, which visited Thursday Island in April 1901 after touring India. Beresford specialised in 'skate and pedestal and Hungarian top-boot dancing' and comedy, while Miss Mande Stamer was 'an accomplished singer soprano and pianiste'.[10] Two years later, it was reported that the Carl Zell Society Entertainers offered 'brilliant entertainment of music, mirth, and mystery', presenting to local audiences 'Magic that has bewildered thousands! Music, vocal and instrumental, that has pleased thousands!'[11]

Alongside such professional troupes, community-based entertainment was an integral part of the local performance culture, which, out of necessity, had to draw on amateur performers. Asian communities participated directly in local performances and at key public events. Thursday Island's sizeable Japanese community participated in the Diamond Jubilee celebrations for Queen Victoria in June 1897.

IN HONOUR of the CELEBRATION of
the DIAMOND JUBILEE of HER
MAJESTY the QUEEN of GREAT BRITAIN
———
The Japanese of Thursday Island will give a
DRAMATIC AND HUMOROUS
ENTERTAINMENT,
IN THE SCHOOL OF ARTS,
ON MONDAY EVENING NEXT,
At 8 o'clock.
Door opens at half-past seven.
Admission free.
The Committee reserve
the right of exclusion to anyone.
THE JAPANESE SPORTS COMMITTEE[12]

A review of the event appeared in the next issue of the *Torres Straits Pilot*. It reported that the event was well attended and 'strictly carried out after the Japanese fashion of portraying tragedy and comedy', with the 11 acts featuring a large cast 'of more or less grace and beauty'.[13] At its conclusion, the Japanese present cheered in honour of Queen Victoria. The prominent businessman, Torajiro Sato, commented on the significance of the event.[14] On behalf of the Japanese community, he expressed love and respect for the Queen and also said how glad they were that 'their lot is cast among such loyal subjects of Her Majesty's in this colony of Thursday Island'.[15]

In 1902, the Japanese community mounted another performance linked to British royalty. Although it was labelled an 'opera', it may have been a version of the kind of entertainment found in the rural area of Wakayama Prefecture where many of the Japanese migrants originated.[16] The audience was told the 'opera' was composed especially for the coronation of the new British king. The *Torres Straits Pilot's* reviewer admitted no understanding of its aesthetic merits beyond surmising they 'were undoubtedly high … if the appreciation of the large Japanese audience is to be a standard of judgement' and, overall, 'the whole performance in every detail was illustrated [sic] of the finer and higher side of Japanese life'.[17] Of particular interest in the context of local politics was the donation of the performance's proceeds to the local Anglican Quetta Parish Institute. It suggests a conscious effort to ameliorate the perception that the Japanese community did not readily integrate, even though they were at that time by far the largest Asian population in Torres Strait as maritime workers and merchants.

Thursday Island musicians. From left: Hismile (Izzie) Shibasaki,
Henry (Seaman) Dan, Eveness (Jerry) Lewin and George Dewis (now deceased), c.1990–91.
Courtesy of Karl Neuenfeldt.

Migrants from Sri Lanka, described variously as Singhalese or Cingalese, also presented public performances. One was the tale of Prince Ramlan and Princess Pew-lina. The *Torres Straits Pilot*'s reviewer observed: 'It is not often that Thursday Island, not withstanding its large share of people of Eastern nationalities, sees a play, or a musical drama, for their amusement.'[18] The play was first read out in English and the reviewer commented on how well the actors acquitted themselves, with accomplished dancing, attractive dresses and makeup that was 'very handsome, as becomes the nature of all oriental people'. The account of another Sri Lankan performance also mentioned the contribution of £1.15 to the local hospital, analogous to Japanese donations to the Anglican Church's Quetta Parish Institute. The 'operas' were described as 'curiously oriental in their character' and were 'undoubtedly appreciated by the coloured element', although 'their efforts to please were responded to only in the main by coloured people'.[19]

In 1903, a 'goodwill visit' by Japanese naval vessels was accompanied by several musical events, which included repertoire based on the British brass-band tradition: 'the band was brought up from the ship and provided music of a high class character. There was evident enjoyment and a full appreciation of a Japanese war ship's band playing at the Grand Hotel on Friday afternoon.'[20]

The importance of music to the pageantry and the success of the visit was remarked widely. The *Torres Straits Pilot* recorded how 'the interest in the visit was considerably enhanced by the band, the like of which was never before heard here, and it may be a long time ere such music may be heard again'.[21] Months later, favourable remarks were still being made about the quality of the Japanese naval band, which had set a standard of comparison for local bands. Commenting on a local band, it was said: 'The ... band has made wonderful progress ... and they now perform in a style which places them in a high class ... said some one on Thursday evening last at the concert, "they remind you of the Japanese band" which was not bad.'[22]

By the 1930s, Asian migrants and their descendants had become very active in community performances on Thursday Island, in some ways challenging the previous Anglo-European dominance. One example of this was a 'Grand Concert' put on by the Merry Magpies at the Town Hall on Monday, 3 September, 1934. Included in the program were dance items such as a 'Malay dance', 'ribbon dance' and a 'paddle dance', performed by community-based entertainers with Asian family names: Ahfat, Bargo, Bin Garape, Sariman and Subideen. The program also included plantation songs out of the North American minstrelsy tradition, such as *Kentucky Home* performed by 'Sambo and Alabama'. One can only speculate as to whether the singers and dancers of Asian heritage 'blackened up' to perform the plantation songs.

Overall, archival newspaper evidence substantiates the claim that Asians, whether presenting their own or imitating other music, contributed to the historic performance culture of Torres Strait and complemented the performance traditions of the dominant (but minority) Anglo-European community. Although direct Asian influence waned with regional and national political, social and economic changes after World War II, traces of Asian musicality and repertoire endure in Torres Strait today, in old and new songs.

Examples of Contemporary Asian Elements in Performance Culture and Musical Repertoire

The following songs are examples of mainly South-East Asian influences in the contemporary music repertoire of Torres Strait Islander communities and performers in Torres Strait and on the mainland. Some biographical information about the Asian heritage of various singers and writers is also given as context. What are often referred to locally as 'Malay' songs can be typified as romantic or nostalgic songs with memorable melodies.[23] Musically and lyrically, they evoke a certain cultural and geographic ambience associated with present-day Indonesia and the Philippines. Linguistically, they often combine 'Malay' and English words, as few contemporary performers are fluent in modern-day Bahasa Indonesia or the Filipino Tagalog language. Depending on the origin of their parents and grandparents, elderly performers and composers may, however, have learned and spoken one of many regional Asian languages and dialects. Nonetheless, the use of 'Malay' words and phrases signifies an overt Asian connection.

Eveness (Jerry) Lewin (born 1927) traces his family's Asian heritage to present-day Indonesia.[24] Along with other non-combatants living on Thursday Island at the outset of the Pacific War, his family was evacuated to the Australian mainland in January 1942.[25] He remembers that before they left he often heard 'Malay' songs at house parties frequented by migrant maritime workers. He recalls, in particular, hearing the well-known Indonesian song, *Bengawan Solo*, written by Gesang Martohartono in 1940. He must therefore have heard it just before his family was evacuated. He recalls it being sung during the war years along with other 'Malay' songs that reminded evacuees of home. While on the mainland he worked in various manual jobs in south-eastern Queensland, but also learned music, especially from Filipinos attached to the US military. When Jerry returned to Torres Strait in the late 1940s, like many other men of his generation, he worked in the maritime industries. One of the boats he worked on was called the *Bada Kris*, a '*kris*' being a kind of knife. It was a barge converted for trochus-shell harvesting and carried a crew of 10 men. It would return to port when it had a full load of trochus shells or when it needed provisions. He wrote a song about it in 1950 when working the Great Barrier Reef out of Cairns, north Queensland. In 2002, Jerry recorded the song for a community CD called *Sailing the Southeast Wind: Maritime Songs from Torres Strait*:

> *Jangan lupa nona manis / classie Bada Kris / belung slamat tinggal / kita skarang mau blihar / tinggal nona nona samuah / susah hati te dalam ada sato / bulan kita con balek*

> Translation: Don't forget my sweetheart the barge *Bada Kris* / saying goodbye to you / we shall be going / be going to our sweethearts in Cairns / I love her with all my heart / she is the only one / I shall return on the first moon and I'll be back in Cairns.

George Dewis (1935–99) traced his family's Asian heritage to the Ambon region in Indonesia and to Timor. He was one of the few Thursday Islanders of Asian descent to visit Indonesia, which he recalled was an interesting experience because some of the music was familiar as were other cultural practices.[26] He was also recognised for his Asian-influenced cooking skills, which were put to good use first while working as a cook on pearling and trochus boats and later at community events. He was a skilled musician and singer and recorded a version of the well-known Indonesian song, *Nona Manis*, for a community CD called *Strike Em!: Contemporary Voices from Torres Strait*.[27] It combines 'Malay' and English words:

> Goodbye to you my *Nona Nona Manis* / Don't you forget *junang lupa kapada siam* / but in your eyes you will always think of me *saya da limpe kapada siam*.

An indication of the continuing significance of such Asian-influenced songs is that his recorded version of *Nona Manis* was played at his tombstone unveiling ceremony in 2002, the key Torres Strait Islander social event that marks the end of the mourning period.[28]

Ernest Ahwang (born 1941) traces his family's Asian heritage to the Singapore Strait settlement. He was just a baby in 1942 when his family was evacuated on the small pearling lugger, *Goodwill*, the same boat Jerry Lewin's family was on. He was raised in Mackay, Queensland, where he learned 'Malay' songs at community events and from his uncle, Norunnie (Rocky) Ahwang. Ernest recorded an instrumental version of *Terang Bulang* for the National Museum of Australia's Torres Strait Islander exhibition *Paipa/Windward*. He also recorded another song he titled *Bala Ernest*. It is based on South-East Asian guitar styles known loosely in the community as '*kronchong*' songs, although they are not overly similar to the well-known Indonesian style. Because the 'Malay' songs have memorable melodies, they lend themselves either to instrumental versions or to new songs, in the sense that they combine some of the 'Malay' words with new English ones.

Hismile (Izzie) Shibasaki (born 1929) traces his family's Asian heritage to Japan and Malaka.[29] His family was also evacuated in early 1942 and spent the war years mostly in the Bundaberg area of Queensland. As a Japanese citizen, Izzie's father, Kyukichi, was interned as a prisoner of war, but was allowed to return to Thursday Island after the war because his wife was born in Torres Strait and he was a skilled pearl diver. Izzie recalls that before evacuation and during the war years 'Malay' music in particular was an important part of social life. His mother sang 'Malay' songs to him as a child and they were sung at house parties. A particular favourite was *Nona Manis Siapa Yang Punya*,[30] which Izzie still sings when performing. The version below is from a Japanese-based web site.[31] It is interesting that the lyrics are in Bahasa Indonesia and English, similar to the transliteration routinely heard in Torres Strait songs:

Nona Manis siapa punya / Nona Manis siapa punya / Nona Manis siapa punya / Rasa sayang sayange / Baju merah siapa yang punya / Baju merah siapa yang punya / Baju merah siapa yang punya / Rasa sayang sayange / Ingat ingat it remember / *Jangan lupa itu* don't forget / *Aku cinta itu* I love you / *Hanya kamu* only you.

Translation: Pretty girl whose fiancee is she / She is very charming / Wearing white dress whose fiancee is she / She is very charming

Wayne See Kee (born 1971), who traces his family's Asian heritage to China, completed a university degree in Asian studies. He has been involved in Torres Strait Islander music as a radio broadcaster, performer and writer and wrote a contemporary romantic song called *Saya Patu Kamu*, which translates from 'Malay' to English as 'I love you'. He recalls: 'I wrote it as a love song, and I was looking for a Torres Strait language to use, but couldn't find an appropriate phrase. I noticed a lot of the Malay descendants on Thursday Island still used this phrase with little children so I decided that it sounded good in the song.'[32]

When will you say you love me *saya patu kamu* / When will you say you care for me *saya patu kamu* / When will you say you want me *saya patu kamu* / When will you say I'm the only one *saya patu kamu* / Though the world could stand still I'll be waiting here for you / Just to hear three special words that will tell me you're so true / When will you say you love me *saya patu kamu*.

There is at least one song in the older Torres Strait repertoire associated with Japan, a song called *Japanese Rumba*. Edwards typifies it as a Japanese folk song and, according to an Islander informant, 'the dance that was associated with it also owed something to the oriental style of dancing, with the actions being very formal'.[33] The lyrics are:

Japanese rumba *ia ia i* / Japanese rumba *ia ia i* / Japanese rumba *ia ia i* / *suda nassi, suda resun / combowa, combowa / whya suda remus* HA.[34]

Another song with a possible connection to Japan is a boat song called *Hossack H*, which was recorded for the National Museum of Australia's Torres Strait Islander exhibition, *Paipa/Windward*, in 2002. Informants in Mackay, where it was recorded, suggested it might be a transliteration of 'Osaka'. Given the dominance of Japanese in the maritime industries, it is understandable that aspects of their music would be learned or assimilated by Islanders. Hayward and Konishi include songs that were written by Japanese maritime workers about their life in Torres Strait.[35] The traffic in songs went both ways: elderly Japanese ex-divers remembered Islander songs when interviewed in 1999.

Conclusion

Some songs in the current Torres Strait Islander repertoire show clear Asian influences, mostly in versions of songs popular when migration from Asia was common. Most of the older songs in the repertoire have been indigenised in the sense that there has been language substitution and in some cases localisation of themes. Large-scale migration all but ceased with the outbreak of World War II and consequently few, if any, new Asian songs have been introduced since then. Current recordings of some of the songs are reintroducing them to new audiences and performers and they may well remain as a reminder of the cultural impact of Asia on Torres Strait and Torres Strait Islander performance culture.

Footnotes

[1]   Beckett, J. R. 1987. *Torres Strait Islanders: custom and colonialism*. Cambridge University Press.

[2]   Ganter, R. 1994. *The Pearl Shellers of Torres Strait: resource use, development and decline 1860s–1960s*. Melbourne University Press.

[3]   It needs to be noted that Torres Strait is not the only region of northern Australia where Asian-influenced music and dance are still performed. For example, during the Darwin Festival of Arts in the Northern Territory in August 2002, two performances were linked overtly to Asia. A Filipino shake-hand dance was performed and the Rondella String Band played music in the style of Filipino string bands. In Western Australia, Broome has long celebrated its Asian linkages in the music of artists such as the Pigram Brothers, who write about the mixed heritage of the community using 'Malay' words and phrases that have become part of the local language. Historical examples of these linkages are noted in Bain, M. 1982. *Full Fathom Five*. Perth: Artlook Books.

[4]   *Torres Straits Pilot* 13 May, 1899. p. 1.

[5]   Mullins, S. 1995. *Torres Strait: a history of colonial occupation and culture contact 1864–1897*. Rockhampton: Central Queensland University Press. Ganter, R., *The Pearl Shellers of Torres Strait*.

[6]   Eykyn, T. 1896. *Parts of the Pacific*. London: Swan Sonnenschein. p. 99.

[7]   Haddon, A. C. 1901. *Head-Hunters: Black, White, and Brown*. London: Methuen. pp. 36–7.

[8]   *Torres Straits Pilot*, 7 November, 1903. p. 1.

[9]   See, for example, Bandmann, D. 1886. *An Actor's Tour or Seventy Thousand Miles with Shakespeare*. New York: Bretano Brothers. Mullins, S. and K. Neuenfeldt. 2001. 'The "saving grace of social culture": early popular music and performance culture on Thursday Island, Torres Strait, Queensland.' *Queensland Review*, Vol. 8, No. 2. pp. 1–20.

[10]   *Torres Straits Pilot*, 18 April, 1901. p. 1.

[11]   *Torres Straits Pilot*, 21 November, 1903. p. 1.

[12]   *Torres Straits Pilot*, 19 June, 1897. p. 1.

[13]   *Torres Straits Pilot*, 26 June, 1897. p. 1.

[14]   Hayward, P. and J. Konishi. 2001. 'Mokuyo-to no ongaku: music and the Japanese community in the Torres Strait (1890–1941).' *Perfect Beat*, Vol. 5, No. 3. p. 48.

[15]   *Torres Straits Pilot*, 26 June, 1897. p. 1.

[16]   Hayward, P. and J. Konishi, 'Mokuyo-to no ongaku'.

[17]   *Torres Straits Pilot*, 5 July, 1902. p. 1.

[18]   *Torres Straits Pilot*, 18 May, 1901. p. 1.

[19]   *Torres Straits Pilot*, 1 February, 1902. p. 1.

20 *Torres Straits Pilot*, 4 July, 1903. p. 1.

21 *Torres Straits Pilot*, 11 July, 1903. p. 1.

22 *Torres Straits Pilot*, 31 October, 1903. p. 1.

23 See Neuenfeldt, K. 2002. 'Examples of Torres Strait songs of longing and belonging.' *Journal of Australian Studies*, No. 75. pp. 111–16.

24 Jerry Lewin, pers. comm., 2002.

25 Osborne, E. 1997. *Torres Strait Islander Women and the Pacific War*. Canberra: Aboriginal Studies Press.

26 George Dewis, pers. comm., 1999.

27 Neuenfeldt, K. 2001. 'Cultural politics and a music recording project: producing *Strike Em!*: *Contemporary Voices from the Torres Strait.*' *Journal of Intercultural Studies*, Vol. 22, No. 2. pp. 133–45.

28 Fuary, M. 1993. 'Torres Strait cultural history.' In N. Loos and T. Osanai (eds), *Indigenous Minorities and Education*, Tokyo: Sanyusha. pp. 165–86.

29 Hismile Shibasaki, pers. comm., 2003.

30 Edwards, R. 2001. *Some Songs from the Torres Strait*. Kuranda: Ramskull Press. pp. 148–9. Edwards claims that *Nona Manis Siapa Yang Punya* was adopted and adapted by Australian troops during World War II. Kartomi (cited in ibid., p. 149) says the song originated in Maluku in Ambon and became ubiquitous in Indonesia after 1949.

31 http://www.alles.or.jp/~longisl/ songe.html

32 Wayne See Kee, pers. comm., 2003.

33 Edwards, R., *Some Songs from the Torres Strait*, p. 75.

34 There were Okinawan divers in Torres Strait after World War II and P. Hayward and J. Konishi, 'Mokuyo-to no ongaku', p. 64, note there is some dispute over the exact origins of the song, citing the work of Hosokawa, S. 1999. 'Soy sauce music: Haruomi Hosono and Japanese self-orientalism.' In P. Hayward (ed.), *Widening the Horizon: exoticism in post-war popular music*, John Libbey/Perfect Beat Publications. pp. 114–44.

35 Hayward, P. and J. Konishi, 'Mokuyo-to no ongaku', pp. 56–8.

Roman Catholic Church, Thursday Island, 1906.
Courtesy of John Oxley Library, Brisbane (Item No. 1618).

CHAPTER 12

Voices from Torres Strait

For all of its history, Torres Strait has been a site of confluence and contestation, linking the currents of the world's two largest oceans, as well as the inhabitants of insular South-East Asia and the Pacific, and the two opposing mainlands of Australia and New Guinea.

Our book has focused on the significant encounter between the Torres Strait Islanders and Asian immigrants. In this final chapter, we proffer eight voices belonging to contemporary Torres Strait Islanders, whose parents or grandparents were members of the Asian communities featured in the preceding chapters. Their distinctly personal stories complement and contextualise the intricacies of the Chinese, Filipino, Malay, Japanese and Sri Lankan diasporic experience in Torres Strait. Multiple viewpoints emerge from these stories, a consequence of individual circumstances and life ways, as well as generational and gender differences.

The personal narratives of the prewar generation of Asian heritage illustrate vividly the choices faced by marginalised people struggling to survive and prosper in a new society they helped create at Australia's northern boundary — a society that was multicultural, yet internally segregated by race and class. For the postwar generation, a self-assured, blended form of Torres Strait-Asian identity is accentuated, informed by memories of childhood, family and community experiences; and by reflection on the myriad intersections of family, community and nation. Apparent in all the stories, however, are the challenging yet rewarding personal journeys made by Torres Strait Islanders of diverse ancestries, journeys that mirror the navigation of community boundaries, which has emerged as a defining aspect of this work as a whole.

The editors of this book offer this final chapter in sincere acknowledgement that it is the people who have shared their stories here, their families and their ancestors, who are truly the authors of the rich and remarkable Asian diasporic experience of Torres Strait.

Eva Salam Peacock is the daughter of Batcho Mingo from Makasar, Sulawesi, Indonesia, and Annie Randolph from Darnley Island, of Torres Strait Islander, Danish and Sri Lankan descent. She was born on Thursday Island in 1924. Eva married Uley John Peacock in Mareeba during the war. She is the mother of eight children, grandmother of 24 and great-grandmother of three.

I was born on Thursday Island and grew up on Thursday Island, Wednesday Island and Hammond Island. On Thursday Island, we lived way up near the Hocking station, what they used to call Hockings Point. You go past all the boat slips, where the Japs were, down near the waterfront. We could just hop and jump into the water. Dad was a mechanic and worked on Hocking's launch engine. He could take the motor apart and fix it and put it back together. After he retired, he took us to live on Wednesday Island, where he cut timber for the pearling luggers and stacked the wood up in cords on the shore above the sand. I started school on Thursday Island, but I went to live on Wednesday Island just after I started school — I must have been about seven or eight. I didn't stay there, just went there for school holidays. We were sent to Hammond Island for school. My older sisters were married and already living there.

My mother was born on Nepean Island — you can see it from Darnley Island. Her mother, my grandmother, was a very tall woman named Balo from Darnley. That's what my mother has on her marriage certificate. My mother didn't know her own mother; she was only two years old when her mother passed away giving birth to her youngest child. My mother was Annie Randolph and she had two full sisters, Sophie and Fanny, and an adopted sister, Harriet. Mum didn't know where her own mother came from: different ones tell her this and that. She was young, and you don't know much. People tell me that Balo was one of three daughters born to Konai, a Torres Strait lady from Bumeo on Darnley Island and her Sri Lankan husband. They had three daughters: Balo, Sophie and Morabisi. Balo married Thomas Randolph from Denmark, but he died when my mother was about only 10 years old, she said. He was on his way to Thursday Island with the four girls when he died on board the *Pirate* — that was the name of his lugger — in 1897. After Randolph died, the girls were looked after by the Sinclairs, who were his friends. The Sinclairs took the four girls and raised them with their own family on Thursday Island. His wife wanted them. My mother told me that John Douglas attended Tom Randolph's funeral and stood there with his arms around the girls.

The Catholic religion came from the Filipino. Mum was an Anglican. She turned Catholic to marry her first husband. He wanted her to, so they could get married in the church. One thing about Sinclair, he always tried to do the right thing for them, because he thought if they went to White people to work and they started working, they probably wouldn't be treated well, you know. So he found jobs for them with the Coloured race. That's how they got to know the Filipinos. Harriet had a job with the Filipinos and so did Mum. I can't remember their names, but Harriet married a Filipino and went back with him to the Philippines and we never heard any more from them. I can't remember what his name was.

Mum was working for a Filipino family and that's how she met Lopez Delacruz. Everybody thinks they were two people, Lopez and Delacruz, but Lopez was his first name. Lots of people got mixed up with it. They thought, 'Oh, Mum's got so many husbands.' So that's how it came about. They had five children. And he died. He was with the

Eva Salam, taken in Darwin, c.1941.
Courtesy of Eva Salam Peacock.

pearling, he was a diver. I don't know how he died. He was in Darwin and was in a fight and was stabbed to death. He's buried in Darwin. So she was left with this young family but then Haji Salam took over. He came to her rescue and married her. That's how we got the name Salam. And she had three children with Salam. That's Siat (Josie), Amelia and Hardie. Amelia died when she was about three or four years old; she had pneumonia. Mum said it broke her heart. She told us all these sad stories. I always remember those sorts of things, you never forget it.

Haji Salam was working on the pearling. She met him and they got married and she had the three children to him. They married in the Catholic Church. I think they could marry in the Catholic Church but not in front of the altar. Haji had to be sent back to Singapore, his 10 years were up. Ten years I think they had. He said, 'Oh well, you can come with me, I'll send your fares. You'll be all right in Singapore.' So Mum was quite happy about that. She loved him. Anyway, he went home and he sent her the money, also a letter explaining that he already had two wives over there. He didn't let her know in the first place. And she didn't know how to take it. She was really upset and she said, 'No', she said she couldn't share him. She said, 'I'll stay here and starve', because

there was no pension or anything like that in those days. Johnny was working — that's the eldest Delacruz boy. He had a job on the pilot launch. He was the only one who brought in some money and kept them from starving. But she said, 'No.' She wrote and told him that she can't go, she couldn't live that way. So that was the end of that. And so she stayed a couple of years, I suppose, and then my Dad came along and wanted to marry her. She said, 'I'm already married, I'm not divorced. I'll get into trouble if I marry again.' And he said, 'No you can marry now', because he went to the magistrate to find out. Anyway, she was afraid that she might get put in jail or something. She always thinks things that way. Poor old Dad was so disgusted, you know. He wanted his children to have his name, but Mum just left it at that. So we had to take the name 'Salam'.

Dad was a Muslim but he didn't mind if we were Catholic. He didn't mind us going to a Catholic school. He was a good provider, anyway. He'd always see that we had food and clothing. He came from the Celebes. He wasn't indentured like Salam, because Hocking got him, him and Tommy Loban. I think he came at the same time as Tommy Loban, because Ellie, his daughter, showed me a photograph of the boys that came during that time. He and Tommy Loban were very good friends. So Hocking sent them back to the place in Indonesia where they thought this British boat went down. They wanted proof to show that it did and asked them to get evidence and they did. They got the name of it, I think, the boat, and they smuggled it back to Thursday Island. So that's why they gave them the freedom to stay. He was something like an undercover spy. But he used to be proud to say he was in the Australian Navy during the war and he was on this boat — it must have been a patrol boat, the coast guard. I don't remember the name, but I remember seeing the photo. He had it on the wall, all the navy men on deck on that boat. He was there and also in the corner of that same picture there was inserted a chest photo of himself wearing navy uniform. We didn't take the picture with us when we were evacuated, we thought we were going to go back to Thursday Island after the evacuation.

Dad was a diver for Reg Hocking. They had a dormitory and the men stayed there. That was at Hocking's pearling station on Thursday Island, down where they had the boat slips. That's where they lived when they were on shore. They had a cook there, someone cooking for them, and I used to sneak up to have some curry and rice with them. It was not far, just round the point. I'd go up there to get a dinner, then I'd come home and have another one. My Dad used to be so proud of me. He used to love watching me. He looked after all the others, too, he was good to them all. He wasn't a very religious man. I didn't see him do all the things that religious Muslims do, but he wouldn't eat pork. But he loved camp pie. Everybody would look at him and say, 'You're Muslim, eh? You don't eat pig, eh?' I'd say, 'Well, what are you eating there?' He'd say, 'Meat.'

He didn't know. He didn't drink beer, like some of the other Muslims, but he'd drink neat rum — that's a tradition from the navy.

When I left Hammond Island, I was about 14. I stayed one year on Thursday Island and I worked for Jenap Jia. Jenap was part-Islander and part-Malay and her sister, Doseena, married Assan, who was a Mohammedan priest. She had a laundry and she used to do all the laundry from the ships that came in to the island, the coastal boats. She wasn't the Jenap who is well-known for her long soup. Sang Kee was the one who made the long soup, the Chinese man. He was very, very famous for his long soup. He married Atima Ahwang. We all went to see them get married but he ran away, he cleared off, but they did marry. I was only very young at the time. They weren't young. She already had her children then.

Mrs Jenap lived in town, not far from the town hall. Yokohama was near the boat slips, near the water. The road went through where the Japs were to get to town. Malaytown was more or less across the road, the tarred road, from Japtown, going down towards the point. The Malays were on that side of the road, the Japs were on the other side, near the water. The Japs were closer to the water, because they worked on the boats. The Chinese didn't live down there, they were more or less going towards the Catholic Church way. Mainly the main street, they were, on Douglas Street. You know where the picture show was? Well, just around there. Chee Quee had that shop near the picture show. And down further, across the road that goes to the water, that's where another Chinese shop was. And Chinese across the road. Mendis was across from the Metropole Hotel. It later burned down. There was another Chinese shop, Lai Foo, up from the jetty and Mendis was along there. There was another Sri Lankan there, the dentist Saranealis. He was not far from the Metropole Hotel, on Douglas Street. The Europeans lived mostly up behind the town, going towards the state school, along that area, and up towards the church. There was the Grand Hotel up on the hill, and there was a Burns Philp shop down from that. And there was another hotel down there, too, McNulty's Hotel. There must have been everybody from around the world living there on that little island.

Monica Walton Gould was born on Thursday Island in 1927, the daughter of William Walton and Gregoria (Guria) Assacruz. Of Torres Strait Islander, Aboriginal, Filipino and English heritage, she married Harold Andrew Gould in Brisbane after the war. Monica has eight children and 17 grandchildren.

I was born on Thursday Island. I don't know if it was in hospital or at home, probably at home. We lived in John Street, not in Malaytown. Malaytown was up the other end past the Post Office. John Street was nearer the shopping centre, in Douglas Street, in the middle. We didn't go down to Malaytown. In our days, Catholics mixed only with Catholics. I don't know why. There was something about religion in those days.

I remember that house we lived in in John Street. It had bare walls, bare floors. We slept on the bare floors on mats, on island mats. That place was fairly big. It was lowset, but there was enough room just to crawl under. We used to crawl under and hide, you know, play hide and seek. We had no fear of spiders or snakes or anything like that. The house had wooden stumps, I remember, and wooden floors and we used to put the mats down at night to sleep. Mum rolled them up in the morning; she was very tidy and clean and I think she used to just roll them up and put them away until night-time. But I remember that house in John Street. This was before myself and my four sisters had to go to the convent for school. I was five, that was the normal age. We boarded at the convent with lots of other girls. I boarded at the convent night and day — I hated it. We worked very hard. We were on our hands and knees scrubbing the wooden floors and verandahs of the presbytery with a scrubbing brush. We used to do the washing in a wood copper, turning a huge handle for the nuns' habits and the priests' habits and vestments. The senior girls starched and ironed the nuns' veils. After I went to the convent to board to go to school, Mum and Dad shifted to Horn Island, and we just went home for school holidays.

Mum was always busy, cooking dampers, cooking the fish, cooking the rice. I didn't know her parents, they weren't alive by then. Mum never spoke about her family. Dad was a very strict man and he had this little sailing boat, *Valmay*. Dad used to go across to Thursday Island every day to work and then he'd come back and we'd see his sailboat getting closer and closer to Horn Island and we'd say, 'Here's Daddy, here's Daddy coming. Wonder if he's got lollies for us.' And he did have lollies for us. Dad worked as a wharf labourer and at one stage he worked for Customs. He used to bring back sacks of potatoes and onions in the boat from Thursday Island, but we had our own vegetables, sweet potatoes and fruit.

Dad sometimes used to make *tuba*; he was no innocent. I remember seeing him take a hanging bunch of coconut blossoms, tying them all together and bending them over an earthenware pot. The juice dripped into the pot and, when it was fermented enough, they drank it. Dad used to be very happy some evenings. Mum asked him to keep some of it for her to ferment more to make vinegar. She used to make coconut oil to wash our hair. You let it boil and boil and it turns into coconut oil. You can cook with it, use it on the skin to counteract the heat, and use it for washing your hair.

There was a well where Daniel Hodges lived on Horn Island; as far as I know, that was the only well in that vicinity. My mother used to get water from the well in a bucket to do her washing, because it was fresh water, drinking water. We also had two water tanks attached to our house. Mum used to get the water out of the well, fill the tub and do the washing. She got the bucket with the rope on the handle and she'd somehow manage to tip it and get the water up. No problems with water, the well was always full.

The two Canendo brothers — they were much older than us — they used to go crayfishing and they'd catch a lot of crayfish and muddies (mudcrabs) and they'd share them, like all the families would share. Dad used to go fishing, take *Valmay* out in the passage, just straight out from our place. We weren't interested in whether he caught fish, all we were interested in was having a swing on the tree and running around and swimming. Then Dad would come back and Mum would have the rice cooked and Dad cleaned the fish and scaled the fish — I can still see it. They had an open fire downstairs and Mum used to roast them over the hot coals. It was really tasty. I told my doctor this and she said, 'That's what gave you the start of a healthy life, having fish from the start of your life.'

I think it was Mr Vidgen — he owned a lot of cattle — who had a place there where they slaughtered the animals for the meat for the butchers. Dad used to go and help Mr Vidgen put the bulls in the shed. Not far from the slaughter yards there were lots of mango trees. I think they were planted, there were lots of them there. The Filipino men might have planted them. There were posts nearby, as if there were houses there once, near the slaughter yards at the same end as *Tiyo* Dualdo. I remember all these mango trees; they were special mangoes, not the ordinary plain mangoes, and very, very sweet. The skins were just really dark green and we called them 'black mangoes'. We'd race along to where we knew the mangoes were and give the lowest branches a shake and the ripe mangoes would fall down and we'd pick them up. Just a few and we were right. We were never, ever hungry. I saw some again in 1998 when my sister and I went up to Thursday Island. They were growing in a vacant allotment between the Rainbow Motel and See Kee's shop. We used to look at the trees, just laden with these mangoes. And if we had stayed on for about another month, I think we would have had a mango feast.

When we were home for school holidays, my sisters and I used to play with Francis Seden. We'd have breakfast and go over to Francis's place. They lived down towards the other end of the island, where *Tiyo* Dualdo lived. Francis was an only child. His stepfather had made him a little boat, just big enough to fit two or three of us children. At the back of their house was a sort of a lagoon and there was a creek leading up to this lagoon. We would play all day when the tide was in. Mum never said to us, 'Be home by four' or 'Be home by five' or anything like that. I think because she knew we weren't in any danger.

Those days were different. And, at the end of the day, we just went home, maybe because we were tired and needed to jump in the tub and were looking forward to Mum's fish and rice. We lived on rice, even in the convent. After supper we'd sit around with the kerosene lamp and read comics. All of us sisters and Reggie and Gertie Lee, they'd come over and read comics with us. Then they'd run back home, 'See you, see you, *yawo*.' And that was our life.

> **Kyôzô Hirakawa** originated from Okinawa and came to Thursday Island in 1958 and in 1960 he married Kathleen Seden. He was naturalised in 1965. Kyôzô and Kathleen went on to have five children and currently have eight grandchildren. Kyôzô is a crayfisherman and, during the off-season, he stays home and often looks after his grandchildren.

I came to Thursday Island with other Okinawan men in 1958. We worked in the pearling industry and stayed in the dormitory. Many of us were not happy with the contracts under which we were employed and so many returned to Okinawa after about one year. I came back to Thursday Island in 1960 with another friend and worked with another pearling company. I worked on a boat with six other people. I met my wife then, who was working for the same company.

At the time, Thursday Island had a very multicultural population and I was able to mix with many cultural groups. Although some attitudes towards Japanese people were difficult, this changed when Australia's relationship with Japan changed as Japanese manufactured goods were introduced.

There are not enough Okinawans to form a club on Thursday Island. When I first arrived on Thursday Island, there were about 160 there. They made *shamisen* (stringed instruments) and sang songs thinking about Okinawa, but I was never, never homesick. Maybe I was too young. Now there are no *shamisen*, no music, but I still listen to cassette tapes of Okinawan songs.

While Okinawan festivals are not celebrated, the three remaining Okinawans stick together. Sometimes we use Okinawan language with them. Nowadays when speaking Okinawan, it feels a bit funny to me as I have used English in my work for over 40 years. My children do not speak Japanese or Okinawan, but one of my granddaughters has learnt Japanese at school and went to Japan on a school tour.

Sometimes Okinawans make the trip to Thursday Island to visit their deceased relatives buried in the Japanese section of the cemetery. The Japanese Memorial at the Thursday Island cemetery is very good as families of those buried there can come and visit.

Elizabeth Mary (Betty) Ah Boo Foster is the daughter of William Manup Ah Boo and Almira Mayor, both from Thursday Island. Betty was also born on Thursday Island in 1936 and is of Torres Strait Islander, Malakan, Javanese and Filipino heritage. She married Thomas Douglas Foster in 1956 and they had seven children.

Paula Foster was born on Thursday Island in 1970. She is the youngest of seven children. Her parents are Betty Foster née Ah Boo and Thomas Foster, who changed his surname from Farquhar. Paula is therefore of Torres Strait Islander, Filipino, Malayan, Scottish and New Zealand descent. She is married to Mark French and has a daughter and a son. She is currently working as a teacher coordinator with RATEP [Remote Area Teaching Education Program] in Napranum.

It was during World War II, in 1942, that the people living on Thursday Island were evacuated to the mainland. My mother, Betty Ah Boo, was one of the many who was evacuated south with her family. Prior to the evacuation, there was great fear among my grandparents, Almira née Mayor and Manup Ah Boo, and my great-grandparents Lass Sedan and Assan Ah Boo. Prince of Wales Island, being the largest island in the Torres Strait, seemed the most appropriate place to hide from the army. The army consisted largely of Europeans; however, Torres Strait Islanders and a mixture of Torres Strait Islanders with Malaysian, South Sea Islander and South-East Asian descendants were also enlisted. Before the enlistment there was much controversy over whether or not non-Europeans could be trusted. Hall writes, 'The conscription of non-European was barred by the Defence Act, but many Aboriginals and Torres Strait Islanders managed to enlist, particularly after Japan entered the war.' The army was responsible for ensuring that the people on Thursday Island were evacuated.

According to my mother, the two months that they lived in hiding on Prince of Wales were the most difficult months of her life. She told me of the American bombers that flew over Prince of Wales, vibrating the island and leaving everyone scared. As a child of seven, my mother, and her family, had to wake early in the mornings — about three o'clock each day — to go into the bush to hide; they would then return to their camp when it was dark. Their camp was made out of bush timber and mangrove wood. Mangrove leaves were used for the roof so that the army would not find them.

While my mother and her family were living on Prince of Wales Island their diet consisted of Sao biscuits and tinned beef with vegetables. The food supplies were bought from the store on Thursday Island before they moved to Prince of Wales. For water, they had three dug-out wells, which had been built by my mother's father, grandfather and uncle.

Eventually, my mother, her family and the other Malaysian families were found by the army. One of the men in the army was part-Malaysian and he had relatives living on Prince of Wales. He reported them to the officials and they were then tracked down. The reason the army gave my mother and her family as to why they had to go south was because the Japanese planes might fly over and bomb Prince of Wales Island. Five minutes were given to my grandparents, great-grandparents and the other Malaysian families to pack one small suitcase per family. In my mother's family, she had one younger brother and sister; her mother, Almira née Mayor, was pregnant with another child. After being taken over to Thursday Island in a launch by the army, my grandfather, Manup Ah Boo, was conscripted as a cook in the army. It was 26 February, 1942, when my mother and the rest of her extended family were put on the schooner, *Goodwill*, to be shipped to Cairns.

On their arrival in Cairns, they were put on to a train for Murgon. At each of the stations at which the train stopped, the Red Cross provided food and clothing to the evacuees. After reaching their destination at Murgon, my mother, and the rest of her extended family, as well as the Malaysian families, were loaded on to big trucks. These trucks took them inland to Cherbourg, which was to become their new home. My mother's first impression of Cherbourg was that it was a 'creepy place'.

Cherbourg had nearly 7,000 acres of land. The settlement had been formed originally by bringing together Aborigines from southern Queensland. Aborigines who were considered to be unhealthy were sent to Fraser Island Mission in 1897, from 1902 to Durundur, then later to Cherbourg. It was in 1931 that the settlement became officially known as Cherbourg. Prior to that, Cherbourg was a government settlement known as Barambah. Originally, it consisted of 2,805 hectares in two sections near Murgon and Wondai. In 1904, Barambah was a grazing property that had an economic basis in agriculture.

It was late in the night when the big trucks pulled into Cherbourg. My mother and her family were taken to a two-storey dormitory. The living conditions were cramped and overcrowded in the dormitory; there was one family to a room. The night they arrived they were given scones, syrup, black tea, unbleached sheets, grey blankets, pillows and pillow slips. No mattresses were given out. This was their temporary accommodation. My mother and her family lived in the dormitory for about three months.

In 1934, an act was amended so that the Chief Protector had the right to control any 'half-castes'. J. W. Bleakley was the Chief Protector from 1913 to

1942, but in 1942, Mr O'Leary took over. In 1937, Bleakley had attended a conference in Canberra. The major issue that was discussed was the need to find a national view on Aborigines. The Queensland opinion was greatly different from that in the rest of Australia. This was partly because the Queensland Government also dealt with Torres Strait Islanders and part-Aborigines. Bleakley held negative views about racial mixing and intermarriages. He suggested two solutions to the situation. One of the solutions was the removal of 'quadroons' and light-coloured people from Aboriginal environments, and the other solution was to leave half-castes and darker people to be cared for by the Government. After much discussion, the conference disagreed with Bleakley and a policy of assimilation of Aborigines into European society was agreed on. In 1939, the 1897 Protection Act was replaced by the Queensland Aboriginals' Preservation and Protection Act. This new act was an extension of powers held under previous legislation and the Chief Protector was responsible for its administration.

In Cherbourg, my mother and her family had to adapt their lifestyle, which had been independent and centred on the sea, to an isolated rural lifestyle, which was dominated by the Chief Protector. The many adjustments made by my mother and her family seemed inevitable, one example being the use of coupons. The Chief Protector issued each family with a coupon booklet. Each coupon had an amount on it. Each family was allowed to get only as many goods as the coupon figure showed. The store contained food, tobacco, toiletries and clothing and the basic foods were supplied free to the people who lived at Cherbourg from a ration store. This makes it seem as though the people had an unlimited supply of food, but this was not the case as each family was restricted in what they could have by the use of coupon booklets. Another example of the restrictions that came with living at Cherbourg was the use of permits. A permit was needed if a person wanted to go off and on to a settlement. My mother told me of her friend who left the mission without permission. My mother described the girl as being 'pretty with long hair'. When her friend came back to Cherbourg, she was taken to get her head shaved. This was done so that everyone living at Cherbourg knew what the girl had done. It also showed the people that they would get the same treatment if they did what the young girl did. The permit system was established in Queensland in 1897. The 1939 act also set out the conditions of mobility. Aborigines could not leave or 'escape' without permission, nor could they go on to other settlements without permission or a removal order from somewhere else. If anyone did not comply with the rules on the reserve, he/she could be put off the reserve. Other adjustments that my mother and her family, as well as the other Malaysian families, experienced was their changing diet. Prior to the evacuation, seafood was the main source of protein. At Cherbourg, the main source of protein was beef. The climate was another adjustment that the people from Thursday Island experienced. Winter was a totally new experience as there is no such thing as winter on Thursday Island. According to my mother, there was not much interaction between the Aborigines living at Cherbourg and the people from Thursday Island. My mother told me that the Aborigines kept to themselves.

The accommodation at Cherbourg was insufficient. There were four types of houses there: one was the officials' house, which was occupied by the people in charge of the settlement. The other three types of houses were for the Aborigines. The first category were small shacks, which had no floor covering, no ceilings, corrugated iron for the roofs and shutters. These shacks were the oldest type of housing. The second category of housing was more recent. These were conventional three- to four-bedroom houses. The first and second category of housing suffered from poor building standards. The houses were prone to leak and to be draughty. The third category was a modern housing commission-style of home built for the community council chairman. During the time that my mother lived at Cherbourg, two to three families were forced to live together. My mother's description of the house in which she lived fits the second category of housing. My mother's family and two other Malaysian families lived in a four-bedroom house which was built out of wood from the forest.

During my mother's stay at Cherbourg, her mother gave birth to a baby boy. My great-grandmother, Lass Ah Boo, delivered the baby. There were other Malaysian ladies who also had babies at Cherbourg. At the end of the war, the birth rate at Cherbourg had overtaken the death rate. Population figures for the period 1940 to 1945 are not available but, if they were, they would perhaps have showed a decrease in population when the men from Cherbourg left to join the army and residents found work for themselves in other towns during the war years. However, perhaps the population may have increased when the people from Thursday Island were evacuated to Cherbourg in 1942.

My grandfather, Manup Ah Boo, was discharged from the war a year later in 1943. Once discharged, he went to Cherbourg to take my mother and the rest of the extended family off the reserve. My mother's family then moved to Bundaberg where my grandfather was employed as a cane-cutter. The Ah Boo family lived in Bundaberg for seven years. It was not until 1949 that the family returned to Thursday Island. The reason for returning to Thursday Island was because the family missed their home, an independent lifestyle, the seafood and their friends. My mother has not returned to Cherbourg since the day that her father took her and the rest of the family off the settlement.

My mother went to the Catholic school when she returned to Thursday Island but she only went as far as Year 3. This was equivalent to Year 7 in today's education. In those days, this was seen as the normal thing to do. At the age of 17, my mother was employed by the Farquhars, who owned a store on the waterfront. She met my father, Thomas Farquhar, while working in the shop. Despite family opposition, my mother and father were married five years later in 1956 on Thursday Island. After getting married, my father decided to change the family's surname to Foster as he did not want to be a part of the Farquhar family. This was done through the Courthouse. In 1959, my mother had her first child, Deborah. Deborah was the eldest of six other children who followed. After Deborah came Thomas, Stephen, Kevin, Sharron, Trevor, then myself, Paula. Before my mother retired, she worked at the same site where she was employed many years ago, although in a different building on the same waterfront. She was employed by the Aboriginal Hostels as an assistant manager in the Jumula Dubbins Hostel. My mother is now a grandmother to 24 children and has seven great-grandchildren.

> **Billy Isao Shibasaki** is a *Nisei* (second generation) of Japanese and Malay/Islander origin. He married Seriba Bin Garape of Malay/Torres Strait origin in 1963. They have four children and seven grandchildren. He served as Deputy Mayor for Torres Strait Shire Council from 1997 to 2000 and as a Councillor until March 2003.

I was born in 1940 on Thursday Island. My dad was born in 1900 in Wakayama and came as a diver to Torres Strait when he was a young man. My mum was born on Horn Island and was of Malay/Islander origin. When the war broke out, I was a one-year-old baby. Dad was taken away and interned separately from us during the war. Therefore, I spent my early childhood not knowing him at all. Soon after his release from the internment camp in 1946 he visited us briefly in Bundaberg before returning to Thursday Island to continue working in the pearling industry. On his arrival in Bundaberg, I asked my mother who this man was. After my mother, brothers, sisters and I all returned to Thursday Island in 1947, we became a whole family again and re-established our close ties with our father.

Again life was unkind to my recently reunited family as my dad died from cancer three years later in 1950. By this time there were eight of us. Another sister and brother were born after the war. It was hard on Mum. Two of my older brothers had to seek employment to provide for the family. They followed in our father's footsteps and became pearl-shell divers.

My father was of average height and well-built. He promoted his country through his respect, friendliness and kindness. Before the war, my father worked as a pearl diver in the Darnley Deeps off Darnley Island and visited Yorke Island regularly. The old timers on Yorke Island still remember him well. He looked after his fellow workers well and everyone called him 'Kew'.

When Dad was working, he was gone for months at a time and so we grew up not knowing much about our Japanese heritage. We were brought up by our Mum's culture, which was predominantly Malay, and this was greatly influenced by the fact that my grandparents were living with us and practised their culture.

I was fortunate to have visited Japan and to meet up with my uncles, aunts and cousins. The family has not established contact with any of my Malay relatives overseas. I believe that if it was financially possible other members of my family would visit with our relations in Japan.

I enjoyed my school years and continue to have fond memories of those precious years. I mixed with boys and girls of different races and religions. I loved parties and was a member of a band called the Checkers in the 1960s with my cousin, Martin, and five other young people. When I finished school, I worked in the shipping and airline industries; local hospital administration, pearling industry, and the pearl-culture industry. I became the managing director of Oceangem Pearls Pty Ltd., a joint venture company with the Kakuda Australian Pearl Co. in Japan, until the companies were taken over by Kyushu Pearl Co. Ltd. Japan. I remained with the industry until 1997.

When our father's generation was alive, they drank beer together and kept regular contact with each other, but we, the second generation, are fragmented. In the old days, there was a Japanese society and an established clubhouse. I think it would be interesting to have a society of Japanese descendants on the island. Although there is a cultural festival held biannually and was to include all cultures, the emphasis is on Torres Strait Islander culture and too little is known about the Asian heritage of a lot of the people living on Thursday Island. The new Gub Titui Gallery was built with funds allocated to the Indigenous people of the Torres Strait and therefore will showcase only Aboriginal and Torres Strait Islander arts and crafts. But I also think it's vitally important that our Asian cultural heritage be preserved.

Mahendra Mendis was born in Brisbane in 1949, the son of Nissanka and Amara Mendis and grandson of Punchi Hewa Mendis, a Sri Lankan business pioneer in Torres Strait. He grew up on Thursday Island before attending boarding school in Ravenshoe on the Atherton Tableland. Returning to Thursday Island, he joined the Queensland Department of Aboriginal and Islander Affairs and later worked for Comalco for 25 years. After his father's death in 1989, he and his mother went to live in Victoria Point, near Brisbane. Mahendra now works for Blue Care, Brisbane South Region.

I was born in Brisbane, but we went up to Thursday Island on the *Elsanna* when I was about six months old. Grandad had a business there and Mum and Dad helped him out. We were down near the Customs House in those days, across from the Post Office: there was a building on the opposite side of the bank, the same block as the Customs House but on the other end of it. The Customs House is on the water end, on the main street there, and there was a long building where Mum and Dad and Grandad used to sort shell.

Grandad was a big influence on my early life. He came to Thursday Island in 1898, but Mum and Dad didn't come until after the war in 1947. Grandad had gone back to get married and he had two children in Sri Lanka.

Punchi Hewa Mendis and his grandson,
Mahendra Mendis, c.1950s.
Courtesy of Mahendra Mendis.

The eldest one, my uncle, came out before the war, but my Dad stayed in Sri Lanka. Afterwards, the other brother got married as well and they all came out together and lived in Brisbane for a while. My Dad stayed on here, but later Grandad wanted someone to look after him and he asked Mum if she would. They went up to Thursday Island just after the war, when they were rebuilding Thursday Island and Grandad was re-establishing the business.

Grandad got into pearling a while before, in the early 1900s. He began as a printer's assistant and then he had a little general store and he worked in a pub for a long time. People say he never drank alcohol, didn't smoke or anything like that. A lot of the older people said that he was probably the smartest of the lot, because he saved his money, whereas everyone else was busy working hard to collect money and then spent it gambling and drinking. Thursday Island was known for that in those early days.

The key to his success was a pearl. He had become pretty knowledgeable about pearls and he bought this one for about £40, a lot of money at the time, with the bank manager's help. The bank manager, as far as we can gather, knew Grandad pretty well. Grandad had made an arrangement with the travellers who sold watches: he used to take a few watches and he'd say, 'Look, I'll sell them and give you the money when you come back.' His employer at the hotel told the travellers he was trustworthy. Grandad always came good and he gained a good reputation. Going up and asking the bank manager for £40, it was a lot of money, but the bank manager trusted him. At that time you had to send pearls to London and a very long time later he got back a cheque for £600. That's what started him off on his own and he went and established a pearling company. He had several luggers and was the first to send trochus shell to Japan. He also sent Sunshine milk to Sri Lanka.

My grandfather had relatives in Japan and Singapore, even as far away as the US. They came from Galle: it's a fishing port, so a lot of ships used to come through and they used to catch a ship from there and they'd go. It was part of the British Empire at that time and a lot of people went to Singapore also. My grandfather wasn't a jeweller by profession, but on Mum's side they were jewellers and a lot of the other families that went to Singapore became jewellers; whether they were jewellers before or learned the trade there, I'm not sure.

My earliest memories of Thursday Island are that there were a lot of transient people, very different types of people, people from all over the place and travellers who kept going and coming. It was a real port of call and they'd come to the shop to buy a paper. We were lucky, we'd see a lot of people. Mum, especially, kept in touch with a lot of people: in those early years she knew hundreds of people. Grandad was pretty shrewd and he developed things all the way through that period. He went from where we were first, moved to another shop and bought a few other places, but he was very discreet.

Nothing was on paper. I remember a lot of transactions were just a handshake. No one ever knew how that transaction was handled, just the two people involved. It was amazing that so many big things were completed that way. Obviously, you have to trust the person in order to lend, for example, start-up capital for a business. But money changing hands, you wouldn't have any idea of what was going on if you weren't directly involved. We've lost that trust in people today. Grandad tried to help a lot of people all the way through, but some of them didn't do very well by him, family members who got their first opportunity from him.

I've met a few uncles who were with him during the war. When they evacuated Thursday Island, Grandad had to go somewhere else, so he went to Darwin and opened up a business there. He built a new shop and he stayed right up until the bombings, because it was difficult getting out of Darwin: the older people and the women and children were flown out first. His eldest son was with him and a cook and another relative, members of his extended family, were working in the shop, selling things to the troops. During that period, even when Grandad was there, they were selling magazines and jewellery and all sorts of strange things. They could never get rid of the soldiers out of the shop in the evening. The soldiers just kept coming in and buying things because there was no competition, apart from a few Chinese people who they knew pretty well. So the old cook used to get a pan and put chilli in it and then fry it. People couldn't stand those fumes so they'd leave and then they could lock the door and go to bed.

When we went to Thursday Island we lived with my grandfather. We moved from one shop in the main street to another shop he had built and we lived on top and built another extension out. That's where Col Jones is now. He's built his shop right across the whole of that area, whereas we just had that bit on the top and at the side and a big yard at the back. That yard with the big mango tree was my playground. Alan Taylor lived next door with his mother, Auntie Kay. Her mother was Mrs Jenap, Auntie Jenap. She made the best long soup on the island and they all used to go with little billies to collect it. She made the noodles herself.

There were some really wonderful people around us: Uncle Connie and Auntie Lullie Filewood, Uncle Dan and Auntie Bulla McGrath, Mr and Mrs Bintahel and Calammi Pilot. The kids we knocked around with were Alan Taylor and there was Vic, Carol and Larry McGrath at the back and then down the street and across the road there was Bruce, Alan and Neil Filewood and then across the back of that were the Bintahals, Toby and all those, and then there was Philip Mosley. The Mosleys used to run the Grand Hotel. And down a little bit further from us was Teddy Abednego and then Richard Barba, who was on the main street as well and lived with Dato Jia, Auntie Jenap's brother. That was our gang: a good mix of people. Vic took me and Carol to school on my first day. I don't remember, but they tell me that I couldn't speak a word of English. We had just come back from Sri Lanka after a year away, when Dad thought we might go back and live there. I don't know how we all got through that.

There weren't so many Torres Strait Islanders on Thursday Island then, although there were a fair few around the back of the island in Tamwoy Town. I remember the buildings were old and dilapidated, but the whole area was always very clean and the area around the houses was carefully swept. We would wander along the ridge of hills down to the fort, but the cemetery was a taboo area. The main thing to remember about that time is that it didn't matter where we went or who we were with, all the adults were like our real parents in that they wouldn't allow us to do certain things: we were reprimanded for things wherever we went. You were always on your best behaviour when you were around adults. They all seemed to have the same ideas about being strict.

At an early age, I was very conscious that we had money but a lot of people didn't. But I don't ever remember an instance where that was brought up. If you went to someone's place, you had a drink and a biscuit or whatever was going. If it was lunchtime, they'd make you lunch. No one ran home or rang up or said, 'They're down here'. You had to be home by five o'clock in the evening and that was the only stipulation. Most times people knew where we were. I suppose we must have had some sort of routine about where we were or what we were doing. There was an old Malay man called Rompong. He was retired by then and lived next door to us in the boarding house with Mrs Jenap and Auntie Kay. He was the loveliest man, our guardian angel, wherever we went, he was always not far behind. You would never see him, but he'd pop up out of the blue and herd us up at 5pm, saying, 'Bath-time, bath-time, boys.'

We had a marvellous life. I never felt unsafe. We used to wander off down to Jumula Dubbins' place down the end of John Street. It was a huge house near the Post Office, part of Yokohama and she had five rooms for boarders. In front of her place was the road that went past See Hop's and out towards Hocking Point. We would cross the road and go swimming on those wonderful days when the tides were high and the water was perfectly clear and warm. You could see the white sand at the bottom. We would play for hours. Auntie Jummie had a little shed out the back with a shower. She would make us all have a shower, dress us, feed us and send us home for our afternoon nap. Auntie Jummie was very influential in my life. There was always wonderful music coming from her place. Her daughters, Auntie Lullie and Auntie Bulla, played the piano and they and Auntie Joy and the boarders sang all the old songs.

We would always get into trouble for not wearing shoes. We used to get out the back and just take our shoes off. We'd usually leave them there and then pick them up on the way home. We kids used to wander everywhere. We'd get a nail in the foot probably about once a week. Once, when we were cleaning bottles to sell to the soft-drink factory, I got a roofing nail in my foot. An old Islander man came out of the factory and got it out of my foot. He then took a weed, a little bush, that used to grow there and squeezed the leaves into his hands, rubbed them on the wound, tapped it with a small stick and in a couple of days I didn't even have a sore.

When I was about seven, I used to creep out on the roof overlooking Douglas Street and watch the fight every Saturday night between the half-castes and another group. It usually began in front of Wally Woods' place. A lot of people would remember Wally: he made water tanks and married one of the Saranealis sisters. There was a streetlight just in front of his house. I don't know if they were Aboriginal or Islander people, it's a bit hazy. Someone would call the police and everyone melted away into the night.

I last went up in 1989 and it's become a completely different type of place. It seems that people are still divided, but differently from the way it used to be. It's the same divide but it's the Europeans taking the back seat. The major difference is that now everyone can have a say and express their views and it'll be in the papers. When I was growing up, it was very much suppressed. People saw things and were very upset about them, but they wouldn't have brought it up. Ted Loban used to rock the boat and many people disliked him for it, although they secretly agreed with him.

I think the younger group don't have the same fun as we used to. In the 1950s and 1960s, there was a vibrant musical scene. People really enjoyed making music in their homes and there were great bands that played at dances and at parties in people's backyards. Every time the *Elsanna* was in port, its band would play at the Town Hall dances, mainly dance and jazz music with piano and violins and occasionally you could go and hear visiting musicians. That was when Seaman Dan, George Dewis, Jerry Lewin and Billy Shibasaki had a band. I remember Karim Binawel was a great guitarist. The music changed in the 1960s, when everyone could go to pubs. With the pub scene, the music changed to rock'n'roll and more guitar playing. The See Kee brothers played well and Riti Doolah was the leader of one group. Vic and Larry McGrath and the Galea brothers played in a band called the Hungry Eyes, which was excellent. They all played by ear. Fun now is associated with drinking, whereas fun in those days was associated with music and dancing. People probably drank when they went out, but you didn't see drunk people.

When I was growing up, distance wasn't a problem. You walked everywhere. That's another big difference: all the cars in the street and the safety factor. Another change is in the structure of the town: there were far more old things then — houses, shops, sheds — but now you've got very modern buildings. The other main difference is in the schools, which used to be segregated. We went to the school on the hill, but that was European and half-caste. There was another school that was all Torres Strait Islanders.

I went away to boarding school and my best friends there were from Thursday Island, Peter Ahloy and Allan Samuel. After I came back, I believed very strongly that it was good to go away to school. I wish they'd all come away with me, I just thought they would have been a lot better off.

I went to work for the department after I finished high school and one of my jobs was to help people get government pensions. What struck me was how many people didn't want pensions. They were living on the basics but they were happy with what they had. I had to convince them to apply. Those old people were extremely kind and generous and I admired them very much. Some of them helped me a lot, people like Arthur Ahmat, Abigail Bann, Lui Bon, Elsie Harry, Mrs Daisy Laifoo, Dato Frank Mills and Tanu Nona. Some of my co-workers were absolutely brilliant, but where's the opportunity? Robert Mye was the most brilliant person I've ever worked with. He had a fund of local knowledge and a photographic memory. He could remember every case, what file and even what page something was on.

That's why I think the Islanders should be educated not only in their own culture, but in the way other people deal with things. You can't just ignore that, because there could be better solutions to problems. Torres Strait is an isolated place and it's easy to be isolated, so Islanders need to be self-sufficient in some way, find some economic niche. There's a lot of talk, but not enough action. There are good leaders, people who are trying to make changes, but it takes time.

I think we have to have some autonomy. It's a bit like Singapore, it needs strong leadership to bring everyone together and get everyone working in the same direction. Nowadays you see some of the things that come out of Torres Strait and there's no comparison with before. For instance, they used to make things out of shell that were absolutely brilliant. You can't get things of that quality now. They have some of the best musicians and sportspeople in the whole world. If you had 15 famous Torres Strait Islanders, they could raise millions of dollars and really get things going.

> **Martin Nakata** is Visiting Professor at Jumbunna Indigenous House of Learning at the University of Technology, Sydney. Of Torres Strait Islander, Japanese and Samoan descent, he was born on Thursday Island after the war and is married with two daughters. His 'voice' is adapted from an article he first published in 1995 in *Re Publica* 2, pp. 61–74, entitled 'Better', and it is reproduced here with his kind permission.

My father is Japanese and was, in my early years, a pearl diver. My mother is a Torres Strait Islander who grew up on Naghir Island in the central Torres Strait region. Her grandfather was a prosperous and enterprising Samoan. When he died early this century, his assets, including £10,000, were left to his family. We never saw it. It was irrecoverable, lost in the maze of so-called 'protection' offered by the Department of Native Affairs or whatever it was called at the time. The family, of course, felt that they had been robbed, but weren't quite sure how it was done. For my mother's father, who became the chief of Naghir Island, and who was my grandfather and an influence on me throughout my life, education — White man's education and knowledge and languages, that is — became a matter of great importance. Education was needed not just for economic development, but also to understand and know the White man well so he could not rob us again. We needed to understand how it was that they did things that seemed to advantage them but not us. To put my grandfather's thoughts into political terms, he believed that to negotiate our position in the islands we needed the White man's languages. To put it simply, he wanted an insider's view of the White world. I don't want anyone to think I grew up in a family that was openly hostile to the White world. I grew up watching this Christian hospitality benefiting everyone except us.

Because my grandfather was so keen for his children, including his daughters, to receive the best education, my mother and her twin sister were sent away at the age of seven to board at the convent school on Thursday Island. This was in the mid-Thirties, well before citizenship and well before any Commonwealth funding. My mother learnt to read and write and do basic maths and received an education to Year 4 level. And, of course, she also learnt to boil up the nuns' habits and linen in the copper, to mend, starch, iron and scrub, to prepare food, to wait on priests at tables, to garden and to milk goats. As a teenager, she became, without any training, the teacher at the small school on Naghir Island and remained there until her marriage in the early Fifties. This school, one of the first primary schools in the strait, had been conceived, built and paid for by her grandfather in 1904, and had been staffed at various times by the Department of Public Instruction.

So, you see, we weren't exactly sitting under coconut trees waiting for handouts.

In 1964, my grandfather made the momentous decision to abandon his island. Anyone who understands the attachment we have for land, sea and way of life could perhaps understand the incredible pain and pressure my grandfather had to confront. But the fact was that the war changed a lot for Torres Strait Islanders, and the economic and educational opportunities were much better on Thursday Island. It was the younger generation — my generation — about whom he was concerned. Whenever I'm struggling with my academic work, I often think of my grandfather. I think of his generous nature, and his bitterness and suppressed anger and confusion over the intrusions of White control into his community. I think of his efforts to build on his own father's perceptions, that a White man's language and education would give us equal passage in the world, and the aspirations he held for his children. And I think of the hopes he had for all his grandchildren that we could do 'better'. And his sadness towards the end of his life when he realised that despite some successes, despite the fact that, yes, things had changed and that we were able to go away to school in the south, that we had 'more' education and some of us eventually made it to tertiary level, that relative to Whites, we were not really in a much better position than we had been all those years ago. His biggest sadness, though, was due to the doubts he had about giving up his island for this other dream. And what for?

My own education occurred mainly on Thursday Island, from the early Sixties to the early Seventies. This was well before any 'special' programs became available to us. We had the straight Queensland curriculum, taught by White teachers who had no special preparation, who probably didn't know we existed until they found out they had a transfer to the region. There was no recognition that English wasn't our language. In those days, I think, Torres Strait Creole, our local language, was not considered to be one, but rather broken, bad English instead. I learnt to read on *Dick and Dora*. I started off at the same convent school my mother went to, which is still there today. My father took us out of there, after arguing with the priest about how much of school time was spent building the stone wall at the back of the church. I then went to the state primary school and I did pretty well by the teacher's standards, though I never understood anything much. But I did learn to read and compute in a basic sort of way. To this end, he'd always speak English to us and encourage us to speak and read it. All my Japanese has been learnt, not from my own father, but from other Japanese people since.

We were continually exhorted by our parents to do 'better'. My memories of school are always of trying, trying, trying, of never getting it quite right, of never knowing what it was that I didn't quite get right, of never being able to make myself understood, of always knowing that I wasn't understood. (These feelings persist, even today, even when I'm with the people I know, who are close to me and care. That frustration I felt in the primary school classroom I still feel on a daily basis in the university, even though I have proved myself in the White world, even though I have a first-class Honours degree and am doing doctoral research.)

I did badly in high school, hindered as I was by my 'bad' attitude — I was so pissed off by now with school and learning and teachers — and I had to repeat Year 10. I did much better the second time and, when well-meaning teachers wanted to take me to boarding school in Maroochydore, on the Australian mainland, as there was no schooling beyond Year 10 in the Torres Strait, my parents, who always wanted the best for me, thought that this was a good opportunity. I attended two schools in that year — I ran away from the first. Again, I understood nothing in the classroom. I understood nothing of what the teacher was teaching. I understood nothing of what we were required to read nor why. I did learn to build fences, to fix broken-down garages, to change nappies and so on. 'Homesickness' they called it, that's all. I ran away from my caretakers and made it to Brisbane, to relatives who helped me get home. My father would not let me give up school and I was sent the next term to the Christian Brothers school in Yeppoon. This was probably the time when I first took up sports as a survival strategy, but I still understood little of what went on in the classroom and, by the end of Year 11, I gave school away for good. I did various jobs — packing shelves, driving trucks and forklifts for a food storage company, fixing small engines for another joint and, later on, some clerical work with an agency for Ansett. With each change of job, I was trying to 'better' myself. At school, I'd wanted to be an architect. I wasn't without aspirations and I didn't need a role model to dream.

In 1980, I joined the Commonwealth Government as a travel officer, moving all the boarding school students from the strait and Cape York to southern mainland schools and back. In 1986, I moved back to Thursday Island as an Education Officer for the Commonwealth Government. It was in this position that I really began to think seriously about studying. The job ordinarily required teaching qualifications, but I had got it on account of my local knowledge. Part of the job involved liaising with teachers in the high school, and with students who were experiencing difficulties in their schooling. After all, I knew a lot about experiencing difficulties in schools. About a year later, it became obvious to me that my input was discounted at all turns, that I was there primarily as an avenue for the funding that came with the job; my local knowledge and understanding of Islander students in classrooms counted for nothing — that is, the 'Torres Strait' component of my job was merely a token.

I began to wonder whether, with qualifications equal to the teachers', I wouldn't be able to do my job much more effectively and be able to push the Torres Strait Islander perspective more insistently. So, having unsuccessfully completed Year 11, having read nothing apart from the prescribed Shakespeare and Dickens (which I never understood a word of) and local newspapers and a few adventure novels, I applied to James Cook University in north Queensland for entry into the Bachelor of Education program as a mature-age student.

When I started studying, I had to read everything at least five times before I could understand a word, and I had to keep a dictionary with me at all times. Writing was the same. I could never be sure whether I'd written a sentence or not. I couldn't believe that there was so much to know. It was a real struggle, but it gradually became easier and, for the first time in my life, I felt that I was making sense of stuff, that I was learning and that I was going to be able to do it. I was also learning to write what I wanted to say and, although it was a difficult and frustrating process, I began to feel excited about what I was doing and very stimulated to learn more and I worked pretty hard.

At this time, my eldest child was learning to read and I was also truly amazed by this process. I was very keen for my girls to do well (we're into the fourth generation now where English and education are to be our salvation) and I was often disappointed with my wife because she never seemed to me to be pursuing this cause very keenly. She'd read to them and talk to them, but

I wanted to see them *taught*. You know? The alphabet and things? And she would say, 'No, no, don't worry, these children will read.' And, do you know, to my amazement, they did. It was a time of great excitement for me to witness the ease with which my children were inserted into the world of print and texts, which has resulted in their success at school.

I did begin to believe, in my second year, that what we really needed was a revolution. I was thinking more deeply about issues in cross-cultural education and I was beginning to feel a sense of dissatisfaction and impatience with some of the stuff I was reading. But I met a lecturer who has had a big impact on my life. This guy, a guy of colour, gave me something that no one else had ever given me in all of my schooling years. For the first time in my life, another person (an authority-type person) responded to me as if I was a capable, knowing person, as if I was a person who didn't have to be put on probation before I was allowed to proceed as mainstream people did. It is a hard thing to explain. Perhaps it is a thing that only people of colour can truly understand, I wouldn't know. I don't think it was so much because he took down a barrier for me. I think that he just didn't put one up. On the basis of my work, he enrolled me in an Honours program, because by this time I was sure that I wanted to go on and research rather than go into a classroom or return to my former job.

It was also about this time, in the second year of studies, that I began to feel uneasy whenever I read about people 'in the margins' — a strange sensation you get when you read about what is supposed to be a representation of yourself in a text. It can give you a sick feeling when you're thinking, 'But this isn't me' or, 'This isn't how I perceive my position' or, 'This wasn't my experience'. And then comes the related anxiety, of course: 'Is this how others see me?' 'How do others see me?' 'And all Torres Strait Islanders?'

Well, from my reading of the literature, the others see lots of things. But, overwhelmingly, I think, they see a group of people who 'lack'. Along with Aboriginal people, Islanders have probably at some stage or other been represented as having lacked everything there is to have. If the experts have named it, then we lack it. We have, at various times, lacked intellect, language and education. We have lacked control over alcohol, finances, land and sea. We have lacked as fathers and mothers. We have lacked as children. We have lacked as students. We have lacked so-called mainstream experiences. This was first noted and written about the time of the first anthropological expedition by Haddon in the 1890s and, more than 100 years later, Western experts can still name it and write it, and so we still lack it. Let me simply ask: from whose point of view are these 'lacks' inscribed on us?

Lynda Ah Mat is the daughter of Phyllis Ah Mat from Thursday Island, of Indian, Indonesian, Torres Strait Islander and Aboriginal descent, and Gary See Kee, of Chinese, Filipino and Welsh descent. She was born in Brisbane in 1964 and educated in Thursday Island and Cairns. She now lives permanently in Cairns and is Manager, Indigenous Studies Product Development Unit, Tropical North Queensland TAFE. She has a daughter, Shari, aged 13.

Lynda Ah Mat with brother,
Gary See Kee, and grandfather,
Arthur Ah Mat,
Thursday Island c.1965.
Courtesy of Lynda Ah Mat.

I was born in Brisbane as Linda Marjorie See Kee to Phyllis May Ah Mat and Gary Robert See Kee, both from Thursday Island. My parents eloped to Brisbane but, as my mother was under-age, she needed her parents' consent, which they agreed to in a letter. Soon afterwards my eldest brother, Gary, was born on 11 April, 1963, on my grandad's birthday — Arthur Ah Mat — and I was born on 2 May, 1964. Gary and myself are the eldest boy and girl grandchildren of the Ah Mat and See Kee families of Thursday Island. My mother Phyllis is the second-eldest of nine children born to Arthur Usop Ah Mat and Emily Marjorie née Agale, seven girls and two boys: Marie (Brown), Phyllis (Gosney), Daisy (Ah Mat), Jacqueline (Backhouse), Michael, Frances (Visini), Sharon (Lediott), James and Veronica (Keane).

My maternal grandfather, Arthur Usop Ah Mat, was born on Thursday Island on 11 April, 1917, and died there on 29 May, 1979, the eldest son of eight children born to Amcia Usop and Ah Mat India. His siblings are Mercia, Petrie, Paul, Joseph, Julie, Portia and Francesca. My grandfather's father was known as Ah Mat India and he first came to TI as an ice-cream hawker. He was born in Delhi, India, the son of Mohama and Lacho. Ah Mat married Amcia Usop, born on Thursday Island. Amcia was the eldest of three sisters, the other two being Barria and Napsia, daughters of Moona and Ussup Sulu. Amcia's mother, Moona, was a full-blood Aborigine born at Batavia River (now known as Mapoon near Weipa). Amcia's father, Ussup Sulu, was born in Sandakan, Malay Archipelago. I believe he came to Torres Strait on a boat to fish for bêche-de-mer and pearl shell.

My maternal grandmother, Emily Marjorie Ah Mat née Agale, was born on Thursday Island on 9 November, 1919 to Gana Fred Agale of Murray Island (Mer) and Felecia née Ah Boo of Mabuiag Island. My grandmother is the third-eldest child, and her siblings are Uncle Maurice; Edna May, known to me as Aunty Nena (whose first marriage was to Raymond Arabena and her second to Michelangelo Lanzafame); Pauline Rose, known to me as Aunty Polly (who married Frank Romano); and Elsie Williams (traditionally adopted, who married Carl Smith). All the children spoke their traditional language, Meriam Mir. My grandmother is the only one of her siblings still alive. Nena, Emily and Polly were recognised back then as the 'princesses of Murray Island' as they are descendants of Harry Buziri, the '*Mamoose*' (traditional leader) of Murray Island of that era.

My father, Gary Robert See Kee, was one of eight children of Arthur Tsing See Kee, born in Cooktown, and Linda nee Laifoo, born on Thursday Island. Their children include Arthur Richard, Karl, Anthony, Gary, Shirley, Francis, John and Winston. Arthur Tsing was the child of Tsing See Kee, born in Hong Kong, and Mary Espanies Ga, born on TI. Mary Espanies Ga was the daughter of Carlos Ga from Finagat, the Philippines, and Mary Anne née Bunyan from Caermarthenshire, Wales. Linda See Kee née Laifoo was the daughter of Laifoo from Canton, China, and Mary from Hong Kong. Linda's siblings were George, Stanley, Harry, Claudie, Sidney, Mabel, Bonnie and Nellie, all from Thursday Island.

I can't tell you much more about the See Kee family. I knew very little about them because my parents' marriage broke down when I was quite young. Looking back at it now, it seems to be an interracial issue possibly of that era, maybe even a status thing — who knows? — as soon afterwards my father's two older brothers, Karl and Arthur Richard, were sent to China to bring back Chinese wives. When I was about five or six, my parents' relationship was on and off and we moved back and forward from my Ah Mat grandparents' residence to my father and to Cairns and back.

My family moved to Cairns from Brisbane and I started school in Cairns at the Balaclava State School. My parents were still together and about Grade 2 or 3 my mother, brother and myself moved back to TI on a prawn trawler, the *Kuzi*, owned by Snowy Whittaker, to help my mother save money. This was about 1972. We moved into my grandparents' home on TI, located below the old high school in Hargrave Street. Our extended family lived there: as well as my grandparents were Dato Peter, Uncle Purrie, a couple of my mother's younger sisters and a brother still at home, and my first cousins, the children of my mother's eldest sister, Aunty Marie, who resided in Cairns. The rest of the family would come back and forward to visit and it was kind of cool to have so many aunties and uncles around and cousins to play with. Our family set up one area with curtains to make a room, as my grandparents not only had their own families but also from time to time took in other people in need of a place to stay, including Guru and Jimmy Baira.

My father followed my mother back and they tried to make things work again, moving us out to live with him at the back of Richard See Kee's shop, opposite the Post Office on Douglas Street. They owned two duplexes in the back area, making us neighbours to Karly See Kee and his family. This arrangement didn't last for very long and we were soon back living with my grandparents.

We come from a Catholic family background and my mother and her siblings went to Our Lady of the Sacred Heart convent school. Apparently, it used to be a Catholic dormitory for orphans and others who needed to live there to attend school. It is the same school that my brother and I attended through to Grade 7. In those days, 'the cane' was the most popular form of discipline used by the nuns who taught us.

My grandfather was the head of the house, an honest, hardworking man with a very cheerful disposition. His beautiful dark skin always shone from head to toe with coconut oil and he always dressed appropriately according to the occasion; a proud man, very well spoken and a very strict man. On a number of occasions I have seen him wipe a cousin's mouth with fresh chilli straight off the tree if he caught him speaking back disrespectfully or swearing; and making another cousin smoke a whole packet of cigarettes until he or she was physically ill if caught smoking in or behind the toilet situated about 30 metres down the backyard of the house; or even punishing a cousin for not having a shower of a morning in the outside bathroom, which had no hot water.

My grandfather was known as one of the best fishermen in his time and everyone who could was taught to catch, clean, gut and fillet fish from an early age. I was told my grandfather was also a good boxer, a practice the local men followed on TI in the early days to win money, while most of the women played cards, also for money. He was also the secretary for the Waterside Workers' Federation and went to meetings down south from time to time bringing us back lots of Chinese goodies like salty plums, preserved mangoes, plums and kunji mangoes to save us buying them at the local stores. He would also bring back lots of Chinese delicacies, as he loved to cook a mixture of Asian foods including Indian, Japanese, Chinese and Malaysian foods. He was the best cook that I know of. He was always entertaining his friends with his cooking, even though we only had a wood stove. His children, the youngest two close in age to my brother and I — Aunty Bonnie and Uncle Jimmy — and all us grandchildren and cousins learnt to sing and dance from an early age to entertain him and his guests. We were a very musical family: four out of my mother's seven sisters could play the piano and guitar or ukulele and both brothers played the guitar; all could sing and all the girls, including us grandchildren, could hula.

Christmas time was the best. We would all help with the food preparation and all the kids would get to chase the chosen nanny goat — the one that was fattened up especially all year round for my grandfather's famous curry — around the house and up the hill. Then we would help catch the chooks that we fed and grew from chicks. My grandmother would have the big outside boiler on, she would chop their heads off with one blow, dip them in the boiling water and let us pluck them. My grandfather and the other men, including Uncle Dewi, Guru, Uncle Jim, would prepare the pig: first the warm blood from the pig was congealed to make a popular Torres Strait dish called *dinagwan*, then the rest of the pig was prepared for other dishes.

My grandfather used to make all of us go to church every Sunday, even though he didn't go himself. There would be lots of us, because our family and all my cousins lived in the one house, so we all marched up the hill past Laifoo's and Takai's and down the hill to the Catholic Church on a Sunday night. When we got home he use to line us all up and ask us, 'Who's the Lord and Raja?' We would all sing out, either 'You, Dad' or 'You, Grandad' and he would reward us with chips and soft drinks. I think it gave us incentive to go to church on Sundays when we were feeling slack. The day sermon was no good to us, as my grandparents had land down at Long Beach on Prince of Wales and we used to load up the *Jacqueline* (named after Aunty Jacqui), my grandfather's putt-putt motorboat and go camping most weekends. We had chores to do before we could play, swim and go up the rocks to fish and collect sea snails and crack oysters. We used to help clear and clean the land, plant coconut trees and other fruit and vegetable trees, drag for mullet; then if we were lucky, fish off the rocks for *bilas* using periwinkle for bait, and crack heaps of oysters and collect periwinkles and cats-eyes to take back to camp to throw on the fire or boil in a billy can to eat. My grandmother would carry heaps of safety pins so that we could all pick out the sea snail meat from the periwinkles and cats-eyes. It was not only good fun but very tasty. The men would get deer and sometimes dugong or turtle and, if it was the 'turtle fast' season, we would go round Prince of Wales looking for turtle tracks to dig up turtle eggs that were best eaten on hot rice with soya sauce. That is only some of the sea food we use to catch and eat. My grandfather taught us well and made sure we all could gather food to feed ourselves. We ate like kings and queens: no one young or old was ever deprived of good food.

I grew up as Linda Marjorie See Kee, not Lynda Marjorie Ah Mat. Linda was the first name of my father's mother and Marjorie the second name of my mother's mother. My brother, Gary Robert, was named after my father, Gary Robert See Kee. After my parents split up, we had nothing to do with the See Kees: we never spoke to any of them and we didn't go into any of their shops;

there seemed to be too much tension. We'd walk past the shops and go to See Hops, Laifoos and Peddells or Col Jones instead, we would not even look sideways at them. I used to always wonder what people thought: the old lady, Linda See Kee, used to sit outside her main shop and see us walk past and she would just stare. There was no conversation, there was no 'hullo' and we weren't game enough to look anyway. That's how we grew up. On the odd occasion our father used to deliver prawn baskets of Easter eggs to the school and tell them to give it to us — once he even brought bicycles — and that's how we would get things from him, not that we accepted any of it that I can remember. My mother was very strict and she taught us to make do with what we had and we learnt to work and support each other from an early age. Both my brother and I were responsible for many chores: we could cook and clean and had set chores every day. I learnt to cook rice and fry sausages, fish and eggs and iron clothes from the age of eight. Now I love cooking and cook without recipe books or measuring utensils. I can practically cook with my eyes closed, even on an open fire.

So, by the time I grew up, became a hairdresser and came back to TI and had my own hairdressing salon, I took it upon myself to change my name. I felt honoured to make the decision to change my name to Lynda (with a 'y') Marjorie Ah Mat, as I didn't feel like I was a See Kee. I knew as little about them as they knew about me and it didn't seem right to open a business where the majority of businesses were either See Kees or Laifoos; plus the struggles my mother, my brother and myself experienced made us closer and we stuck together through thick and thin. All my family and cultural values came from my Ah Mat upbringing and I felt that my mother and her family deserved the recognition and credit for bringing me up the way they did. My mother struggled to give us what we needed to become respectable, honest, hardworking, proud adults today. She worked very hard and got no support outside of her own family and in those days there was no such thing as child maintenance. My mother was just like her parents, strong, proud and strict but with a friendly disposition. She was a people's person like her father and also very much like her own mother, loyal, hardworking, a proud woman who gave all for her children. My grandmother at the age of 84 is still living on TI, still very strong and a hard worker, beautiful and regal.

My mother was taken out of school at the age of 15 to help my grandfather put food on the table for the rest of the family. She started out working as a cleaner for the Four Winds owned by Jim and Ivy Cadzow. She did odd jobs including cleaning, scrubbing, cooking and ironing for five pounds 10 shillings a week, which went straight to my grandfather. At night, she had a part-time job babysitting for the Mosleys, who then owned the Grand Hotel.

She also waitressed at the Royal Hotel, before moving on to a hospital job, where she started out filling in for the X-ray nurse, working in the medicine dispensary and pathology. She left home to marry, but on her return to TI in the early 1970s, she again picked up her job in the pathology, where she stayed until we left in 1978.

My mother found happiness once again in her marriage to John Gosney and soon came my youngest brother, Lyndon, born in 1974. I had a new father figure: he has been our dad ever since and still is. It was a huge change for me but I managed to cope, and so did my brother. In 1976, my mother sent my eldest brother to an all-boys' boarding school in Cairns, St Augustine's, but I continued my schooling on TI to be closely watched. You know, being a girl and all, I was there to help my mother. We stayed on TI up until about Grade 9 and then my family decided to move to Cairns in 1978, where I continued my education at St Monica's Girls' College. Sadly, my grandfather passed away in 1979 and we went back for his tombstone opening in 1981 or 1982.

Both my brother and I spoke Broken English, as did all the local kids on TI, but the adults in the family didn't always agree with it. I'm glad that I can speak and understand the basics, as I feel I have an advantage over those kids who weren't allowed to speak it. We used to play with our friends in the neighbourhood and speak it anyway behind our elders' backs and, before you knew it, no one sounded any different in the neighbourhood or at school. My parents and my grandmother would always tell us, 'Speak English!' when we talked Broken among ourselves. My grandmother could speak the proper Meriam Mir traditional language fluently. I really would have liked to have learnt it but she never taught any of her children to speak her language, apart from a few words here and there. She tells me the language they speak out at Mer now is not the true language she was brought up with. She used to tell me that at school on Murray Island they made them speak English, but when she went home she would speak her own language. She feels that everyone benefited from learning to speak English and I agree with her now that I'm older, but I still think it is also beneficial to preserve her traditional language. She never taught it to any of her children and I don't believe it is still as strong as it used to be: my grandmother believes it is broken down with Torres Strait Creole. My grandmother always praised the Coming of the Light, as she believes this was a good thing for the Torres Strait, teaching the people to wear clothes and speak English, the White man way.

Now I'm more aware of how and maybe why my grandparents thought the way they did. My grandmother was raised on Murray Island and her way of thinking was a little bit different, old fashioned to today's generation. She didn't agree with wearing togs, or showing too much of the body. She believed a woman's place was in the home learning to cook and clean first, before going out styling up for man. My grandfather was born on TI and his background was Indian, but he had a really different outlook on life. He associated mainly with the Europeans. He did have his Malay friends and Chinese friends, like Uncle Putt Ahmat down the road, Uncle Ali Drummond, Uncle Tommy Fujii and many more — they would exchange food and recipes continually and stuff like that.

Both my grandparents seemed to want their girls to marry White men, to have a better life. So the way of thinking back then was quite different to what you find now. In that era, if a mixed-race or light-skinned girl was dating an island boy, there was always talk in the house, for example, 'Oh, what them pla bunging on, going out with all *ailan* boy, all no shame, all come from good family?' These sorts of comments were common throughout my upbringing and most of my mother's sisters and my mother in her second marriage actually did marry White men. That was the era I grew up in, although by the time I was in high school lots of my friends were rebelling and going out with whoever they wanted to, regardless of what was being said around town.

In my days there, TI seemed to be made up of many divisions and many mixed races across both TI and Hammond Island. I guess being a part of the Catholic Church and school and hanging out at the close-knit community functions you tended to have more to do with what was known in those days as 'half-caste' people. Although a derogatory term today, it is still mostly used by the older generation when trying to explain the light-skinned or mixed-race Torres Strait Islanders. For example, the Hammond Islanders have a distinct Filipino descent bloodline with other Torres Strait Islander mixes. Some of the main families were the Sabatinos, Dorantes, Ah Wangs, Bobongies, Davids, Garniers, Ambers, Bowies and Dans. On TI itself there were distinctions between the people from Malaytown and Tamwoy Town, which still exist today. The majority of the mixed-race families lived in Malaytown on the front side of TI. Some of the Malay families that I grew up around were the Lobans, Bin Dorahos, Bin Awels, Bin Garapes, Lewins, Bin Judas, Shibasakis and Filewoods.

TI had various racial mixtures including Chinese, Japanese, Indian, Malay, Filipino, European and Aboriginal people mixed with Torres Strait Islanders, making them a really multicultural racial mix of people. I've just come back from Bali and it reminded me so much of Thursday Island when I was growing up: the resemblance of the people, the words they used, like *makan* for eat, *talinga* for ears, *susu* for breast, *bibi* for auntie, and the food markets were very similiar to the bring-and-buy food markets in the 1970s. We used to go down Yamashita's street with containers and plastic bags to buy long soup, *simur* chicken and coconut curry and other goodies in front of houses. The community and even us as kids use to take prawn baskets filled with mullet or dugong on strings of iron and sell them by the string through the neighbourhood. The Sacred Heart convent school was mainly made up of people of mixed Asian heritage and White kids; whereas the primary school was mainly kids from Waiben and Tamwoy Town and the rest of the people who weren't Catholics. It was an interesting mix. I had friends at primary school as well, who lived in my neighbourhood and we used to go down to the old Wongai basketball courts to play with them.

When we were kids, we used to go up into the bushland at the back of Summer Street, where my grandfather's brother, Uncle Petrie Ah Mat, lived next door to Uncle Talipasa Nona and his family. We used to follow Uncle Jimmy, my mother's youngest brother, to shanghai birds. We'd get one, pluck it as best we could and stick it on a piece of wood, light a fire and roast it and we would share this one little bird among four of us. As Uncle Jim was the eldest and the leader — more like our idol, who we used to all look up to and take his advice — he would decide who does what, who goes where and who gets what and how much of it. It was an honour to be allowed to follow Uncle Jim.

As there were very limited things to do as children, we used to take empty, cleaned-out food tins or plastic containers and steal fresh tar from the bitumen roads, after the council workers put it down. The boys would get old sheets of copper from the side of the house or the roof or the dump — wherever they could — and get two pieces of wood and bend the copper up making a *kapa kenu* (copper canoe). They would nail the wood to each end and any holes in the copper would be tarred up so the canoe would float. Then we would carry the canoe down to the beach or even the small wharf, where the baths (rock pool) were, where the local kids used to swim and sometimes test the canoes. The big wharf was mainly for the big boats and we would get in trouble if we were caught by the waterside workers. Some of the canoes sank to the bottom and I'm sure they're still down there. Well, they've probably put cement over the top of them, as it is now a car park. The more daring ones would canoe out to the buoys about 40–50 metres out from the wharf. If they got caught by the adults, they would get in big trouble and warned about sharks going to eat them.

Mango season was the best time. Mangoes used to come into season about Christmas time, the same time as the king tides, swimming season. We used to get the mangoes raw and scrape off the top where the milk comes out. We would smash the mangoes against the concrete, so they broke into pieces and then we would take them out with us in the salt water sailing and we'd keep wetting them in the salt water and eating them. It was like marinating them all day long. Those were the green mangoes — they're everywhere on TI. Then tamarind season would come along and we would get bags of tamarinds and shell them and put soy sauce and sugar on them and put them in big bottles and let them sit and then we would share them around the neighbourhood. I reckon these are influences from Asia. Our tastebuds are Asian, because everyone cooks with a lot of soy sauce and garlic, ginger and onion and chillies and vinegar. We eat lots of hot dishes like sambal, *namas*, as well as *simur*, curries, sopsops, dampers, kapmauris and lots of rice, to mention just a few of the Asian dishes that are commonly served at most celebrations, parties, tombstone openings, etc., and are recognised as TI recipes.

When I lived on TI in the 1970s, they had no TV, no videos and we went to the open-air 'picture show'. Friday nights featured movies with Elvis Presley and Bruce Lee and westerns with stars like John Wayne. Before each performance everyone would stand for *God Save the Queen*. The cinema was segregated then: upstairs was for mixed-race and White people, and downstairs was for all others. The people who sat upstairs would really dress up. I was close friends with Paula Clark and would sit upstairs with her family. At half-time everyone would rush out for snacks and quickly rush back for the next movie. When you sat upstairs you weren't watched at all but downstairs you were watched by a man with a torch, who we called Uncle Porgy. Patimah Malone used to be in the ticket box and my mother's sister, Jacqueline, also worked there as a ticket girl. Uncle Porgy stood at the door with a torch and, if he heard any noise, he would shine the torch on you, but that was for downstairs only. If you sat upstairs, you wouldn't get wet from the rain, because it was under cover. But downstairs it was open and all the lovers used to sit in the back row because they had double canvas seats for two people. By the end of the late 1970s, getting close to the 1980s, anybody could sit wherever they wanted.

By the late 1980s, when I returned to live on TI as a hairdresser, the climate felt different. I guess that was because political shifts, land claims, talk of independence and other influences of the time had changed the old TI that I once knew and loved. Although friends and family, the food, the fishing and so forth were the same, there was an influx of European government workers and more Torres Strait Islanders from the outer islands, making accommodation harder to find for the young local couples with families. The Government seems to be buying everything for either the government workers or public housing to benefit mainly the outer Islanders.

There seemed to be a slight change in attitudes: social issues were more obvious and more people sat in the pubs than went camping and fishing; more shops meant more convenience, but it seemed a real shame. The old picture theatre had closed, so more kids hung outside pubs or gathered in the parks drinking and smoking and causing trouble. There were more drinking parties when the pubs closed.

It is not like it was before. In the pubs, the outer Torres Strait Islander people under the influence would whisper, 'What all style po, themfla no kam from dis pleis, all apkas.' They look at your skin and hair and make you feel unwelcome. In a way I'm sorry my daughter won't experience the same childhood as I had, but then again she is lucky to have the opportunity to be educated on the mainland and still learn her culture from her grandmother. She was born on TI in 1990 and identifies as a Torres Strait Islander, as she has every right to. Although people raise an eyebrow when we tell them we are from the Torres Strait and have lived the experience as Torres Strait Islanders, you can see people have trouble working out how we are descendants from the Torres Straits. But I have nothing to hide: I know where I'm from and the evidence is there running through my veins in my blood and I am proud to say who I am. My family is just one of the many true TI people from the 'old TI' and we are Torres Strait Islanders.

> **Wayne See Kee** was born on Thursday Island and has lived in the local community for most of his life. His education was a mixture of public and private schooling on Thursday Island and in Cairns. After secondary school, he studied and completed a Bachelor of Arts in Modern Asian Studies at Griffith University in Brisbane, majoring in Chinese Language and Politics. Wayne then worked in the media industry for 10 years as a journalist, broadcaster and radio station program manager. He is employed by the Torres Strait Regional Authority, which is an Australian Government agency based on Thursday Island.

My father used to tell us stories about how hard it was for the Chinese because English for them was a second language when they first came here. I suppose it was pretty hard being Chinese, copping flack from the local people here and also the European people who were here. My father is actually third generation from Thursday Island, I think his grandparents were living here for a while and they were travelling back and forth to Hong Kong. When my father was born they got caught in Hong Kong during World War II. He told me how hard it was for them when they returned after the war, as a couple of fires went through their property and they lost everything twice and had to start from scratch on each occasion — that was really hard for them. My father only went through the first two years of secondary school and that was it, he just spent the rest of his time working. He got a lot of support from his parents and everybody helped each other until all of the family members were established and went their own way. The way of life during this period didn't give them much time to mix with other groups in the community other than through work.

It was a lot different for me growing up, the attitudes were a lot different. I went to school here from kindy right up, primary, secondary school — half in Cairns, half here — university in Brisbane. I studied Chinese at university: I was looking for something to do, it was good fun. I didn't do it for family reasons, I did it because I did Asian studies and I majored in Chinese politics and I thought if I ever wanted to go further with this study I'd better know how to speak it. My *paw-paw* (grandmother) spoke Cantonese. My parents and grandparents were always working so we didn't get that exposure to them talking or my *paw-paw* talking. My dad's older brothers can all speak or understand Cantonese and one of them also knows Mandarin.

While I was growing up, there was also my mother's Islander background that my sisters, brother and myself needed to understand. There were our immediate relatives and other relatives who we came to know. The kinship system up here is pretty different and quite complex, the extended family is a major part of people's lives. That didn't really happen with my father's side, in the Chinese way of things. It was pretty hard to understand at a young age. It was pretty difficult actually. It wasn't until I went to uni and came back again when I was 21, 22 that I started to really understand. I found that going away for a while and talking with other people down south helped to put things in perspective and made it a lot easier to understand when I came back. My father was always working in the business, and building a future for our family. As children, we also had to work and help. Those years of working in the shop established many of the values that I carry today, especially my work ethic and team approach to doing things.

A lot of the interaction that kids get nowadays with their relatives on their Islander side we didn't get very much, because we lived on Thursday Island and would rarely see my mother's family, as many of them still lived on the outer islands or down south. We would get to see some of them when they were passing through town. For my younger brother and sister it was somewhat different, because by then the shop started to slow down and they had more contact with our other relatives, especially through high school. They also had more time to socialise because they didn't have to work in the shop like my other sister and I — it was easier for them to get to know all their relatives.

When I think back about how you don't understand both cultures properly, it's pretty hard to mix the two cultures together and sometimes you just feel like stepping back. Coming into contact with extended family who help explain things to you makes it easier to comprehend what you're in the middle of here. You start to see the forest from the trees and understand what the kinship system means, why this person is related to you, why you're supposed to call this person 'Uncle' or 'Auntie', etc. On my mother's side, you can go right back to three or four generations and know exactly who everybody is. I want to ensure that my kids will be more aware of their heritage than I was, because, from my experience, I have an idea of what they need to know so that they don't forget any part of their family background. I consider myself fortunate to have learned about two unique cultures in my youth and to continue to be a part of both — I get the best of both worlds.

> **Jason Christopher** is a fourth-generation Thursday Islander of Japanese, Chinese, German and Danish origin. He was born in Cairns in 1974, but spent his childhood and early school years on Thursday Island. He is married and currently studying at James Cook University to become a pharmacist.

I was born in Cairns in 1974. My mum is a *Sansei* (third generation) of Japanese and Chinese origin born on Thursday Island and my dad is of Danish/German heritage born in Townsville. Nana was born in Smithton, Tasmania, to Priscilla Sherman and Andy Nielsen, timber millers. Harumi or Phylis Ahloy (née Yamashita) is my grandmother. I call her *Obâsan*. She is the second-oldest daughter of the Yamashita family. She married William Ahloy, a Chinese from Canton, in 1950. I was their first grandchild. *Gesan* (Grandad) used to show me kung-fu movies and explained them to me in English, but that was just about as far as it got with my Chinese influence other than spending time with my great uncle Ahbuck, who owned the Kowloon Restaurant in Cairns along with my *Gesan*. Since he passed away, I have had very little to do with the Chinese side of my cultural heritage.

I went to primary school on TI until Grade 5, when my parents tried to import us into the mainstream society in Cairns, but we were unable to adapt and returned by March of the same year. We made another attempt the next year and my mum insisted we try to adapt and kept us very busy with many different sports and activities to enable us to make friends and adapt to what was very foreign to us. In TI, because we lived 100 metres from the beach, we spent all of our spare time looking for monkey-fish, crabs, playing football and playing on the beach.

I settled in Cairns for Grade 6 onwards, first at Edgehill State School, and then in Grade 8 I moved on to Trinity Anglican High School. My parents didn't want to educate me in TI because we, as children, were not exposed to different influences. They thought we needed to have a variety to be able to learn and prosper, not in wealth, but in knowledge and the hunger to investigate the world. If there was only the TI way of living, my parents would have left us there, but we needed to go out and experience. It was not as though we cut ourselves off from TI: no, quite the opposite. We had the best of both worlds. Staying in TI would have restricted our knowledge and adventures. I studied Japanese at school, as they started teaching Japanese not Chinese. In Year 8, I did really well, but in Years 9 and 10 I didn't do so well. Mum said I had to continue, so I went on with it, but I nearly failed in Year 11. I wanted to go to Japan and didn't want to go to uni. I continued to have a strong interest in Japanese history and language.

After my return, I decided to go to university. I studied Japanese as part of my BA at the University of Queensland. When I finished, I went back to TI and helped my father work on the boat. I worked on TI for two years and decided to apply to go on the JET (Japan Exchange Teachers) Program. I was successful and got a position as a coordinator of International Affairs in Nonao City in Ishikawa Prefecture, where I spent three years.

On completion of my contract, I was offered an extension to stay, but my partner was not, so we decided to come back to Australia. I ran a tour company for a few months in Cairns and finally decided to get married to my partner, who is German/Australian. We moved to TI, where my wife was placed as a second-year teacher and I assisted in the bakery for my *Obâsan*. I then moved over to the boats and skippered our family lobster-fishing boat for some months. But things changed quickly when I was accepted into uni again. We decided to move to Townsville and I am back studying again, this time pharmacy at James Cook University. Studying is one of my hobbies. I have the need to be indulging myself with more knowledge. I hope one day to open my own pharmacy with my sister, who is studying with me.

Among my great-uncles on my maternal side, Shigeru is the only one who is strongly interested in Japan. He studied science at a Japanese university in Tokyo and married a Japanese lady, Hiroko. My oldest great-uncle married Aunty Blanche, who is of Aboriginal/Scottish descent, and has nine children. He has never left the island. The only daughter of the Yamashita family who remained on the island is my *Obâsan*. All the other sisters, my great-aunts, lived elsewhere after marriage. Yoshiko, who married a TI-born Japanese, moved to Sydney; Sadako married a Japanese pearl technician and now lives in Cairns; and Takeko, who was born in the internment camp, married an Englishman and now lives in Britain.

Obâsan is the strongest. She is the pillar of stability. Everything revolves around her. When something goes wrong, she is always the one who remains strong. I don't believe it, but *Obâsan* truly believes that she has inherited Japanese strength in her. Hours she works, very few hours she sleeps; seven days a week and 365 days a year.

She not only runs the shop, but boats, real estate and a bakery. She must have 50 to 100 people working for her. I respect her more than anybody in the world. But there is a limit and she is getting old and she must slow down. Even though she strongly associates herself with Japanese strength and stuff, things that are happening in Japan or are said about Japan never affect her or us. She doesn't know what's going on or isn't worried about who the current Emperor is. TI is isolated and not much is said about Japan on TI.

TI is diverse, with lots of different ethnicities. There is no clear cut in these things. Who is 'Islander'? There is a lot of grey area — 'Australians', 'Islanders' and 'Asians'. Where does it stop and where does it start? The Yamashita family, who started out as a Japanese family more than one century ago, is now so mixed through marriage with partners of different ethnic background on the island. I have a mixed heritage — Japanese, Chinese and Danish, German — but all my life up to now, I've regarded myself as a 'Thursday Islander' because that is where my heart is. I find it a place to reflect and it is not a commercialised society. Things run according to TI time and no one on Earth will be able to change that about TI.

TI my beautiful home. TI, my home sweet home.

Figure A: Map of South-East Asia and Torres Strait

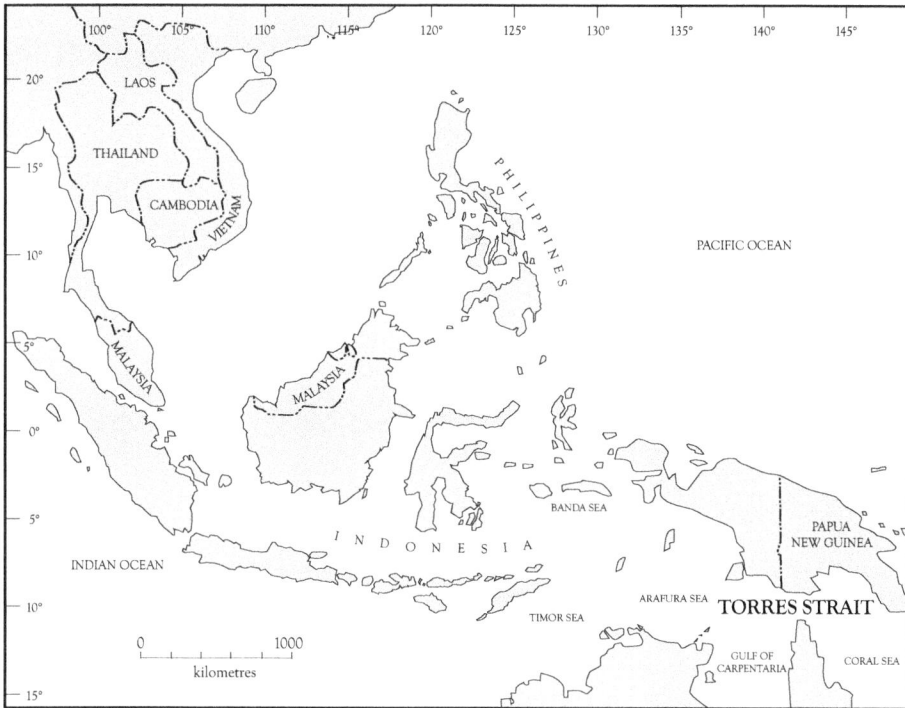

Figure B: Map of the islands of Torres Strait

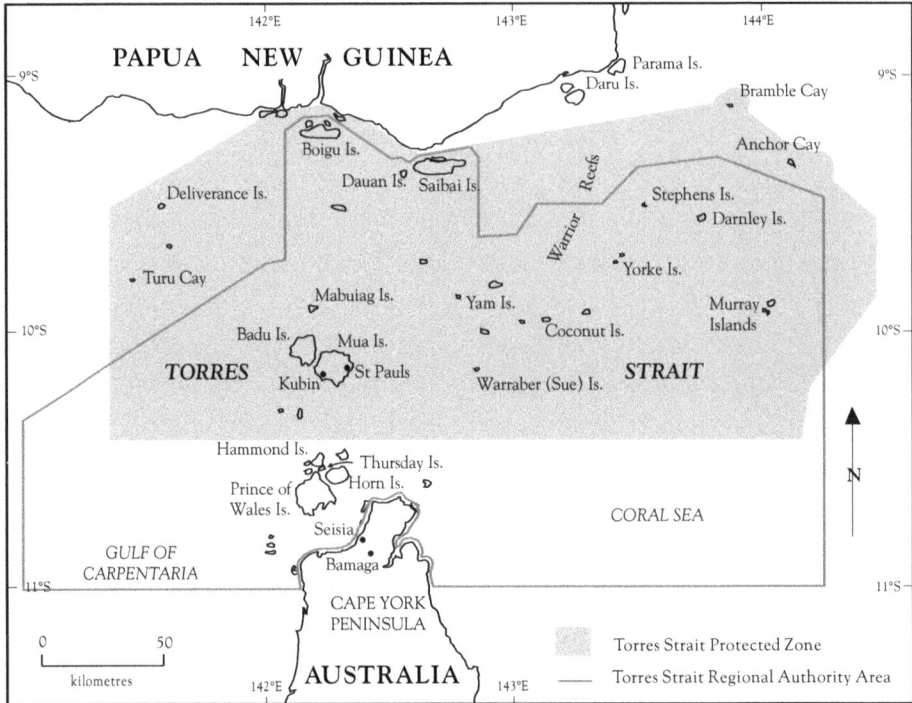

Figure C: Map of Thursday Island, 1890s

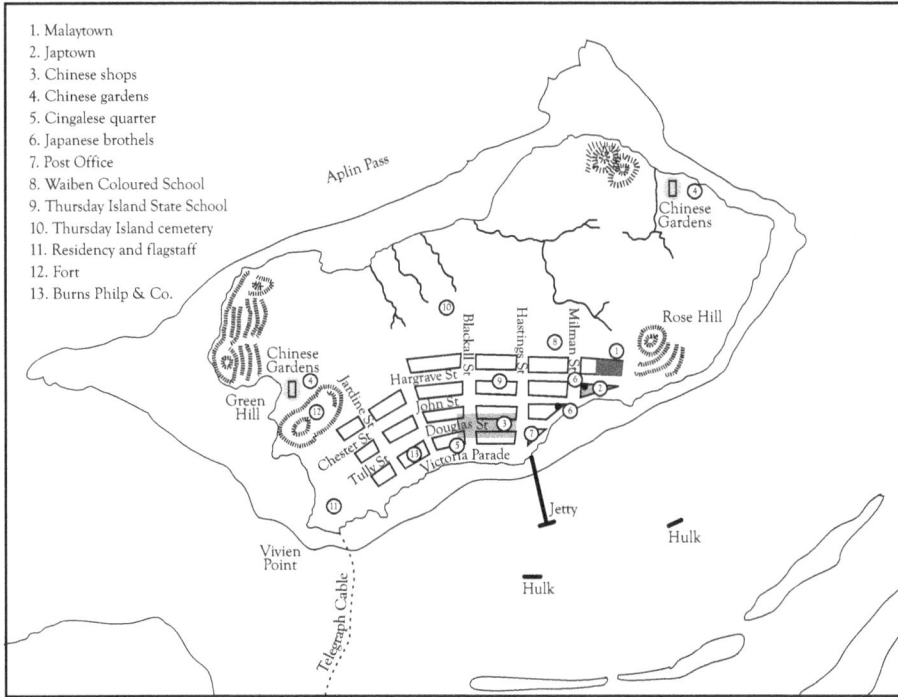

1. Malaytown
2. Japtown
3. Chinese shops
4. Chinese gardens
5. Cingalese quarter
6. Japanese brothels
7. Post Office
8. Waiben Coloured School
9. Thursday Island State School
10. Thursday Island cemetery
11. Residency and flagstaff
12. Fort
13. Burns Philp & Co.

Figure D: Map of Filipino and Malay communities in Torres Strait, 1890s–1942

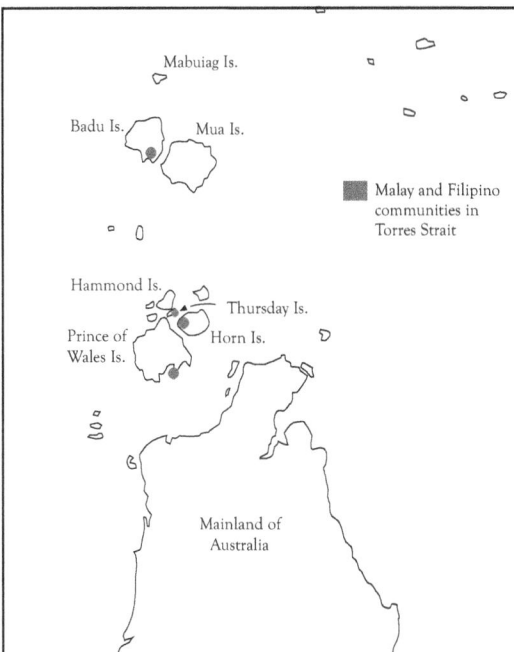

a) Horn Island was Filipino b) Port Lihou was not Malay until 1930s

Index

Biographies

Dr Paul Battersby is program coordinator for the Bachelor of Arts (International Studies) and BA (International Studies) Hons in the School of International and Community Studies, RMIT University. He teaches courses in global risk and governance, international education, intercultural management and South-East Asian studies. He completed his doctorate at James Cook University and has been published in books and leading international journals on topics ranging from Thailands' international relations to work-integrated learning.

Dr Regina Ganter is a Senior Lecturer in Australian History and Convener of the Bachelor of Arts program in the School of Arts, Media and Culture at Griffith University. Her doctorate on Queensland's pearling industry, published as *The Pearl-Shellers of Torres Strait* (1994), received the Australian Historical Association prize in Australian history in 1992. She has just completed a large Australian Research Council project on Asian/Aboriginal contact in northern Australia, and has published widely on that topic, including the forthcoming *Mixed Relations* (UWA Press).

Jeremy Hodes is Assistant Director, Training Initiatives Section, Vocational Educational and Training Group at the Department of Education, Science and Training in Canberra. Previously, he was the institute librarian at the Tropical North Queensland Institute of TAFE, where he set up the Far North Queensland Collection, a resource containing more than 50,000 items on Torres Strait and north Queensland. He has travelled and written widely on Torres Strait and is currently completing a doctorate on John Douglas, 19th-century Queensland Premier and Government Resident in the Torres Strait from 1885–1904.

Professor Reynaldo C. Ileto was educated at the Ateneo de Manila and Cornell University. Among his many publications are two prize-winning books: *Pasyon and Revolution: Popular Movements in the Philippines, 1840–1910* (1979, 5th printing, 1997) and *Filipinos and Their Revolution: Event, Discourse, and Historiography* (1998). He is working on a 19th-century history of southern Luzon towns, and a history of nation construction in the Philippines. He was formerly Reader in History at James Cook University and Reader in Asian History at The Australian National University. He is Professor of South-East Asian Studies at the National University of Singapore.

Dr Yuriko Nagata is a Senior Lecturer in Japanese language and culture in the School of Languages and Comparative Cultural Studies, the University of Queensland. Her doctoral work on Japanese internment in Australia during World War II was published as *Unwanted Aliens* (1996) by University of Queensland Press. She researches and publishes locally and internationally on Japanese diasporic experiences in Australia and on the representation of culture and gender in language teaching.

Dr Karl Neuenfeldt is a Senior Lecturer in the School of Contemporary Communications at Central Queensland University, Bundaberg campus. He trained in anthropology and cultural studies and is active as a musician and music producer, especially with Torres Strait Islander musicians and communities.

Dr Guy Ramsay is a Lecturer in Chinese language and studies and Coordinator of the Chinese program in the School of Languages and Comparative Cultural Studies, the University of Queensland. He completed his doctorate in linguistics in 1997, and has since broadened his research focus and published locally and internationally in the areas of cultural identity and Chinese-Indigenous contacts in Australia.

Dr Anna Shnukal is Honorary Research Fellow and formerly ARC Australian Research Fellow at the Aboriginal and Torres Strait Islander Studies Unit, the University of Queensland. A former Senior Lecturer in Linguistics, she is the author of more than 50 publications on aspects of Torres Strait language, culture and history.

Stanley Sparkes was born in Kandy, Sri Lanka, obtaining a degree in economics from London University. Since migrating to Australia more than 25 years ago, he has served as the publications secretary for the Sri Lanka Society of Queensland and completed the historical work, *Sri Lankan Migrants in Queensland in the Nineteenth Century*.

www.ingramcontent.com/pod-product-compliance
Lightning Source LLC
Chambersburg PA
CBHW061217270326
41926CB00028B/4668